Mental Health Tribu

Available as an ebook at www.lag.org.uk/ebooks

The purpose of the Legal Action Group is to promote equal access to justice for all members of society who are socially, economically or otherwise disadvantaged. To this end, it seeks to improve law and practice, the administration of justice and legal services.

Mental Health Tribunal Handbook

Sarah Johnston, Sophy Miles and
Dr Claire Royston

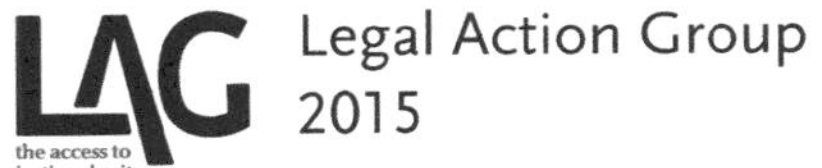

Legal Action Group
2015

This edition published in Great Britain 2015
by LAG Education and Service Trust Limited
3rd floor, Universal House, 88–94 Wentworth Street, London E1 7SA
www.lag.org.uk

British Library Cataloguing in Publication Data
a CIP catalogue record for this book is available from the British Library.

This book has been produced using Forest Stewardship Council (FSC) certified paper. The wood used to produce FSC certified products with a 'Mixed Sources' label comes from FSC certified well-managed forests, controlled sources and/or recycled material.

ISBN 978 1 903307 89 2
E-ISBN 978 1 908407 22 1

Typeset by Regent Typesetting, London
Printed in Great Britain by Hobbs the Printers, Totton, Hampshire

Preface

The Mental Health Act (MHA) 1983 is an Act with exceptional reach. It is a mechanism by which the state can take control of those with mental disorders which place them, or others, at risk. Its use can save lives: but detention under the Act is also one of the most intrusive interventions in a citizen's life.

The use of the MHA 1983 is increasing: in its report on the use of the MHA 1983 in 2013-14 the Care Quality Commission found that use had increased by nine per cent since 2010.

We wanted to write this book because all authors – Sarah, Sophy and Claire – know that representing a patient at a mental health tribunal is a difficult, though rewarding, task. We have all presented cases from both sides of the table, representing patients over many years, in different settings and sitting on the mental health tribunal panel, Sarah as a salaried tribunal judge, Sophy as a fee-paid judge and Claire as a medical member.

It is 14 years since *R (Mackintosh and Duncan) v Legal Aid Board and the Lord Chancellor* in which Lord Justice Brooke said about the challenges of this area of law:

> We are worried, however, that the [Legal Aid] Board has not yet appreciated how difficult mental health law is, and how generalist solicitors cannot pick up the expertise needed to serve their clients effectively unless they have a strong educational and practical grounding in this field of law ...
>
> Mental health law is difficult enough today. Reading the report of a psychiatrist, identifying its areas of weakness, commissioning evidence from the appropriate expert to challenge it, and representing a client at a tribunal requires expert professional skills born, as we have said, of education and practical experience. It is not like going down to the magistrates' court as a duty solicitor, arduous though those duties are.[1]

1 [2000] EWHC 294 (Admin) at paras 569, 571.

Referring to what were then forthcoming changes to the law through the implementation of what became the Mental Capacity Act 2005 and the Human Rights Act 1998, Brooke LJ made the following prescient comments:

> In the fairly near future the demands made on skilled solicitors in this field are going to increase exponentially ... Everyone, including the mentally incapacitated, will have the Convention rights mentioned in section 1(1) of that Act, and it will be unlawful for any public authority to act in a way which is incompatible with a Convention right (see section 6(1)). The rights and freedoms identified in the Convention may not be limited or restricted or interfered with except on one or more of a number of clearly defined grounds, and any such restriction or limitation or interference will have to be objectively justified (see Schedule 1, Article 8(2), 9(2), 10(2) etc) ... a lot still needs to be done to empower premier league mental health solicitors to expand their practices and to make their skilled services more readily available ...[2]

We agree with his Lordship. In addition to the need for a solid understanding of the Mental Health Act, its Code of Practice and the Tribunal Procedure Rules 2008, successful practitioners need a working knowledge of the Mental Capacity Act 2005, a knowledge of domestic and European case-law as well as an acquaintance with psychiatric concepts. Practitioners need to be able to build a case and plan the points they will argue before the tribunal. To this needs to be added real communication skills as well as the ability to ask focused questions of experienced professional witnesses on their own 'turf'. Last year, between April 2014 and September 2014, approximately 8,780 tribunal hearings were held and of those only 920 found in favour of the applicant. These figures show how hard representatives have to work to persuade the tribunal of their client's case.

The relative informality of tribunal proceedings is deceptive. To carry out this work effectively requires a high level of preparation, care and strategic thinking. But it can make a difference, as the experience of John (interview at chapter 9) makes clear.

Sadly, the last fourteen years has not seen the expansion in skilled legal services that Lord Justice Brooke hoped for. Always attracting lower rates of legal aid payments, tribunal work has often been a poor relation, subsidised, where possible, in firms by other better paid areas. While non-means tested legal aid remains available for representation at mental health tribunals, this is paid at rates that many firms find unsustainable.

2 At para 572.

Our experience of sitting on the tribunal panel is that all too often this work has been delegated to inexperienced unqualified staff, who have not been given the training and support to allow them to provide the level of skilled representation their clients deserve given the seriousness of the infringement of their liberty. Recent changes in contracting requirements may result in improvement, now that firms must always ensure that tribunal advocates are accredited by the Law Society, but an advocate can only do so much and the key to effective representation is preparation that has been informed by a thorough understanding of the issues and – crucially – a relationship of trust with the client whose liberty is at stake. A tribunal will be very stressful for a patient who will listen to their life being picked over in front of strangers. Many will be hopeful of a decision to discharge but the tribunal's discharge rate is low. Part of the task of the practitioner is managing those expectations as well as giving the patient a voice.

We hope that this book will help those who are new to this demanding, fascinating and rewarding area of practice and also that it will provide an accessible reference point for the experienced practitioner. We hope it will also assist Independent Mental Health Advocates in their important role.

The book is divided into four parts: the first part (chapters 1–7) is an introduction to key concepts, followed by overview of the relevant provisions of the Mental Health Act 1983. Chapter 7 introduces the practitioner to the Mental Capacity Act 2005 with particular reference to the Deprivation of Liberty Safeguards and their interface with the Mental Health Act 1983, and chapter 8 attempts to bring together some of the issues relating to representing children and young people.

Part 2 (chapters 9–14) considers the regulatory framework under which most mental health representation takes place, the funding available and the procedural steps to take a case from initial instructions through to hearings and, where necessary, to appeals to the Upper Tribunal.

Part 3 deals with mental disorder. Chapter 15, 'Understanding mental disorder' written by Dr Claire Royston, introduces the non-medically qualified practitioner to the categories, diagnosis and treatment of common mental disorders. Part 4 covers important cases that are useful to practising mental health law.

Many people have helped us to write this book. Special thanks are due to Debbie Postgate, who kindly read the complete first draft and provided a valuable editorial overview, and to Roger Pezzani who provided essential comments on the law, from his huge experience in this area. We would also like to thank the following friends and colleagues for their input: Alison Callcott, Richard Charlton, Christopher Curran, Tam Gill, Tim McInerney, Camilla Parker, Floyd Porter, Alex Ruck Keene, Angela Truell, Aswini Weereratne and Jonathan Wilson.

We would particularly like to thank John who shared his experience as a patient of being at the centre of the tribunal process. We hope his frank comments help the reader in understanding what is at stake for him and others who seek to regain their liberty through the tribunal process.

Sophy would like to dedicate this book to Guy, Frank and Rebecca.

Sarah would like to dedicate this book to Clare, Kate, Georgie and Alex.

Claire would like to dedicate this book to all the patients she has met as part of a tribunal process whose experiences have contributed to her professional insight and development as a psychiatrist.

We would lastly like to thank LAG's Esther Pilger, our editor, for her thoroughness, patience and support.

Sarah Johnston
Sophy Miles
Claire Royston

March 2015

Authors

Sarah Johnston was called to the Bar in 1989 in New Zealand where she practised family and criminal law until 1993. She then worked for the Global Alliance against Traffic in Women in Thailand until she came to the UK in 1997 where she worked as a mental health and public law solicitor and was awarded an LLM in Human Rights Law in 2001. Sarah was head of the mental health department at Scott Moncrieff Harbour and Sinclair from 2003, representing patients in the tribunal and in judicial review proceedings, and while there led the Legal Services Commission's Specialist Support in mental health. She was appointed as a salaried judge of the First-tier Tribunal (Mental Health) in 2009 and was one of the first tribunal judges to sit on restricted cases. She now also sits in the Special Educational Needs Tribunal. Sarah is also an appraiser and trainer of other judicial office holders within the mental health jurisdiction.

Sophy Miles qualified as a solicitor in 1989. She was a founding partner at Miles and Partners LLP where she led the mental health and capacity team for 16 years, before becoming a consultant. She has been involved in significant cases under the inherent jurisdiction and in the Court of Protection, including *JE v DE and others* and *Hillingdon v Neary*. She is a fee-paid judge of the First-tier Tribunal (Mental Health). Sophy is co-author of *Court of Protection Handbook* (LAG, 2014) and writes the regular Court of Protection updates in *Legal Action*. She chairs the Law Society's mental health and disability committee and is an active member of the Mental Health Lawyers Association committee. She is an accredited mediator (Regent's University London). Sophy was called to the Bar in March 2015 and is a member of Doughty Street Chambers, London.

Dr M Claire Royston, MB ChB MSc FRCPsych, qualified at the University of Manchester and was registered as a specialist in General Adult and Old Age Psychiatry in 1997. She was made a Fellow of the Royal College of Psychiatrists in 2005 and was Vice-President of the Royal Society of Medicine between 2004 and 2006. Dr Royston has held a number of senior level positions including lead psychiatrist for the Mental Health Act Commission and medical member and trainer for the First-tier Tribunal (Mental Health). Dr Royston is the Group Medical Director for Four Seasons Health Care, the UK's largest independent health and social care provider with a national network of more than 500 services providing personalised residential, nursing and dementia care and specialist mental health hospitals.

Contents

PART 2: PRACTICE AND PROCEDURE

APPENDICES

Table of cases

Table of statutes

Table of statutory instruments

Abbreviations

AMHP	approved mental health practitioner
AWOL	absent without leave
CCG	clinical commissioning group
CLR	controlled legal representation
CMHT	community mental health team
CMR1	form for making a pre-hearing application
CPA meeting	Care Programme Approach meeting
CQC	Care Quality Commission
CTO	community treatment order
DOLS	Deprivation of Liberty Safeguards
DSM5	Diagnostic and Statistical Manual (5th edition)
ECHR	European Convention on Human Rights
ECT	electro-convulsive therapy
ECtHR	European Court of Human Rights
EDR	early date of release
FTT	First-tier Tribunal
HESC	Health, Education and Social Care Chamber (of the First-tier Tribunal)
ICD-10	International Classification of Diseases (10th revision)
IMHA	independent mental health advocate
LAA	Legal Aid Agency
LASSA	local authority social services authority
LASPO 2012	Legal Aid, Sentencing and Punishment of Offenders Act 2012
MAPPA	multi-agency public protection arrangements
MCA 2005	Mental Capacity Act 2005
MHA 1983	Mental Health Act 1983
MHAA	Mental Health Act administrator
MHCS	mental health casework section (of Ministry of Justice)
MHRT	mental health review tribunal (in Wales)
MHT	mental health tribunal
MoJ	Ministry of Justice
NICE	National Institute for Health and Care Excellence
NR	nearest relative
PHE	pre-hearing examination
RA	responsible authority
RC	responsible clinician
SCT	supervised community treatment

SOAD	second opinion appointed doctor
SRA	Solicitors Regulation Authority
TCEA 2007	Tribunals, Courts and Enforcement Act 2007
The Rules	Tribunal Procedure (First-tier Tribunal) (Health, Education and Social Care Chamber) Rules 2008
UT	Upper Tribunal
VLO	victims' liaison officer

PART 1

The law

CHAPTER 1

Purpose of the Mental Health Act and key concepts

Introduction

1.1 This chapter looks at the purpose of the Mental Health Act (MHA) and introduces the key concepts of 'mental disorder' and 'treatment'.

1.2 Chapters 2–6 provide an overview of the Mental Health Act 1983. These chapters broadly follow the structure of the Act.

Purpose of the Mental Health Act

1.3 The purpose of the Mental Health Act is to provide a legal framework for the care and treatment of those suffering from mental disorder who may pose a risk to themselves or others. The Act delineates the circumstances where mental health professionals may override the wishes of mentally disordered patients to detain them in hospital and provide them with care or treatment without their consent.

1.4 The concept of liberty is fundamental. Magna Carta provides that:

> No freeman shall be taken or imprisoned, or disseised of his freehold, or liberties, or free customs, or be outlawed, or exiled, or any otherwise destroyed; nor will we not pass upon him, nor condemn him, but by lawful judgment of his peers, or by the law of the land. We will sell to no man, we will not deny or defer to any man either justice or right.[1]

1.5 More recently the legal framework is necessary in order for the United Kingdom to comply with Article 5 of the European Convention on Human Rights (ECHR):

> **Article 5 – Right to liberty and security**
> 1. Everyone has the right to liberty and security of person. No one shall be deprived of his liberty save in the following cases and in accordance with a procedure prescribed by law:
> (a) the lawful detention of a person after conviction by a competent court;
> (b) the lawful arrest or detention of a person for non-compliance with the lawful order of a court or in order to secure the fulfilment of any obligation prescribed by law;
> (c) the lawful arrest or detention of a person effected for the purpose of bringing him before the competent legal authority on reasonable suspicion of having committed an offence or when it is reasonably considered necessary to prevent his committing an offence or fleeing after having done so;

1 Magna Carta, 1297, clause 29.

> (d) the detention of a minor by lawful order for the purpose of educational supervision or his lawful detention for the purpose of bringing him before the competent legal authority;
> (e) the lawful detention of persons for the prevention of the spreading of infectious diseases, of persons of unsound mind, alcoholics or drug addicts or vagrants;
> (f) the lawful arrest or detention of a person to prevent his effecting an unauthorised entry into the country or of a person against whom action is being taken with a view to deportation or extradition.
>
> 2. Everyone who is arrested shall be informed promptly, in a language which he understands, of the reasons for his arrest and of any charge against him.
> 3. Everyone arrested or detained in accordance with the provisions of paragraph 1(c) of this article shall be brought promptly before a judge or other officer authorised by law to exercise judicial power and shall be entitled to trial within a reasonable time or to release pending trial. Release may be conditioned by guarantees to appear for trial.
> 4. Everyone who is deprived of his liberty by arrest or detention shall be entitled to take proceedings by which the lawfulness of his detention shall be decided speedily by a court and his release ordered if the detention is not lawful.
> 5. Everyone who has been the victim of arrest or detention in contravention of the provisions of this article shall have an enforceable right to compensation.

1.6 The concept of detention on the basis of being of 'unsound mind' was considered by the European Court of Human Rights (ECtHR) in *Winterwerp v The Netherlands*.[2] In this case the Court formulated what have become known as the 'Winterwerp criteria'.

1.7 Mr Frits Winterwerp had complained that the procedure which had led to his detention in psychiatric hospitals was arbitrary and violated his Article 5 rights as it was not governed by any clearly defined law in The Netherlands and he could not challenge his admission and detention in hospital in front of a court.

1.8 The judgment sets out the following principles if a patient is to be lawfully detained on the basis of unsoundness of mind. These 'Winterwerp criteria' are recognised as the principles on which all detention for mental disorder in the UK must be based:

i) there must be reliable medical evidence that the patient is suffering from a mental disorder;
ii) the mental disorder must be of a kind or degree warranting compulsory confinement; and

2 App No 6301/73, [1979] ECHR 4.

iii) the mental condition must persist throughout the period of confinement.

The Court found that these criteria had been met in Mr Winterwerp's case and his claim that his rights under Article 5(1) had been violated was dismissed.

1.9 In connection with his right to challenge his detention the court held that:

i) the criteria for detention must be 'prescribed by law', that is to say, be set out in legislation, so that the patient knows what they are and can bring effective proceedings to challenge his detention;
ii) the person concerned must have access to a court and the opportunity to be heard in person or where necessary through some form of representation;
iii) the person concerned does not need to have 'substantial and well-founded grounds' in order to challenge their detention – that is the decision of the court; and
iv) the person concerned does not have to take the initiative in instructing a lawyer before having recourse to a court.

The system at the time of the case in The Netherlands meant that on some occasions Mr Winterwerp's requests for discharge were forwarded by the hospital to the regional prosecutor, who exercised his discretion not to refer the requests to the court on the basis that the request for discharge was unfounded. The fact that his requests never even reached a court led the ECtHR to decide that Mr Winterwerp was deprived of access to a court and his claim for violation of his rights under Article 5(4) was upheld.

1.10 In England and Wales the purpose of the Mental Health Act is to provide the 'procedure prescribed by law' required by Article 5(1) and defined by *Winterwerp*. It gives patients access to a court where they can challenge their deprivation of liberty. The Mental Health Act 1983 replaced the Mental Health Act 1959 and has itself been amended, most recently by the Mental Health Act 2007 and Tribunals, Courts and Enforcement Act (TCEA) 2007. The Mental Health Act 2007 made a number of significant changes perhaps most controversially the introduction of Community Treatment Orders (CTOs). For a potted history of mental health legislation going back to the fourteenth century readers are recommended to the introduction to *Blackstone's Guide to the Mental Health Act 2007.*[3]

3 P Bowen, OUP, 2008.

The Code of Practice and the Welsh Code

1.11 It is essential for representation of patients in mental health tribunals to have a good working knowledge of the MHA 1983 and the Code of Practice.

1.12 The Code of Practice derives from section 118 of the MHA 1983 which requires the Secretary of State and, as appropriate, the Welsh Ministers to prepare a Code of Practice. The Code provides guidance to registered medical practitioners, approved clinicians, hospital managers and hospital staff in relation to the admission of patients to hospital and registered establishments under the Act and also in relation to guardianship and community treatment orders.[4] It also provides guidance to 'registered medical practitioners and members of other professions in relation to the medical treatment of patients suffering from mental disorder'.[5] This means it applies to doctors and other professionals providing medical treatment (as defined in the MHA 1983 and discussed at paras 1.26–1.30 below) to patients who are informal and also to patients who are not in hospital at all. For example in *R (C) v A Local Authority*,[6] the court held that the Code's provisions which relate to seclusion applied to a child with severe autism in a residential special school, who was being regularly secluded.

1.13 The status and importance of the Code was considered by the House of Lords in *R (Munjaz) v Mersey Care NHS Trust*.[7] The House of Lords stated in strong terms that the Code should be followed unless there were cogent and convincing reasons not to follow it:

> The Court of Appeal said in para 76 of its judgment that the Code is something that those to whom it is addressed are expected to follow unless they have good reason for not doing so: see *R v Islington London Borough Council ex p Rixon* (1996–97) 1 CCLR 119, per Sedley J at p123. [...] I would go further. They must give cogent reasons if in any respect they decide not to follow it. These reasons must be spelled out clearly, logically and convincingly. I would emphatically reject any suggestion that they have a discretion to depart from the Code as they see fit. Parliament by enacting section 118(1) has made it clear that it expects that the persons to whom the Code is addressed will follow it, unless they can demonstrate that they have cogent reasons for not doing so. This expectation extends to the Code as a whole, from its

4 MHA 1983 s118(1)(a).

5 MHA 1983 s118(1)(b).

6 [2011] EWHC 1539 (Admin).

7 [2005] UKHL 58.

statement of the guiding principles to all the detail that it gives with regard to admission and to treatment and care in hospital, except for those parts of it which specify forms of medical treatment requiring consent falling within section 118(2) where the treatment may not be given at all unless the conditions which it sets out are satisfied.[8]

1.14 Section 118 requires the Code to set out guiding principles.[9] It further requires the Secretary of State to consult on the preparation of possible amendments.[10]

1.15 The English Code has recently been revised as part of the Government's response to the Winterbourne View scandal where patients were routinely and severely abused by staff at Winterbourne View hospital.[11]

1.16 The guiding principles in the Code are set out as follows and are aimed to set the standards by which all care, support and treatment under the Act are to be provided:[12]

- empowerment and participation – ensuring that patients, their families and carers are fully involved in decisions about care, support and treatment
- least restrictive option and maximising independence – all care, support and treatment should wherever possible be as least restrictive as possible, ensuring the autonomy of the patient
- respect and dignity – ensuring that patients, their families and carers are listened to by professionals and included in decisions about care and treatment
- purpose and effectiveness – decisions about care and treatment must be appropriate to the patient, must be performed to national guidelines and standards and must be expected to work, and
- efficiency and equity – the quality of commissioning and provision of care services should ensure that all professionals involved in a patient's care are involved and that physical, mental health and social care needs are equally considered.

The guiding principles are thus an important tool for the practitioner.

8 [2005] UKHL 58 at para 69.

9 MHA 1983 s118(2A).

10 MHA 1983 s118(3).

11 *Transforming Care: A National Response to Winterbourne View Hospital*, Department of Health, December 2012.

12 Code of Practice: Mental Health Act 1983 – www.gov.uk/government/publications/code-of-practice-mental-health-act-1983.

Who does the Mental Health Act apply to?

Part 1 – application of the Act

Definition of mental disorder: section 1

1.17 This part of the MHA 1983 contains only one section which sets out the limits of the application of the MHA 1983. It should be read in conjunction with Chapter 3 of the Code. The Act applies to the:

- reception (into hospital);
- care; and
- treatment

of mentally disordered patients.

1.18 Section 1(2) provides a single definition of mental disorder as 'any disorder or disability of the mind'. This definition includes illnesses such as schizophrenia and bipolar affective disorders as well as personality disorders.[13]

1.19 The definition in section 1 is wide. There are two points to be aware of in the definition section. The first of these is that being addicted to alcohol or drugs is not a mental disorder under the MHA 1983.

1.20 Section 1(3) provides that dependence on drugs or alcohol is not a disorder or disability of the mind. This means that if a person's *only* diagnosis was of drug or alcohol dependency then the MHA 1983 cannot be used. It does not exclude treatment under the Act for mental disorders which arise from the use of alcohol or drugs such as withdrawal state with delirium or with associated psychotic disorder, or some organic disorders associated with longstanding use of alcohol or drugs. A drug-induced psychosis is still a mental disorder.[14]

1.21 Sections 2A and 2B exclude some learning disabled patients from the definition of mental disorder, for the purpose of the longer term sections.

1.22 A learning disability is defined as:

> ... a state of arrested or incomplete development of the mind which includes significant impairment of intelligence and social functioning' (s1(4)).

1.23 A patient with a learning disability can only be treated under the longer term treatment provisions: under guardianship or on a CTO

13 See chapter 15 for an explanation of the more common mental disorders.

14 *Secretary of State for Justice v MP and Nottinghamshire Healthcare NHS Trust* [2013] UKUT 025 (AAC).

if their learning disability is 'associated with abnormally aggressive or seriously irresponsible conduct on his part'. This is an additional requirement: the patient also needs to satisfy the criteria needed before a section can be imposed.

1.24 However, a patient with a learning disability which was not associated with such conduct could still be detained under sections 2, 4 and 5: the 'short term sections'. Such a patient would still need to meet the criteria for detention under these sections: see paras 2.4–2.17, 2.32–2.38.

1.25 The definition of learning disability does not include autistic spectrum disorders (Code of Practice 2.17). A person with an autistic spectrum disorder could therefore be regarded as mentally disordered and detained under section 3 even if their condition is not associated with abnormally aggressive or seriously irresponsible conduct. The Code of Practice recognises that this is rarely likely to be justified: 2.14–2.16. Again, the criteria in section 3 would still need to be satisfied.

Definition of treatment: section 145

1.26 'Treatment' is a key concept. Section 145(1) provides that medical treatment includes 'nursing, psychological intervention and specialist mental health habilitation, rehabilitation and care' and section 145(4) provides that a reference to medical treatment for mental disorder shall be construed a reference to 'medical treatment the purpose of which is to alleviate, or prevent a worsening of, the disorder or one or more of its symptoms or manifestations'.

1.27 'Appropriate medical treatment', which must be available for a patient admitted to hospital under the longer term sections of the MHA 1983, is defined in a somewhat circular fashion in section 3(4) as 'medical treatment which is appropriate in his case, taking into account the nature and degree of the mental disorder and all the other circumstances of his case'.

1.28 The Code of Practice considers the appropriate treatment test in Chapter 23. The following entries are noteworthy:

- 'Purpose' is not the same as 'likelihood' (para 23.4).
- Interventions may exist that represent appropriate treatment for a particular mental disorder even if the disorder is likely to persist or get worse (para 23.6).
- 'All the other circumstances' of the patient's case might include his physical health; culture and ethnicity; gender, identity and sex-

ual orientation; implications for his family including his role as a parent; the consequences for the patient or others if the patient does not receive the treatment (which could include imprisonment) (para 23.12).

- Where normal treatment approaches would aim (and be expected) to alleviate or improve the patient's condition significantly then treatment which simply aims to prevent deterioration is unlikely to be appropriate; but in some cases managing the symptoms is all that can be hoped for (para 23.16).
- In some cases treatment which consists of nursing and specialist day to day care under an approved clinician in a safe and structured environment will be appropriate (para 23.17) but simply detaining a patient in hospital is not medical treatment (para 23.18).
- Treatment can be appropriate even if the patient refuses to engage with it (paras 23.19–23.20).

1.29 The provisions in the Code of Practice for Wales are broadly similar and appear in Chapter 4.

1.30 The definition of 'appropriate medical treatment' has been challenged in several cases. The appropriate treatment argument has so far been used for those patients who are suffering from severe personality disorders that are very difficult to treat and where the patient has refused to undertake any therapy in hospital. Such patients may be on life sentences and transferred to hospital later in their sentence or near the end or their fixed sentence and are believed to remain dangerous to the public. These cases are reasonably few in number. However, the argument that there is no appropriate treatment available is difficult to make, as is illustrated by the following cases:

MD v Nottinghamshire Health Care NHS Trust[15]

This case concerned a patient who was detained at Rampton Secure Hospital following convictions for child cruelty. He appealed against the refusal of the First-tier Tribunal to discharge him from MHA 1983 ss47 and 49, on the basis that the tribunal erred in finding that the appropriate treatment test was met. Judge Jacobs referred to the provisions of the Code of Practice in force at the time, which were broadly as set out in para 1.28. He held that it was for the tribunal to consider on the facts of each case where the boundary between treatment and containment lay.

15 [2010] UKUT 59 (AAC).

DL-H v Devon Partnership NHS Trust and Secretary of State for Justice[16]
A patient with a diagnosis of anti-social personality disorder appealed against a tribunal's refusal to discharge him. Judge Jacobs recognised:

> ... the danger that a patient for whom no appropriate treatment is available may be contained for public safety rather than detained for treatment. The solution lies in the tribunal's duty to ensure that the conditions for continued detention are satisfied. The tribunal must investigate behind assertions, generalisations and standard phrases. By focusing on specific questions, it will ensure that it makes an individualised assessment for the particular patient. What precisely is the treatment that can be provided? What discernible benefit may it have on this patient? Is that benefit related to the patient's mental disorder or to some unrelated problem? Is the patient truly resistant to engagement? The tribunal's reasons then need only reflect what it did in the inquisitorial and decision-making stages.'

See also *MD v Merseycare NHS Trust.*[17]

Capacity and the Mental Capacity Act 2005

1.31 We have emphasised the particular feature of the Mental Health Act 1983 which allows the detention and treatment of some patients, even if their decision-making is unimpaired.

1.32 However, the question of whether a patient has capacity to consent to a particular course of action arises in connection with:

- the decision to admit patients under the Mental Health Act 1983 rather than informally (see paras 2.24, 2.47);
- the possible use of the Deprivation of Liberty Safeguards (see chapter 7);
- the consent to treatment provisions (see chapter 4); and
- the decision to appoint a representative to conduct the tribunal (see chapter 11).

1.33 The Mental Capacity Act 2005 provides a legal framework for making decisions in the best interests of those who are unable to make the decisions themselves. It is essential to have a working knowledge of its provisions and guiding principles and readers are referred to chapter 7 which summarises the relevant provisions of the Mental Capacity Act 2005 as well as its interaction with the Mental Health Act 1983.

16 [2010] UKUT 102 (AAC); [2013] UKUT 500 (AAC).
17 [2013] UKUT 127 (AAC).

CHAPTER 2

Civil sections: admission, transfer and community treatment

continued

Introduction

2.1 This chapter summarises and explains the key provisions in Part 2 of the Mental Health Act 1983, that is those sections (sometimes known as 'civil sections') that deal with patients who are admitted to hospital or guardianship by mental health professionals rather than through the criminal justice system. See chapter 3 for the provisions affecting patients involved in the criminal justice system.

2.2 Part 2 covers the following topics:

- Procedure for hospital admission: sections 2–6
- Guardianship: sections 7–10
- General provisions regarding applications and recommendations: sections 11–15
- Leave and Community Treatment Orders: sections 17 and 17A
- Return and re-admission of patients absent without leave: section 18
- Transfers between hospitals and between hospitals and guardianships: section 19
- Duration of orders, renewal and discharge: sections 20–25
- The nearest relative: sections 26–30
- Supplemental provisions: sections 30–34.

Procedure for hospital admission

2.3 Sections 2–6 cover the criteria for, and effect of, compulsory admission to hospital. This Part of the Act should be read in conjunction with Chapter 14 of the Code or Chapter 5 of the Code of Practice for Wales.

Admission for assessment: section 2

2.4 Section 2 is likely to be used for patients who have not been in contact with mental health services before or where there has been some change in the patient's presentation.

2.5 Section 2 provides for admission to hospital for assessment for a period not exceeding 28 days. The 28 days begin with the day of admission. It cannot be renewed. This means that once the 28 days are over the section 2 order will expire at 12 midnight on the 28th day. There is one exception to this at section 29(4). This section applies where county court proceedings have commenced to displace the patient's nearest relative and this is considered at para 2.239.

2.6 A patient detained under section 2 could be placed under section 3 during the course of the 28 days.

2.7 A patient may be detained under section 2 if:

- they are suffering from mental disorder of a nature or degree which warrants detention in hospital for assessment – or assessment followed by medical treatment – for at least a limited period, and
- they ought to be so detained in the interests of their own health or safety or with a view to the protection of other persons.

2.8 Section 2 introduces the key concepts of the 'nature' and 'degree' of the relevant disorder. Paragraph 14.6 of the Code defines 'nature' as 'the particular mental disorder from which the patient is suffering, its chronicity, its prognosis, and the patient's response to receiving treatment for the disorder' while 'degree' refers to 'the current manifestation of the patient's disorder'. These concepts are discussed in more detail at paras 5.34–5.44, in the context of the test to be applied by tribunals, and also in chapter 14, 'The hearing'. The Code suggests that section 2 should not be used to detain patients whose condition and treatment needs are known: para 14.27.

2.9 The question of what constitutes being 'warranted' was considered by Charles J in *AM v South London and Maudsley NHS Foundation Trust and Secretary of State for Health.*[1] The judge said:

> ... for detention in hospital to be 'warranted' it has to be 'necessary' in the sense that the objective set out in the statutory test cannot be achieved by less restrictive measures ... the relevant aim is to seek to identify the least restrictive way of best achieving the proposed assessment or treatment.

Who makes the application?

2.10 An application for admission is made by an approved mental health practitioner (AMHP) or by the patient's nearest relative. The definition of the nearest relative, and their role is described at para 2.11. It is unusual for the patient's nearest relative to apply for detention under section 2 or section 3 and in the vast majority of cases an AMHP will make the application. The Code of Practice states that doctors who are approached by nearest relatives should advise the nearest relative that it is preferable for the AMHP to make the application and

1 [2013] UKUT 0365; see also para 2.20.

of their right to require an AMHP to consider the patient's case (in section 13(4), see below para 2.87).[2]

2.11 An AMHP is defined at section 114. Before the amendments made by the Mental Health Act 2007, applications were made by Approved Social Workers (ASWs). These were, as the name suggests, social workers approved by the local social services authority (LSSA) as having appropriate competence in dealing with persons suffering from mental disorder. The 2007 Act broadened the range of professions which could be approved so that applications for admissions could be made by occupational therapists, psychiatric nurses and others.

Regulations govern the requirements and processes of approval.[3] The decision to apply for admission is a matter for the independent personal judgment of the AMHP, who cannot be instructed to make an application. The Code states that the role of the AMHP is to 'bring an independent decision about whether or not there are alternatives to detention under the Act, bringing a social perspective to bear on their decision'.[4]

2.12 The Code of Practice for Wales states that the AMHP 'plays a significant part in the assessment process as they should bring a social perspective to a process where the other participants are doctors. This variety of expertise is intended to promote a holistic approach to the consideration of a person's needs'.[5]

2.13 The application for admission under section 2 is founded on recommendations by two registered medical practitioners. The medical recommendations and the applications are made on standard forms. The medical practitioners do not need to examine the patient together but if they do not then there must be no more than five clear days between the examinations.[6]

2.14 Section 12(2) provides that one of the two medical recommendations must come from a practitioner approved by the Secretary of State as having special experience in the diagnosis and treatment of mental disorder (referred to as 'section 12 approved') and if the section 12 doctor does not have previous acquaintance with the patient then the other medical practitioner should, if practicable.

2 Code of Practice paras 14.30–14.32.

3 Mental Health (Approved Mental Health Professionals) (Approval) (England) Regulations 2008 SI No 1206; Mental Health (Approval of Persons to be Approved Mental Health Professionals) (Wales) Regulations 2008 SI No 2436.

4 Code of Practice para 14.52.

5 Code of Practice for Wales para 2.33.

6 MHA 1983 s12(1).

2.15 If the patient is under 18, at least one of the three professionals assessing the patient should be a clinician specialising in Child and Adolescent Mental Health Service (CAMHS).[7]

When can the patient appeal to the mental health tribunal?

2.16 A patient admitted under section 2 can apply to the mental health tribunal during the first 14 days of admission: s66(1)(a), (2A) and see also table 4 at para 5.11. If the period expires on a day when the tribunal office is closed then the period is automatically extended to the following business day: see *R (Modaresi) v Secretary of State for Health*.[8] The position concerning patients lacking capacity to make applications to the tribunal was considered by the European Court of Human Rights in *MH v United Kingdom*[9] and is discussed at paras 5.19–5.21 and 16.44–16.60 below. A patient who has missed the deadline may ask the Secretary of State to refer the case to the tribunal. See para 5.17 onwards.

Who can discharge the section?

2.17 The responsible clinician (RC) can discharge a patient detained under section 2 at any time during the section (s23 and see paras 2.117–2.118). A patient's nearest relative can discharge a patient who is detained under section 2 by giving notice to the managers (s23(2)(a)). This is subject to the RC's power to block the discharge if he or she considers that the patient is likely, if discharged, to act in a manner that is dangerous to himself or others (s25). This is discussed further at paras 2.117–2.119.

2.18 As an order under section 2 cannot be renewed, once it expires there is no authority for the patient to be detained unless he or she has been detained under another provision of the MHA 1983 (for example section 3) or under another legal framework such as the Mental Capacity Act 2005: see chapter 14. The 28 days begins with the date upon which the patient was admitted. In *R v East London and*

7 Code of Practice para 14.39, Code for Wales para 33.19. The English Code also refers to other groups where particular expertise is needed (for example patients with learning disabilities). If one of the assessors does not have such expertise then a professional with this expertise should be consulted: para 14.40.

8 [2013] UKSC 53.

9 [2013] ECHR 1008.

the City Mental Health Trust ex p Brandenburg,[10] the House of Lords considered the case where a patient detained under section 2 was discharged by the tribunal but was shortly afterwards re-sectioned. Lord Bingham said:

> ... an [AMHP] may not lawfully apply for the admission of a patient whose discharge has been ordered by the decision of a mental health review tribunal of which the [AMHP] is aware unless the [AMHP] has formed the reasonable and bona fide opinion that he has information not known to the tribunal which puts a significantly different complexion on the case as compared with that which was before the tribunal. It is impossible and undesirable to attempt to describe in advance the information which might justify such an opinion.

Admission for treatment: section 3

2.19 Section 3 is usually used for a patient who has had contact with mental health services before and has an established diagnosis. This is reflected in the guidance given by the Code of Practice: paras 14.27–14.28.

2.20 Section 3 provides for admission to hospital for treatment for up to six months. An order under section 3 can be renewed. The threshold for admission under section 3 is often seen as higher than for admission under section 2, because of the use of the word 'necessary' in section 3(2)(c).

2.21 In *AM v South London and Maudsley NHS Foundation Trust Secretary of State*,[11] Charles J suggested that the term 'warranted' in section 2 implied that detention had to be 'necessary'. The key difference is perhaps not the use of the different terms but the purpose of the two sections. In *Re MM* the Upper Tribunal held:

> Once it is known that a patient requires treatment for the effects of a mental disorder, the criteria can be, and are, appropriately exacting. But detention for assessment must, of necessity, be less exacting, since the need for treatment is not then known. Assessment under section 2 may, as an essential preliminary to establishing the need for treatment, be necessary in order to render section 3 effective for some patients. To that extent, it plays an important role in protecting the health and safety of those patients and the protection of others. This does, of course, reduce the protection for the patient, but that is

10 [2003] UKHL 58.

11 [2013] UKUT 0365; see paras 14.95–14.98 and 16.32–16.36.

balanced by the fact that, unlike section 3, detention under section 2 is limited by the need for an assessment and for a period of 28 days.[12]

2.22 As with section 2 *all* the conditions must be satisfied:

- the patient is suffering from mental disorder of a nature or degree which makes it appropriate for them to receive medical treatment in hospital (s3(2)(a)), and
- it is necessary for the health or safety of the patient or for the protection of other persons that the patient should receive such treatment (s3(2)(c)) and it cannot be provided unless he or she is detained under this section, and
- appropriate medical treatment is available to the patient (s3(2)(d)).

The criteria for sections 2 and 3 are largely mirrored in section 72, which sets out the test which tribunals should apply: see para 5.34.

2.23 As set out in chapter 1, section 145(1) defines treatment and the definition is very wide: see para 1.26.

2.24 'Necessary' is a high standard. Necessity is not the same as desirability: *Reid v Secretary of State for Scotland*.[13] Professionals should consider whether treatment could be provided by informal admission rather than use of the MHA 1983. This should include consideration of whether the patient has capacity to consent to informal admission, and whether the Mental Capacity Act 2005 could be used, including if appropriate the Deprivation of Liberty Safeguards, and if so whether this would be a less restrictive alternative. For more detail about the relationship between the MHA 1983 and DOLS and other provisions of the Mental Capacity Act 2005, see chapter 7, paras 7.67–7.98. The Code suggests alternatives that could be considered for example management in the community by a crisis team, in a crisis house or with host family.[14]

Who makes the application?

2.25 As with section 2, an application for detention under section 3 can be made by an AMHP or (unusually) a nearest relative founded on recommendation by two medical practitioners, on standard forms, which must address all the criteria including alternatives to detention and why they are not appropriate (s3(4)(b)). The medical practitioners may examine the patient separately but there must be no more

12 (2013) MHLO 150 (UT).

13 [1999] 1 All ER 481.

14 Code para 14.11.

than five clear days between the examinations.[15] If the application is made by an AMHP he or she must have consulted the patient's nearest relative (s11(4)). This important safeguard is considered at paras 2.228–2.242.

2.26 Section 12(2) provides that one of the two medical recommendations must come from a practitioner approved by the Secretary of State as having special experience in the diagnosis and treatment of mental disorder (referred to as 'section 12 approved') and if the section 12 doctor does not have previous acquaintance with the patient then the other medical practitioner should, if practicable, have such acquaintance.

2.27 If a patient who is detained under section 3 had previously been detained under sections 2, 4 or 5 or subject to guardianship these earlier orders shall cease to have effect (s6(4)).

When can the patient appeal to the mental health tribunal?

2.28 The patient can appeal in the first six months, the second six months if the section is renewed, and yearly after that.[16] If they do not appeal within six months of the date of admission they will be referred to the tribunal. If they are long term patients and have not had a tribunal for three years they will also be referred.[17]

Who can discharge the section?

2.29 The section can be discharged by the RC, the hospital managers, the MHT or the nearest relative.[18] For further discussion of these powers see paras 2.117–2.242.

Section 2 or section 3?

2.30 The Code of Practice and the Code of Practice for Wales both give examples of pointers towards detention under section 2 or section 3 respectively.

15 MHA 1983 s12(1).
16 MHA 1983 s66.
17 MHA 1983 s68.
18 MHA 1983 ss23, 72.

2.31 Section 2 is indicated where the patient's condition, prognosis, response to treatment or willingness to accept voluntary treatment are unclear. The Code for Wales also suggests section 2 is indicated where the patient has not previously been admitted to hospital and has not been in regular contact with the specialist psychiatric services and it has not been possible to formulate a treatment plan. Section 3 is indicated if the patient is already detained under section 2 or the nature and degree and elements of treatment are established.[19]

Cases of urgent necessity: section 4

2.32 Section 4 deals with admission to hospital for assessment in cases of emergency for no more than 72 hours.

Who makes the application?

2.33 The AMHP or nearest relative may apply, in cases of 'urgent necessity' (s4(1)) certifying that compliance with the provisions of Part 2 of the Act would cause 'undesirable delay' (s4(2)). The application can be founded on one medical recommendation, if practicable from a medical practitioner with previous acquaintance with the patient, who must also certify that a obtaining a second medical recommendation would involve undesirable delay. An emergency admission under section 4 can be converted to section 2 if the second medical recommendation is given and received by the managers within 72 hours from the time when the patient is admitted to hospital, and in that case the 28 days will run from the time of admission to hospital under section 4.

2.34 The Code of Practice considers applications under section 4 at chapter 5. Para 5.6 provides that to be satisfied that a 'genuine emergency' has arisen, both the AMHP and the doctor making the recommendation will need to have seen evidence of:

- an immediate and significant risk of mental or physical harm to the patient or others;
- danger of serious harm to property; or
- a need for physical restraint of the patient.

The Code of Practice for Wales makes the same points.[20]

19 Code of Practice paras 14.27–14.28, Code of Practice for Wales paras 5.2–5.4.

20 Code of Practice for Wales paras 5.6, 5.7.

When can the patient appeal?

2.35 The patient can appeal to the tribunal or the detained under section 4.[21] However, if a second medical recommendation is made then the patient is automatically detained under section 2 and in practice this would happen before a tribunal could be convened. If the second medical recommendation is not made then the patient will no longer be detained and any application to the tribunal would lapse.

Who can discharge the section?

2.36 The RC can discharge the patient from this section which would also lapse if a decision is taken that the patient should not be detained under section 2 of the MHA 1983.

Holding powers for informal patients: section 5

2.37 Section 5(1) allows for the detention of patients who are already in hospital on a voluntary basis and who can subsequently be detained under sections 2 or 3. Note that the section 5 powers can be exercised in any hospital setting (for example, a maternity or surgery ward).

Who is responsible for detaining the patient?

2.38 Section 5(2) allows the registered medical practitioner or approved clinician in charge of a voluntary patient (ie, who is not detained under this Part of the Act or subject to a CTO) who is already in hospital to furnish to the managers a written report to the effect that an application for compulsory admission should be made. The effect of furnishing the report is to allow the patient to be detained for up to 72 hours. This power can be delegated to no more than one person at a time (s5(3)) who must be a registered medical practitioner or approved clinician on the staff of the hospital (s5(3A)).

2.39 Section 5(4) allows a nurse 'of the prescribed class' (by an order of the Secretary of State (s5(7)) to record in writing the fact that it appears to him or her that a patient is 'suffering from mental disorder to such a degree that it is necessary for his health or safety or for the protection of others for him to be immediately restrained from leaving hospital' (s5(4)(a)) and it is not practicable to secure the

21 MHA 1983 s66(1)(a).

immediate attendance of a practitioner or clinician who could exercise the power to detain under section 5(4).

2.40 Writing the record allows the patient to be detained for a maximum of six hours, or less if the clinician arrives to complete the report required by section 5(2) within that period. If a report is then made by the clinician, the 72 hours allowed by section 5(2) runs from the time the nurse exercised the 'holding power'. Use of the holding powers does not confer the power to treat a patient without their consent.

2.41 The Regulations provide that a nurse of the prescribed class means a nurse registered by the Nursing and Midwifery Council of Level 1 or 2, whose field of practice is shown as either mental health or learning disabilities nursing.[22] Both Codes make it clear that the decision to exercise the power is for the nurse, who cannot be instructed to use it.[23]

2.42 The Code of Practice provides guidance on the use of holding powers at chapter 18. The Welsh Code deals with this at chapter 5. There are no rights of appeal as the time of the detention is so short. Again the patient can be discharged by the RC but it is more likely if the patient does not meet the section 2 or 3 criteria that the section will lapse.

Effect of applications

What happens after the applications are made?

2.43 Section 6 deals with the effect of applications for admission to hospital.

- A duly completed application for admission allows the applicant or any person authorised by them to 'take and convey' the patient to the hospital named in the application at any time within 14 days beginning with the date of the last medical examination in the case of sections 2 and 3 (s6(1)(a)), or in the case of an emergency admission, within 24 hours of either the medical recommendation or the application, whichever is the earlier. Reasonable force may be used.[24] Guidance as to the conveyance of patients is

22 Mental Health (Nurses) (England) Order 2008 SI No 1207; Mental Health (Nurses) (Wales) Order 2008 SI No 2441.

23 Code of Practice para 18.27, Code of Practice for Wales para 8.21.

24 MHA 1983 s137(2).

contained in chapter 17 of the Code of Practice and chapter 9 of the Code of Practice for Wales. The Code of Practice states that patients should be conveyed in the manner most likely to preserve their dignity and privacy (para 17.3). The Code for Wales at para 9.5 refers to the responsibility to ensure that patients are conveyed in the most humane and least threatening manner consistent with ensuring that no harm comes to the patient or others. It is for the doctors who make the recommendation to ensure that a suitable hospital bed is secured, unless local policies provide otherwise: Code para 14.77.

- Once the patient is admitted to hospital within these time periods, or detained after having been admitted informally, the application is 'sufficient authority' for the managers to detain the patient in accordance with the Act (s6(2)).
- The managers of the hospital can act on what appears to be a duly made application, based on the necessary medical foundations, without requiring further proof of the signature or qualifications of the recommendations or application, or of anything stated in the recommendation or application (s6(3)).

2.44 This means that if the application has not in fact been duly completed, then the applicant or, their delegate, does not have authority to take and convey the patient to hospital. The LSSA or whomever the AMHP acts for could be liable for unlawfully detaining the patient.

2.45 However, if the application and medical recommendations *appear* to be duly completed, they can be relied upon by the hospital managers who can then act upon them once they are received. The hospital managers are then required to scrutinise the application (after the detention has begun). Section 15 allows some irregularities in the application or recommendations to be amended, within 14 days beginning with the date on which the patient was admitted. However, if it becomes clear on proper scrutiny that the application or recommendations are fundamentally defective, then the patient's detention should be brought to an end.

2.46 In *TTM v Hackney LBC*,[25] an AMHP completed an application that was unlawful. The AMHP had stated that the patient's nearest relative did not object to detention under section 3. The AMHP and TTM's nearest relative had a number of conversations and the AMHP believed in good faith that the nearest relative no longer objected to the admission. The court found, on an objective assessment of the conversations, that it was clear that the nearest relative

25 [2011] EWCA Civ 4.

did still object. Although the hospital managers were entitled to rely on the application, the patient's detention was unlawful, both under common law and through breach of TTM's Article 5 rights. Section 6(3) exonerated the hospital from liability. The LSSA was liable for the unlawful detention because it had caused the hospital to detain TTM.

2.47 Chapter 14 of the Code provides guidance on applications for admission and re-affirms the need to consider alternatives to detention such as informal admission or use of a home treatment team (para 14.11). In the case of patients lacking capacity to consent to admission to hospital, the AMHP should consider whether the treatment can be given using sections 5 or 6 of the MCA 2005, or the Deprivation of Liberty Safeguards (see chapter 14). Paragraph 14.9 of the Code provides a checklist of factors which must be considered, including the patient's wishes, views of their own needs, cultural background, and the impact on the patient's children, relatives or carers if he or she deteriorates or does not improve. The Code also provides guidance as to how Mental Health Act assessments should be set up and carried out (paras 14.38–14.56). Specific guidance as to the assessment of patients who are deaf appears at paras 14.115–14.119; and paras 14.120–14.125 give guidance as to assessing patients with dementia. Paragraph 14.88 of the Code requires the AMHP to ensure, before making an application, that appropriate arrangements are in place for any dependent children of the patient, and for any adults who rely on the patient for care. The Code for Wales provides guidance at Chapter 2.

2.48 It is essential to satisfy yourself that the requirements of the Mental Health Act 1983 and the relevant Code have been complied with in every case and the best way of doing this will be to check the section papers. Guidance as to how to approach this important task is at chapter 11, para 11.37 and see checklist at appendix E.

2.49 The Mental Health (Hospital, Guardianship and Treatment) (England) Regulations 2008[26] set out procedures for service and delivery of documents (regulation 3) and for records of admissions (regulation 4).

2.50 The Mental Health (Hospital, Guardianship and Treatment) (Wales) Regulations 2008[27] set out procedures for service and delivery of documents (regulation 3) and for records of admissions (regulation 4).

26 SI No 1184.

27 SI No 2439 (W212).

2.51 Both sets of regulations prescribe specific forms which must be used in each case.

Reception into guardianship

2.52 Guardianship is a community section which does not deprive a patient of his or her liberty. It is relatively rarely used.

2.53 Sections 7–10 deal with the power of guardianship. Guardianship can be used in respect of a patient who is:

- at least 16 years old (s7(1)); and
- suffering from mental disorder of a nature or degree which warrants his reception into guardianship(s7(2)(a))

and it is necessary in the interests of the welfare of the patient or for the protection of others that he is received into guardianship (s7(2)(b)). A ward of court cannot be received into guardianship (s33(3)).

2.54 Chapter 30 of the Code of Practice deals with guardianship. The purpose is described as 'to enable patients to receive care outside hospital when it cannot be provided without the use of compulsory powers' (para 30.2), and it is described as 'an authoritative framework for working with a patient, with a minimum of restraint, to achieve as independent a life as possible within the community'. The Code for Wales contains similar provisions.[28] Paragraph 30.5 reads 'Guardianship must not be used to impose restrictions that amount to a deprivation of liberty'.

Effect of the Guardianship Order

2.55 Guardianship does not involve admission to hospital but gives the guardian (who can be any person but is frequently the local social services authority):

- The power to require the patient to reside at a place specified by the guardian (s8(1)(a)).
- The power to require the patient to attend at specified places and times for medical treatment, occupation, education or training.
- The power to require access to the patient to be given, at any place where he or she is residing, to any registered medical practitioner, AMHP or any other specified person.

28 Code for Wales para 6.2.

2.56 A guardian who is not the LSSA is referred to as a private guardian.[29] Such a guardian must comply with certain duties including appointing a general practitioner (GP) for the patient, keeping the LSSA informed as they require and following the LSSA's directions in exercising the guardian's powers and duties[30]

2.57 If a patient subject to guardianship leaves their required place of residence without permission, section 18(3) permits an officer of the LSSA or person authorised by the LSSA, or a constable, to take the patient into custody and return him, either within six months starting with the day of his absence or within the duration of the guardianship order (whichever is the later). Section 18(7) provides that this power can also be used to take the patient to their new placement for the first time. Section 137(2) provides that reasonable force can be used because it gives those exercising powers to take and convey under the Act the same powers as a constable has within the area where he or she acts.

Who makes the application?

2.58 The application is made by an AMHP or the patient's nearest relative (s11(1)) and must be supported by two medical recommendations (s7(3)). There must be no more than five clear days between the examinations.[31] The Regulations prescribe the forms to be used.[32]

2.59 If the applicant is the nearest relative and wishes to appoint the local authority as guardian then the application must be accompanied by a written statement confirming the local authority accepts the appointment, or the application will not take effect (s7(5)).

2.60 The application must be forwarded to the local social services authority within 14 days of the latest of the medical recommendations (s8(2)). As with applications for admissions for treatment an application that appears to be duly made can be acted upon by the local authority. Section 8(4) allows for the correction of defective applications within 14 days of acceptance.

29 Mental Health (Hospital, Guardianship and Treatment) Regulations 2008 reg 2.

30 Mental Health (Hospital, Guardianship and Treatment) Regulations 2008 reg 22. Mental Health (Hospital, Guardianship, Community Treatment and Consent to Treatment) (Wales) Regulations 2008 reg 11.

31 MHA 1983 s12(1).

32 Mental Health (Hospital, Guardianship and Treatment) Regulations 2008 reg 52. Mental Health (Hospital, Guardianship, Community Treatment and Consent to Treatment) (Wales) Regulations 2008 reg 9.

When can the patient appeal to the tribunal?

2.61 A patient subject to guardianship may apply to the tribunal for discharge of the order. See table 4 at para 5.11 for details.

Who can discharge the order?

2.62 A patient subject to guardianship may be discharged by his nearest relative.[33] There is no equivalent to the RC's power under section 25 to make a 'barring order' (see para 2.233) but a nearest relative of a guardianship patient may be displaced: see below para 2.238.

2.63 If a guardian, who is not the LSSA, dies or wishes to relinquish guardianship then the guardian's powers vest in the local authority (s10)(1)), who will also exercise the guardian's powers in the event the guardian is incapable of doing so (s10(2)). An AMHP can apply to the county court for transfer of a guardianship order if a non-LSSA guardian is exercising his or her powers negligently or against the interests of the patient's welfare (s10(4)).

The tribunal can discharge the order: s72(4), see para 5.54.

Can guardianship be used to impose a move to a new home or to deprive a person of their liberty?

2.64 A controversial aspect of guardianship has been the extent to which it provides the power for the guardian to determine whether the patient should move from their home, and whether it can be used to deprive the subject of his or her liberty. In connection with patients who lack capacity to make decisions about where they should live, in *C (by his litigation friend the Official Solicitor) v Blackburn with Darwen Borough Council and others*[34] Peter Jackson J commented that:

> ... it is not in my view appropriate for genuinely contested issues about the place of residence of a resisting incapacitated person to be determined either under the guardianship regime or by means of a standard authorisation under the DOLS regime. Substantial decisions of that kind ought properly to be made by the Court of Protection.[35]

2.66 The Code provides that the power to return patients should not be used to restrict their freedom such that they are effectively detained (para 30.30). The power to require patients to live in a specified place

33 MHA 1983 s23(1).
34 [2011] EWHC 3321 (COP).
35 [2011] EWHC 3321 (COP) at para 37.

may not be used to deprive them of their liberty unless this is separately authorised (para 30.31). Paragraph 30.37 continues:

> If a patient consistently resists exercise by the guardian of any of their powers it can normally be concluded that guardianship is not the most appropriate form of care for that person and the guardianship should be discharged.

Support for the proposition that the guardianship powers do not extend to deprivation of liberty can be found in *NL v Hampshire CC*.[36]

Community Treatment Orders or Supervised Community Treatment: section 17A

2.67 Community Treatment Orders (CTOs) were one of the most controversial amendments of the Mental Health Act 2007 and were opposed by many, including the Royal College of Psychiatry. CTOs provide another legal framework for treating patients in the community.

2.68 At the time of the debates over the Mental Health Bill 2007, the government's position was that CTOs would be used for a relatively small number of 'revolving door' patients. In fact the use of CTOs far outstripped this. In 2012/13 there were 4,647 uses of CTOs, the highest figure since their introduction. In 2013/14 there were 4,434 CTOs.[37]

2.69 Chapter 29 of the Code deals with Community Treatment Orders. Paragraph 29.2 describes the purpose of CTOs as:

> ... to allow suitable patients to be safely treated in the community rather than under detention in hospital, and to provide a way to help prevent relapse and any harm – to the patient or others – that this may cause. It is intended to help patients to maintain stable mental health outside hospital and to promote recovery.

2.70 A randomised controlled trial, funded by the National Institute of Health Research, of patients discharged under CTOs and patients discharged under section 17 leave found that the number of patients re-admitted did not differ between the groups. This was interpreted as showing that in well co-ordinated mental health services the imposition of compulsory supervision does not reduce the rate of readmission of psychotic patients.[38]

36 [2014] UKUT 475 (AAC).

37 *Monitoring the Mental Health Act in 2013/14*, Care Quality Commission.

38 See *The Lancet* vol 381: http://dx.doi.org/10.1016/S0140-6736(13)60107-5.

2.71 Patients who are 'liable to be detained in a hospital in pursuance to an application for admission for treatment' may be made subject to CTOs.[39] This includes those detained under section 3 but not section 2. Schedule 1, Part 1, para 1 provides that the CTO provisions also apply to patients subject to hospital orders (discussed in chapter 3).

2.72 Patients subject to CTOs are referred to in the Mental Health Act 1983 as 'community patients' (s17A(7)).

Who makes the application?

2.73 The RC can discharge a detained patient from hospital, subject to the patient remaining liable to recall (in other words onto a CTO) if the following criteria, set out in section 17A(5) are met (and with the agreement of an AMHP, see below):

- The patient is suffering from mental disorder of a nature or degree which makes it appropriate for him to receive medical treatment; and
- It is necessary for the patient's health or safety or for the protection of other persons that he should receive such treatment; and
- The treatment can be provided without the patient continuing to be detained in a hospital, provided he remains liable to recall; and
- It is necessary that the RC should be able to exercise the power of recall; and
- Appropriate medical treatment is available for him.

2.74 When deciding whether the power of recall is necessary the RC must consider what risk there would be of the patient's condition deteriorating if he or she were not in hospital (for example as a result of him or her refusing or neglecting to receive treatment). The RC must have regard to the patient's history of mental disorder and any other relevant factors (s17A(6)).

2.75 An AMHP must state in writing that he or she agrees that the criteria are met and that it is appropriate to make the order.

2.76 The Code states that 'a CTO may only be used if it would not be possible to achieve the desired objectives for the patient's care and treatment without it. In particular, the RC should consider whether the power to recall the patient is necessary and whether the patient can be treated in the community without that power. Consultation at an early stage with the patient and those involved with the patient's

39 MHA 1983 s17A(1) and (2).

care will be important' (para 29.10). The patient's views should also be taken into account: see para 29.15.

2.77 A CTO must always contain a condition which requires the patient to make himself available for examination in two situations: the first is when the RC has to examine the patient in order to decide whether to renew the CTO (s20A) and the second is when a Second Opinion Appointed Doctor (SOAD) has to examine the patient to provide a certificate under Part 4A where this is required in order to treat the patient. See chapter 4, 'Consent to treatment' at para 4.54 onwards. If the patient does not comply with either of these conditions, the RC may recall the patient (s17E(2)). Other conditions may be imposed only if the RC and the AMHP think them necessary or appropriate for one or more of the following:

- Ensuring medical treatment (s17B(2)(a)).
- Preventing risk of harm to the patient's health or safety (s17B(2)(b)).
- Protecting other persons (s17B(2)(c)).

When can the patient apply to the mental health tribunal?

2.78 A patient can apply to the MHT within six months beginning with the day on which the CTO was made[40] and in any successive periods for which the CTO is renewed.[41]

Who can discharge the Community Treatment Order?

2.79 The CTO will remain in force until:

- six months has elapsed and the order has not been extended (s17C(a), s20A);
- the patient is discharged by the RC, the hospital managers or the tribunal (s17C(b));
- the application for treatment otherwise ceases to have effect (s17C(c));
- the order is revoked under section 17F (s17C(d) and see below para 2.85).

2.80 Section 20A allows the extension of the CTO for a further six months and then for periods of a year at a time.

40 MHA 1983 s66(2)(ca).

41 MHA 1983 s66(2)(fza).

2.81 The Regulations prescribe the forms to be used.[42]

2.82 It is important to be aware that while the patient remains on a CTO the section 3 order for treatment is suspended but comes into effect if the CTO is revoked (s17D). Different provisions as to consent to treatment apply to community patients and to detained patients: see chapter 4, 'Consent to treatment'.

Power of recall

2.83 The core of the powers attached to a CTO is the power of recall. The power of recall can be exercised if in the RC's opinion:

- the patient requires medical treatment in hospital for his mental disorder, and
- there would be a risk of harm to the health or safety of the patient or to other persons if the patient were not recalled to hospital for treatment.

As set out in para 2.77 above the RC can recall the patient to hospital if the patient has not complied with the mandatory conditions in section 17B(3).

2.84 The Regulations prescribed the forms to be used on recalling a patient and how the patient should be notified.[43] The Code of Practice provides further guidance.[44]

2.85 It will be seen therefore that the threshold for admitting a patient on a CTO to hospital is lower than for admitting a patient under sections 2 and 3. Once a patient has been recalled the RC must decide within 72 hours whether to revoke the CTO. If this happens, the patient is then treated as if they had been detained under section 3 (or section 37) on the day on which the order is revoked (s17G(5)). The hospital managers must refer the case of a patient whose CTO has been revoked to the MHT (s68(7)).

42 Mental Health (Hospital, Guardianship and Treatment) Regulations 2008 reg 6; Mental Health (Hospital Guardianship, Community Treatment and Consent to Treatment) (Wales) Regulations 2008 reg 16.

43 English reg 6, Welsh reg 19.

44 Code 29.45–29.51; Code for Wales paras 30.63–30.71.

Assessing the lawfulness of the patient's admission: how applications and recommendations should be carried out

2.86 Sections 11–16 contain important provisions as to how applications and recommendations should be carried out. Familiarity with these sections is important so that practitioners are able to assess whether their client's admission has been lawful. Where appropriate these have been included in the paragraphs dealing with the procedure for admission or guardianship. The provisions relating to the nearest relative are considered in more detail at paras 2.228–2.242.

2.87 Additionally the following requirements should be noted:

- **Section 11(1A)** prohibits AMHPs from applying for admission or guardianship where there is a potential conflict of interest; and section 12(3) prohibits medical practitioners from making recommendations where there is a potential conflict of interest. The Mental Health (Conflict of Interest) (England) Regulations 2008[45] and the Mental Health (Conflicts of Interest) (Wales) Regulations[46] define circumstances in which potential conflicts arise for financial, business, professional and personal reasons and are made under section 12A. Chapter 39 of the Code of Practice also summarises the provisions (chapter 3 of the Code for Wales). There will be a potential conflict of interest if the patient is to be admitted to an independent hospital and both medical assessors are on the staff of that hospital. There will also be a potential conflict if all three assessors are members of the same team. Both Codes make it plain that conflicts of interests may arise in other circumstances as well.
- **Section 11(2)** requires that the application for admission shall be addressed to the managers of the hospital and the guardianship application sent to the LSSA who is the guardian or the LSSA where the patient resides.
- **Section 11(3)** requires an AMHP to take 'such steps as are practicable' to inform the person appearing to be the nearest relative that an application for admission for assessment (ie, under s2) has been or is to be made.
- **Section 11(4)** prohibits an AMHP from applying for admission for treatment (s3) or guardianship (s7) if the nearest relative objects

45 SI No 205.

46 SI No 2440.

(s11(4)(a)) or if the AMHP has not consulted the person appearing to be the nearest relative, unless it appears to the AMHP that consultation is not reasonably practicable or would involve unreasonable delay (s11(4)(b)). (See discussion of *TTM* at para 2.46 above.) The decision on whether it is practicable to consult can include consideration of the patient's wishes which would be more than a passing comment, possible harm to their health, whether contact would serve no purpose or merely allow the NR the opportunity to interfere in the patient's life. In *TW v Enfield Borough Council*[47] the Court of Appeal held that the AMHP should weigh up the interference in the patient's Article 8 rights which would be involved in consulting a nearest relative against the patient's Article 5 rights and *R(E) v Bristol City Council*[48] should not be followed[49] The Court further held that at the time the Code of Practice on this point was incomplete.[50] This is now addressed in the Code at paras 14.57–14.65. Note that this subsection does not apply when the patient is a ward of court (s33(1)) because the leave of the court is required to apply for the ward's admission.

- **Section 11(5)** provides that no application for admission under sections 2, 3 or 7 may be made unless the applicant (whether AMHP or nearest relative) has personally seen the patient within 14 days ending with the date of the application.
- **Section 12(1)** requires medical recommendations to be carried out together or not less than five days apart.
- **Section 12(2)** provides that one of the two medical recommendations must come from a practitioner approved by the Secretary of State as having special experience in the diagnosis and treatment of mental disorder (referred to as 'section 12 approved') and if the section 12 doctor does not have previous acquaintance with the patient then the other medical practitioner should, if practicable.
- **Sections 12ZA, 12ZB and 12ZC** allow the Secretary of State to arrange for the approval functions to be exercised by third parties and were added by the Health and Social Care Act 2012.
- **Section 12A** allows the Secretary of State to make regulations about the circumstances which mental health professionals would be considered to have conflicts of interests.

47 [2014] EWCA Civ 362.
48 [2005] EWHC 74 (Admin).
49 [2014] EWCA Civ 362 at paras 26–31.
50 [2014] EWCA Civ 362 at para 54.

- **Section 13(4)** compels a local social services authority, if required by the nearest relative of a person living in the authority's area, to arrange for an AMHP to consider the person's case with a view to an application for admission. If the AMHP decides not to make the application they must give the nearest relative reasons in writing. This provision that can be useful if you are asked to advise a client who is concerned about the mental health of one of their family; see also section 14 below.
- **Section 14** requires the managers to notify the LSSA if a patient is detained following an application by a nearest relative, and the LSSA must then arrange for an AMHP to interview the patient and prepare a social circumstances report for the managers.
- **Section 15** is an important provision that deals with the ability of the detaining authority to rectify some defects in applications for admission, within 14 days beginning with the date of admission. Note that no provision is made for renewals of detention which are defective to be rectified. Nor are there provisions for CTO documentation to be rectified. See also the note at para 2.60.

When can the patient leave the ward? Section 17 leave

2.88 Practitioners will frequently be asked to advise about the important issue of leave for detained patients.

2.89 Section 17 provides the RC with the power to grant detained patients leave of absence, during which time the patient can be recalled by the RC if it appears necessary to do so in the interests of the patient's health or safety or the protection of others (s17(4)). The consent of the Secretary of State is required in the case of restricted patients: Schedule 1 Part 2 paras 2 and 3. This is discussed at para 3.15 below.

2.90 Leave cannot be granted to patients remanded to hospital under sections 35 or 36 of the Act, or to those subject to interim hospital orders under section 38 (Code para 27.4). Only the RC or an approved clinician acting as the patient's RC (for example if the RC is on leave) may grant section 17 leave.[51]

2.91 This power can be used to grant trial leave to another hospital (usually from a high secure to a medium secure hospital): s17(3). The RC must consider using a CTO (see paras 2.67–2.85 above)

51 Code of Practice para 21.6. See also Code of Practice for Wales para 28.3.

before granting 'longer term leave' (where leave of absence will total more than seven consecutive days: s17(2B). (This requirement will not apply to patients who would not be eligible for CTOs, ie patients detained under section 2 or restricted patients.)

2.92 The Code of Practice provides guidance on when to use longer term leave at para 31.5.

2.93 See paras 27.22–27.37 of the Code of Practice for important guidance on the planning, recording and organisation of leave and chapter 31 on the question of deciding between leave or CTO.

2.94 In practice patients may start with some form of escorted leave and move to unescorted leave at a later stage. The decision to grant this is entirely within the discretion or the RC for unrestricted patients.

2.95 In restricted cases the Ministry of Justice will explain to the RC what their reasons are for not granting leave. This will enable the RC to reapply with extra information or have the patient address through some sort of therapy the concerns they have. The Ministry of Justice has provided guidance for the RC when making applications for leave to the MHCS[52] and practitioners can help by following up the applications and calling the case worker at the MHCS for a decision.

2.96 The Code for Wales deals with leave at chapter 28.

Patients who leave hospital or the place[53] where they are required to live in the community without prior permission

2.97 Section 18 contains the various powers to return patients who are absent without leave (AWOL). These powers apply to detained patients who either leave hospital without permission, or fail to return when required from at the conclusion of their leave, or who leave without permission a place where they are required to reside by virtue of conditions of leave (s18(1)). The powers also apply to community patients who have been recalled, and to those received into guardianship who absent themselves without permission from the place where they are required to live by the guardian.

Who can return the patient?

2.98 Section 18 empowers an officer of the detaining authority or person authorised by the managers of the hospital, an AMHP or a constable

52 See appendix C.

53 MHA 1983 s18(1)(c).

to take the patient into custody and return them. In the case of a patient subject to guardianship, the power can be exercised by any officer of a local social services authority, any constable or any person authorised in writing by the guardian or the local social services authority. See also paras 2.64–2.66.

For how long does the power to return the patient apply after they have gone AWOL?

2.99 If the patient was detained under sections 2, 4 or 5 then he may not be taken and returned after the expiration of the period of detention authorised by the section (s18(5)). In other cases the power can be exercised until the later of either the expiry of the section, or six months beginning from the day of their absence (s18(4)). Detention or guardianship cannot be renewed while a patient is absent without leave (ss18(4A) and 18(4B)). Restricted patients can be re-taken at any time while the restrictions remain in place.

The transfer of patients

2.100 Section 19 deals with transfers between hospitals and between guardianship and hospitals, and empowers the Secretary of State to make regulations as to the management of such transfers. In *R (L) v West London Mental Health NHS Trust*[54] the Court held that a common law duty of fairness was engaged by the decision to transfer a patient from medium security to a high secure hospital, because of the serious implications for the patient. The Court of Appeal agreed that such a duty was engaged.[55] The Court of Appeal said that the gist of the letter of referral by the medium secure unit to the high secure unit, and the assessment carried out by the clinician from the high secure hospital, should be disclosed to the patient and/or his or her representative. This should happen unless precluded by urgency, security or a clinical reason. The patient and/or the representative should be informed in writing that they may make recommendations to the admissions panel which will decide whether to accept the patient. If the doctor who assessed the patient is to attend the meeting it may be appropriate for the patient to participate.

2.101 The Court of Appeal noted that the current version of the Code did not provide adequate guidance about transfers to high secure

54 [2012] EWHC 3200 (Admin).

55 [2014] EWCA Civ 47.

hospitals. The guidance given by the Court of Appeal is now reflected in the Code at para 37.22:

> In the case of transfers to high security psychiatric hospitals, unless the circumstances are urgent or there would be clinical risks to the patient or others or there is some other significant reason to make it inadvisable, the relevant hospital managers should:
>
> - give the patient and/or their representative sufficient information and opportunity to make written representations to the admissions panel of the receiving hospital. At a minimum this will be a summary (if the documents are not provided) of:
>   - the letter of reference from the hospital that wishes to transfer the patient to the high security hospital
>   - the assessment by the clinician from the high security hospital; and any other accompanying reports/documents the hospital managers think should be shared in the interests of fairness
> - if the assessing doctor is invited to attend the deliberations of the admissions panel, the hospital should consider whether the patient and/or their representative should be invited to attend or be represented at those deliberations.

Duration of orders, renewal and discharge: sections 20–25

Renewals

2.102 The remainder of Part 2 of the Mental Health Act 1983 deals with the duration and renewal of detention, discharge of patients and the important provisions relating to 'nearest relatives'.

2.103 Section 20 deals with the duration of applications for admission for treatment and guardianship.

Section 3 and Community Treatment Orders

2.104 An application for treatment (s3) or guardianship lasts for six months beginning with the date of admission or guardianship (s20(1)) but the application can be renewed for six months (s20(2)(a)) and subsequently for periods not exceeding a year (s20(2)(b)). This is mirrored for patients on CTOs (s20A).

2.105 In the case of detained patients, and those on CTOs, the renewal is the decision of the RC who must satisfy themselves that the appropriate criteria are met by examining the patient within the two months ending on the last day of the original period of detention (ss20(3) and 20A(4)). The criteria concerned are the same as the criteria for a section 3 admission or being made subject to a CTO (ss3(2) and 20(4) and ss17A(5) and 20A(6)).

2.106 The RC must also consult at least one other person from another profession who has been professionally concerned with the patient's medical treatment before furnishing their report to the managers renewing the detention or CTO. That person must be from a different profession to the RC (s20(5), (5A)). In the case of a CTO patient the RC's report must be accompanied by a statement from an AMHP confirming that the criteria for continuing the CTO are met and that it is appropriate for the CTO to be extended (ss20A(4)(b), (8)).

2.107 The furnishing of the report to the managers has the effect of renewing the period of detention or CTO (ss20(3); 20A(10)). Note that section 15 does not apply to renewals so defects in renewals cannot be subsequently amended.

Guardianship

2.108 A similar process takes place for patients subject to guardianship save that the examination is carried out by the relevant practitioner and the report furnished to the LSSA and no other professional needs to be involved.

2.109 On receipt of the RC's or practitioner's report the hospital managers or LSSA must consider whether to discharge the patient under section 23.

Renewing the section of a patient on leave

2.110 It is lawful for the detention of a patient who is on leave at the time to be renewed, as long as hospital treatment forms a significant component of the patient's treatment plan: *R (DR) v Mersey Care NHS Trust*;[56] *R (CS) v Mental Health Review Tribunal*.[57] Hospital treatment can include out patient treatment carried out at a hospital: see *KL v Somerset Partnership NHS Foundation Trust*.[58]

2.111 Chapter 32 of the Code of Practice considers renewal. Note paragraph 32.9 which reads that:

56 [2002] EWHC 1810 (Admin).

57 [2004] EWHC 2958 (Admin).

58 [2011] UKUT 233 (AAC).

Unless there are exceptional circumstances, the decision of the identified second professional should be accepted, even if the responsible clinician disagrees with it.

2.112 The Code for Wales provides guidance as to the role of the RC in connection with renewals at para 12.17 onwards.

If the patient is AWOL does their section expire?

2.113 There are special provisions for those patients who are absent without leave when either their detention, CTO or guardianship is due to expire: see sections 21 and 21A. In brief these provisions have the effect of extending the duration of the original authority until after the patient returns, or is returned, within the time limits of section 18 discussed above.

2.114 If the patient has been absent for more than 28 days the relevant practitioner must examine the patient within a week of the day of return and report to the managers if he considers the relevant criteria to be satisfied (ie, the criteria for detention, CTO or guardianship). If no such report is furnished within seven days then the detention, guardianship or CTO will cease to have effect (except in the case of a CTO patient whose CTO is revoked). If the report is furnished then the authority to detain (or for CTO or guardianship) is renewed. The renewal will take effect from the date that the original authority would have expired.

2.115 If a patient subject to detention, guardianship or a CTO is detained in custody pursuant to a court order or sentence for more than six months the application will expire at the end of the six months. This provision does not apply to restricted patients[59] so they will remain subject to the application and restrictions.

2.116 If the period in custody is less than six months the following provisions apply:

- The patient will be treated as if the order for detention or the CTO were in force until the end of the day on which he is released even if it has in fact expired: s22(5).
- The day of release from custody shall be treated as if the patient had gone absent without leave on that day: s22(6).
- The patient can be taken into custody within 28 days beginning from the date of release: s22(7).
- A CTO will come to an end if the underlying section 3 application has come to an end.

59 MHA 1983 Sch 1 Part 2 para 6.

Discharge of patients

2.117 Section 23 of the Mental Health Act 1983 provides that the powers to discharge patients from detention, guardianship or CTOs may be exercised by RCs, hospital managers and (subject to section 25) nearest relatives. This power does not apply to patients remanded to hospital, those on interim hospital orders or to restricted patients.

Responsible clinicians

2.118 Paragraph 32.18 of the Code provides guidance and specifies that responsible clinicians (RCs) must keep the appropriateness of compulsory powers under review and discharge patients if their use is not warranted. Paragraph 12.27 of the Code for Wales gives similar guidance.

2.119 A refusal by a second professional to support renewal of detention, guardianship or a CTO, or the refusal of an AMHP to support extension of a CTO, should prompt the responsible clinician to review the appropriateness of compulsory powers.

The hospital managers

2.220 The hospital managers' power of discharge is an important safeguard. Managers may review a patient's detention at any time and can carry this out themselves or authorise a panel to review detention.

2.221 The Code of Practice provides guidance as to when detention or a CTO should be reviewed: para 38.11. It must be reviewed when the responsible clinician submits a report renewing either detention or a CTO. Managers should consider reviewing detention when they receive a request from, or on behalf of, a patient asking for discharge; and when they receive a report from a responsible clinician barring discharge by a nearest relative (see para 2.233). See also chapter 27 of the Code of Practice for Wales.

2.222 The review is generally carried by a panel of three persons conducting an oral hearing who can be authorised by the detaining authority for that purpose.

2.223 The MHA 1983 does not specify the criteria to be applied by hospital managers in exercising the power of discharge, or the form in which the decision should be taken.

2.224 The Code at chapter 38 describes how managers' panels should be configured (paras 38.3–38.9) and the procedure to be adopted (38.24–

38.50). It is important to be familiar with these provisions before representing at a managers' hearing. Paragraph 38.37 provides:

> Members of managers' panels will not normally be qualified to form clinical assessments of their own. They must give full weight to the views of all the professionals concerned in the patient's care. If there is a divergence of views amongst the professionals ... managers' panels should reach an independent judgment based on the evidence that they hear. Regard should be had to the least restrictive option and maximising independence principle. In some cases it might be necessary to consider adjourning to seek further medical or other professional advice.

2.225 The Code sets out the criteria to be considered by the managers at paras 38.16–38.18 (paras 27.15 and 27.16 in the Code for Wales) and it will be seen that these mirror the criteria for admission or for the imposition of a CTO respectively. If three or more members of the panel do not agree that the criteria are satisfied then the patient should be discharged (para 38.19): *R (Tagoe-Thompson) v The Hospital Managers of the Park Royal Centre.*[60] Note that the Code suggests that when the managers discharge a patient who lacks capacity to decide where the live 'the hospital managers may request that consideration be given to making a DOL authorisation or a DOL order'.

2.226 The manager should also convene when a barring order is issued by the RC. This will be discussed under nearest relatives in the section below.

2.227 Managers must give reasons for their decisions: see Code at paras 38.47–38.49. If the reasons are inadequate the decision may be unlawful: see *R (O) v West London Mental Health NHS Trust.*[61]

The nearest relative

2.228 The term 'nearest relative' (NR) derives from the 1983 Act. In most cases a patient subject to the provisions of the Act will have a family member to whom the Act assigns certain rights and powers. It will already have been seen for example that section 11(4) requires the AMHP to consult with the person appearing to be the nearest relative before making an application for admission, subject to certain exceptions (see para 2.87).

2.229 The nearest relative can exercise a pivotal role. Practitioners should be alert to the possibility of conflict of interest if considering

60 [2003] EWCA Civ 330.

61 [2005] EWHC 604 (Admin).

representing both patient and nearest relative and this is discussed at para 7.32.

2.230 If the patient is a ward of court, then the powers of the nearest relative are exercised by the court.[62]

2.231 The table overleaf sets out the key provisions which apply to the nearest relative.

62 MHA 1983 s33(4).

Table 1: role of the nearest relative

Role	Provision
Can make an application for detention under ss2 or 3	s11(1)
Can make an application for guardianship	s11(1)
Must be consulted by AMHP unless impracticable before s3	s11(4)
With the patient's consent, should be provided with copies of information about the patient's status and about rights to appeal that is provided to the patient.	s132 (detained patient), s132A (community patient)
As long as the patient does not object, should be informed of patient's discharge (including discharge onto a CTO).	s133
Unless the patient requests otherwise, managers must take reasonably practicable steps to inform the person who appears to be the NR of a patient's transfer, renewal of detention, extension of CTO, transfer to/from guardianship.	Mental Health Regs reg 26 Mental Health (Wales) Regs regs 8.22
Unless patient requests otherwise, LSSA to provide information about patient subject to guardianship	Mental Health Regs reg 26 Mental Health (Wales) Regs reg 15
Can require LSSA to arrange consideration of patient's case by AMHP, with a view to assessment for admission by LSSA; entitled to written reasons if AMHP does not make an application.	s13(4)
Can discharge patient from ss2 and 3 subject to RC's power to bar	s23(2), s25(1)
Can discharge from CTO subject to RC's power to bar	s23(2), s25(1A)
Can discharge from guardianship – no power to bar	s23(2)
Can obtain examination by registered medical practitioner, who may see patient's records and examine him in private, for purpose of deciding whether to exercise power to discharge	s24
Can delegate powers in writing	Mental Health Regs reg 24 Mental Health (Wales) Regs reg 33
Can be displaced by county court	s29
Can apply to MHT in respect of patient under s3 or community patient where discharge has been barred by RC	s66(g)
Can apply to MHT for discharge of patient detained under s37	s69
MHT shall notify NR of application, subject to patient with capacity requesting otherwise.	Tribunal Procedure Rules 2008 r33 Mental Health Tribunal Rules for Wales r16

The application for discharge by the nearest relative

2.231 The NR may discharge a patient detained in hospital under sections 2 or 3, subject to the RC's power to bar discharge under section 25(1) (see para 2.233). The NR may also discharge a patient from a CTO (subject to s25) or guardianship. This is an important safeguard and it is therefore necessary correctly to identify the nearest relative and advise the patient of his or her power, and, with the patient's agreement, the nearest relative themselves. (See chapter 11 for more guidance as to how this may work in practice). The 'pecking order' is set out in section 26(1) but note that this is elaborated in subsections (2)-(7). Sections 27 and 28 deal with the nearest relative for children or young people in care and for minors under guardianship.

The limits on the powers

2.232 The limits on the nearest relative's power to discharge and the patient's right to apply for a different nearest relative to be appointed are considered at para 2.238. The notice of discharge by the nearest relative must be in writing. Managers should offer nearest relatives any help they require (para 32.25 of the Code of Practice) such as giving them a standard letter. The Code has an illustrative standard letter which could be adapted for use (para 32.25). The Code considers the provision of information to nearest relatives at paras 4.31–4.36 and the assistance they may require at para 32.23.

2.233 The power to discharge a patient from detention or from a CTO is subject to the RC's power to issue a barring order within 72 hours after notice has been given to the managers by the nearest relative (s25(1)). The RC can bar discharge if they report that in their opinion the patient is likely, if discharged, to act in a manner dangerous to other persons or themselves. Paragraph 32.23 of the Code notes that 'this question focuses on the probability of dangerous acts such as causing serious physical injury or lasting psychological harm, not merely on the patient's general need for safety and others' general need for protection'. In addition it removes the necessity for detention on the grounds of health alone.

2.234 In *K (by his litigation friend) v The Hospital Managers of the Kings—wood Centre and Central and North West London NHS Foundation Trust,*[63] K sought an order of habeas corpus. K's mother, his nearest relative, had given notice by fax only of her intention to discharge K.

63 [2014] EWCA Civ 1332.

The fax was addressed to the Mental Health Act Administrator marked 'Private and confidential. To be opened by addressee only'. The administrator worked part-time and the notice did not come to her attention until after the 72 hours had expired. The 2008 Regulations[64] contain provisions for service under which the nearest relative's discharge order can served by delivery to the authorised officer, pre-paid post or – with the agreement of the managers – internal mail. Notices sent by first class post are deemed to have been served on the second business day following the day of posting; and on the fourth business day following the day of posting where second class post is used. The Regulations do not provide for service by fax or other means such as email. The Court of Appeal held that the hospital was responsible for putting into place systems to deal with documents that are served using the methods set out in the Regulations, but not when documents were served using methods not prescribed in the Regulations. Had the letter also been sent by first class post it would have been 'deemed' to have been served on the second business day following the day of posting whether the administrator had been at work or not. Because a method outside the regulations was used, the 'deeming provisions' did not apply and the time for the RC to consider whether to make a barring order did not begin to run until the administrator actually received the fax.

The managers' duty to consider the barring order

2.235 Where the RC has issued a 'barring order' under section 25 of the MHA 1983 the managers must consider whether the patient would, if discharged, be likely to act in a manner that is dangerous to himself or other people (Code para 38.20). If three or more members of the panel who comprise a majority do not consider that this had been made out then the patient should usually be discharged, but the managers retain a discretion not to discharge if there are 'exceptional reasons' why the patient should not be discharged. See *R (Huzzey) v Riverside MH Trust*[65] and *R (SR) v Huntercombe Maidenhead Hospital and others.*[66]

64 Mental Health (Hospital, Guardianship and Treatment) Regulations 2008 SI No 1184; Mental Health (Hospital, Guardianship, Community Treatment and Consent to Treatment) (Wales) Regulations 2008 SI No 2439 reg 3.

65 [1998] EWHC 465 (Admin).

66 [2005] EWHC 2361 (Admin).

Applications to the tribunal

2.236 If the application is made by the nearest relative following a barring order the MHT should consider the dangerousness criterion: see para 5.35. The details of when the NR can apply to the tribunal are set out in table 4 at para 5.11. See para 2.87 as to the need to consult with the NR; table 1 at para 2.231 for a summary of the NR's powers; para 2.238 for a discussion of section 29 and the powers of the county court to appoint a substitute NR.

An examination by a different medical practitioner on behalf of the nearest relative?

2.237 Section 24 of the Mental Health Act 1983 allows registered medical practitioners or approved clinicians to visit and examine in private and view the hospital and section 117 after-care records of a patient detained for treatment, or subject to guardianship or a CTO, in order to advise a nearest relative as to whether to exercise their powers under section 23.

Can the NR be replaced?

2.238 Section 29 of the Mental Health Act 1983 allows the county court to replace the person defined by the MHA 1983 as nearest relative and appoint a suitable person to act in their place, on the application of the patient (s29(2)(za)); a relative of the patient (s29(2)(b)); any other person with whom the patient resides or was residing before admission (s29(2)(c)); or an AMHP (s29(2)(d)). The grounds for applying are set out at section 29(3).

What if the NR refuses to consent to an order under section 3 when a patient is detained under section 2?

2.239 Section 29(4) deals with the position where a patient is detained under section 2 and the nearest relative refuses consent to an order under section 3. Provided that the application to displace is made within the currency of the section 2 order, detention under section 2 will be extended until the application is finally disposed of (including the expiration of time to appeal) or seven days after any order under section 29 is made. An automatic referral to the tribunal will be made six months after the date of detention (s68(2)). See paras 5.14–5.22

below for a detailed discussion of this subject and the impact of *MH v United Kingdom*.[67]

2.240 Section 30 of the Mental Health Act 1983 deals with the provisions for discharge or variation of an order under section 29 while section 31 provides for rules to regulate the determination of applications in the county court: see Civil Procedure Rules PD8A para 18.

2.241 Chapter 5 of the Code of Practice deals with the nearest relative. In particular it provides at paragraph 5.14 a non-exhaustive list of factors an AMHP might consider when deciding whether to apply to displace a nearest relative and these include any reason to think the nearest relative (or someone close to them) has abused the patient; any reason to think that the patient is afraid of the nearest relative or distressed at the prospect of the nearest relative being involved in their live; or where the relationship between patient and nearest relative is distant or has broken down. Paragraph 5.13 draws attention to the fact that some patients who wish to apply to displace the nearest relative may be deterred from doing so by the need to apply to the county court. The decision to apply is for the AMHP personally (para 5.15); and the AMHP should consider alternatives such as agreed delegation of the nearest relative's role or supporting the patient to make the application.

2.242 The Code of Practice for Wales directs the AMHP to consider the views of the patient and to distinguish between the patient's concern about the person and their concerns about the role of the nearest relative.[68]

67 [2013] ECHR 1008.

68 Code for Wales para 23.23.

CHAPTER 3

Mentally disordered offenders

Mental Health Act 1983 Part 3

3.1 Part 3 of the Mental Health Act 1983 deals with the admission and treatment of mentally disordered offenders (ss35–55). The patients can be called 'Part 3 patients' or, if they are subject to a restriction order, 'restricted patients'. A restriction order can be made under sections 41 and 45A of the Act and the Criminal Procedure and Insanity Act (CPIA) 1964. In addition, a patient who has been transferred from prison will normally have a restriction order until the early date of release and if they are on a life sentence the restriction lasts until discharge although the life licence continues after that.

3.2 The MHA 1983 Code of Practice emphasises the right of those subject to criminal proceedings to psychiatric assessment and treatment (para 22.3 of the Code) and the need for speedy assessment to prevent deterioration and promote a quicker trial process. The hospital wing of a prison is not a hospital for the purpose of the MHA 1983 and the consent to treatment provisions of Part 4 do not apply. In practice this means that a patient who is in prison and is unwell can only be treated with his consent (para 22.30 of the Code) or under the provisions of the Mental Capacity Act 2005 or the common law doctrine of necessity.

The patient remanded to hospital

3.3 The patient who is remanded to hospital for a report, or for treatment, is entitled to an independent report on their condition from a doctor of his or her choosing, either at the patient's own expense or through legal aid (s35(8), s36(7)) and the Code requires hospital managers to help patients exercise this right by enabling patient to contact 'a suitably qualified and experienced solicitor or other adviser'.

Types of Part 3 patients

Unrestricted patients

3.4 A person may be sentenced to a hospital order under section 37. If the court does not impose restrictions then they are in a similar position to a patient detained under section 3 except that they cannot apply to the tribunal in the first six months of the order being made. If a patient is on a time limited sentence and has reached the early date release (EDR) – the details of which the Mental Health Casework

Section (MHCS) should have – then they become an unrestricted patient on that day. Again, they are in a similar position at that stage to a patient detained under section 3.

3.5 A patient who does not have the capacity to form intent to commit a crime but has in fact committed the act of which they are accused (the 'actus reus' of the crime) can have a hospital order imposed on them either with or without a restriction. In law the intent is called the 'mens rea'. For example if a patient assaulted someone but was very psychotic at the time, they could be convicted of doing the act but due to their extreme psychosis at the time were unable to form the intent or did not have the mens rea to commit the crime.

3.6 The magistrates' court can sentence a person for the act even without the intent under section 37(3) of the Mental Health Act 1983 by imposing a hospital order without convicting a person. The court needs to be satisfied that the offence involved could be punished by imprisonment on conviction and that the person did the act or made the omission concerned. This allows hospital orders to be made in respect of those who – perhaps as a result of their mental state – cannot be shown to have had the necessary mens rea to be convicted. The Crown Court can do the same under the Domestic Violence, Crime and Victims Act 2004.

Restricted patients

3.7 A restricted patient is different in that their freedom on leave or on discharge is not a decision of the responsible clinician (RC). The Secretary of State, in practice through the MHCS, has the ultimate decision on leave and on transfer to another hospital. The MHCS can also discharge, as can the tribunal, but the RC cannot. Restricted patients have no nearest relative.

3.8 Table 2 below sets out the relevant sections of Part 3 of the Mental Health Act, who imposes the section and on what grounds, how long the section lasts and who can discharge the patient.

Table 2: Part 3 patients

Section	Court/Secretary of State	Patient
s35: remand for report on accused's mental condition	Crown Court (CC) or magistrates' court (MC) (s35(1))	An accused person awaiting trial or awaiting sentence in the CC for an imprisonable offence (s35(2)(a)), other than a sentence fixed by law (s35(3)) (ie awaiting trial for murder) can be remanded to hospital but not after conviction Person convicted by the MC of an imprisonable offence; or charged with such an offence if the court is satisfied that the act or omission were committed; or has consented to the exercise by the court (s35(2)(b))
s36: remand to hospital for treatment	CC only (s36(1))	A person awaiting trial or in the course of a trial in the CC but before sentence for an offence punishable by imprisonment (but not where the sentence is fixed by law): s36(2)
s37: hospital order/ guardianship	MC or CC	Person convicted before the CC of offence punishable by imprisonment with a sentence not fixed by law (s37(1)) (other than offences set out in s37(1A); or person convicted by the MC with offence punishable with imprisonment; or person appearing before MC with sentence punishable by imprisonment and court has not convicted but is satisfied that the person did the act or made the omission concerned (s37(3))

Grounds	Duration	Discharge by?
Court satisfied on the evidence of a registered medical practitioner (RMP) that the patient may be suffering from mental disorder (s35(3)(a)) and it would be impracticable for a report to be made if on bail (s35(3)(b)), and that arrangements have been made for admission to that hospital within 7 days beginning with the date of the remand (s35(4))	28 days at a time maximum of 12 weeks (s35(7)); further remands can be made in absence of patient if represented (s35(6))	The court at anytime by terminating the remand (s35(7))
Evidence of 2 RMP's that: • person is suffering from mental disorder of a nature or degree which makes it appropriate for him to be detained in hospital for medical treatment (s36(1)(b)), and • appropriate medical treatment is available (s36(1)(b)), and • evidence that arrangements have been made for admission to that hospital within 7 days beginning with the date of the remand (s36(3))	28 days at a time (s36(6)); maximum of 12 weeks (s36(6)) on the evidence of the RC (s36(4)); further remands in absence of patient if represented by an authorised person who is able to be heard (s36(5))	Court can terminate remand at any time (s36(6))
Evidence of 2 RMPs that: • the offender is suffering from mental disorder of a nature or degree which makes it appropriate for him to be detained in hospital for medical treatment and appropriate medical treatment is available to him (s37(2)(a)(i)); or • the offender is 16 or older and the mental disorder is of a nature and degree which warrants his reception into guardianship (s37(2)(a)(ii)), and (in both cases) • an order under this section is the most suitable way of disposing of the case (s37(2)(b)) and • evidence that arrangements have been made for admission within 28 days beginning with the date of the order (s37(4)). Note s37(5): Secretary of State can direct admission to a second hospital if it is impracticable to arrange to the first within 28 days. In the case of guardianship the court must be satisfied that the local social services authority or person named as guardian is willing to receive the offender	For 6 months, if renewed another 6 months and then renewal yearly (s20) unless accompanied by a restriction order	Can be discharged by RC if not with a restriction order and by the MHT with or without a restriction order can be discharged by the MHCS of the MoJ or the MHT

Section	Court/Secretary of State	Patient
s38: interim hospital orders	CC or MC	Person convicted of offence punishable by imprisonment by either CC or MC (other than a sentence fixed by law) (s37(1))
s41: restriction order	CC only (s41(1)) MC may commit in custody, (or direct admission to hospital under s44) if offender is 14 years old or above and if the conditions for a hospital order are satisfied but the court considers a restriction order should also be made (s43(1)). The order could be made in the person's absence if it is impracticable to bring him or her to court if proper and they are satisfied of the medical requirements of s37 (s51(7))	Hospital order is made (s41(1))
s45A: hospital and limitation direction	CC only	Offender convicted of offence for which the sentence is not fixed by law where the offender is mentally disordered but the court decides a sentence of imprisonment is appropriate and directs the transfer of the offender to hospital with restrictions under this section

Grounds	Duration	Discharge by?
Court is satisfied on the evidence of 2 RMPs that: the offender is suffering from mental disorder (s38(1)(a)), and the mental disorder is such that it may be appropriate for a hospital order to be made and the court is satisfied on evidence from the future RC who is to have responsibility, or that arrangements have been made for admission within 28 days beginning with the date of the order (s37(4))	A specified period of no more than 12 weeks (s38(5)(a)); which can be renewed for periods of no more than 28 days if warranted on the evidence of the RC (s38(5)(b)); to a maximum of 12 months can be renewed in the patient's absence as long as he is represented by counsel or a solicitor who has the opportunity of being heard (s38(6))	Terminated by the court on making a hospital order or disposing of the case in some other way (s38(5))
If it is necessary for the protection of the public from serious harm for the person to be subject to special restrictions, having regard to the nature of the offence, the antecedents of the offender and risk of the person committing further offences if set at large (s37(1)) court must have oral evidence from one of the practitioners specified in s37(2)(a)	Since 2007 indefinite/ may be some time limited restrictions left although unusual even when possible	Secretary of State or tribunal only
Court satisfied the evidence of 2 RMPs (one giving oral evidence s45A(4)) that: the offender is suffering from mental disorder of a nature or degree which makes it appropriate for him to be detained in hospital for available appropriate medical treatment to be given (s45A(2)). The court considers making a hospital order but imposes a sentence of imprisonment s45A(1)(b); Arrangements must be in place to admit the patient within 28 days beginning with the date of the direction (s45A(5)); the Secretary of State can direct a different hospital	The section does not expire	The tribunal considers detention under s74 and so makes a recommendation to the Secretary of State who then has the case considered by the Parole Board

3.9 The greater the potential interference in the patient's rights, the higher the threshold and the higher the authority of the court required to authorise it. Therefore it must be easier to satisfy a court of the need for a remand to hospital for a report than of the need for a remand to hospital for treatment.[1] The purpose of the power to remand for reports is to inform the court of a defendant's fitness to plead and his diagnosis, not to advance one party's claim, for example by obtaining evidence of his ability to form the intention to commit a particular crime.[2]

The effect of a hospital order

3.10 The effects of orders made under sections 35, 36, 37 (other than for guardianship) and section 38 is to give authority for the person to be conveyed to hospital within seven days in the case of remands under sections 35 and 36, and 28 days in the case of orders under sections 37 and 38 and for the managers of the hospital to detain him in accordance with the provisions of the MHA 1983 (see s35(9) and (10); s36(8); s40(1)).

The effect of a guardianship order

3.11 A guardianship order under section 37 provides the guardian with the same authority as they would have had the person been received into guardianship under section 8 (see paras 2.55–2.57).

3.12 The differences for patients who are on hospital orders to their Part 2 civilly detained counterparts are set out below.

3.13 Patients who are detained in hospital or received into guardianship as a result of orders made under section 37, are treated broadly as if they had been detained under section 3 or section 7, with some differences which are provided for by Schedule 1.[3]

3.14 In summary the differences are:

- A patient detained under a section 37 hospital order can apply in the second 6 months of detention: s69(3)–(5). If the patient is made subject to a guardianship order then they can apply within the first 6 months: s69(1)(b).

1 *MS v North East London Foundation Trust* [2013] UKUT 092 (AAC) where the section 2 criteria were found to be less exacting than those under section 3.

2 *R (M) v Crown Court at Kingston upon Thames* [2014] WLR (D) 328.

3 MHA 1983 Sch 1 Part 1.

- If the patient is subject to a section 37 their nearest relative does not have the right to order discharge under section 25 but after 6 months can apply directly to the tribunal: s69(1)(a).
- If the patient is placed on a guardianship order their nearest relative can apply once yearly: s69(1)(b)(ii).
- Note that the RC and hospital managers retain the power to discharge the patient, so in the first 6 months the managers can consider an appeal against detention.
- CTOs are still available for patients detained under hospital orders, but not for those subject to restriction orders.[4]

The effect of a restriction order

3.15 The imposition of a restriction order on a patient made the subject of a hospital order will have the following effect:

- The hospital order does not need to be renewed as long as the restriction order remains in force: s41(4).
- The nearest relative provisions do not apply: s41(3)(a).
- A patient can only be given leave outside the hospital grounds with the permission of the Secretary of State: s41(3)(c)(i).
- The Secretary of State must agree to transfer: s41(3)(c)(ii).
- The Secretary of State must agree to discharge either conditionally or absolutely unless ordered by the tribunal: s41(3)(c)(iii).
- The Secretary of State retains a separate power to discharge the patient either absolutely or conditionally, independently of the RC: s42(2).
- The Secretary of State can recall a conditionally discharged patient at any time: s42(3). In effect this means if something is reported to the Secretary of State they can recall the patient against the advice of the RC.
- The Secretary of State has the power to bring the restriction order to an end if he or she is satisfied that it is no longer necessary to protect the public from serious harm although this rarely happens: s42.
- Both the Secretary of State and the RC have the power to recall from leave or take into custody if the patient absconds: s41(3)(d).
- The patient cannot be placed on a CTO: s41(3)(a).
- An application to the tribunal can only be made after the first 6 months under s70 unless they have been transferred from prison

4 Sch 1 Part 1 para 1 which provides that the CTO provisions apply without modifications to Part 3 patients who are not restricted.

and then they can make an application in the first 6 months: s69(2).

- The RC is obliged to examine and send reports on the patient to the Secretary of State at intervals directed by the Secretary of State which will be no more than a year: s40(6).

3.16 Table 3 below sets out the sections, patients, grounds, duration and discharge of a prisoner transferred to hospital.

3.17 The impact of a 'restriction direction' is to have the same effect as a restriction order under section 41 (s49(2)). The difference is that the tribunal cannot discharge a sentenced patient subject to section 47/49 but can only make a recommendation under section 74 that the patient would have been entitled to a conditional discharge if detained under section 37 or 41 but if not discharged they can recommend that they should remain in hospital. If the patient is a post-tariff prisoner (in other words, if the patient has served the minimum amount of the sentence directed by the court) then the Secretary of State would normally automatically refer the case to the Parole Board. If the Parole Board does not release the patient then if a recommendation is made by the tribunal that they should remain in hospital if not discharged they would remain in hospital.

3.18 If the patient is pre-tariff (in other words if the patient has not served the minimum amount of the sentence directed by the court) then he or she would return to prison unless the tribunal has made a recommendation that he or she does not. If the tribunal recommends the patient is entitled to an absolute or conditional discharge and does not make a recommendation that the patient stay in hospital then he or she is returned to prison to apply for a Parole Board hearing if so entitled. If the patient is not entitled at that stage he or she remain in prison until released. For an example of how this can work in practice, see *R (LV) v (1) Secretary of State for Justice, (2) the Parole Board*.[5]

5 [2014] EWHC 1495 (Admin). See also *R v Vowles and others* [2015] EWCA Crim 45 for guidance to sentencing judges. The effect of this may be that more patients are made subject to section 45A.

Table 3: transfers from prison

Section	Patient	Grounds	Duration	Discharge
s47	Serving a sentence of imprisonment (s47(1)). This includes anyone who is sentenced by a criminal court, those committed to custody for breach of bind-overs by magistrates and those committed to custody for failure to pay fines (s47(5))	Secretary of State is satisfied by reports from at least 2 RMPs that the patient is suffering from mental disorder of a nature and degree which makes it appropriate for him to be detained in a hospital for medical treatment and appropriate treatment is available to him and the Secretary of State is of the opinion that is expedient to transfer the patient having regard to the public interest and all circumstances (s47(1)(a)–(c))	Order lapses if not in the named hospital within 14 days from the date it was issued	As per hospital order, or if with a restriction order then a recommendation can be made to the Secretary of State under s74 and the matter is usually then dealt with by the Parole Board
s48: transfer of remand prisoners	Those detained in prisons or a remand centre who are not sentenced; remanded in custody by MCs (not CCs who have their own powers); civil prisoners who do not fall within s47; those detained under the Immigration Act 1971 or Nationality, Immigration and Asylum Act 2002 s8(2). If still awaiting sentence or committed by the magistrates then a section 49 order must be made as well (s49(1))	If Secretary of State is satisfied by reports from at least 2 RMPs that the person is suffering from mental disorder of a nature or degree which makes it appropriate for him to be detained in a hospital for medical treatment (s48(1)(a)) and he is in urgent need of such treatment (s48(1)(b)) and appropriate medical treatment is available (s48(1)(c))	Order lapses if not in the named hospital within 14 days from the date it was issued (s48(3))	Order ceases to have effect where case is disposed of by the court (s51(2)). An order can be made in his absence (s51(5)). If the Secretary of State is informed that the person no longer needs to be in hospital then they can direct remission to a place of detention and on arrival the transfer direction ceases (s51(3)). The sentencing court may also either remit to an institution or release on bail (s51(4)). The transfer direction ceases to have effect when the period of remand ends or they are committed in custody to the Crown Court (which can be done in the person's absence if he is represented or the magistrates' court can direct the transfer direction ceases to have effect if satisfied that the person needs treatment in hospital (s52(4)).

Section	Patient	Grounds	Duration	Discharge
s49: 'restriction directions' on transferred prisoners	Patient subject to transfer under s47 or s48	If seen fit by Secretary of State (s49(1))	Restriction direction expires on release date (see s50(3)) thereafter patient becomes a 'notional s37' (s41(5))	An RC or an AC may notify Secretary of State that person no longer requires treatment in hospital or that no effective treatment is available in the particular hospital and Secretary of State may remit him to custody or exercise power to release on license or discharge under supervision (s50(1)), or a tribunal can recommend to the Secretary of State under s74 can be made that the patient would be entitled to a conditional discharge. The matter is usually then dealt with by the Parole Board but the person could be released by the Secretary of State: see paras 5.70–5.74.

CHAPTER 4

Consent to treatment

Consent to treatment: Parts 4 and 4A of the Mental Health 1983

4.1 This chapter examines the treatment that can be given under the Mental Health Act (MHA) 1983 to patients suffering from mental disorder. Chapter 15 'Understanding mental disorder' considers common forms of treatment.

4.2 Compulsory treatment can amount to an interference with a person's rights under Article 8 ECHR which guarantees the right to respect for private and family life, home and correspondence). The state can interfere with Article 8 rights only if the interference is:

- in accordance with the law, and
- necessary in a democratic society in the interests of national security, public safety or the economic well-being of the country, for the prevention of disorder or crime, for the protection of health or morals or for the protection of the rights and freedoms of others.

4.3 The importance of procedural safeguards for patients receiving psychiatric treatment in hospitals was vividly illustrated in *X v Finland*[1] where the applicant, a paediatrician, alleged that her rights under Article 8 had been violated when she was forcibly administered medication while detained in hospital. The Court said:

> The Court considers that forced administration of medication represents a serious interference with a person's physical integrity and must accordingly be based on a 'law' that guarantees proper safeguards against arbitrariness. In the present case such safeguards were missing. The decision to confine the applicant to involuntary treatment included an automatic authorisation to proceed to forced administration of medication when the applicant refused the treatment. The decision-making was solely in the hands of the treating doctors who could take even quite radical measures regardless of the applicant's will. Moreover, their decision-making was free from any kind of immediate judicial scrutiny: the applicant did not have any remedy available whereby she could require a court to rule on the lawfulness, including proportionality, of the forced administration of medication and to have it discontinued.[2]

4.4 The MHA 1983 sets out procedural safeguards which are explained in this chapter. On admission under section 2 or a treatment section a patient can be treated without their consent for three months

1 App No 34806/04, [2012] ECHR 1371.
2 [2012] ECHR 1371 at para 220.

before a second opinion by a doctor appointed by the Care Quality Commission (CQC) is required (ss63 and 58).

4.5 After three months in most cases the MHA 1983 sets out a process of certification often by a doctor appointed by the CQC: a Second Opinion Appointed Doctor (SOAD).[3] There are prescribed forms for these certificates.[4] It is important to be aware however that many of these safeguards can be over-ridden to give treatment that is 'immediately necessary'. See paras 4.44–4.46.

4.6 Mental health tribunals do not have the power to make decisions about treatment plans and the only remedy available to a patient seeking to challenge treatment under the MHA 1983 is judicial review. This was confirmed in two recent Upper Tribunal decisions: *SH v Cornwall Partnership NHS Trust*[5] and *GA v Betsi Cadwaladr University Local Health Board*.[6] However, compulsory treatment for mental disorder is an intrusive intervention and practitioners are very likely to be asked to advise clients about their rights as far as treatment is concerned, and what treatment can be imposed without their consent.

4.7 Parts 4 and 4A of the Act deal with the patient's consent to psychiatric treatment. Some provisions apply to any patient, whether they are in the community, in hospital informally, detained or subject to CTOs. Others apply only to those who are being treated under the MHA 1983. Different rules apply to those subject to CTOs and these are set out in Part 4A.

4.8 'Consent' is defined by the Code of Practice at paragraph 24.34 as:

> the voluntary and continuing permission of a patient to be given a particular treatment, based on a sufficient knowledge of the purpose, nature, likely effects and risks of that treatment, including the likelihood of its success and any alternatives to it. Permission given under any unfair or undue pressure is not consent.[7]

The Code draws attention to the importance of provision of sufficient information to enable the patient to make a decision and to the importance of properly maintained treatment plans.[8]

4.9 The Care Quality Commission's report *Monitoring the Mental Health Act in 2011/12* found that in almost half the cases they considered there was no evidence that doctors had talked to patients

3 MHA 1983 s58(3).

4 Form T1.

5 [2012] UKUT 290 (AAC).

6 [2013] UKUT 280 (AAC).

7 The definition is repeated in the Code for Wales para 16.29.

8 Code paras 24.36–24.39.

about whether they consented to the treatment that was proposed.[9] In 2013/14, the CQC found no evidence of assessment of capacity to consent to treatment in 25 per cent of cases.[10]

4.10 Parts 4 and 4A of the Act frequently refers to the patient's capacity to consent to a particular form of treatment. The test is whether the patient is capable of understanding the nature, purpose and likely effects of the treatment concerned. The capacity of patients who are 16 or older should be assessed with reference to the Mental Capacity Act (MCA) 2005. For those under 16 consideration should be given to whether the child is 'competent' namely whether the child has sufficient understanding and intelligence to enable him or her fully to understand the proposed treatment.[11] This is known as 'Gillick-competence'.[12]

4.11 See chapter 14 which discusses the key concepts of the MCA 2005 in more detail.

Part 4: treatment under the MHA 1983

4.12 For the purpose of consent to treatment, section 56 defines 'detained patients' as those liable to be detained in hospital under any section of the MHA 1983, including supervised community treatment (SCT) patients who have been recalled to hospital[13] but excluding:

- those detained under section 4 and awaiting second recommendation;[14]
- those detained under section 5 (holding powers);[15]
- those remanded to hospital for reports under section 35 (remand to hospital for reports);
- those detained in hospital as a place of safety under sections 135 and 136;[16]

9 *Monitoring the Mental Health Act in 2011/12*, CQC, page 69. In a sample of 2,500 records, 45 per cent showed no evidence of consent to treatment discussions before the first administration of medication to a detained patient.
10 *Monitoring the Mental Health Act in 2013/14*, CQC.
11 Code para 24.33; Code for Wales para 16.12.
12 From *Gillick v West Norfolk and Wisbech Health Authority* [1986] AC 112 and discussed below at paras 8.10–8.13.
13 MHA 1983 s56(4).
14 MHA 1983 s56(3)(a).
15 MHA 1983 s56(3)(b).
16 MHA 1983 s56(3)(b).

- patients awaiting admission to a named hospital following orders under section 37(4) or section 45A;[17] and
- conditionally discharged restricted patients who have not been recalled to hospital.[18]

4.13 As explained below, some treatment regulated by Part 4 applies to all patients, whatever their legal status. Note that the definition of 'patient' in section 145 is 'a person suffering or appearing to be suffering from mental disorder'.

Application of Part 4

4.14 The provisions in section 57 apply to all patients. The special provisions about electro-convulsive therapy (ECT) for those under 18 (s58A) apply to all patients under the age of 18, not simply those detained under the MHA 1983. All the other treatment provisions apply only to those detained (as defined by section 56) or subject to CTOs (Part 4A).

Invasive or irreversible treatment: section 57

4.15 Section 57 regulates particular forms of treatment which are highly invasive or irreversible. It is uncommon for patients to be given treatment under this section. For this reason the requirements apply to detained, informal and SCT patients alike. The section applies to neurosurgery for mental disorder and certain other forms of treatment listed in regulations made by the Secretary of State. Currently the forms of treatment in the Regulations are limited to surgical implantation of hormones to reduce the male sex drive.[19]

4.16 Such treatment is not permitted without:

- *The patient's capacitous consent.* The patient's capacity to consent must be certified by three independent persons appointed by the CQC, one of whom is a registered medical practitioner;[20] and
- *Certification in writing by the registered medical practitioner that the treatment is appropriate.* The registered medical practitioner must first consult with two other persons professionally concerned with

17 MHA 1983 s56(3)(b).

18 MHA 1983 s56(3)(c).

19 Mental Health (Hospital, Guardianship and Treatment) (England) Regulations 2008 reg 26; Mental Health (Hospital, Guardianship, Community Treatment and Consent to Treatment) (Wales) Regulations 2008 reg 38.

20 MHA 1983 s57(2)(a).

the patient's treatment. One must be a nurse and the other must be neither a nurse nor a registered medical practitioner. Neither must be the responsible clinician (RC) or the person in charge of the treatment in question.[21]

4.17 This section applies to an informal patient or a patient in the community. If such a patient does not have capacity to consent to the treatment then, quite simply, it cannot be given. Section 28 of the Mental Capacity Act 2005 prohibits giving or consenting to treatment when the person's treatment is regulated under Part 4 of the MHA 1983. Therefore a patient lacking capacity cannot be given section 57 treatment under either MHA 1983 or MCA 2005, nor can an attorney or deputy consent to it.

4.18 This section is subject to the emergency provisions in section 62 – see paras 4.44–4.46 below. Given the nature of the treatments regulated by section 57 it is hard to envisage when the emergency provisions could apply.

Medication and section 58

4.19 For a discussion about the treatment of common mental disorders see chapter 15.

Section 58 permits the administration of medication to detained patients (as defined by s56) after three months from the day on which any form of medication for mental disorder was first administered during the current period of detention. Section 58 treatment can be given provided that:

- either the RC or a SOAD have certified that the patient is capable of understanding the nature, purpose and likely effects of the treatment and has consented to it;[22] or
- a SOAD certifies that the patient is not capable of understanding the nature, purpose and likely effects of the treatment but that it is appropriate for the treatment to be given.

4.20 The Code of Practice states that the SOAD should consider the both clinical appropriateness and appropriateness in the light of all the other circumstances of the patient's case. As in all cases where a SOAD is asked to approve treatment, the SOAD must consult with two other professionals before providing the certificate.[23] Paragraphs

21 MHA 1983 s57(2)(b).

22 MHA 1983 s58(3)(b).

23 MHA 1983 s58(4).

25.25–25.71 of the Code provide guidance to SOADs. Chapter 18 of the Code for Wales provides guidance for SOADs.

4.21 This section 58 procedure is subject to the urgent treatment provisions in section 62: see below at paras 4.44–4.46.

Electro-convulsive therapy (ECT)

4.22 Special provisions apply to this form of treatment which is governed by section 58A. ECT includes medication used in connection with ECT. There are different requirements for adult patients and for patients who are under 18.

Adult patients

4.23 By virtue of section 56, the provisions that relate to ECT for adult patients only come into play if the patient is detained for the purpose of Part 4 (see above, para 4.12).

4.24 ECT may not be given to any patient with capacity to consent without his or her consent.[24]

4.25 In the case of an adult patient who has capacity to consent to ECT, and who does consent, the clinician in charge, or a SOAD, must certify that the patient is capable of understanding the nature, purpose and likely effects of the treatment and has consented to it.[25]

4.26 ECT may be given to an adult patient lacking capacity in the following circumstances:

- the patient is detained,[26] and
- a SOAD certifies that that a) the patient lacks capacity to consent to the treatment and b) that the treatment is appropriate and c) giving ECT would not conflict with a valid and applicable advance decision, or a decision of a donee or court appointed deputy.[27]

The SOAD must consult with two other professionals before providing the certificate.[28] This is subject to the emergency provisions in section 62. See paras 4.44–4.46.

24 MHA 1983 s58A(3), (4).
25 MHA 1983 s58A(3).
26 MHA 1983 s56(3).
27 MHA 1983 s58A(5).
28 MHA 1983 s58A(6).

Patients under 18

4.27 The position for patients under 18 years old is different. Section 56(5) provides that the requirements of section 58A also apply to patients who are under 18, even if they are not detained nor subject to a CTO. They could for example be treated in hospital informally or as an outpatient.

Under 18 *with* capacity to consent

4.28 In the case of a patient under 18 (who need not be detained[29]) a SOAD must certify that the patient is capable of understanding the nature, purpose and likely effects of the treatment and has consented to it. The SOAD must also certify that it is appropriate for the treatment to be given.[30]

Under 18 *without* capacity to consent

4.29 The provisions of section 58A(5) apply to both adult patients and those under 18. Therefore a patient who is under 18 and lacks capacity to consent to ECT may be given ECT if a SOAD certifies in writing that the patient is not capable of understanding the nature, purpose and likely effects of treatment, but that it is appropriate for the treatment to be given.

4.30 Again the SOAD is required to consult with two professionals.[31]

4.31 However, section 58A(7) provides that the SOAD's certificate alone does not provide authority to administer ECT to such patients unless they are detained.

4.32 A patient under 18 who is receiving treatment as an outpatient cannot be given ECT if he or she cannot consent to it, unless some alternative legal authority is in place. The Reference Guide suggests that the authority might be a court order or, in the case of a young person aged 16–17, the provisions of the MCA 2005.[32]

4.33 The Code of Practice at paras 19.40 and 19.43 considers whether consent could be given by a person with parental responsibility for a patient under 18. There is nothing in the MHA 1983 which prohibits this but the Code notes that such a decision is likely to be outside what is termed the 'zone of parental control'. A decision is likely to be within the zone of parental control if:

29 MHA 1983 s56(5).
30 MHA 1983 s58A(4).
31 Section 58A(6).
32 Reference Guide to the Mental Health Act paragraph 23.50.

a) it is a decision that a parent would be expected to make having regard to social norms and any relevant human rights decisions made by the courts, and
b) there are no factors which may undermine the validity of parental consent.[33]

4.34 A patient under 18 who discusses the possibility of section 58A treatment with a registered medical practitioner or approved clinician is entitled to an Independent Mental Health Advocate (IMHA) even if not subject to any orders under the MHA 1983.[34]

The patient's right to change their mind

4.35 If a patient has consented to treatment under sections 57, 58 or 58A, then he or she may withdraw consent at any time. Those sections will then apply as if the remainder of the course of treatment were a separate form of treatment.[35] If instead the patient becomes unable to understand the nature, purpose and likely effects of the treatment before it is completed, then he or she will be treated as having withdrawn consent and again the remainder of the treatment will be considered a separate form of treatment.[36] This is subject to section 62, see paras 4.44–4.46 below.

4.36 If the patient had been certified as unable to understand the nature, purpose and likely effects of treatment under section 58 or section 58A, but then gains the ability to understand these matters before the treatment is completed, then the certificate is of no effect. The provisions of section 58 or section 58A will then apply to the remainder of the treatment as if it were a separate form of treatment.[37] Again this is subject to section 62.

4.37 Any patient who has consented to a plan of treatment may withdraw his or her consent at anytime, subject to section 62.

4.38 If the patient has withdrawn his or her consent, or is treated as having withdrawn consent under section 60, or if a certificate granted by a SOAD ceases to have effect before a programme of treatment has finished then in certain circumstances the treatment can continue pending compliance with the relevant provisions (for example obtaining a further certificate). The treatment can continue if the

33 Code para 19.41; Code for Wales para 16.23.

34 MHA 1983 s130C(3)(b).

35 MHA 1983 s60(1).

36 MHA 1983 ss60(1A) and 60(1B).

37 MHA 1983 s60(1A) and 60(1D).

approved clinician in charge of the treatment considers that it would cause serious suffering to the patient if the treatment were to be discontinued.

4.39 Treatment is irreversible if it has unfavourable, irreversible physical or psychological consequences.[38] It is hazardous if it entails significant physical hazard.[39]

4.40 The position of a patient who has been recalled from a CTO or whose CTO has been revoked is dealt with at section 62A.

When must treatment be reviewed?

4.41 Section 61 provides an additional safeguard for certain forms of treatment, which requires the approved clinician in charge of the treatment to report on the patient's treatment and condition to the Care Quality Commission. This applies to the following patients:[40]

- A patient who is receiving treatment under section 57(2): currently this refers to hormone implantation reducing the male sex drive.
- A detained patient receiving medication under section 58(3)(b), where a SOAD has provided a certificate.
- A patient who is under 18 and receiving ECT under section 58A(4) in other words with his consent and who may or may not be detained.
- A detained patient lacking capacity to consent and receiving ECT under section 58A(5) where a SOAD has provided a certificate.

4.42 The CQC can require a report at any time.[41] The approved clinician must provide a report at the following times:

- When the RC next provides a report to the managers which renews the patient's detention.[42]
- When the RC next provides a report to the managers which renews the patient's CTO.[43]
- If the patient returns to hospital after having been absent without leave for more than 28 days, when the RC provides a report to the managers.[44]

38 MHA 1983 s62(3).
39 MHA 1983 s62(3).
40 MHA 1983 s61(1).
41 MHA 1983 s61(1)(b).
42 MHA 1983 s61(1)(a).
43 MHA 1983 s61(1)(a).
44 MHA 1983 s61(1)(a).

- In the case of restricted patients, at the end of the first six months from the order and thereafter when the RC provides yearly reports to the Secretary of State.[45]

The above provisions for mandatory reviews will only apply to those detained under the MHA 1983 or subject to CTOs. For other patients, such as under 18s receiving ECT, reports would have to be specifically requested by the CQC.

4.43 Under this section the CQC can direct that a certificate which has been given authorising treatment shall no longer apply. This means that either a new certificate must be sought or the treatment cannot continue.[46]

When can urgent treatment be given? Section 62

4.44 Section 62 provides that the provisions of sections 57 and 58 do not apply to treatment to which is:

- immediately necessary to save the patient's life; or
- is immediately necessary to prevent a serious deterioration of the patient's condition and is reversible; or
- is immediately necessary to alleviate serious suffering by the patient and is neither irreversible nor hazardous; or
- is immediately necessary and is the minimum interference necessary to prevent the patient from behaving violently or being a danger to himself or others, and is neither irreversible or hazardous.[47]

4.45 If the treatment concerned is ECT then the provisions of section 58A do not apply to treatment that is:

- immediately necessary to save the patient's life; or
- is immediately necessary to prevent a serious deterioration of the patient's condition and is reversible.[48]

4.46 Note that treatment under section 62 can only be provided to detained patients. It applies to patients of all ages.

45 MHA 1983 s61(2).
46 MHA 1983 s61(3).
47 MHA 1983 s62(1).
48 MHA 1983 s62(1A).

Section 63: the first three months

4.47 Section 63 permits treatment without consent to detained patients for 'the mental disorder from which he is suffering' which does not fall within sections 57, 58, or 58A if this is given by, or under, the direction of the approved clinician in charge of the treatment. Note the wide definition of 'treatment' in section 145 of the MHA 1983. This would include medication administered during the first three months after treatment begins, before the requirements of section 58 come into effect.

4.48 Treatment under this section has also been held to include 'acts ancillary to' the patient's core treatment and relieving the symptoms of the disorder and the physical consequences of the symptoms: see *B v Croydon Health Authority*[49] which involved use of a naso-gastric tube in the case of a patient with a personality disorder. More obvious examples include monitoring blood levels of medication to ensure the patient has been taking what is prescribed or to look at whether there is enough or too much medication in the patient's blood which would require a change in medication. See section 145(4) and the discussion about medical treatment at paras 1.26–1.30.

4.50 In *R v Collins ex p Brady*,[50] Ian Brady was on hunger strike following his move to a different ward in Ashworth Hospital. The Court held that he could be fed through a tube under section 63 because the hunger strike was a manifestation and symptom of his personality disorder.

4.51 Section 63 was also considered in *A NHS Trust v Dr A*.[51] Dr A was on hunger strike in an attempt to recover his passport from the UK Border Agency who had refused his application for asylum. He received nutrition via a naso-gastric tube. He was detained under section 2 and then section 3 of the MHA 1983. He had delusional disorder and was found to lack capacity to decide about nutrition and hydration. His views as to the continuation of his hunger strike did not change with the fluctuations of his mental state. Baker J accepted the view of the treating psychiatrist that providing Dr A with artificial nutrition and hydration was treatment for physical disorder arising from his decision to refuse food, even though the decision to refuse food was flawed, because of Dr A's mental disorder. The judge said that 'the physical disorder is thus in part a consequence of his mental

49 [1995] 1 All ER 683.
50 (2000) 58 BMLR 173.
51 [2013] EWHC 2442 (COP).

disorder, but, in my judgment, it is not obviously either a manifestation or a symptom of the mental disorder'. The judge also noted that it was undesirable to extend the meaning of medical treatment under the MHA 1983 too far. In borderline cases an application should be made to the court to approve the treatment.

4.52 *Nottinghamshire Healthcare NHS Trust v RC*[52] concerned a patient with a longstanding and severe personality disorder who had become a Jehovah's Witness. He regularly harmed himself, including by slashing his artery. He made a valid advance decision to refuse transfusions of blood or blood products to treat his wounds. Holman J said that where a responsible clinician decides – as she had in this case – not to impose life-saving treatment under MHA 1983 s63 the NHS Trust concerned would be 'well-advised' to apply to the court for declaratory relief, because the patient's rights under Article 2 ECHR (the right to life) are engaged. Holman J agreed that the patient's wound, which resulted from self-harm, was a 'symptom or manifestation of the underlying personality disorder'. Section 63 could therefore be used to treat it, including through transfusions. However, the judge agreed with the decision not to impose treatment on RC given that he currently had capacity to refuse it and had made a valid advance decision. In these circumstances it would be an abuse of power 'even to think about imposing a blood transfusion'.

4.53 Treatment for unrelated physical disorder for a patient detained under the Mental Health Act 1983 and lacking, for whatever reason, capacity to consent to the treatment should not be provided under the Act.[53]

Part 4A: treatment of community patients not recalled to hospital

4.54 The medical treatment of a patient subject to a CTO is regulated by Part 4A of the MHA 1983. The exception to this is section 57 treatment (neurosurgery and hormonal implantation). The special requirements of section 57 also apply to patients subject to CTOs.

4.55 Part 4A uses the term 'relevant treatment' which is described as being medical treatment for the mental disorder from which the patient is suffering, and which is not section 57 treatment.[54]

52 [2014] EWCOP 1136.

53 Such treatment should be provided under MCA 2005 s5.

54 MHA 1983 s64A.

4.56 Part 4A refers to 'section 58 type treatment' and to 'section 58A type treatment'. Section 58 type treatment is treatment that would come under section 58 if, instead of being on a CTO, the patient were detained in hospital, in other words medication after the first three months (as long as this is an unbroken period of detention and CTO). Section 58A type treatment, by the same token, is treatment that would come under section 58A if the patient were detained in hospital, namely ECT and medication used in connection with ECT.[55]

4.57 In all cases the person giving the treatment must have authority to do so and in most cases there is also a requirement for a certificate to be given by a SOAD along with the consent of the patient. As with Part 4 SOADs, the SOAD providing a certificate for a patient on a CTO must consult with two other persons who have been professionally concerned with the patient's treatment.[56] Note that a certificate is not required if the patient is either within the first three months of medication having been administered during an unbroken period of detention (or detention and community treatment) or during the first month beginning with the date of the CTO but only if the patient consents.[57] For example a patient may be detained on section 3 for two months and discharged subject to a CTO. A certificate is not required on the CTO for another month.

4.58 The position for patients over 16 years of age differs to the position for those under 16. Again, it is helpful to consider the provisions for adult patients and for patients under 16 separately, and then to consider the position for those in both groups who have capacity to consent and those who lack capacity to consent.

4.59 As with Part 4 treatment there are different provisions for urgent treatment.

Adult (over 16) CTO patients with capacity

4.60 An adult CTO patient with capacity may consent to treatment and this will provide the authority needed to treat him or her.[58] This cannot be overridden even in an emergency, unless the patient is recalled to hospital.

55 MHA 1983 s64C(3).
56 MHA 1983 s64H(3).
57 MHA 1983 s64B(1), (5).
58 MHA 1983 s64C(2)(a)

4.61 This then leaves the certificate requirement. This can be provided by the approved clinician in charge of the patient's treatment certifying that the patient has capacity to consent to the treatment and has consented to the treatment.[59] This is subject to one exception: where the patient is between 16 and 18 and the treatment concerned is ECT then a certificate that the treatment is appropriate must be provided by a SOAD.[60] A SOAD can in any event provide a certificate that the treatment is appropriate rather than the approved clinician.[61]

4.62 In some cases a certificate is not necessary. In an emergency, treatment (either section 58 type treatment or section 58A type treatment) that is immediately necessary can be given without the certificate, as long as the patient consents.[62]

4.63 'Immediately necessary' means in the case of section 58 type treatment that the treatment is immediately necessary to:

- save the patient's life, or
- prevent a serious deterioration in the patient's condition and is not irreversible; or
- alleviate serious suffering by the patient and is not irreversible or hazardous, or
- prevent the patient from behaving violently or being a danger to himself or others and is not irreversible or hazardous and represents the minimum interference necessary.[63]

If the treatment is section 58A type treatment then one of the first two conditions above must apply.[64]

4.64 Where the section 58 type treatment is medication then the certificate is not needed for the first month beginning with the day when the CTO started.[65]

Adult (over 16) CTO patient lacking capacity to consent to treatment

4.65 Again there are two types of requirement before section 58 type treatment or section 58A type treatment can be administered. The first is

59 MHA 1983 s64C(4)(a).
60 MHA 1983 s64C(4)(b).
61 MHA 1983 s64C(4).
62 MHA 1983 s64B(3)(b).
63 MHA 1983 s64C(5)
64 MHA 1983 s64C(6)
65 MHA 1983 s64B(4).

the requirement that there is authority to treat.[66] The second is the certificate requirement.

4.66 The authority to treat can be provided in several ways. A donee or deputy or the Court of Protection can consent to it on the patient's behalf.[67] As a person under 18 cannot grant a lasting power of attorney this will only arise in the patient is 18 or over. Alternatively, treatment can be given if:

- reasonable steps have been taken to establish that the patient lacks capacity (s64D(2)), and
- there is no conflicting valid and applicable advance decision or objecting deputy or donee (s64D(6)), and
- the person seeking to treat the patient is the approved clinician in charge of the treatment or someone acting on that person's behalf, and[68]
- there is no reason to believe the patient objects to the treatment, or if he or she does object, force is not needed.

In deciding whether the patient objects or not the person seeking to treat shall consider all the relevant circumstances as far as it is appropriate, including the patients behaviour, wishes, feelings, views, beliefs and values (s64J).

There is no definition of force in the MHA 1983 but the Code defines it as 'actual use of physical force on the patient' (Code para 23.17).

4.67 The certificate requirement will be met if a SOAD certifies that it is appropriate for the treatment to be given. The SOAD can specify conditions in his or her certificate, and if he or she does these must be met for the treatment to be given.[69] No certificate is needed for the administration of medication in the first month beginning with the date on which the CTO is made.[70]

Urgent treatment for adult (over 16) CTO patients lacking capacity to consent

4.68 There is also authority to treat the patient in an emergency. This is governed by section 64G. This provides that a person is authorised to give 'relevant treatment' to a patient on a CTO who is over 16

66 MHA 1983 s64B.
67 MHA 1983 s64C(2)(b).
68 MHA 1983 s64D(5).
69 MHA 1983 s64C(4).
70 MHA 1983 s64B(4).

if certain conditions apply. The treatment must be immediately necessary to:[71]

- save the patient's life; or
- prevent a serious deterioration in the patient's condition and is not irreversible; or
- alleviate serious suffering by the patient and is not irreversible or hazardous or;
- if it is not irreversible or hazardous, it is immediately necessary and is the minimum interference necessary to prevent the patient behaving violently or being a danger to himself or others.

If the treatment is ECT then one of the first two conditions must apply.[72]

4.69 The person seeking to give the treatment must reasonably believe that the patient lacks capacity to consent to the treatment.

4.70 Force can be used if necessary, on the conditions that the treatment needs to be given to prevent harm to the patient and that the use of force is a proportionate response to the likelihood of the patient suffering harm and to the seriousness of the harm.

4.71 Note that if the conditions set out in section 64G are met, treatment can be authorised even if giving the treatment conflicts with a valid and applicable advance decision or the decision of a donee or deputy. Nor does the treatment need to be given by, or under, the direction of the approved clinician.

4.72 In an emergency the certificate requirement is also relaxed, as is the case with adult patients with capacity to consent.

4.73 Treatment (either section 58 type treatment or section 58A type treatment) that is immediately necessary for any of the purposes set out in para 4.68 can be given without the certificate with the consent of a donee, a deputy or the Court of Protection.[73]

If the treatment is section 58A treatment then the treatment must be immediately necessary to save the patient's life or prevent a serious deterioration in his/her condition.[74]

4.74 A situation can arise where there is authority to treat the patient because the emergency conditions of section 64G are met, but there is no consent from a deputy, donee or from the Court of Protection. In this case the treatment can still proceed without the certificate.[75]

71 MHA 1983 s64G(5).

72 MHA 1983 s64G(2).

73 MHA 1983 s64(3)(b)(ii).

74 MHA 1983 s64C(6).

75 MHA 1983 s64B(3)(a).

Child (under 16) CTO patient who is competent to consent to treatment

4.75 A child CTO patient who is under 16 and who is competent can be given treatment if there is authority to treat him and in most cases there is also a requirement for a certificate from a SOAD.

4.76 A competent child can consent to section 58 type treatment or section 58A type treatment and this will provide authority for the treatment to be given.[76]

4.77 A certificate from a SOAD is not required for the administration of medication for the first month beginning with the day when the CTO is made.[77]

4.78 In other cases (apart from urgent treatment which is immediately necessary) a certificate is required. A SOAD's certificate must certify that the treatment is appropriate. If the SOAD has specified conditions then these must be met.[78] A SOAD must provide the certificate if the treatment is section 58A type treatment (ECT).[79] However, as with adult patients who have capacity, the approved clinician in charge of the treatment can satisfy the certificate requirement by certifying that the patient is competent and has consented to section 58A type treatment.[80]

4.79 As with an adult CTO patient who has capacity to consent to treatment, there is no authority to treat a competent CTO child patient without his consent, even in an emergency. This could only be done if the patient were recalled to hospital. However, if the child has consented then treatment that is immediately necessary can be given without a certificate.

4.80 In the case of section 58 type treatment that the treatment must be immediately necessary to:

- save the patient's life, or
- prevent a serious deterioration in the patient's condition and is not irreversible; or
- alleviate serious suffering by the patient and is not irreversible or hazardous or

76 MHA 1983 s64E(6).
77 MHA 1983 s64E(4).
78 MHA 1983 ss64E(7), 64C(4).
79 MHA 1983 ss64E(7), 64C(4B).
80 MHA 1983 ss64E(7), 64C(4A).

- prevent the patient from behaving violently or being a danger to himself or others and is not irreversible or hazardous and represents the minimum interference necessary.

If the treatment is section 58A treatment then one of the first two conditions above must apply.

Child (under 16) CTO patient who is not competent to consent to treatment.

4.81 Authority to treat such patients is provided by section 64F. Treatment can be given if the following conditions are satisfied:

- The person takes reasonable steps before giving the treatment to establish whether the patient is competent to consent.
- When giving the treatment he reasonably believes the patient is not competent to consent to the treatment.
- He has no reason to believe that the patient objects to the treatment or if he does have reason to believe that the patient objects it is not necessary to use force to give the treatment.
- He is either an approved clinician in charge of the treatment or is under the direction of that clinician.

4.82 The certificate requirements in respect of child patients who lack capacity are as follows:

- No certificate is needed for the administration of medication for the first month from the date the order is made.[81]
- In all other cases apart from treatment which is immediately necessary, a SOAD must certify the treatment is appropriate and any conditions set must be met.[82]

Note that the provisions of section 64G apply to child patients lacking competence as well as adult patients lacking capacity.

4.83 The provisions of section 64FA deal with what happens if a patient:

- withdraws his consent to a programme of treatment to which he had agreed, or
- loses capacity or competence to consent to treatment where he had previously consented.

The remainder of the treatment has to be dealt with as if it was a separate form of treatment. However, if the approved clinician in charge

81 MHA 1983 s64E(4).

82 MHA 1983 s64C(4).

of the treatment certifies that it would cause serious suffering to the patient if treatment were to be discontinued, then the treatment can continue pending compliance with the requirements of Part 4A.[83]

4.84 Section 64H provides that the SOAD's certificates, which are referred to as 'Part 4A certificates' can cover a treatment plan which includes one or more forms of section 58 type treatment or section 58A type treatment.[84] It must be in a prescribed form.[85] The SOAD must consult with two others who have been professionally concerned with the patient, one of whom can be a registered medical practitioner, but neither of whom can be the RC or clinician in charge of the treatment.[86]The CQC may require periodic reports on the patient's condition (there is no mandatory requirement as with section 61).[87]

4.85 The CQC can at any time direct that a certificate shall cease to have effect on a given day and in that case the relevant section needs to be complied with again. If the patient is still on a CTO this will be section 64B or section 64E (depending on his age). If the patient has been recalled to hospital, or the CTO revoked, then the hospital will need to comply with section 58 or section 58A.[88] Treatment can continue pending compliance if the approved clinician certifies that discontinuance would cause the patient serious suffering.[89]

4.86 If the patient is recalled to hospital, or the CTO revoked, then it is important to remember that section 17E(6) provides the hospital with the legal power to detain the patient. This power lapses 72 hours after recall unless the CTO has been revoked. The power to detain provides the authority to treat the patient without consent provided the requirements of Part 4 are complied with as the patient's treatment will now regulated by Part 4 rather than Part 4A. There are some differences to the certificate requirements.

4.87 If the patient has a Part 4A certificate which expressly covers section 58 type treatment or section 58A type treatment in the event of recall or revocation, then that certificate can be relied on.[90] A section 58 (1)(b) certificate is not needed if the patient is recalled or revoked within a month beginning from the date that the CTO was made, or

83 MHA 1983 s64FA(5).
84 MHA 1983 s64H(1).
85 MHA 1983 s64H(2).
86 MHA 1983 s64H(3).
87 MHA 1983 s64H(4).
88 MHA 1983 s64H (5), (6), (7).
89 MHA 1983 s64H(8).
90 MHA 1983 s62A(5)(a).

within three months of the first administration of medication whilst subject to compulsory powers.[91] However, if the patient's CTO is revoked then treatment can only continue pending compliance with section 58.[92]

4.88 Section 58A treatment which is expressly allowed to continue after recall or revocation by the Part 4A certificate can continue.

4.89 If the Part 4 certificate does not expressly allow treatment – whether section 58 type treatment or section 58A type treatment – to continue after recall or revocation, or if the certificate has been withdrawn by the CQC but treatment is continuing on the basis of section 64H(8), then it may still continue pending compliance if the approved clinician certifies that discontinuance would cause serious suffering to the patient.[93] Likewise if the certificate requirement had been met by the approved clinician certifying the patient's capacitous or competent consent to treatment and the patient is recalled or the CTO revoked, the approved clinician may certify that discontinuance of treatment would cause serious suffering. If the certificate is no longer valid – perhaps because the patient has lost capacity or now refuses to consent – treatment can continue pending compliance with section 58 or section 58A.[94] If the treatment is ECT and the patient has capacity to consent to ECT but does not do so, the treatment cannot be continued. This is because section 58A will not permit a SOAD to certify ECT for a capacitous patient who does not agree to it, so section 58A could never be complied with.

91 MHA 1983 s64A(3)(b).

92 MHA 1983 s62A(7).

93 MHA 1983 s62A(6).

94 MHA 1983 s62A(6A).

CHAPTER 5

Mental health tribunals

Background

5.1 The Mental Health Review Tribunal was established by the Mental Health Act 1959. Amendments to its functions were made by the Mental Health Acts 1983 and 2007. England and Wales have different arrangements.

5.2 The current structure of the Tribunals Service in England derives from the Tribunals, Courts and Enforcement Act (TCEA) 2007. Her Majesty's Courts & Tribunals Service administers the operation of tribunals which comprise a First-tier Tribunal (FTT) and an Upper Tribunal (UT).

5.3 The term 'Mental Health Review Tribunal' is no longer used when referring to the relevant tribunal in England. The First-tier Tribunal (Mental Health) is part of the Health, Education and Social Care (HESC) Chamber. Its operations are described in chapter 14. It is sometimes also referred to as the Mental Health Tribunal or MHT as it has been in this book. Its procedures are governed by the Tribunal Procedure (First-tier Tribunal) (Health, Education and Social Care Chamber) Rules 2008.[1]

5.4 The Mental Health Review Tribunal for Wales is not part of the HESC but operates independently by virtue of Mental Health Act (MHA) 1983 s65. Its Rules, the Mental Health Review Tribunal for Wales Rules 2008, are provided for by MHA 1983 s78.[2]

5.5 The Rules for both the MHT and MHRT for Wales are considered in chapter 9.

5.6 Before the TCEA 2007 the only means of challenging the decision of a tribunal was through judicial review. This was often a slow process and the new structures were meant to bring about speed. There is now a review procedure where a judge of the First-tier Tribunal can set aside a decision if there is a clear error of law and can grant leave to appeal to the Upper Tribunal. The Upper Tribunal now hears appeals from both the First-tier Tribunal and the Mental Health Review Tribunal for Wales. The Upper Tribunal can also grant leave to appeal and can treat an application as a judicial review.

5.7 The jurisdiction and procedure of the Upper Tribunal is considered at chapter 12.

1 SI No 2699.
2 SI No 2705.

Routes to the tribunal

5.8 A patient's case can come before a tribunal by the following routes:

- an application by the patient or in some cases the nearest relative (s66);
- automatic referrals by the hospital managers (s68) or the Ministry of Justice (s70);
- discretionary referrals by the Secretary of State for Health (s67) or Ministry of Justice (s71(2)).

5.9 Section 77 explains which tribunal should deal with a patient's case:

- If the patient is liable to be detained in a hospital in England then the application or reference will be heard by the FTT (s77(3)(a)).
- If the patient is liable to be detained in a hospital in Wales then the application or reference will be heard by the MHRT for Wales (s77(3)(a)).
- If the patient is subject to a CTO then the location of the responsible hospital determines which tribunal hears the application, irrespective of where the patient resides. So if the responsible hospital is in Wales then the MHRT for Wales will hear the application or reference and if the responsible hospital is in England the relevant tribunal will be the FTT (MHA 1983 s77(3)(b)). (See chapter 6 for cross-border matters.)
- If the patient is subject to guardianship and resides in Wales the relevant tribunal will be the MHRT for Wales. If the patient is subject to guardianship and resides in England then the relevant tribunal will be the FTT (s77(3)(c)).
- If the patient is a conditionally discharged patient who has not been recalled then if he resides in Wales the relevant tribunal will be the MHRT for Wales, but the FTT if he resides in England (MHA 1983 s77(4)).

5.10 Sections 66 sets out when patients detained under Part 2 and community patients are entitled to apply to tribunals. Section 69 sets out the entitlement of those who are subject to hospital or guardianship orders and section 70 provides for applications by restricted patients.

5.11 The effect of these provisions is summarised in table 4 below.

Table 4: applications to the tribunal

Patient subject to:	Provisions	Who can apply	When
ss2, 4 subsequently detained under s2	s66(1)(a), (2)(a)	patient	Must be within 14 days beginning with date of admission
s3: first 6 months (does not include CTO patient who is recalled under s17E)	s66(1)(b), (2)(b), (2A)	patient	Patient: within 6 months beginning with date of admission
Patient detained under hospital order under s37 (including 'notional section 37' patient)	s69(1)(a), s66(1), (2)(f), Sch 1 Part 1 para 9	patient and nearest relative	Period for which authority is renewed (ie 2nd 6 months and yearly thereafter). No application in first six months from order
Detained (including s37) patient whose detention is renewed under s20 and is not discharged under s23	s66(1)(f), (2)(f); Sch 1 Part 1 para 9	patient	During the period/s for which authority for detention is renewed
Detained (including s37) patient who has • been AWOL for more than 28 days but • has either been returned or returned himself and • detention would otherwise have expired but has been renewed under s21B(2)	s66(1)(fa), (2)(f); Sch 1 Part 1 para 9	patient	During the period for which detention has been renewed
s7(guardianship): first 6 months	s66(1)(c), (2)(c)	patient	Within 6 months beginning with the day on which the application is accepted
s7 or s37: guardianship renewed under s20 and not discharged under s23	S66(1)(f), (2)(f); Sch 1 Part 1 para 9	patient	During the period/s for which authority for guardianship is renewed

Patient subject to:	Provisions	Who can apply	When
s7 or s37: guardianship patient who has • been AWOL for more than 28 days and • has either been returned or returned himself and • Guardianship would otherwise have expired but has been renewed under s21B(2)	s66(1)(fa), (2)(f); Sch 1 Part 1 para 9	patient	During the period for which authority for guardianship is renewed
Guardianship patient transferred to hospital under s19 (whether admitted under s7 or s37)	s66(1)(e), (2)(e); Sch 1 Part 1 para 9	patient	Within 6 months beginning with the day on which the patient is transferred
Patient placed under guardianship order under s37	s69(b)	patient and nearest relative	Patient within 6 months beginning with date of guardianship order; nearest relative within 12 months beginning with the date of the order and in any subsequent period of 12 months
CTO – first 6 months	s66(1)(ca), (2)(ca)	patient	Within 6 months beginning with the day on which the CTO is made
CTO – renewed under s20A and not discharged under s23	s66(1) (fza), (2)(fza)	patient	During the period for which the CTO period is extended.
CTO – revoked under s17F	s66(1)(cb), (2)(cb)	patient	Within 6 months beginning with the day on which the CTO is revoked
CTO patient who has been AWOL for more than 28 days but has either been returned or returned himself and whose CTO would otherwise have expired but has been renewed under s21B(2)	s66(1)(faa), (2)(fza))	patient	During the period for which the CTO has been renewed

Patient subject to:	Provisions	Who can apply	When
Detained patient or CTO patient where nearest relative has attempted to discharge and been barred under s25	s66(1)(g), (2)(d)	Nearest relative	Within 28 days beginning with the day when the NR is informed of barring order
Where a county court has displaced the nearest relative on the basis of s29(3)(c) or (d) and Part 2 patient is liable to be detained, or subject to guardianship or a CTO patient or subsequently becomes liable to be detained or subject to guardianship	s66(1)(h), (2)(g)	Nearest relative (though patient will have their own separate entitlement)	Within 12 months beginning with the date of the order and in any subsequent 12 month period while the order is in force
'Restricted patient' (subject to restriction order or limitation direction or restriction direction)	s70	patient	During the period between the expiration of 6 months and 12 months, beginning with the date of the hospital order, hospital direction or transfer direction
Patient transferred under ss47, 48 or 47/49	s69(2)(b)	patient nearest relative only in the case of transfer patients who are not subject to restrictions	Within 6 months of direction; between 6 and 12 months and thereafter at yearly intervals
Conditionally discharged restricted patient recalled to hospital	s75 (1)	patient	Within the 2nd 6 months beginning with the date of recall and thereafter yearly
Conditionally discharged restricted patient who has not been recalled	s75(2)	patient	Within the second period of twelve months beginning with the date of his actual release from hospital and once in each subsequent period of two years

5.12 If a statutory time limit expires on a day when the court office is not open, then the time is extended to the next business day: *R (Modaresi) v Secretary of State for Health*.[3]

5.13 There is a duty to refer cases to the tribunal at certain intervals. In the case of Part 2 and non-restricted Part 3 patients this is exercised by the hospital managers (s68). In the case of restricted patients this is exercised by the Ministry of Justice (s71).

The hospital managers' duty to refer

5.14 The hospital managers must refer a patient's case to the tribunal in the following circumstances:

- On the expiry of six months beginning with the date of admission to hospital of a patient detained under either section 2 or section 3, provided that the patient, or their nearest relative, has not already exercised the right to apply to the tribunal, or that the case has not been referred to the tribunal under section 67, unless the referral was made during the currency of a section 2 order (s68(1)(a), (1)(b), (3)). If the patient has made but then withdrawn an application to the tribunal this does not count as exercising his or her right to apply and the referral must still be made: s68(4). This will include those under section 2 orders which have been extended through the use of section 29(4).
- On the expiry of six months beginning with the date of admission to hospital on either section 2 or section 3 (whichever is the earlier) of a patient who is now subject to a CTO, or a CTO patient whose CTO has been revoked (s68(1)(c), (1)(d)), subject to the exceptions listed above.
- On the expiry of six months from the date of transfer from guardianship to hospital (s68(1)(e), (5)(d)) again with the same exceptions.
- As soon as possible after the revocation of a CTO under section 17F (s68(7)).
- In the case of a detained or community patient or patient whose CTO has been revoked, if more than three years has elapsed since the patient's case was last considered by a tribunal (or one year if the patient is under 18) (s68(6)).

5.15 It will be seen that a patient made the subject of an order for admission under section 37 will only have the case referred to the tribunal

3 [2013] UKSC 53.

if the patient, or their nearest relative, has made at least one application, because the requirement to refer is counted from the date when the patient's case was last considered by the tribunal. If the patient lacks capacity to apply to the tribunal this lack of an automatic referral may be unlawful. In *MH v United Kingdom*[4] the fact that section 66 did not provide an incapacitated patient detained on section 2 access to a court was found to violate Article 5(4) ECHR which says that anyone who is deprived of their liberty has the right to take proceedings to a court to determine the lawfulness of the detention.

5.16 There is no provision for automatic referral to the tribunal of a patient who is subject to guardianship.

The Secretary of State's discretion to refer

5.17 The Secretary of State for Justice may refer the case of a restricted patient to the tribunal at any time.[5] The Secretary of State must refer a restricted patient's case to the tribunal in the following circumstances:

- within one month of the recall of a conditionally discharged restricted patient to hospital (s75); and
- where the patient's case has not been considered by a tribunal within the last three years (s71(2)).

5.18 The Secretary of State for Health has the discretion to refer the case of any patient to the tribunal at any time. This power arises in respect of patients and those subject to guardianship under Part 2, and community patients under MHA 1983 s67.

5.19 This is an important safeguard the use of which should be borne in mind particularly when representing a patient who lacks capacity to decide to appeal to the tribunal. As said above it has been held in the ECtHR that the lack of access to a court for a patient without capacity detained under section 2 violates Article 5. However, the legislation still stands. The same case in the House of Lords before it went to the ECtHR found that the MHA 1983 could be read so as not to violate the Convention. In *R (MH) v Secretary of State for Health*[6] the patient, who lacked capacity to apply to the tribunal, was detained under section 2. During the currency of the order an application was made to the county court to displace her nearest relative. MH's

4 App No 11577/06, (2013) ECHR 1008.

5 MHA 1983 s67(1).

6 [2005] UKHL 60.

detention under section 2 was extended by section 29(4). She could not apply to the tribunal because of the operation of section 66(2)(a) (application to be made within 14 days of detention under section 2).

5.20 Holding that section 29(4) was capable of being operated compatibly with the patient's rights under Article 5(4), Baroness Hale referred to the Secretary of State's power under section 67(1) and said at para 30:

> ... But the Secretary of State is under a duty to act compatibly with the patient's Convention rights and would be well advised to make such a reference as soon as the position is drawn to her attention. In this case this happened at the request of the patient's own lawyers. Should the Secretary of State decline to exercise this power, judicial review would be swiftly available to oblige her to do so. It would also be possible for the hospital managers or the local social services authority to notify the Secretary of State whenever an application is made under section 29 so that she can consider the position. These applications are not common: they no longer feature in the annual published *Judicial Statistics*, but when they did feature they tended just to make double figures every year. So the burden on the authorities, the Secretary of State and the tribunals would not be high.

This paragraph refers specifically to the position of a patient whose detention under section 2 has been extended by an application under section 29. Although the ECtHR disagreed with the Supreme Court, it may be useful to refer to it in other cases where the patient lacks capacity to apply to the tribunal and where there is a good reason for his case to be considered before the next automatic reference is due.

5.21 In *MH v United Kingdom*[7] the ECtHR held that the lack of an automatic referral to the tribunal whilst MH was detained under section 2 violated her rights under Article 5(4) but dismissed the remainder of her claims.

5.22 However, in R *(Modaresi) v Secretary of State for Health*,[8] the tribunal (wrongly) treated an application for a tribunal by a patient detained under section 2 as out of time. The patient asked the Secretary of State to refer her case to the tribunal. The Secretary of State refused because she had by now been detained under section 3 and become eligible to appeal against section 3. The Secretary of State indicated that he would consider a further request for a referral. The Supreme Court held that Mrs Modaresi had not been deprived of her

7 App No 11577/06, (2013) ECHR 1008.

8 [2011] EWHC 417 (Admin).

access to a court to challenge her detention and that the Secretary of State had acted lawfully.[9]

If the patient's section changes does the application continue?

5.23 If a patient is detained under section 2 and by the time of the tribunal is detained under section 3, the tribunal still proceeds.

5.24 If a patient is detained under section 3 and appeals, or is referred to the tribunal, but is placed under a CTO before the hearing takes place, then the application remains valid but the tribunal will consider the criteria for continuation of the CTO rather than the section 3 criteria: *AA v Cheshire and Wirral Partnership NHS Foundation Trust.*[10]

5.25 Section 77 provides that no application to a tribunal can be made other than when expressly provided for by the Act. In *DP v Hywel DDA Health Board*[11] the person who was believed to be the nearest relative applied to the tribunal following a barring order under section 25 by the patient's responsible clinician (RC). But when it emerged that in fact the applicant was not the nearest relative then the tribunal had no jurisdiction

What can the tribunal do? Powers of tribunals

5.26 The powers of tribunals are set out in sections 72–75 of the MHA 1983. The tribunal's jurisdiction is limited to these provisions and it does not have jurisdiction to rule on other issue such as consent to treatment: *SH v Cornwall Partnership NHS Trust*[12] and *GA v Betsi Cadwaladr University Local Health Board.*[13]

5.27 The tribunal must apply the civil standard of proof on the balance of probabilities and the burden of proof is on the detaining authority: see *R (N) v Mental Health Review Tribunal (Northern Region)*.[14] However, it should also be borne in mind that the tribunal is inquisitorial

9 [2013] UKSC 53.
10 [2009] UKUT 195 (AAC).
11 [2011] UKUT 381 (AAC).
12 [2012] UKUT 290 (AAC).
13 [2013] UKUT 280 (AAC).
14 [2005] EWCA Civ 1605.

and can use its powers to obtain information.[15] In a criminal case if the Crown has failed to put forward enough evidence to show the accused committed the crime a no case to answer submission could be made. There is no such thing as a submission of no case to answer in a tribunal.

5.28 As is set out below, the position differs between applications and references concerning unrestricted patients and those concerning restricted patients. Some of the key cases which concern the interpretation of the statutory criteria are considered below. See also chapter 16.

Non-restricted patients: discharge from detention

5.29 The tribunal has in all cases a discretion to discharge the patient (s72(1)). In *GA v Betsi Cadwaladrv University Local Health Board*, the Upper Tribunal commented that the discretionary power:

> ... allows a tribunal to direct discharge even when this is not required by section 72(1)(c). It must therefore allow the tribunal to take account of factors other than the criteria that justify detention. Otherwise it would be redundant. It is not possible as a matter of interpretation to exclude issues of consent from the jurisdiction of the tribunal in exercise of that power.[16]

5.30 When exercising its discretion to discharge the tribunal must act in a way that is consistent with its findings. The Upper Tribunal described the power of discretionary discharge as one to be exercised in exceptional circumstances only. This is because it is not easy to envisage a set of facts where a tribunal decides to exercise its discretion to discharge which would not also involve a finding by the tribunal that detention (or liability to recall for CTO patients) was not 'necessary' – in which case the tribunal would be compelled to discharge anyway because of section 72(1).

5.31 If the tribunal is not satisfied that the criteria set out in the Act for continued detention – or for continuation of guardianship or a CTO – are met then the tribunal must discharge the patient. These conditions, usually referred to as the 'statutory criteria', vary depending on the status of the patient and effectively reflect the criteria for admission.

5.32 A patient detained under section 2 must be discharged unless the tribunal is satisfied (s72(1)(a)):

15 Tribunal Procedure (First-tier Tribunal) (HESC) Rules 2008 r15.

16 [2013] UKUT 280 (AAC) at para 21. See also paras 16.26–16.31 below.

(i) that he is then suffering from mental disorder or from mental disorder of a nature or degree which warrants his detention in a hospital for assessment (or for assessment followed by medical treatment) for at least a limited period, or

(ii) that his detention as aforesaid is justified in the interests of his own health or safety or with a view to the protection of other persons.

This wording makes it clear that the tribunal must be satisfied in respect of both tests, or the patient must be discharged. Note the use of the word 'then': the tribunal must consider the position as it is at the time of the hearing.

5.33 In respect of a patient detained 'otherwise than under section 2 above' (in other words a patient detained under section 3 (including a community treatment order patient whose CTO has been revoked) or section 37), the test that the tribunal must apply is more stringent. Such a patient must be discharged unless the tribunal is satisfied (s72(1)(b)):

(i) that he is then suffering from mental disorder or from mental disorder of a nature or degree which makes it appropriate for him to be liable to be detained in a hospital for medical treatment; or

(ii) that it is necessary for the health or safety of the patient or for the protection of other persons that he should receive such treatment; or

(iia) that appropriate medical treatment is available for him; or

(iii) in the case of an application by virtue of paragraph (g) of section 66(1) above, that the patient, if released, would be likely to act in a manner dangerous to other persons or to himself.

This refers to an application by a nearest relative who has sought to discharge the patient from detention and where the RC has issued a barring certificate under section 25(1).

5.34 These criteria do not entirely mirror the criteria in section 3 as section 72(1)(b)(i) refers to the appropriateness of continued *liability* to detention. This allows for example a tribunal to find that the criteria are met in respect of a patient who is on section 17 leave at the time of a hearing, as long as there is a significant element of hospital treatment in the patient's treatment plan (because 'such treatment' in section 72(1)(b)(ii) refers back to 'treatment in hospital for mental disorder'): see R *(DR) v Mersey Care NHS Trust,*[17] *R (CS) v Mental Health Review Tribunal and others*[18] and *KL v Somerset Partnership*

17 [2002] EWHC 1810 (Admin).

18 [2004] EWHC 2958 (Admin).

NHS Foundation Trust.[19] In *KL* the patient was on section 17 leave, attending the CMHT base fortnightly for medication and outpatient reviews. The base where he attended was maintained by the responsible authority: it was 'an adult community mental health centre providing assessment and treatment through individual, group and family therapy intervention, which is maintained by the Trust in connection with its inpatient units, one of which is ... where the appellant was admitted as an inpatient'.[20] The patient's care was under the same RC who had been responsible for his inpatient treatment. The Upper Tribunal upheld the First-tier Tribunal's finding that the patient was receiving hospital treatment.

5.35 Note that if the application is made by a patient rather than the nearest relative (NR) following a barring order then the MHT are not obliged to order discharge if the dangerousness criterion is not met but can take this into account in exercising their discretion: *R(W) v Mental Health Review Tribunal.*[21] If the application by the nearest relative is made after displacement by the county court then the MHT address the usual section 72(1)(b) criteria. It is only in the case of an application by a nearest relative whose attempt to discharge the patient has been blocked by the RC using the powers under section 25 that a tribunal has to consider the additional criterion of dangerousness.

5.36 It will be recalled that the degree of the mental disorder refers to 'the current manifestation of the patient's mental disorder'.[22] This requires the tribunal to assess the extent of the patient's symptomatology at the time of the hearing. The nature refers to the 'particular mental disorder from which the patient is suffering, its chronicity, its progress and the patient's previous response to receiving treatment for the disorder'.[23]

5.37 Two important cases provide guidance as to how the tribunal should assess the question of whether the nature of the disorder in the case of the patient whose case they are considering should be assessed. This is especially important in cases where the patient is stable at the time of the tribunal and the responsible authority do not seek to rely on the degree of the illness. Given that many disorders are relapsing in nature how should the tribunal decide whether the

19 [2011] UKUT 233 (AAC).
20 [2011] UKUT 233 (AAC) para 9.
21 [2004] EWHC 3266 (Admin).
22 Code para 4.3.
23 Code para 4.3.

nature in the case they are hearing makes continued liability to detention appropriate?

5.38 The first is the case of *R v London and South West Region Mental Health Review Tribunal ex p Moyle.*[24] This concerned a patient with a history of relapsing. The court held:

> The correct analysis, in my judgment, is that the nature of the illness of a patient such as the applicant, is that it is an illness which will relapse in the absence of medication. The question that then has to be asked is whether the nature of that illness is such as to make it appropriate for him to be liable to be detained in hospital for medical treatment. Whether it is appropriate or not will depend upon an assessment of the probability that he will relapse in the near future is he were free in the community.

5.39 The second is *CM v Derbyshire Healthcare NHS Foundation Trust*[25] where the Upper Tribunal emphasised that the assessment of the probability of the patient's non-compliance with medication after discharge and the risk of consequent relapse must relate to the 'near future' (paras 10 and 27 where the words 'in the near future' are emphasised by the Upper Tribunal Judge).

5.40 If the evidence suggests that the patient's mental disorder is of a nature but not a degree to make continued liability to detention appropriate, the tribunal should then consider whether it is necessary in the interests of the patient's health, safety or the protection of others that he receives treatment in hospital for mental disorder. Necessity rather than desirability is the standard (see *Reid v Secretary of State for Scotland*[26]) and the tribunal should consider each of the three 'risk criteria' separately.

5.41 The question of after-care may be relevant to the tribunal's assessment of the statutory criteria and the tribunal can adjourn to obtain further information about this: *R (Ashworth Hospital Authority) v Mental Health Tribunal for West Midlands and Northwest Region.*[27] Tribunals will not always be willing to adjourn to obtain evidence as to after-care. In *AM v West London Mental Health NHS Trust*[28] the Court of Appeal held that there will be some cases where it is:

> ... properly open to the First-tier Tribunal to conclude that there was no possibility of discharge at that stage, whatever information about

24 [1999] MHLR 195. See also paras 16.2–16.6 below.
25 [2011] UKUT 129 (AAC). See also paras 16.7–16.9 below.
26 [1998] UKHL 43.
27 [2001] EWHC 901 (Admin).
28 [2012] UKUT 282 (AAC).

after-care might be provided. That, as it seems to me, is the basis on which the tribunal dealt with the question of adjournment.

5.42 The availability of an order under the Deprivation of Liberty Safeguards can be relevant: see para 7.94. For a discussion of what constitutes appropriate available treatment see paras 1.26–1.30.

Discharge of patients on CTOs

5.43 A patient on a CTO can be discharged under the tribunal's general discretion in section 72(1) and must be discharged if the tribunal is not satisfied (s72(1)(c)):

(i) that he is then suffering from mental disorder or mental disorder of a nature or degree which makes it appropriate for him to receive medical treatment; or
(ii) that it is necessary for his health or safety or for the protection of other persons that he should receive such treatment; or
(iii) that it is necessary that the responsible clinician should be able to exercise the power under section 17E above to recall the patient to hospital; or
(iv) that appropriate medical treatment is available for him; or
(v) in the case of an application by virtue of paragraph (g) of section 66(1) above, that the patient, if discharged, would be likely to act in a manner dangerous to other persons or to himself.

5.44 Again the tribunal must be satisfied of each element of the criteria although it will be seen that (v) will only fall to be considered in the case of an attempted discharge by a nearest relative which has been barred by the responsible clinician. When considering the necessity of the power or recall the tribunal must consider 'in particular, the patient's having regard to the patient's history of mental disorder and any other relevant factors, what risk there would be if a deterioration of the patient's condition if he were to continue not to be detained in a hospital) as a result, for example, of his refusing or neglecting to receive the medical treatment he requires for his mental disorder)' (s72(1A)).

5.45 The power to recall is the most likely of the criteria that will be challenged in front of the tribunal.

Deferred discharges and recommendations

5.46 If the tribunal discharges the patient it may defer the discharge to a future date which it must specify (s72(3)). The discharge will take effect on the date given, regardless of any change in circumstances.

In *MP v Merseycare NHS Trust*[29] the First-tier Tribunal deferred discharge and at the same time invited the care team to consider making a CTO. This was not expressed as a formal recommendation. The CTO was made but at the date of the deferred discharge the underlying section 3 came to an end, which brought the CTO to an end as well: see also *Bostridge v Oxleas NHS Foundation Trust*.[30]

5.47 A tribunal may only defer discharge for the purpose of making arrangements and cannot be used to test the patient: *CNWL NHS Foundation Trust v H-JH*.[31]

5.48 Where the tribunal decides not to discharge the patient, it may make statutory recommendations for the patient to be given leave of absence or transferred to another hospital or to guardianship. Such recommendations must be 'with a view to facilitating his discharge on a future date' and not for any other purpose. If the recommendations are not complied with the tribunal may further consider the patient's case (s72(3)). The tribunal will consider whether to reconvene and must give its reasons. In *RB v Nottinghamshire Healthcare NHS Trust*[32] the tribunal made a recommendation which was not followed. However, the tribunal did not reconvene. In the appeal observations were made by the Head of Mental Health Policy at the Ministry of Justice about the purpose of the power to reconvene. The judge noted the following observations:

> Clearly, the Department cannot speak to the intentions of those who proposed and accepted this amendment in 1982. However, it appears to us that the intention (and effect) of what is now section 72(3) is to put in statute the power of the tribunal to make recommendations about certain matters for certain purposes, and to give added weight to those recommendations by allowing (but not requiring) the tribunal to return to the patient's case if the recommendations are not followed. The mere possibility that the tribunal could return to the case – whether or not there is any realistic possibility that the patient would, in fact, then be discharged – seems to have been designed to ensure that the tribunal's recommendations, once given, did not simply disappear into the ether.[33]

29 [2011] UKUT 107 (AAC).

30 [2014] EWCA Civ 1005. See also [2015] EWCA Civ 79, in which the Court of Appeal concluded that the claimant should receive only nominal damages.

31 [2012] UKUT 210 (AAC).

32 [2011] UKUT 73 (AAC).

33 [2011] UKUT 73 (AAC) para 9.

5.49 The judge commented that the discretion to make a recommendation should be exercised judicially and once embarked on it should be followed through. He said:

> The experience of this case may, though, provide a useful lesson for the future. It is surely undesirable to give a patient false hope. The first question is whether to make a recommendation at all. The more obvious the recommendation, the more likely it is that the authority will consider it anyway. So recommendations are likely to be made in those cases where the authority has not considered the possibility or would be unlikely to do so. If the tribunal does make a recommendation, it has to take account of the tenuous nature of its control. This makes it essential to consider very carefully the timescale and the directions that the tribunal might give in order (i) to apply its moral pressure on the authority and (ii) to be fully informed by the time it has to decide whether to reconvene. It may, for example, be appropriate for the tribunal to direct that a progress report be provided shortly before a specified date so that it can decide if there is any practical purpose in reconvening. Finally, the tribunal has to decide whether to reconvene. In making that decision, it has to decide what practical value this would serve. It has no power to enforce the recommendation and is not reconvening for that purpose. It has the power to embarrass the authority into explaining its thinking or, possibly, into compliance. But it has to make a judgment on what it can practically achieve, if anything.[34]

If the tribunal does reconvene it will have the same powers as it did at its original hearing and so could discharge the order.

5.50 Section 72(3A) deals with the position when a tribunal considers that it might be appropriate for the patient to be discharged under a CTO. If this is the case the tribunal is not required to discharge the patient but instead can recommend that the responsible clinician consider whether to make a CTO, and may (but need not) reconvene if no CTO is made. In *MP v Merseycare NHS Trust* (see above para 5.46) the tribunal made a deferred discharge having stated that the criteria for continued liability for detention were not satisfied. The tribunal did not make a formal recommendation under section 72(3A) but invited the care team to consider a CTO. The judge held that once the tribunal had found that the criteria for continued detention were not satisfied, the tribunal was under a duty to discharge the patient (whether deferred or not) and the power to make recommendations under section 72(3A) was irrelevant and in any event a CTO would cease to exist on the discharge date.

34 [2011] UKUT 73 (AAC) para 16.

5.51 The tribunal does not have the power to discharge directly onto a CTO.

Discharge of patients subject to guardianship

5.52 The tribunal must discharge a patient subject to guardianship if it is satisfied that the patient is not suffering from mental disorder and that it is not necessary in the interests of the patient's welfare or for the protection of other persons, that the patient should remain under guardianship (s72(4)). The tribunal can discharge the patient under its discretion in any event.

5.53 Note that in these cases the wording is reversed, in that it is the patient who must satisfy the tribunal that he or she does not fulfil the criteria. In *NL v Hampshire CC*[35] the Upper Tribunal held that a) the burden of proof does not rest on the detailing authority as it does in detention because guardianship does not involve deprivation of liberty, and b) the comments in *GA v Besti Cadwaladrv University Local Health Board* about discretionary discharges apply in guardianship cases (see para 5.29).

Restricted patients

5.54 Section 73 deals with the position concerning patients subject to a restriction order. The tribunal does not have the general discretion provided for in respect of non-restricted patients but must follow the statutory criteria, as modified, below. The important difference is the availability to the tribunal of a conditional discharge, which as has been seen is not available to a tribunal considering the case of a non-restricted patient.

5.55 The tribunal must discharge a patient if it is not satisfied:

- that he is then suffering from mental disorder or from mental disorder of a nature or degree which makes it appropriate for him to be liable to be detained in a hospital for medical treatment; or
- that it is necessary for the health or safety of the patient or for the protection of other persons that he should receive such treatment; or
- that appropriate medical treatment is available for him.

If the tribunal is not satisfied that it is appropriate for the patient to remain liable to recall to hospital for further treatment, the patient must be absolutely discharged (s73(1)). This brings to an end the

35 [2014] UKUT 475 (AAC).

hospital order and the restriction order. If the tribunal is satisfied that it is appropriate for the patient to remain liable to recall they should discharge the patient conditionally (s73(2)). It is possible for a tribunal to discharge a patient conditionally without imposing specific conditions: see para 5.60.

5.56 There is no power to defer an absolute discharge. Section 73(7) gives the tribunal the power to defer the direction for conditional discharge until arrangements have been made to the tribunal's satisfaction. These are provisional decisions and the tribunal can reconvene to monitor progress and has the same powers as at its original hearing: *R(H) v Ashworth Hospital Authority*.[36] However, they are decisions and the tribunal cannot go back on them. Once a deferred conditional discharge decision has been made, unless the conditions cannot be fulfilled or there is some material change in circumstances such as the patient becoming unwell, the decision will remain.

5.57 In *EC v Birmingham and Solihull Mental Health NHS Trust*[37] the Court of Appeal held that there is no equivalent in section 73 to the provisions in section 72(3)(a) (the power to make recommendations in non-restricted cases). However, in cases where the patient is seeking support from the tribunal for leave, the tribunal can be asked to consider leave as part of the question of whether appropriate treatment is available.

5.58 The tribunal cannot impose conditions that would entail a deprivation of the patient's liberty: *Secretary of State for Justice v RB*[38] and *Secretary of State for Justice v SB*.[39] But a patient who has been conditionally discharged may also be deprived of his liberty using the Deprivation of Liberty Safeguards if this is necessary to give effect to a best interests decision about how the patient should be cared for: see paras 7.77–7.82.

5.59 In *Secretary of State for Justice v MP*,[40] MP was made the subject of a conditional discharge without conditions. The tribunal recorded that it was not satisfied that he had ever suffered from mental disorder whilst recognising the possibility that he did. For this reason the tribunal considered that MP should be liable to recall. After his discharge the Secretary of State imposed conditions on MP and he was recalled to hospital. His case was referred to the tribunal and he was

36 [2003] 1 WLR 127.
37 [2013] EWCA Civ 701.
38 [2011] EWCA Civ 1608.
39 [2013] UKUT 320 (AAC).
40 [2013] UKUT 025 (AAC).

not discharged. In the meantime the Secretary of State appealed the original decision to discharge MP. The Secretary of State argued that by concluding that it was not satisfied that MP had ever had a mental illness, the FTT was seeking to go behind the decision to admit MP in the first place. The Upper Tribunal rejected this, but held that the FTT's reasoning for not imposing conditions had been inadequate:

> A tribunal has power to make a patient's discharge conditional even if the patient does not have a mental disorder: *R v Merseyside Mental Health Review Tribunal ex p K* [1990] 1 All ER 694 at 699–700. A conditional discharge is so named because the patient is liable to recall. It is permissible to direct a conditional discharge without imposing any further conditions, as envisaged by section 73(4)(b). A tribunal is under a duty to explain its decision, including a decision not to impose further conditions. In some cases, the circumstances alone may be sufficient to show why the tribunal did not impose conditions. This is not such a case. The tribunal found that Mr P had a drug-induced psychosis and that he had continued to use drugs. Indeed, he said that he would do if he were discharged. The tribunal found that that involved a risk of self-neglect. In those circumstances, the tribunal was under a duty to explain why it did not impose conditions.[41]

5.60 The tribunal may not make a deferred conditional discharge if it cannot formulate the conditions to be imposed. In *DC v Nottinghamshire Healthcare NHS Trust and the Secretary of State for Justice*[42] the FTT had twice adjourned DC's case which had been referred to the tribunal. The first paragraph in the adjournment notice read:

> Having heard all the evidence available to it, the tribunal concludes that, with the exception of the availability of suitable after-care for the Patient, none of the criteria for his detention in hospital for treatment are met.[43]

DC appealed on the basis that he should have been granted a deferred conditional discharge.

5.61 The Upper Tribunal analysed the position:[44]

> **Adjournment**
>
> 23. The First-tier Tribunal has the power to adjourn as one of its case management powers under rule 5(3)(h) of the Tribunal Procedure (First-tier Tribunal) (Health, Education and Social Care Chamber) Rules 2008 (SI No 2699). The power must be exercised judicially and in accordance with the overriding objective in rule 2. As a procedural

41 [2013] UKUT 025 (AAC) para 20.
42 See [2012] UKUT 92 (AAC) para 5.
43 [2012] UKUT 92 (AAC) para 23.
44 [2012] UKUT 92 (AAC).

> power, it cannot be exercised to override the provisions of the substantive legislation. In particular, a tribunal cannot adjourn if it is obliged to give a decision under section 73 of the 1983 Act.
>
> **Section 73**
>
> 24. Section 73 contains conditions and consequences. The conditions are set out in section 73(1). The consequences depend on which conditions are met. If and only if the tribunal is satisfied that the patient should not be detained but should be subject to recall, these two consequences follow. The first consequence is a duty – the tribunal must direct a conditional discharge under section 73(2). The second consequence is a power – the tribunal may defer that direction under section 73(7).
>
> 25. The language of section 73(7) is important. The tribunal does not defer the patient's conditional discharge. It defers the direction for the discharge. That is what section 73(7) says and it is significant. That presupposes that there is a direction to discharge ready to take effect. Until there is, there is nothing to defer. That means that the conditions for discharge must be identified and included in the direction. The deferral allows time for the necessary arrangements to be made. That means the arrangements necessary for the conditional discharge. And it is impossible to make those arrangements without knowing what the conditions for the discharge are. Section 73(7), by its terms, operates until the tribunal is satisfied that the arrangements are in place. Once it is, there is nothing left for the tribunal to do except to lift the deferral.
>
> 26. In summary, the tribunal cannot exercise the power in section 73(7) unless it finds that the patient should not be detained but should be subject to recall and it formulates a direction, including conditions for discharge, that can take effect if the necessary arrangements can be made. Until then, it is free to adjourn.

5.62 The Upper Tribunal emphasised that a deferred conditional discharge should not be used to gather information:

> It is only permissible to use section 73 when (a) it is able to find, on the balance of probabilities, that the patient should not be detained but should be subject to recall, and (b) it has drafted the conditions for the discharge.[45]

In that case the tribunal was not in a position to make a deferred conditional discharge and had properly adjourned the case.

45 [2012] UKUT 92 (AAC) para 28.

The effect of a conditional discharge

5.63 The effect of the conditional discharge is that the patient can be recalled by the Secretary of State and must comply with the conditions set down by the tribunal or subsequently by the Secretary of State who has an ongoing power to vary the conditions (s73(5)).

5.64 If the patient is recalled to hospital the Secretary of State must refer his case to the tribunal within a month of the day on which the patient was recalled.

5.65 A conditionally discharged restricted patient can apply to the tribunal during the second twelve months of his conditional discharge and in any subsequent period of two years (s75(2)). In this case rather than applying section 72 or section 73, the tribunal has the power to vary any of the existing conditions or impose new ones, or discharge the restriction order altogether, so that the patient is absolutely discharged.

What should the tribunal consider when asked for an absolute discharge?

5.66 In *R (SC) v MHRT*[46] SC challenged the lack of any statutory criteria for the tribunal to apply, on the basis that this did not protect him against arbitrary decision-making, because section 75 was insufficiently precise. Dismissing the application Munby J (as he then was) held that the relevant factors for a decision under section 75 could be readily identified.

5.67 The judge said the tribunal would need to consider:

> ... the nature and gravity of his mental disorder, past, present and future, the risk and likelihood of the patient re-offending, the degree of harm to which the public may be exposed if he re-offends, the risk and likelihood of a recurrence or exacerbation of any mental disorder, and the risk and likelihood of his needing to be recalled in the future for further treatment in hospital. The tribunal will also need to consider the nature of any conditions previously imposed, whether by the tribunal or by the Secretary of State, under sections 42(2), 73(4)(b) or 73(5), the reasons why they were imposed and the extent to which it is desirable to continue, vary or add to them.[47]

5.68 The judge went on to comment:

> I agree ... that this broad discretion serves to ensure that the tribunal can respond flexibly and appropriately to the varied and potentially

46 [2005] EWHC 17 (Admin).
47 [2005] EWHC 17 (Admin) para 57.

> complex situations which may arise when a restricted patient has been conditionally discharged. This enables the tribunal to ensure that both the interests of the patient and the interests of public safety which arise in the case of a restricted patient are adequately served. In practice ... such an exercise is fact-intensive and strongly dependent upon the clinical details of each particular case – as, indeed, the decision of the tribunal in the present case illustrates.[48]

Patients transferred from prison

5.69 Section 74 governs the position of patients subject to restriction directions and limitation directions. In these cases the tribunal's powers are more limited. The tribunal must notify the Secretary of State whether the patient would be entitled to either a conditional or absolute discharge, had he been subject to a restriction order rather than a restriction direction (s74(1)). The tribunal must also notify the Secretary of State whether, in the case of a patient whom the tribunal considers would have been entitled to a conditional discharge, the tribunal recommends he remains in hospital if he is not discharged under the provisions set out below.

5.70 If the tribunal notifies the Secretary of State that the patient would be entitled to an absolute or conditional discharge and the Secretary of State gives notice within 90 days that the discharge may take place, then the tribunal must direct the absolute or conditional discharge, (unless the patient is transferred pursuant to section 48 – remand prisoners – in which case special provisions apply by virtue of s74(4)). However, if the Secretary of State does not give notice that the transfer may take place within 90 days then the managers must transfer the patient to a prison or other institution where he can be dealt with as if he had not been removed to hospital (s74(3)), unless the tribunal has also recommended under section 74(1)(b) that he should remain in hospital if not discharged.

5.71 In the case of prisoners transferred under section 48, the 90-day period does not apply and the patient will simply be transferred to prison or another institution and will be dealt with as if he had not been removed to hospital (s74(4)), unless the tribunal has made a recommendation that the patient should remain in hospital if not discharged.

5.72 If the tribunal recommends that a patient subject to a restriction direction or a limitation direction should remain in hospital if he is not discharged, then the Parole Board retain jurisdiction to consider

48 [2005] EWHC 17 (Admin) para 58.

his case and in the event that the Parole Board or the Secretary of State make a decision which would have allowed him to be released absolutely or on licence from prison, then the effect of that decision is that the patient will remain in hospital as a 'notional section 37' patient but without the restriction or limitation direction.

5.73 The tribunal's role is advisory and it cannot take account of what decisions might or might not be made by the Parole Board: *AC, Partnerships in Care Ltd v Secretary of State for Justice.*[49] See also *R (LV) v (1) Secretary of State for Justice and (2) The Parole Board.*[50]

5.74 Section 76 permits a registered medical practitioner or approved clinician to visit and examine a patient detained in hospital or subject to a CTO or guardianship for the purpose a tribunal application. The visiting practitioner may have access to the patient's records.

49 [2012] UKUT 450 (AAC).

50 [2013] EWCA Civ 1806 and *R v Vowles and others* [2015] EWCA Crim 45.

CHAPTER 6

Mental Health Act 1983 Parts 6–10

6.1 This chapter summarises the key provisions of Parts 6–10 of the Mental Health Act (MHA) 1983:

- Part 6 – cross-border issues
- Part 7 – management of patient's finances (repealed by the Mental Capacity Act 2005)
- Part 8 – functions of local authorities and the Secretary of State
- Part 9 – offences
- Part 10 – includes provisions for independent mental health advocates, informal admission, information and accessing the patient at home or in public.

Part 6: removal and return of patients within the United Kingdom

6.2 This Part of the Mental Health Act 1983 governs the position of patients who are removed within the UK or abroad. In general the Act permits the removal of patients within the UK when it is in the patient's interests and when sufficiently similar corresponding arrangements are in place for the patient's care and treatment. Note that the patient's consent is not required for the exercise of these powers. Once a patient is removed from England or Wales either within the UK or abroad under this Part of the MHA 1983, the original order for detention, community treatment or guardianship will cease to have effect.[1] There is one exception to this and that is when a patient subject to an order under section 37 or 41 is removed from the UK under section 86, the restrictions will remain in force if he or she returns to the UK.[2]

Within the United Kingdom

Scotland

6.3 Patients (other than those detained under sections 35, 36 or 38, whose criminal cases are still pending) can be removed to Scotland from England or Wales if the Secretary of State considers this to be in the patient's interests and if arrangements have been made for him to be admitted and detained there (s80). Responsibility for a community patient who has not been recalled to hospital can be transferred

1 MHA 1983 s91(1).
2 MHA 1983 s91(2).

to Scotland if it appears to the Secretary of State to be in the patient's interests, and arrangements are in place to deal with him or her under corresponding or similar provisions in Scotland (s80Z). A conditionally discharged restricted patient can be transferred in his or her interests with the consent of the Minister exercising corresponding functions in Scotland.

6.4 Patients can be moved from Scotland to England or Wales through regulations made under section 290 (1)(a) of the Mental Health (Care and Treatment) (Scotland) Act 2003, if they were detained either under that Act or under the Criminal Procedure (Scotland) Act 1995 and if they are admitted to hospital in the UK (s80B).

6.5 A patient who is admitted to an English or Welsh hospital from a Scottish hospital will be treated as if he or she were detained under the closest English equivalent power, as from the date of his or her admission to hospital in England or Wales.

6.6 A patient subject to community treatment powers in Scotland who moves to England or Wales will be treated as if on the day of arrival in England he or she was admitted to the responsible hospital there and then immediately discharged on a community treatment order (CTO) (s80C). The new responsible clinician (RC), with the agreement of an approved mental health practitioner, must specify conditions as soon as practicable after the patient arrives (s80C(5) and (6)).

6.7 A conditionally discharged restricted patient transferred from Scotland will be treated as if he or she had been subject to an order under section 37 or 41 and been conditionally discharged on the day of arrival (s80D).

Northern Ireland

6.8 Section 81 allows the transfer of patients to Northern Ireland who are detained in England or Wales or subject to guardianship, again with the exception of those with pending criminal cases who are detained under sections 35, 36 or 38, as long as it is in the patient's interests and arrangements have been made to admit him or her to hospital or receive him or her into guardianship in Northern Ireland. These patients will be treated as if they had been admitted under the closest corresponding measure in Northern Ireland.

6.9 A patient detained in England or Wales and then moved to Northern Ireland and admitted there will be treated as though he or she had been admitted under the equivalent provision in Northern Ireland, on the day of admission in England or Wales: section 81(4) and

81(5). Section 81(ZA) provides that a community treatment patient would be treated as if he or she had been made subject to an equivalent order in Northern Ireland, on the day on which the English CTO was made. However, as there is currently no equivalent regime, such patients could be transferred under section 81 and detained in Northern Ireland as if they had not been subject to a CTO. A guardianship patient moving from England or Wales to Northern Ireland will be treated as if a guardianship order under Northern Ireland provisions had been made on the date of arrival at his or her new residence (s81(3)). A conditionally discharged restricted patient can be moved to Northern Ireland with the consent of the corresponding Minister in Northern Ireland, and if a time-limited restriction direction, the date of expiry will not be affected by the transfer (s81(3)).

6.10 Patients may be removed to England or Wales from Northern Ireland if is considered in their interests and arrangements for either detention in hospital or admission to guardianship have been made (s82(1)). A detained patient is treated on arrival as if he or she had been detained under the corresponding English and Welsh provision on the day that he or she was admitted in Northern Ireland (s82(2), (4) and (4A)). By contrast, guardianship patients are treated as though the guardianship order had been made on the day they arrived at their new residence. Sentenced offender patients are treated as though their sentences had been imposed in Northern Ireland and the expiry of any time limited restriction order or direction imposed in Northern Ireland is unchanged. Conditionally discharged patients can be transferred in their interests with the consent of the Secretary of State and are treated as though they were conditionally discharged on the day of their arrival. There is no equivalent to a CTO in Northern Ireland.

The Channel Islands and the Isle of Man

6.11 A patient detained or subject to guardianship in England and Wales can be transferred to the Channel Islands or the Isle of Man if it is in his or her interests and if arrangements have been made to receive the patient (s83). Under section 83ZA, the provisions as to detained patients also apply to community patients in England and Wales who can be removed to the Channel Islands or the Isle of Man. There is no provision for CTOs in the Channel Islands or the Isle of Man so these patients would simply be detained on their arrival. However, section 83ZA provides that if an equivalent regime to the CTO regime were to come into force in the Isle of Man or the Channel Islands then that regime would apply to a CTO patient transferred there from England or Wales.

6.12 Conditionally discharged patients can be transferred in their interests to the Channel Islands or the Isle of Man with the consent of the corresponding authority there.

6.13 Offenders found by courts in the Channel Islands or the Isle of Man to be insane and ordered to be detained during Her Majesty's Pleasure can be removed to hospital in England or Wales and will then be treated as if detained under sections 37/41 of the MHA 1983. Such a patient can be returned to the island by warrant of the Secretary of State and dealt with as if he had never been removed (s84).

6.14 A detained patient who arrives from the Channel Islands or the Isle of Man will be treated as if he or she had been detained under the English or Welsh equivalent on the day of admission (s85(2)). Guardianship patients are treated as if they were received into guardianship on the day of their arrival (s85(3)). Sentenced offender patients will be treated as if they had been sentenced in England or Wales (s85(4)). Time-limited restricted patients will have the same expiry date as would have applied had they not been moved (s85(5)).

6.15 A conditionally discharged restricted patient transferred from the Isle of Man or Channel Islands is treated as if he or she had been conditionally discharged on the date of transfer.

6.16 Section 85(ZA) provides for the potential transfer of CTO patients from the Isle of Man or Channel Islands, in the event that such a regime comes into force.

6.17 Conditionally discharged patients will be treated as if subject to the corresponding provision in England and Wales.

6.18 Patients who abscond from hospitals can be returned to England and Wales from Northern Ireland (s87). Those absent from hospitals in the Channel Islands and the Isle of Man can be returned to the Channel Islands or the Isle of Man from England and Wales (s89). None of these provisions apply to those subject to guardianship (ss87(2), 89(2)).

Removal of aliens

6.19 Section 86 allows the removal from the UK, Isle of Man or Channel Islands of inpatients receiving treatment for mental disorder in hospitals in England and Wales, who are not British citizens or Commonwealth citizens with the right of abode in the UK. This can be arranged if the Secretary of State considers it to be in the patient's interest and if 'proper arrangements' have been made for their removal, care and treatment. The Secretary of State must first obtain the approval of the appropriate tribunal. This power does not apply to those subject to guardianship or CTOs.

6.20 Patients can also be voluntarily repatriated with their consent.

Part 7: management of property and affairs of patients

6.21 This Part of the Act dealt with the management of patients' finances and was repealed by the Mental Capacity Act 2005.

Part 8: functions of local authorities and the Secretary of State

6.22 This Part of the Act deals with functions of local authorities and the Secretary of State.

6.23 Section 114 deals with the provision of training for approved mental health professionals (AMHPs).

6.24 Section 115 provides a power of entry to any AMHP to enter and inspect any premises other than a hospital in which a mentally disordered person is living, at all reasonable times and on production of appropriate identification. This does not permit the AMHP to enter by force or without the consent of the owner. Nor is there any power to remove the patient under this section.

6.25 Section 116 applies to certain more vulnerable patients and imposes additional duties on local authorities. It applies to:

- children under a care order pursuant to the Children Act 1989 (or the Social Work (Scotland) Act 1968);
- patients subject to guardianship;
- patients in whose case the local social services authority exercises the functions of the nearest relative.

When a patient in any of these categories is admitted to a hospital, independent hospital or care home the local authority must arrange visits to the patient and take such steps 'as would be expected to be taken by his parents'. This section is not limited to patients admitted under the MHA 1983. See also chapter 15 on children and young people.

After-care: section 117

6.26 Section 117 places a duty on the Clinical Commissioning Group (CCG), local health board (in Wales) and local social services authority to provide after-care to patients who leave hospital following detention under sections 3, 37, 45A, 47 or 48.

6.27 The duty is:

> ... to provide, or arrange for the provision of, in co-operation with relevant voluntary agencies, after-care services until such time as the CCG, local health board and local authority are satisfied that the person concerned is no longer in need of such services; but they shall not be so satisfied in the case of a community patient while he remains such a patient.[3]

6.28 After-care services are described in the English Code of Practice at chapter 33 as 'a vital component in patients' overall treatment and care'.[4] The tribunal will expect to be informed of what services might be provided if the patient were to be discharged so 'some discussion of after-care needs ... should take place in advance of the hearing' (para 33.11 in the Code) and 'the planning of after-care needs to start as soon as the patient is admitted to hospital'.[5] However, the tribunal is entitled in appropriate cases to proceed in the absence of detailed information about after-care: see para 5.41 and the case of *AM v West London Mental Health NHS Trust*.[6]

6.29 The duty to provide or commission the after-care does not take effect until the patient is discharged from hospital.[7]

What is after-care?

6.30 After-care was not defined in section 117 until the Care Act 2014 (see below) and its elements have been considered by the courts.

6.31 In *Clunis v Camden and Islington Health Authority*[8] the Court of Appeal held:

> After-care services are not defined in the Act. They would normally include social work, support in helping the ex-patient with problems of employment, accommodation or family relationships, the

3 MHA 1983 s117(2) amended by Care Act 2014 s75(1).

4 Code para 33.5

5 Code for Wales para 31.7.

6 [2013] EWCA Civ 1010.

7 MHA 1983 s117(1).

8 [1997] EWCA Civ 2918.

provision of domiciliary services and the use of day centre and residential facilities.

The House of Lords approved this concept of section 117 services in 2002 in *R v Manchester City Council ex p Stennett*.[9]

6.32 The question of accommodation under section 117 has been considered by the Court most recently in *R (Tewodras Afework (by his sister and litigation friend Aster Afework Mehare)) v London Borough of Camden*[10] where Mostyn J held that a duty under section 117(2) regarding after-care is only engaged vis-à-vis accommodation if:

i) the need for accommodation is a direct result of the reason the ex-patient was detained in the first place ('the original condition'); and
ii) the requirement is for enhanced specialised accommodation to meet needs directly arising from the original condition; and
iii) the ex-patient is being placed in the accommodation on an involuntary (in the sense of being incapacitated) basis as a result of the original condition.[11]

6.33 The Care Act 2014 amended section 117 and there is for the first time a statutory definition of after-care:

> ... after-care services ... means services which have both of the following purposes –
> (a) meeting a need arising from or related to the person's mental disorder, and
> (b) reducing the risk of a deterioration of the person's mental condition (and accordingly, to reduce the risk of the person requiring admission to a hospital again for treatment for mental disorder).[12]

6.34 The Code gives the following new guidance at para 33.4, which underlines the importance of taking a holistic approach:

> CCGs and local authorities should interpret the definition of after-care broadly. For example, after-care can encompass healthcare, social care and employment services, supported accommodation and services to meet the person's wider social, cultural and spiritual needs, if these services meet a need that arises directly or is related to the patient's mental disorder, and help to reduce the risk of a deterioration in the patient's condition.

Section 117 services can be provided by means of direct payments in appropriate cases: Care Act 2014 s75(7), (8). Services under section

9 [2002] UKHL 34 para 9, per Lord Steyn.
10 [2013] EWHC 1637 (Admin).
11 [2013] EWHC 1637 (Admin) para 19.
12 MHA 1983 s117(6) amended by Care Act 2014 s75.

117 cannot be charged for but patients or third parties can 'top up' payments if they wish to choose more expensive supported accommodation: MHA 1983 s117A.

Who is responsible?

6.35 It is important to establish which bodies are responsible for section 117 after-care for a particular patient. Following amendments by section 75 of the Care Act 2014, the relevant local authority will be the local authority for the area in England or Wales where the patient was 'ordinarily resident' before he was detained.[13] Prior to the Care Act 2014 the responsible local authority was the authority where the patient was 'resident' or 'sent on discharge'. Ordinary residence is not defined in statute and the courts have stressed that in ascertaining where a person is ordinarily resident the words should be given their natural meaning. For adults with capacity to decide where to live the courts have held that:

> ... 'ordinarily resident' refers to a man's abode in a particular place or country which he has adopted voluntarily and for settled purposes as part of the regular order of his life for the time being, whether of short or long duration.[14]

6.36 In the case of adults lacking capacity, it should not be assumed that they will be 'ordinarily resident' with their parents, unless the person concerned has 'at least ... a regular pattern of living with the parents'.[15] Section 39 of the Care Act 2014 contains 'deeming provisions' which also apply to those receiving services under section 117. The effect of these is that if a patient is provided with care home accommodation, 'shared lives scheme accommodation' (sometimes described as adult foster care places) or supporting living,[16] then the patient will be treated as ordinarily resident in the area which arranged the placement and which holds section 117 responsibility, even if that is not the area where the patient in fact lives.

6.37 If a person is ordinarily resident in Local Authority A before being detained, becomes subject to an order under sections 37/41, is conditionally discharged to a hostel in Local Authority B and is

13 MHA 1983 s117(3) amended by Care Act 2014 s75(3).

14 *R v Barnet LBC ex p Shah* [1983] AC 309.

15 *R (Cornwall Council) v Secretary of State for Health and others* [2014] EWCA Civ 12.

16 See Care and Support (Ordinary Residence) (Specified Accommodation) Regulations 2014 SI No 2828.

then recalled to hospital, the placement in Local Authority B will not 'break the chain' and Local Authority A will retain section 117 responsibility. This is because the patient was compelled to live in Local Authority B as a result of the conditions of his discharge.[17]

6.38 The amendments to section 117 by section 75 of the Care Act 2014 also now gives the Secretary of State powers to resolve disputes about section 117 responsibility.[18]

How should it be planned?

6.39 The Code (para 34.19) provides that:

> Care planning requires a thorough assessment of the patient's needs and wishes. It is likely to involve consideration of:
>
> - continuing mental healthcare, whether in the community or on an out-patient basis;
> - the psychological needs of the patient and, where appropriate, of their family and carers;
> - physical healthcare;
> - daytime activities or employment;
> - appropriate accommodation;
> - identified risks and safety issues;
> - any specific needs arising from, for example, co-existing physical disability, sensory impairment, learning disability or autistic spectrum disorder;
> - any specific needs arising from drug, alcohol or substance misuse (if relevant);
> - any parenting or caring needs;
> - social, cultural or spiritual needs;
> - counselling and personal support;
> - assistance in welfare rights and managing finances;
> - the involvement of authorities and agencies in a different area, if the patient is not going to live locally;
> - the involvement of other agencies, eg the probation service or voluntary organisations (if relevant);
> - for a restricted patient, the conditions which the Secretary of State for Justice or the Tribunal has imposed or is likely to impose on their conditional discharge; and
> - contingency plans (should the patient's mental health deteriorate) and crisis contact details.

6.40 To ensure the after-care plan 'reflects the needs of each patient', the following people may need to be involved:

17 *R (Wiltshire Council) v Hertfordshire CC and SQ* [2014] EWCA Civ 712.

18 MHA 1983 s117(4) and (5) inserted by Care Act 2014. See also Care and Support (Disputes between Local Authorities) Regulations 2014 SI No 2829.

- the patient's responsible clinician;
- nurses and other professionals involved in caring for the patient in hospital;
- a practitioner psychologist registered with the Health and Care Professions Council, community mental health nurse and other members of the community team;
- the patient's GP and primary care team, if there is one;
- any carer who will be involved in looking after them outside hospital;
- the patient's nearest relative or other family carers;
- a representative of any relevant voluntary organisations;
- in the case of a restricted patient, the MAPPA co-ordinator;[19]
- a representative of housing authorities, if accommodation is an issue;
- an employment expert, if employment is an issue;
- an independent mental health advocate, if the patient has one;
- an independent mental capacity advocate, if the patient has one;
- the patient's attorney or deputy, if the patient has one; and
- any other representative nominated by the patient.[20]

What if section 117 does not apply?

6.41 Patients detained under MHA 1983 s2 will not be entitled to section 117 after-care, unless they have formerly been detained under the longer term sections and have not been discharged from section 117. Such patients may have a need for social care and support which could be provided under the Care Act 2014. Note that section 9 of the Care Act 2014 obliges local authorities to carry out an assessment if it appears to the local authority that an adult may have needs for care and support, so the threshold at which the duty to assess arises is not high. Some patients with complex mental health needs will be entitled to have care provided under the Care Programme Approach (CPA), which is an 'overarching system for co-ordinating the care of people with mental disorders. It requires close engagement with service users and their carers and includes arrangements for assessing, planning and reviewing care.'[21] Chapter 34 of the Code is devoted to the CPA and explains when it should be used. In Wales, practitioners will need to be familiar with the Mental Health (Wales) Measure 2010.

19 For a discussion of the role of MAPPA see paras 11.124–11.130.

20 Code of Practice 34.12.

21 Code para 34.2.

6.42 The importance of attending after-care planning meetings or section 117 meetings is considered in chapter 9 and is also referred to in the Peer Review Guidance 2011 from the Legal Services Commission as it then was.[22]

The Code of Practice: section 118

6.43 Section 118 requires the Secretary of State to prepare and revise a Code of Practice and sets out the matters which must be addressed in the Code's statement of principles. These are defined in section 118(2B).

6.44 The Secretary of State is also required to have regard to the desirability of ensuring efficient use of resources and the equitable distribution of services.

6.45 Note that the Code does not simply apply to those detained under the Act (s118(1)(a)) but is also:

> [s118(1)](b) for the guidance of registered medical practitioners and members of other professions in relation to the medical treatment of patients suffering from mental disorder.

6.46 See paras 1.11–1.16 for a discussion of the status of the Code. The current version came into force on 1 April 2015.

6.47 Sections 119–120 deal with the regulatory framework and functions of the Care Quality Commission.

Part 9: offences

6.48 Part 9 (ss126–130) creates a series of specific offences including ill-treatment of patients (s127) and assisting patients to absent themselves from hospital without leave (s128). This offence includes giving a patient who has absconded any assistance 'with intent to prevent, hinder or interfere with his being taken into custody or returned to hospital' (s128(3)). Practitioners who are contacted by clients who have absconded must bear in mind this provision. Section 129 creates an offence of obstruction.

22 *Improving Your Quality: a guide to common issues identified through Peer Review – Mental Health*, 3rd edn, April 2011: see appendix C.

Part 10: independent mental health advocates, informal admission, information and accessing the patient at home or in public

6.49 This Part of the Act provides for:

- **Sections 130A–D**: the requirement to provide Independent Mental Health Advocates (IMHAs) to 'qualifying patients' (those detained under any provision other than sections 4, 5(2) or (4),[23] those under guardianship or CTOs,[24] those discussing section 57 type treatments,[25] or those under 18 discussing section 58A treatment ie ECT).[26]
- **Section 131**: informal admission of patients. This section permits the admission to hospital of patients requiring treatment for mental disorder without use of the Act. These patients will be those who have capacity to consent to their admission and do consent or those who lack capacity to consent but do not object. In connection with adult patients without capacity see the section in chapter 1 on the Mental Capacity Act and the Deprivation of Liberty Safeguards. In connection with those under 18, see chapter 8.
- **Section 131A**: duty to ensure that all under 18s admitted to hospital for treatment for mental disorder are in an environment that is suitable having regard to his age (subject to his needs), see further chapter 8.
- **Sections 132 and 132A**: duty of managers to provide information about the right to apply to the tribunal to detained and CTO patients.
- **Section 133**: duty of managers to inform nearest relatives of patients' discharge from detention or CTO, unless requested not to by the patient.
- **Sections 134 and 134A**: provision for withholding correspondence from patients in certain circumstances
- **Section 135**: power of AMHP to apply to magistrates court for a warrant to enter premises and remove a person believed to be suffering from mental disorder and either '(a) (b) A patient removed under these provisions can be detained in a place of safety or places of safety for up to 72 hours (s135(3), (3A), (3B)). Place of

23 MHA 1983 s130C(2)(a).

24 MHA 1983 s130C(2) (b) and (c).

25 MHA 1983 s130C(3)(a).

26 MHA 1983 s130C(3)(b).

safety is defined in section 135(6) and see discussion below, paras 6.53–6.56.

- **Section 136**: power of constable to remove to a place of safety (as defined in s135(6)) any person in a place to which the public has access, who appears to be suffering from mental disorder and to be in immediate need of care and control. See discussion below, paras 6.57–6.59.
- **Section 137** provides that the conveyance of a person under the MHA 1983, or their detention in a place of safety under the Act is deemed to be lawful custody. The police have the same powers, authority, protection and privileges when acting under the MHA 1983 as within the area where they act as constables.
- **Section 138** deals with the arrangements for re-taking patients who have escaped from legal custody.
- **Section 139** provides protection from liability for acts carried out under the MHA 1983 or Regulations and section 139(2) requires leave from the High Court to be obtained before any civil proceedings can be brought in respect of acts carried out under the MHA 1983.

Section 145 deals with interpretation. See in particular section 145(4) defining medical treatment which is considered in chapter 1.

Police powers: ss135–137

6.50 A warrant can be obtained under section 135 from a magistrate. There are two situations in which the magistrate may grant a warrant. The first – an application under section 135(1) – relates to a person who is not yet liable to be detained. The application must be made by an AMHP,[27] and must satisfy the magistrate:

> ... that there is reasonable cause to suspect that a person believed to be suffering from mental disorder–
> (a) has been, or is being ill-treated, neglected or kept otherwise than under proper control, in any place within the jurisdiction of the justice, or
> (b) being unable to care for himself, is living alone in any such place.[28]

27 MHA 1983 s135(1).
28 MHA 1983 s135(1).

If the warrant is granted it authorises a constable to 'enter, if need be by force, any place specified in the warrant'. He or she must be accompanied by an AMHP and a registered medical practitioner.[29]

6.51 The second situation in which a warrant may be issued arises where a person is already subject to the powers of the MHA 1983, or equivalent powers under Scottish legislation, and is liable to be taken or re-taken.[30] This could be a patient who is liable to be detained or is subject to guardianship or a CTO. In this case the warrant can be applied for either by a constable or person authorised under the MHA 1983 or under the Scottish legislation. The criteria are different to those in section 135(1). For a warrant under section 135(2) the magistrate must be satisfied that:

(a) there is reasonable cause to believe that the person is to be found on the premises within the jurisdiction of the justice, and
(b) that the admission to the premises has been refused or that a refusal of such admission is apprehended.[31]

6.52 The warrant issued under section 135(2) allows the constable to enter and remove the patient without other professionals but he or she may be accompanied by a registered medical practitioner or authorised person.

6.53 While there the constable may remove the person to a 'place of safety',[32] or to one or more places of safety.[33] The maximum period for which the person can be detained (whether or not they are moved from one place of safety to another) must not exceed 72 hours.[34]

6.54 A person detained under either of these provisions is held to be in lawful custody.[35] If the person escapes from lawful custody he or she may be re-taken at any time during the 72 hours from either the time of his detention, or the time of his escape, whichever expires first.[36]

6.55 A 'place of safety' is defined as residential accommodation, a hospital, a police station or any other suitable place whose occupier is willing to receive the patient temporarily.[37]

29 MHA 1983 s135(4).
30 MHA 1983 s135(2).
31 MHA 1983 s135(2).
32 MHA 1983 s135(1).
33 MHA 1983 s135(3A).
34 MHA 1983 s135(3), (3A).
35 MHA 1983 s137(1).
36 MHA 1983 s138(3).
37 MHA 1983 s135(6).

6.56 The Code urges the identification in advance of the place of safety, with a view to avoiding the use of police stations other than in exceptional circumstances.[38] The Code gives guidance as to the development of local policies between NHS commissioners, local authorities, police forces and ambulance staff, as well as guidance as to how assessments should be carried out.[39] The Code for Wales gives similar guidance.

Detention under section 136

6.57 Section 136 allows the detention of a mentally disordered person found in a public place. The criteria are that the person is found by a constable 'in a place to which the public have access' and 'appears to him [the constable] to be suffering from mental disorder and to be in immediate need of care and control'. The constable may, if he thinks it necessary in the interests of the person or for the protection of other persons, remove the person to a place of safety. This is defined in section 135(6) and discussed above.[40]

6.58 The person may be detained for up to 72 hours to enable him to be examined by a registered medical practitioner, interviewed by an AMHP and to enable necessary arrangements for his treatment and care to be made.[41] As with section 135 the person may be moved from one place of safety to another within the 72-hour period.[42]

6.59 The guidance in the Code as to the need to avoid use of police cells applies to those detained under either sections 135 or 136. The Code for Wales contains similar provisions at paragraphs 7.11–7.22.

Under 18s and police powers

6.60 The Code states at para 16.44 that a child or young person should not be taken to a place of safety in a police station unless there is no suitable alternative. If a police station is to be used, then placing the child or young person somewhere other than the custody suite should be considered. In December 2014 the government announced the intention to prohibit the use of police cells as places of safety for those under 18.

38 Code para 16.5.
39 Code paras 16.30–16.44.
40 MHA 1983 s136(1).
41 MHA 1983 s136(2).
42 MHA 1983 s136(3) and (4).

CHAPTER 7

Mental Capacity Act 2005 and Deprivation of Liberty Safeguards

7.1 This chapter gives more detail about the provisions of the Mental Capacity Act (MCA) 2005 and the Deprivation of Liberty Safeguards ('DOLS'). It summarises the key principles and looks at how these are likely to arise in the context of a tribunal. It draws on some of the material in LAG's *Court of Protection Handbook*[1] to which readers are referred for a comprehensive account. Readers are also referred to Chapter 13 of the Code of Practice.

The Mental Capacity Act 2005

Background

7.2 The Mental Capacity Act 2005 provides a legal framework for making decisions in the best interests of those who are unable to make the decisions themselves. It is essential to have a working knowledge of its provisions and guiding principles.

7.3 The question of capacity to make a particular decision can arise in the following contexts:

- In connection with the decision to admit patients under the Mental Health Act (MHA) 1983 rather than informally (see paras 2.24, 2.47).
- The consent to treatment provisions (see chapter 4 and paras 7.21–7.26 below).
- Whether a patient has capacity to appoint a representative to conduct the tribunal for them (see paras 9.55–9.58, 11.34 and 11.114).
- Where consideration is being given to using the DOLS (see below at paras 7.28–7.29).

7.4 The Mental Capacity Act 2005 codifies case-law of the courts using their protective powers to make declarations that certain steps were necessary in the best interests of an adult who lacked capacity to make a relevant decision. *In Re F (Mental Patient: Sterilisation)*[2] allowed the Court of Appeal and later the House of Lords to declare that a woman with severe learning disabilities lacked capacity to consent to sterilisation but that such a procedure would be lawful in F's best interests.

7.5 Over the next two decades a series of cases extended the jurisdiction until it could be described by Munby J (as he then was)

1 A Ruck Keene, K Edwards, A Eldergill and S Miles, *Court of Protection Handbook*, LAG 2014. See also www.courtofprotectionhandbook.com/.

2 [1990] 2 AC 1.

as 'indistinguishable from wardship in relation to children': *E v Channel 4*[3] (a case that concerned the question of whether a young woman with dissocial personality disorder had the capacity to consent to the filming and transmission of a documentary about her).

Principles

7.6 Unlike the Mental Health Act 1983, the principles of the Mental Capacity Act are set out in section 1 of the MCA 2005:

> (1) The following principles apply for the purposes of this Act.
> (2) A person must be assumed to have capacity unless it is established that he lacks capacity.
> (3) A person is not to be treated as unable to make a decision unless all practicable steps to help him to do so have been taken without success.
> (4) A person is not to be treated as unable to make a decision merely because he makes an unwise decision.
> (5) An act done, or decision made, under this Act for or on behalf of a person who lacks capacity must be done, or made, in his best interests.
> (6) Before the act is done, or the decision is made, regard must be had to whether the purpose for which it is needed can be as effectively achieved in a way that is less restrictive of the person's rights and freedom of action.

Note that the MCA 2005 does not require that the least restrictive course of action must always be followed as the Code requires in cases under the MHA 1983.

The capacity test

7.7 The definition of a person lacking capacity is set out at section 2:

> A person lacks capacity in relation to a matter if at the material time he is unable to make a decision for himself in relation to the matter, because of an impairment of, or a disturbance in the functioning of, the mind or brain.

7.8 It is important to note that this is time and issue specific. This means that what must be assessed is the person's ability to make a particular decision at the time that it needs to be made.

7.9 However, in order to engage the jurisdiction of the MCA 2005 it is not enough simply to show that the person concerned is unable to make a decision at a particular time. It must also be established

3 [2005] 2 FLR 913.

that the reason that the person cannot make a decision is because of 'an impairment of or disturbance of the functioning of the mind or brain'.[4] Note that this is not the same definition as is used to define mental disorder in section 1 of the MHA 1983 ('any disorder or disability of the mind'). So a person who is unable by reason of intoxication or unconsciousness to make a decision which has to be made could be treated under the MCA 2005, but would not fall within the definition of mental disorder in the MHA 1983.

What does it mean to be unable to make a decision?

7.10 Inability to make decisions is defined in section 3 of the MCA 2005:

> (1) For the purposes of section 2, a person is unable to make a decision for himself if he is unable–
> (a) to understand the information relevant to the decision,
> (b) to retain that information,
> (c) to use or weigh that information as part of the process of making the decision, or
> (d) to communicate his decision (whether by talking, using sign language or any other means).

7.11 Two cases, both involving extreme circumstances, illustrate the approach that the courts have taken in assessing capacity.

7.12 In *Re E (Medical Treatment: Anorexia)*[5] a young woman with severe anorexia was found to lack capacity to make decisions about treatment for severe and life-threatening anorexic. E was articulate and intelligent and could understand and retain the relevant information but the court found that she was unable to weigh or use it because her fear of calories was 'the card that trumps all others'. The Court of Protection found it was in her best interests to receive invasive medical treatment.

7.13 In *Re SB (A Patient: Capacity to Consent to Termination)*[6] the Court of Protection had to assess the capacity of a woman with bipolar affective disorder to decide whether to have her pregnancy terminated. She had welcomed her pregnancy initially. She then discontinued prescribed medication because of her pregnancy and suffered a relapse. She expressed the firm wish to terminate the pregnancy. The judge found that she had the capacity to make the decision noting that she

4 *PC v NC and City of York* [2013] EWCA Civ 478.
5 [2012] EWHC 1639 (COP).
6 [2013] EWHC 1417 (COP).

was able to give range of rational reasons for the decision even if some aspects of her thought process were 'skewed' by paranoia.

Best interests

7.14 The MCA 2005 contains a comprehensive checklist which must be followed in working out the relevant person's best interests. The person lacking capacity is referred to in the MCA 2005 as 'P' and the decision-maker as 'D'

7.15 The 'best interests checklist' appears in MCA 2005 s4:

Best interests

(1) In determining for the purposes of this Act what is in a person's best interests, the person making the determination must not make it merely on the basis of–
  (a) the person's age or appearance, or
  (b) a condition of his, or an aspect of his behaviour, which might lead others to make unjustified assumptions about what might be in his best interests.

(2) The person making the determination must consider all the relevant circumstances and, in particular, take the following steps.

(3) He must consider–
  (a) whether it is likely that the person will at some time have capacity in relation to the matter in question, and
  (b) if it appears likely that he will, when that is likely to be.

(4) He must, so far as reasonably practicable, permit and encourage the person to participate, or to improve his ability to participate, as fully as possible in any act done for him and any decision affecting him.

(5) Where the determination relates to life-sustaining treatment he must not, in considering whether the treatment is in the best interests of the person concerned, be motivated by a desire to bring about his death.[7]

(6) He must consider, so far as is reasonably ascertainable–
  (a) the person's past and present wishes and feelings (and, in particular, any relevant written statement made by him when he had capacity),
  (b) the beliefs and values that would be likely to influence his decision if he had capacity, and
  (c) the other factors that he would be likely to consider if he were able to do so.

(7) He must take into account, if it is practicable and appropriate to consult them, the views of–

7 See also Code of Practice paras 5.29–5.36.

(a) anyone named by the person as someone to be consulted on the matter in question or on matters of that kind,
(b) anyone engaged in caring for the person or interested in his welfare,
(c) any donee of a lasting power of attorney granted by the person, and
(d) any deputy appointed for the person by the court,

as to what would be in the person's best interests and, in particular, as to the matters mentioned in subsection (6).

7.16 'Values and beliefs and other factors which might influence P when he had capacity' in section 4(6)(b) are important but not determinative. The closer P is to having capacity on the relevant issue, the greater the weight to be given to P's wishes. However these are not determinative as Lady Hale observed in *Aintree University Hospitals NHS Trust v James*:[8]

> The purpose of the best interests test is to consider matters from the patient's point of view. That is not to say that his wishes must prevail, any more than those of a fully capable patient must prevail. We cannot always have what we want. Nor will it always be possible to ascertain what an incapable patient's wishes are.

7.17 Section 5 provides a defence to D if D carries out an act that relates to care and treatment for P, as long as D:

- takes reasonable steps to establish whether P has capacity to consent to the matter in question[9]; and
- at the time D carries out the act, reasonably believes that P lacks capacity and that the act is in P's best interests.[10]

7.18 Section 6 allows D to restrain P (described as the use or threatened use of force to do an act which P resists[11]) if D reasonably believes it is necessary to prevent harm to P[12] and if the act is a proportionate response to the likelihood of harm to P and to the seriousness of that harm.[13]

7.19 D may not deprive P of his liberty unless;

- D is giving effect to a relevant order of the Court of Protection;[14]

8 [2013] UKSC 67, (2013) 16 CCLR 554.
9 MCA 2005 s5(1)(a).
10 MCA 2005 s5(1)(b).
11 MCA 2005 s6(2), (4).
12 MCA 2005 s6(2).
13 MCA 2005 s6(3).
14 MCA 2005 s4A(3).

- D is giving effect to an authorisation under Schedule A1 ('Deprivattion of Liberty Safeguards');[15]
- D may also deprive P of his or her liberty to which is necessary to give life-sustaining treatment or do some vital act while a decision is sought from the court.[16]

Excluded decisions

7.20 Some decisions cannot be made on behalf of a person lacking the capacity to make the decision himself. MCA 2005 s27(1) excludes the following decisions from being taken on behalf of a person lacking capacity to make the decision:

(a) consenting to marriage or civil partnership,
(b) consenting to have sexual relationships,
(c) consenting to a decree of divorce being granted on the basis of two years' separation,
(d) consenting to a dissolution order being made in relation to a civil partnership on the basis of two years' separation,
(e) consenting to a child's being placed for adoption by an adoption agency,
(f) consenting to the making of an adoption order,
(g) discharging parental responsibilities in matters not relating to a child's property,
(h) giving a consent under the Human Fertilisation and Embryology Act 1990,
(i) giving a consent under the Human Fertilisation and Embryology Act 2008.

The MCA 2005 and treatment under the MHA 1983

7.21 Section 28 of the MCA 2005 excludes the use of the Act when a person who lacks capacity is having treatment that is regulated by Part 4 of the MHA 1983. Part 4 concerns consent to treatment and is discussed in detail at chapter 4.

7.22 Section 28 also provides that if the patient's treatment is regulated by Part 4 of the MHA 1983, then the MCA 2005 cannot be used to make decisions in the patient's best interests about medical treatment for mental disorder.[17] For the purpose of this section the definition of medical treatment is the definition in MHA 1983 s145

15 MCA 2005 s4A(5).

16 MCA 2005 s4B.

17 MCA 2005 s28(1).

and the definition of mental disorder is the definition of MHA 1983 s1.[18]

7.23 Part 4 of the MHA 1983 applies to some treatments for patients who are not detained under the MHA 1983 and may not even be in hospital. Part 4 applies to the most invasive treatments (such as neurosurgery), regulated by section 57 of the MHA 1983, in respect of all patients, what ever their status. Section 57 provides that this type of treatment can only be given to patients with capacity to consent to the treatment, and who do consent. Section 28 of the MCA 2005 means that a patient who lacked capacity to consent to such treatment cannot receive it under the provisions of the Act.

7.24 See paras 4.15–4.18 for more details about the provisions of MHA 1983 s57.

7.25 There are some exceptions to the rule in section 28(1). Part 4 of the MHA 1983 applies to electro-convulsive therapy (ECT) to patients under 18, even if they are informal.[19] The effect of section 28(1A) however is that informal patients between 16 and 18 years, who lack capacity to consent to ECT, could have this treatment administered to them under the provisions of the MCA 2005.

7.26 The effect of section 28(1B) is that medical treatment for mental disorder (such as medication) cannot be given under the provisions of the MCA 2005 to a patient who is under a CTO, and who has not been recalled, if that patient lacks capacity to consent to the treatment. The provisions of Part 4A of the MHA 1983 must be used instead.

Other provisions in the MCA 2005

7.27 The MCA 2005 also provides for:

- Lasting Powers of Attorney (LPA): ss9–14,22 and 23.
- Welfare and financial deputies, who can be appointed by the Court of Protection and given a remit in which they can take decisions in the best interests of the person who lacks capacity: ss16–20.
- Advanced decisions, where a person with capacity can refuse in advance certain forms of treatment in the event that they lose capacity in future: ss24–26.
- Research: ss30–34.
- Independent Mental Capacity Advocates (IMCAs): ss35–41.
- Offences of ill-treatment and neglect: s44.

18 MCA 2005 s28(2).
19 MHA 1983 s58A(7).

- The Court of Protection and Public Guardian: ss45–61.
- Amendments added by Mental Health Act 2007 relating to powers to deprive adults lacking capacity of their liberty: ss4A, 16A s21A, and Schedule A1.

The Deprivation of Liberty Safeguards

7.28 The Deprivation of Liberty Safeguards are set out in Schedule A1 of the MCA 2005. This Schedule was added to the MCA 2005 by the Mental Health Act 2007.

7.29 The Government decided to amend the Mental Capacity Act 2005 as a response to the legislative lacuna (known as the 'Bournewood Gap') which was exposed in the important case of *HL v United Kingdom*.[20]

7.30 The case concerned Mr L, a man in his 40s with severe autism, who can only communicate non-verbally. He had spent many years in Bournewood Hospital, but was then placed with paid carers, Mr and Mrs E. He lived with them for around four years although his care continued to be managed by Bournewood Hospital rather than the community team. Having become disturbed at his day centre one day in July 1997 Mr L was taken to Bournewood Hospital. He was considered to need inpatient treatment and was admitted as an informal patient under section 131 of the MHA 1983, as he was making no attempt to leave. A decision was taken that Mr and Mrs E should not be allowed to visit as it was considered that this might cause agitation. He was given medication and had he attempted to leave he would have been prevented from doing so, by use of the MHA 1983. Mr L did not have the capacity to consent to admission to hospital.

7.31 Mr and Mrs E applied for judicial review and habeas corpus on HL's behalf. Having been unsuccessful at first instance he was successful at the Court of Appeal. The hospital appealed to the House of Lords where the Court of Appeal's decision was overturned (with a strong dissenting judgment from Lord Steyn).

7.32 Following the decision of the Court of Appeal HL was detained under the Mental Health Act but was discharged in December 1997 and returned to live with Mr and Mrs E. However HL appealed to the European Court of Human Rights (ECtHR) in 1998, asserting that his rights under Article 5 had been violated. The ECtHR found that

20 App No 45508/99, [2004] ECHR 471, (2004) 7 CCLR 498.

HL had been deprived of his liberty for the purpose of Article 5 and that this was not in accordance with a procedure prescribed by law.

7.33 In making this finding the Court commented:

> ... the key factor [is] that the health care professionals treating and managing the applicant exercised complete and effective control over his care and movement ... any suggestion to the contrary is ... fairly described ... as 'stretching credulity to breaking point' and as a 'fairy tale'.[21]

7.34 Because HL had been an informal patient, there had been no formal admission procedure indicating who could propose admission, why, for what reasons, and on what medical findings; and no requirement to fix the purpose of admission (eg assessment) and no limits of time, treatment or care. There had been no requirement to monitor ongoing presence of disorder warranting detention (the 'Winterwerp criteria': see above paras 1.6–1.9). Nor had a representative been appointed for HL.

7.35 This case demonstrated the need for legal safeguards that would allow compliant incapacitated patients to be deprived of their liberty in order to be provided with care and treatment when this was in their best interests, without infringing their rights under Article 5.

7.36 In HL's case the hospital eventually made use of the MHA 1983. However in a further case, *JE v DE, Surrey County Council and EW*[22] the Court found that DE, who lacked capacity to make decisions about where he should live, had been deprived of his liberty in a nursing home, where the MHA 1983 could not have been used to provide authority.

7.37 The Government decided to rectify this by amending the MCA 2005, adding Schedules A1 and 1A and amending other provisions of the MCA 2005, as set out below. The amendments created the Deprivation of Liberty Safeguards ('DOLS'). DOLS can be used to authorise the detention of incapacitated patients in hospitals and care homes, if the requirements are complied with. DOLS cannot be used in supported living or educational establishments.

7.38 The following amendments were made to the body of the MCA 2005:

- Section 4A(3) provides that 'D' may deprive 'P' of his liberty if in doing so, D is giving effect to 'a relevant decision of the Court'. This means an order by the Court of Protection which expressly permits P to be deprived of his liberty and might be used for

21 [2004] ECHR 720 at para 91.

22 [2006] EWHC 3459 (Fam), (2007) 10 CCLR 149.

example in supported living settings where the DOLS procedure cannot be used.

- Section 4A(5) provides that D may deprive P of his liberty if this is authorised by Schedule A1 (ie if an standard or urgent authorisation under DOLS is in place).
- Section 4B permits D to deprive P of his liberty to enable P to receive vital or life-sustaining treatment while a decision on a relevant matter is sought from the Court.
- Section 16A makes it clear that if a person is ineligible for a standard or urgent authorisation under DOLS, then this cannot be rectified by the Court of Protection making an order which purports to deprive P of his liberty. (However, following the decision in Dr A, it appears that such an order could be made by the Court using its inherent jurisdiction.)
- Section 21A gives the Court of Protection to determine a range of issues arising from challenges to DOLS authorisations.

7.39 A new Code of Practice, *Mental Capacity Act 2005: Deprivation of Liberty Safeguards Code of Practice*, referred to as the DOLS Code of Practice was produced at the same time.

7.40 DOLS introduced standard or urgent authorisations. Such authorisations allow a 'managing authority' (which will be a hospital or care home) lawfully to deprive P of his liberty, if all the requirements are complied with.

7.41 An urgent authorisation can be self-granted up to seven days (Sch A1 para 78). A standard authorisation can be granted by the supervisory body (now always local authority) up to maximum of one year (Sch A1 para 42(2)(b)).

7.42 A standard authorisation must be requested by the managing authority (who are they) when it appears to the managing authority that P is accommodated in relevant care home or hospital or will be within 28 days; and is or is likely to be a detained resident; and meets or is likely to meet all the qualifying requirements (Sch A1 para 24).

7.43 This requires the managing authority to identify correctly when a deprivation of liberty is occurring. The DOLS Code para 2.5 provides a non-exhaustive list of factors which may be relevant to identifying deprivation of liberty. None are given primacy but the list includes:

- use of restraint including sedation to admit p where p is resisting admission;
- staff exercise complete and effective control over P's care and movement for a significant period;

- staff exercise control over assessments, treatment, contacts and residence;
- a decision has been taken that person will not be released into the care of others or permitted to live elsewhere unless staff ... consider it appropriate;
- requests by carers for person to be discharged to their care is refused;
- the person is unable to maintain social contacts because of restrictions on their access to others;
- the person loses autonomy because they are under continuous supervision and control.

7.44 This now needs to be treated with caution, following the decision of the Supreme Court in *P v Cheshire West County Council and Chester Council.*[23] In this case Lady Hale adopted what she described as an 'acid test': Is P under continuous supervision and control and not free to leave?[24] This had the effect of bringing within the protection of Article 5 a large number of individuals whose living arrangements had previously not been seen to engage Convention rights.

7.45 As a result of the Supreme Court's judgment there has been a substantial increase in the number of applications for authorisations under DOLS.

7.46 An application must be made where it appears to the managing authority that (P is or will be a detained resident, ie will be deprived of his liberty for the purpose of Article 5 (s64(5));

Requirements for a standard authorisation

7.47 The six requirements for a standard authorisation are set our below:

- **Age requirement**: over 18 (Sch A1 para 13).
- **Mental health requirement:** P must have a mental disorder for the purpose of the MHA 1983. If this is a learning disability it need not be associated with abnormally aggressive or seriously irresponsible behaviour (Sch A1 para 14).
- **Mental capacity requirement:** P must lack capacity to decide whether or not he should be accommodated in the relevant hospital or care home for the purpose of being given the relevant care or treatment (Sch A1 para 15).

23 [2014] UKSC 19, (2014) 17 CCLR 5.
24 [2014] UKSC 19 at para 49.

- **Best interests requirement**: It is in P's best interests to be a detained resident and it is necessary and proportionate to the risk of harm to P (Sch A1 para 16).
- **Eligibility requirement:** P is not ineligible by virtue of Schedule 1A, which deals with the interface with the MHA 1983 (Sch A1 para 17). This is explained at paras 7.71–7.98.
- **No refusals requirement:** There is no valid advance decision that applies to some or all of the relevant treatment; or it would be in conflict with a valid decision (ie within the scope of their authority) of a donee of an LPA or a deputy (Sch A1 paras 18–20).

7.48 All the requirements must be assessed. The mental health assessment and best interests assessment must be done by different people: Sch A1 para 129(5). 'Best Interests Assessors' are required to carry out the best interests requirement.

7.49 Paragraph 50 of Schedule A1 provides that the supervisory body must give a standard authorisation if all assessments are positive ie conclude P meets relevant requirement.

7.50 This was considered in *London Borough of Hillingdon v Neary*:[25]

> The granting of DOL standard authorisations is a matter for the local authority in its role as a supervisory body. The responsibilities of a supervisory body, correctly understood, require it to scrutinise the assessment it receives with independence and a degree of care that is appropriate to the seriousness of the decision and to the circumstances of the individual case that are or should be known to it. Where, as here, a supervisory body grants authorisations on the basis of perfunctory scrutiny of superficial best interests assessments, it cannot expect the authorisations to be legally valid.[26]

7.51 Schedule A1 para 139 provides that the supervisory body must appoint a 'relevant person's representative' (RPR) as soon as possible after an authorisation is granted. (P must also be represented during the assessment process by an IMCA if no other appropriate person: MCA 2005 s39A).

7.52 Paragraph 140 sets out the role of the RPR which is to maintain contact with relevant person, represent and support them in matters related to or connected with this schedule.

7.53 'A Managing Authority' can grant an urgent authorisation when it is required to make a request for a standard authorisation but there is an urgent need for the person to be a detained resident (Sch A1 para 76).

25 [2011] EWHC 1377 (COP).

26 [2011] EWHC 1377 (COP) at para 33.

Challenging an authorisation

7.54 The supervisory body must carry out a review if requested by an eligible person (Sch A1 para 102). An eligible person means P, the RPR, or the managing authority (para 102(3)).

7.55 There is no procedure for an automatic referral to the Court but an application to the COP can be made and section 21A of the MCA 2005 gives the court wide powers including terminating or varying an authorisation if an application is made. A detailed examination of these procedures is outside the scope of this book.[27]

What are the limits of DOLS?

7.56 An authorisation merely regulates the care and treatment of a person lacking capacity where they are deprived of their liberty in a placement. It does not do anything else. In particular it does not authorise interferences with P's rights under Article 8 (right to respect for private and family life).

7.57 The Courts have made it clear that where there is a genuine dispute about where the place of residence of a person who lacks capacity to decide where to live, then an application should be made to the court.

7.58 In *London Borough of Hillingdon v Neary*[28] Mr Justice Peter Jackson commented that DOLS 'not to be used by a local authority as a means of getting its own way on the question of whether it is in the person's best interests to be in the place at all'.[29]

7.59 In *C v Blackburn and Darwen Borough Council*[30] the same judge said that it was 'not appropriate for genuinely contested issues about residence of a resisting incapacitated person' to be dealt with via DOLS or guardianship regime.

7.60 Therefore if a local authority or a trust consider that a change in residence is in the best interests of a person who lacks capacity to decide where to live ('P'), then they cannot simply rely on DOLS – or the combination of DOLS and a CTO or guardianship order – to override objections either by P or P's family or carers. The question of the person's residence must be determined by the Court of Protection. If the court determines that the change in residence is in P's

27 Practitioners are referred to Ruck Keene, Edwards, Eldergill and Miles *Court of Protection Handbook*, LAG, 2014.

28 [2011] EWHC 1377 (COP).

29 At para 33.

30 [2011] EWHC 3321 (COP), (2012) 15 CCLR 251.

best interests, then an authorisation under DOLS may be used to authorise any deprivation of P's liberty that may result.

7.61 In *J Council v G U, J Partnership NHS Foundation Trust, CQC and X Limited*[31] the court considered the situation of 'George' who was 'very seriously challenged' and had childhood autism, OCD, personality disorder and paedophilia. George's placement regime involved rigorous restrictions on his contact with others including strip searching, monitoring correspondence and telephone calls to protect the public. George's placement constituted a deprivation of his liberty but also curtailed his rights under Article 8, and had to be 'in accordance with the law' (Article 8(2)).

7.62 Had George been detained under the MHA 1983 in a high security hospital the Safety and Security Directions 2011 would apply.

7.63 The judge commented:

> In contrast (it might be thought surprisingly), there are no equivalent detailed procedures and safeguards stipulated anywhere for persons detained pursuant to orders made under the Mental Capacity Act 2005.[32]

7.64 Detailed policies were agreed to ensure that the interference with George's Article 8 rights was in accordance with the law. These included oversight by the CQC.

What if DOLS cannot be used?

7.65 As we have seen DOLS can only be used in hospitals or registered care homes[33]. What happens if it is necessary to deprive a person lacking capacity to make decisions about residence is another setting such as supported living? In this situation an application must be made to the Court of Protection by the care provider or the relevant public body (local authority or trust). As long as the person concerned is not ineligible then the Court can make an order under section 16(2)(a) of the MCA 2005 which can specifically authorise the deprivation of P's liberty.

7.66 Following the judgment in *Cheshire West* the number of applications under section 16 was projected to increase from around 134 to over 18,000 per year.[34] In *Re X (Deprivation of Liberty) (Nos 1 and 2)*[35]

31 [2012] EWHC 3531 (COP), (2013) 16 CCLR 31.

32 [2012] EWHC 3531 (COP) at para 14.

33 Sch A1 para 1(2).

34 ADASS Press Release, June 2014. The eventual figure was much lower.

35 [2014] EWCOP 25, [2014] EWCOP 37.

the President of the Court of Protection, Sir James Munby, outlined a 'streamlined procedure' for these applications. This is outside the scope of this book.[36]

Where do the MHA 1983 and DOLS overlap?

7.67 *HL v UK*[37] concerned an informal patient in a psychiatric hospital, who had been admitted under section 131 of the MHA 1983.

7.68 Following the 'acid test' in the Supreme Court judgment in *Cheshire West*,[38] many of these informal patients would now be considered to have been deprived of their liberty.

7.69 If a person who lacks capacity to consent to admission to hospital needs to be admitted to hospital for medical treatment for mental disorder, how do those involved decide whether to use the MHA 1983 or the MCA 2005/DOLS?

7.70 Decisions as to which regime applies need to be made by those considering an application for admission under the Act. But in some cases the decision will need to be made by the First-tier Tribunal, because it may need to consider discharging a patient from (for example) section 2 or 3, on the basis that the care and treatment can be given using the DOLS and MCA 2005.

What are the 'eligibility criteria'?

7.71 This section looks at how these decisions should be made and explains what is known as the 'eligibility criteria'. The eligibility criteria are set out in Schedule 1A to the MCA 2005.

7.72 One of the mandatory requirements for a standard authorisation is that the patient is not 'ineligible' to be detained under DOLS. Schedule 1A aims to explain who is eligible and ineligible to be deprived of their liberty under DOLS.

7.73 It is important to be aware that if P is ineligible for detention under DOLS, this also prevents the Court of Protection from making an order depriving P of his liberty.[39]

7.74 The relevant provisions of Schedule 1A are set out below, and then explained, in using case studies to illustrate them.

36 See www.courtofprotectionhandbook.com for further discussion of the streamlined process.

37 App No 45508/99, [2004] ECHR 471, (2004) 7 CCLR 498.

38 [2014] UKSC 19, (2014) 17 CCLR 5.

39 MCA 2005 s16A.

PART 1: INELIGIBLE PERSONS

Application

1 This Schedule applies for the purposes of–
(a) section 16A, and
(b) paragraph 17 of Schedule A1.

Determining ineligibility

2 A person ('P') is ineligible to be deprived of liberty by this Act ('ineligible') if–
(a) P falls within one of the cases set out in the second column of the following table, and
(b) the corresponding entry in the third column of the table – or the provision, or one of the provisions, referred to in that entry – provides that he is ineligible.

	Status of P	**Determination of ineligibility**
Case A	P is– (a) subject to the hospital treatment regime, and (b) detained in a hospital under that regime.	P is ineligible.
Case B	P is– (a) subject to the hospital treatment regime, but (b) not detained in a hospital under that regime.	See paragraphs 3 and 4.
Case C	P is subject to the community treatment regime.	See paragraphs 3 and 4.
Case D	P is subject to the guardianship regime.	See paragraphs 3 and 5.
Case E	P is– (a) within the scope of the Mental Health Act, but (b) not subject to any of the mental health regimes.	See paragraph 5.

Authorised course of action not in accordance with regime

3(1) This paragraph applies in cases B, C and D in the table in paragraph 2.
(2) P is ineligible if the authorised course of action is not in accordance with a requirement which the relevant regime imposes.
(3) That includes any requirement as to where P is, or is not, to reside.
(4) The relevant regime is the mental health regime to which P is subject.

Treatment for mental disorder in a hospital

4(1) This paragraph applies in cases B and C in the table in paragraph 2.

(2) P is ineligible if the relevant care or treatment consists in whole or in part of medical treatment for mental disorder in a hospital.

P objects to being a mental health patient etc

5(1) This paragraph applies in cases D and E in the table in paragraph 2.

(2) P is ineligible if the following conditions are met.

(3) The first condition is that the relevant instrument authorises P to be a mental health patient.

(4) The second condition is that P objects–

(a) to being a mental health patient, or

(b) to being given some or all of the mental health treatment.

(5) The third condition is that a donee or deputy has not made a valid decision to consent to each matter to which P objects.

(6) In determining whether or not P objects to something, regard must be had to all the circumstances (so far as they are reasonably ascertainable), including the following–

(a) P's behaviour;

(b) P's wishes and feelings;

(c) P's views, beliefs and values.

(7) But regard is to be had to circumstances from the past only so far as it is still appropriate to have regard to them.

Case A

7.75 Case A is on the face of it, straightforward. Being 'subject to the hospital regime' means that P is the subject of an order any of the following sections of the MHA 1983: ss2, 3, 4, 35, 36, 37, 38, 44, 45A, 47, 48 or 51. It does not therefore include patients subject to CTOs or Guardianship.

7.76 But to fall within Case A, P must also be detained under that regime.

Example 1

Fred has dementia and a psychotic illness. He lacks capacity to agree to admission to hospital and to make decisions about treatment. Fred is detained in hospital under section 2 of the MHA 1983.

- Fred is both subject to the hospital regime and detained in a hospital under that regime.
- Fred falls within Case A and is ineligible to be detained using DOLS as long as he is detained under section 2. If Fred needs treatment for physical disorder – for example he has a fall and

requires surgery – then he could be treated under the MCA 2005. But if in order to carry out the surgery it was necessary for him to be deprived of his liberty, because he is likely to resist, then this could be achieved by the RC giving him section 17 leave to the general hospital, and an authorisation could allow deprivation of liberty there.

- However, the possible use of DOLS might have to be considered if Fred applies to a tribunal. See below, in the discussion concerning *AM v v South London and the Maudsley NHS Foundation Trust.*[40]

Case B

7.77 Case B applies to those who are subject to the hospital regime. As with Case A it applies to those in respect of whom an order has been made under any of the following sections of the MHA 1983: ss2, 3, 4, 35, 36, 37, 38, 44, 45A, 47, 48 or 51. As with case those under CTOS or guardianship are excluded. However Case B applies to those who are not *detained* under that regime. So it would apply to those who are on section 17 leave or section 73 conditional discharges.

7.78 The Schedule does not provide that all those on section 17 leave or conditional discharges are ineligible to be deprived of their liberty. There are two further points to be considered and both of these are linked to the reason for the proposed authorisation.

The 'authorised course of action'

7.79 The first is whether the 'authorised course of action' conflicts with a requirement that P is already subject to, because of the relevant 'mental health regime'.[41]

7.80 These two concepts recur in other cases within the Schedule. The authorised course of action means, in essence, the proposed plan for P which will involve deprivation of his liberty. This could be declarations about where P should live and about how his care will be delivered, which have been made by the Court.[42]. Or it could mean accommodation of P in a care home under Schedule A1, if the authorisation is granted.[43]

7.81 The 'mental health regime' means either the hospital, guardianship or community treatment regime which P is subject to.[44] A

40 [2013] UKUT 0365. See paras 7.95–7.98.

41 Schedule 1A paragraph 3.

42 Schedule 1A para 13.

43 Schedule A1 para 14.

44 Schedule 1A para 7.

requirement under this regime could include a condition as to where P is to reside.[45]

The relevant care or treatment

7.82 P will be ineligible to be detained using DOLS if the care and treatment that the DOLS would authorise is in whole or in part medical treatment for mental disorder in hospital.

Example 2

Fred in Case A is given leave under section 17. His RC specifies that he should stay at home.

- The requirement to stay at home is a requirement of the 'mental health regime' (in his case section 2 of the MHA 1983). Fred could not be accommodated in a nursing (or care) home using DOLS, because this (the 'authorised course of action') conflicts with the conditions of his leave. Nor could DOLS be used to give him anti-psychotic medication in hospital because the 'relevant care or treatment' is treatment in hospital for mental disorder. (Instead he must simply be recalled from section 17 leave.[46])
- If, however, Fred needs to be deprived of his liberty using DOLS so he can receive hospital treatment for a physical disorder in the general hospital then this can run alongside his section 17 leave, as long as it does not specify that he should live somewhere else.

Example 3

Bill is a patient detained under sections 37/41. He is granted a conditional discharge. One of the conditions is to stay at X Road Hostel. He lacks capacity to make decisions about residence (and is subject to restrictions amounting to a deprivation of liberty).

- He could be made the subject of a standard authorisation depriving him of his liberty at X Road Hostel, if he fulfilled all the qualifying requirements including that such an order was necessary in his best interests. (However it should be noted that a conditional discharge cannot itself contain conditions which amount to a deprivation of liberty: *Secretary of State for Justice v RB and Lancashire Care NHS Foundation Trust*[47]).

45 Schedule 1A para 3(3).
46 MHA 1983 s17(4).
47 [2011] EWCA Civ 1608.

Case C

7.83 A patient who is under a CTO pursuant to section 17A of the MHA 1983 (or any other England and Wales enactment which has the same effect)[48] is 'subject to the community treatment regime'. As with Case B, it is necessary to consider the 'authorised course of action' and whether it conflicts with any conditions attached to the CTO. If there is a conflict then P is ineligible to be deprived of his liberty using DOLS of an order of the Court of Protection[49]. P would also be ineligible if either the standard authorisation or the Court order would authorise – in whole or in part – medical treatment in hospital for mental disorder.[50]

Example 4

Mary has dementia and has recently been discharged from section 3 onto a CTO. She is cared for in circumstances amounting to a deprivation of liberty at a nursing home. A standard authorisation has been granted.

- There is no conflict between the conditions of the CTO and the standard authorisation.
- If Mary's mental health deteriorates and she requires a period of admission in hospital, however, she would be ineligible to be deprived of her liberty through DOLS or an order of the court. Instead she should be recalled to hospital and the standard authorisation should be suspended (and would lapse after 28 days, if Mary has not been discharged again).[51]

Case D

7.84 Case D applies to patients who are 'subject to the guardianship regime' which means that he is under a guardianship order pursuant to section 7 or 37 of the MHA 1983.[52] He can be subject to both a guardianship order and a DOLS authorisation, provided the requirements of each do not conflict with each other.[53]

7.85 However he will be ineligible if all of the following further conditions apply:

48 Schedule 1A para 9
49 Schedule A1 para 3.
50 Schedule A1 para 4.
51 Schedule A1 Part 6
52 Schedule A1 para 10.
53 Schedule A1 para 3.

- that the standard authorisation (or the order of the court) authorises P to be a 'mental health patient',[54] defined as 'a person being accommodated in hospital for the purpose of being given medical treatment for mental disorder;
- that P objects to being a mental health patient, or to some or all of the mental health treatment[55] (ascertained by having regard to all the circumstances including P's behaviour, wishes and feelings, and views, beliefs and values);[56] and
- that no donee or deputy has made a valid decision to consent to each matter to which P objects.[57]

7.86 This places patients under guardianship in a different position to those on CTOs, section 17 leave or conditional discharges. We have seen that DOLS cannot be used to administer inpatient treatment for mental disorder for the latter three categories. But a patient who is under a guardianship could be admitted to hospital for medical treatment for mental disorder as long as P does not object or, if he does, no deputy or donee of an LPA has agreed on his behalf.

Example 5

Amy is under a guardianship order. She needs a period of time in hospital for treatment for mental disorder. She has executed a LPA making her niece Sarah her attorney with a remit to make decisions about medical treatment.

- Amy objects to going into hospital. If Sarah consents on Amy's behalf, however, Amy could still be admitted to and deprived of her liberty in hospital using DOLS.

Case E

7.87 Case E relates to patients who are not subject to any orders of any sort under the MHA 1983, but is 'within the scope of the Mental Health Act'. This is one of the most troublesome definitions in Schedule 1A.

7.88 It is useful to consider the purpose of Case E and this was set out by the Department of Health in a letter referred to in *DN v*

54 Schedule A1 para 5(3).
55 Schedule A1 para 5(4).
56 Schedule A1 para 5(6).
57 Schedule A1 para 5(5).

Northumberland and Wear NHS Foundation Trust.[58] The following passage is relevant:

> The Government's policy intention was that people who lack capacity to consent to being admitted to hospital, but who are clearly objecting to it, should generally be treated like people who have capacity and are refusing to consent to mental health treatment. If it is considered necessary to detain them in hospital, and they would have been detained under the MHA if they had the capacity to refuse treatment, then as a matter of policy it was thought right that the MHA should be used in preference to the MCA.[59]

7.89 The explanation given is at Sch 1A para 12:

> *P within scope of Mental Health Act*
>
> 12(1) P is within the scope of the Mental Health Act if:
>
> (a) an application in respect of P could be made under section 2 or 3 of the Mental Health Act, and
>
> (b) P could be detained in a hospital in pursuance of such an application, were one made.
>
> (2) The following provisions of this paragraph apply when determining whether an application in respect of P could be made under section 2 or 3 of the Mental Health Act.
>
> (3) If the grounds in section 2(2) of the Mental Health Act are met in P's case, it is to be assumed that the recommendations referred to in section 2(3) of that Act have been given.
>
> (4) If the grounds in section 3(2) of the Mental Health Act are met in P's case, it is to be assumed that the recommendations referred to in section 3(3) of that Act have been given.
>
> (5) In determining whether the ground in section 3(2)(c) of the Mental Health Act is met in P's case, it is to be assumed that the treatment referred to in section 3(2)(c) cannot be provided under this Act.

7.90 Breaking this down, a patient without capacity to consent to admission would be 'within the scope of' the MHA 1983 in the following situation:

- P has a mental disorder, and the criteria for admission under either section 2 or 3 are met. There is no reason why an application could not be made under sections 2 or 3. For the purpose of this exercise the fact that there is an alternative to the use of the MHA 1983 should be ignored.

58 [2011] UKUT 327 (AAC).

59 [2011] UKUT 327 (AAC) at para 18.

- The decision-maker (perhaps an AMHP) should work on the assumption that the two medical recommendations for admission have been made, even if they have not.[60]

7.91 P could still be admitted under DOLS if he did not object to being a 'mental health patient' (see above), as long as he does not have a deputy or donee of a LPA who objects on his behalf. This scenario is probably the closest to that of Mr L.

7.92 As the discussion below on *AM v South London and the Maudsley NHS Foundation Trust and the Secretary of State for Health*[61] below illustrates, there will be some cases where the AMHP or tribunal will have to weigh up and decide which framework should be used.

7.93 These complex provisions have been considered by the courts. In *GJ v Foundation Trust, PCT and Secretary of State for Health*[62] the Court of Protection considered whether a patient was a 'mental health patient' for the purpose of Schedule 1A when he was receiving treatment for both mental and physical disorder. In brief the court concluded that P was not a 'mental health patient' if he would not need to be detained in hospital but for his need for the package of physical treatment, and if his need for package of physical treatment was the only reason he needed to be detained in hospital.

7.94 In *DN v Northumberland and Wear NHS Foundation Trust*[63] the Upper Tribunal held that the availability of DOLS to secure the patient's residence as part of his after-care was a relevant consideration for the tribunal when considering discharge from the MHA 1983. The type of case where this could be important might include a patient with a learning disability and challenging behaviour, who has been detained in hospital under section 3 for a long period. A community placement is being put forward. If in order to provide the necessary care and treatment for the patient, those caring for him will deprive him of his liberty, then this can be authorised by a standard authorisation. This is part of the after-care arrangements that the tribunal should consider.

7.95 The question of how decision-makers under the MHA 1983 should approach the possibility of treatment under the MCA 2005 was considered by the Upper Tribunal in a judgment by Charles J in

60 Schedule A1 para 12.
61 [2013] UKUT 365 (AAC).
62 [2009] EWHC 2972 (Fam), (2009) 12 CCLR 600.
63 [2011] UKUT 327 (AAC).

AM v South London and the Maudsley NHS Foundation Trust and the Secretary of State for Health.[64]

7.96 AM argued that she should be discharged from detention under section 2 by a tribunal and her treatment in hospital should be continued using the Deprivation of Liberty Safeguards.

7.97 The judge noted that in bringing in the DOLS, Parliament must have intended to provide an alternative to the MHA 1983 to authorise the detention of an incapacitated person, and that this must have been intended to include occasions where such a person would be detained using DOLS in hospital for mental disorder. Decision-makers under the MHA 1983 (which would include AMHPs and also tribunals) therefore needed to consider the availability of treatment authorised by DOLS.

7.98 In essence the process of reasoning which the judge considered to be required was:

- Is admission to hospital required?
- Will P be a mental health patient and if so does he object to all or part of the relevant treatment? If so he is ineligible for DOLs and the MHA 1983 must be used.
- Does the relevant person have capacity to consent to admission to hospital?
- Can the hospital rely on the provisions of the MCA 2005 to assess and treat the person lawfully? This requires consideration of the likelihood of the person remaining compliant with their treatment (and therefore remain eligible to be deprived of their liberty using DOLS); and also whether there is a risk that cannot sensibly be ignored that the treatment regime will amount to a deprivation of liberty.[65]
- How should the existence of a choice between reliance on the MHA 1983 and the MCA 2005/DOLS be taken into account?[66] This involves the First-tier Tribunal (or earlier decision-maker, for example an AMHP) taking a fact-sensitive approach to try to identify the least restrictive way of best achieving the proposed assessment or treatment.[67] DOLS will not always be less restrictive than the MHA, but may carry less stigma in the eyes of some.[68] An AMHP or a tribunal cannot compel a managing authority to

64 [2013] UKUT 365 (AAC). See also paras 16.32–16.36 below.

65 [2013] UKUT 0365 (AAC) at para 59.

66 [2013] UKUT 0365 (AAC) at para 62.

67 [2013] UKUT 0365 (AAC) at para 73.

68 [2013] UKUT 0365 (AAC) at paras 65–66.

apply for an authorisation or a supervisory body to grant one, so the AMHP or tribunal needs to know whether those who could implement the MCA 2005/DOLS regime are in fact prepared to do so. The two schemes (MHA 1983 and MCA 2005/DOLS) are not mutually exclusive. The question of which regime has primacy over the other in a given case will depend on the circumstances of that case.

DOLS and tribunals

7.99 In reality there will be few cases where it will be appropriate to argue that the 'best and least restrictive alternative' for an incapacitated compliant inpatient will be DOLS rather than the MCA 2005, where the proposal is that P remains in hospital but where this will or is likely to result in a deprivation of his or her liberty. If this argument is to be put however it is important to ascertain before the hearing whether in fact, if the section is lifted, the hospital would agree to apply for an authorisation.

7.100 Practitioners at the tribunal are more likely to come into contact with DOLS or with the need for an application to the Court of Protection in the context of after-care for patients who lack capacity to make decisions about where to live.

7.101 If therefore a community placement is being considered for a patient and it is likely that a legal framework will be needed to avoid a violation of the patient's Article 5 rights, it is helpful to ascertain before the hearing:

- whether there is a dispute over the patient's capacity to decide where to live;
- whether the placement would be willing to apply for a standard authorisation;
- whether an application should be made to the Court of Protection, and if so, whether the local authority or Clinical Commissioning Group is willing to make the application.

CHAPTER 8

Children and young people

8.1 This chapter looks at the key provisions which relate to the admission and treatment of children and young people believed to have mental disorders.

8.2 Practitioners should note that chapter 19 of the Code of Practice deals with children and young people. It is recommended to practitioners in both England and Wales as a clear and detailed guide. Helpful flow charts and case studies appear at the end of the chapter.

Terminology

8.3 The Code of Practice uses the term 'child' to refer to a person under the age of 16 and 'young person' to refer to a person of 16 or 17. In the Code of Practice for Wales the word 'child' is used for all under-18s, although where a provision applies only to 16–17 year olds the term 'young person' is used.[1]

8.4 For the purpose of this chapter a child is a person under 16. A young person is a 16 or 17 year old.

How do the provisions of the Act apply to under-18s?

8.5 There is no minimum age limit for admission to hospital under the Mental Health Act (MHA) 1983 but there are age requirements for some provision, as set out in table 5 opposite. Note that the powers under sections 135 and 136 also apply to children and young people.

1 Code for Wales para 33.2.

Table 5: age limits

Power	Age limit and notes	Provisions
Admission under Part 2	No minimum age; but if the patient is a ward of court the leave of the court must be obtained and the provisions of s11(4) (requirement to consult nearest relative) do not apply. If the patient is subject to a care order then the relevant local authority is the nearest relative, unless the patient is married or in a civil partnership.	ss33(1), s27
Guardianship	Minimum age 16. A ward of court cannot be made subject to guardianship. If the patient is subject to a care order then the relevant local authority is the nearest relative, unless the patient is married or in a civil partnership.	ss7(1), 33(3), 27
CTO	No minimum age. If the patient is subject to a care order then the relevant local authority is the nearest relative, unless the patient is married or in a civil partnership.	s27
Admission under Part 3	No minimum age. Again the nearest relative of a child or young person subject to a care order will be the relevant local authority.	s27
Use of the MCA 2005 (except DOLS)	Minimum age 16 (and patient must lack capacity to make the relevant decision); unless power is being exercised by the Court of Protection in relation to the child's property and affairs, and the sourt considers that the child will lack decision-making capacity when s/he reaches 18.	MCA 2005 ss2(5), 18(3)
DOLS	Minimum age 18, and must lack capacity to decide whether to be accommodated in the relevant care home or hospital for the purpose of being given care or treatment.	MCA 2005 Sch A1 paras 13, 15
Inherent jurisdiction	No age limit.	

What about informal admission?

8.6 Children and young people can be admitted to hospital informally: s131. However, there are a number of factors which need to be considered before this step is taken and these depend upon:

- the age of the patient;
- whether, in the case of a young person, the patient has capacity to consent to admission for the purpose of the MCA 2005;
- whether, in the case of a child, the child is 'Gillick-competent' to consent to informal admission (see below para 15.12); and
- in some cases, the attitude of the person with parental responsibility.

Parental responsibility and the 'zone of parental control'

8.7 The Code summarises the questions that need to be asked to ascertain who holds parental responsibility for a child or young person: paras 19.8–19.13. Practitioners should check that the correct person has been identified, because this is not always immediately obvious and will depend on – for example – whether the parents are married and, if not, whether the father has acquired parental responsibility.

8.8 This is particularly important because in some cases consent of the person with parental responsibility can be relied on to admit a child or young person to hospital or to treat them. However this will only be possible if the decision is one which it is appropriate for the parent to make on behalf of the child: is the decision within what is known as the 'zone of parental control'? This concept is discussed in chapter 4 at para 4.33. It is also considered in detail in the Code at paras 19.38–19.41.

8.9 Importantly, a decision to deprive a child or young person of their liberty is not within the zone of parental control: see *RK v BCC and others*.[2] For a discussion of what constitutes a deprivation of liberty see para 14.44. However, following the decision in *P v Cheshire West and Chester Council and others*,[3] the 'acid test' to be applied is whether the patient is under continuous supervision and control and whether the patient is free to leave. If the answer to the first question is 'yes'

2 [2011] EWCA Civ 1305.

3 [2014] UKSC 19, (2014) 17 CCLR 5.

and the second 'no', then it is highly likely that there is a deprivation of liberty.

Capacity or competence?

8.10 The test to be applied to ascertain whether a child or young person can make a particular decision will depend upon the age of the child or young person.

8.11 The Mental Capacity Act 2005 applies to 16–17 year olds. Therefore a young person's capacity to consent to admission should be assessed using the test in section 2 and 3 of the MCA 2005:

> 2(1) ... a person lacks capacity in relation to a matter if at the material time he is unable to make a decision for himself in relation to the matter, because of an impairment of, or a disturbance in the functioning of, the mind or brain.
>
> 3(1) For the purposes of section 2, a person is unable to make a decision for himself if he is unable –
> (a) to understand the information relevant to the decision,
> (b) to retain that information,
> (c) to use or weigh that information as part of the process of making the decision, or
> (d) to communicate his decision (whether by talking, using sign language or any other means).

8.12 For children under the age of 16 the test is whether they are what is described as 'Gillick-competent'. This term comes from the case of *Gillick v West Norfolk and Wisbech Area Health Authority*.[4] The test is whether the child has sufficient understanding and intelligence to enable them to understand fully what is involved in a proposed intervention. If they do have sufficient understanding then they can consent to the intervention.

8.13 The 'Gillick competence' test is primarily intended to reflect the child's current level of maturity and understanding. It does not contain a diagnostic criterion, although a mental disorder may affect the child's competence. By contrast, in order for a young person to lack capacity for the purpose of the MCA 2005, there must be an impairment of or disturbance in the function of the mind or brain, even if this is temporary.

4 [1986] AC 112.

How does this apply to informal admission?

8.14 16–17 year olds with capacity to consent to admission can be admitted to hospital informally if they consent.[5] If they do not consent to informal admission the person with parental responsibility cannot override this and the patient may not be admitted informally.[6]

8.15 16–17 year olds who lack capacity to consent to informal admission to hospital could be admitted informally using the provisions of the Mental Capacity Act 2005 but not if the admission will deprive the young person of their liberty. It may be possible for the young person to be admitted informally on the basis of the consent of the person with parental responsibility. This will require an assessment as to whether on the facts of the particular case the decision falls within the zone of parental control or not. Even if it does, the person with parental responsibility cannot consent to a deprivation of the young person's liberty.

8.16 A child under 16 who is competent to consent to informal admission may be admitted on the basis of his or her consent. If the child does not consent it would be inadvisable to rely on the consent of the person with parental control. Such a decision is unlikely to fall within the zone of parental control even though it is not specifically outlawed by the MHA 1983.

8.17 A child under 16 who is not competent to consent to informal admission could be admitted informally on the basis of the consent of the person with parental responsibility. This will require an assessment as to whether on the facts of the particular case the decision falls within the zone of parental control or not. Even if it does, the person with parental responsibility cannot consent to a deprivation of the child's liberty.

8.18 Where it is not possible to rely on the consent of the child or young person, or of the person with parental responsibility for them, the MHA 1983 should be used. If the criteria for detention under the MHA 1983 are not met then an application to court would have to be made.

5 MHA 1983 s131(3).
6 MHA 1983 s131(4).

What about consent to treatment?

8.19 Chapter 4 considers how the consent to treatment provisions apply to children and young people.

What special arrangements must be made for children in hospital?

8.20 Section 131A of the MHA 1983 imposes a duty on hospital managers to ensure that any person under 18 admitted to hospital is in an environment that is 'suitable having regard to his age (subject to his needs)'.[7] This applies to all admissions, whether under the powers of the MHA 1983 or otherwise.

8.21 The Code states at para 19.94 that admissions of those under 18 to adult wards is permissible only in exceptional circumstances. If a person under 18 is placed on an adult ward for a continuous period of more than 48 hours the Care Quality Commission must be notified immediately.[8]

8.22 Section 116 of the MHA 1983 imposes certain duties on local authorities when a child or young person is admitted to hospital (whether informally or using compulsory powers. In these circumstances the local authority must arrange for visits to be made for the person and must 'take such other steps in relation to the patient ... as would be expected to be taken by his parents'.[9]

8.23 The Code[10] and the Code for Wales[11] stress the importance of facilitating contact between children and young people in hospital and their family and friends.

8.24 The Code encourages local authorities to consider providing financial support to assist families to visit children and young people who are 'looked after' for the purposes of the Children Act 1989 or accommodated in hospital for more than three months.[12]

8.25 All children and young people are entitled to the support of an independent mental health advocate (IMHA) if they discuss treatment

7 MHA 1983 s131A(2).

8 Care Quality Commission (Registration) Regulations 2009 SI No 3112; Code para 19.93.

9 MHA 1983 s116(1).

10 Code para 19.5.

11 Code for Wales paras 20.8–20.9.

12 Code para 19.122.

to which section 58A applies (ECT) with a registered medical practitioner or approved clinician.[13]

8.26 The Code has a helpful summary of the entitlement of children and young people to education, after-care and transitional arrangements as they move from Children and Adolescents Mental Health Services (CAMHS) to adult services: see paras 19.116–19.120.

Children and young people at the tribunal

8.27 Children and young people have the same rights of appeal to the tribunal or hospital managers as any other patient.

8.28 In addition, the cases of patients under 18 must be referred to the tribunal by the hospital managers if a year has elapsed since the case has been considered by the tribunal (as opposed to three years in the case of an adult).[14]

8.29 Special arrangements have been made by the tribunal so that wherever possible at least one panel member will have experience working with those under 18. The Practice Direction[15] sets out detailed requirements for the reports concerning patients who are under 18. The purpose of these requirements is to ensure that the tribunal is fully informed about what other agencies are involved in the child or young person's care.

8.30 Tribunal hearings may be especially daunting for children and young people. Tribunals ought to be alert to this but it is particularly important for the representative to take steps to explain the procedure in advance and answer any questions about the process, to reduce the anxiety of the patient.

13 MHA 1983 s130C(3)(b).

14 MHA 1983 s68(6).

15 *Practice Direction: First-tier Tribunal (Health, Education and Social Care Chamber): Statements and Reports in Mental Health Cases*, 23 October 2013 available at www.judiciary.gov.uk.

PART 2

Practice and procedure

CHAPTER 9

Regulation, ethics and guidance

9.1 Tribunal representatives should demonstrate the highest standards of ethics and professionalism. Their clients have a right to expect nothing less. This chapter looks at the regulations governing this area of work and considers how to approach ethical dilemmas.

9.2 It considers the importance of mental health awareness and the patient's perspective and includes an interview with a tribunal applicant about his experiences.

The Solicitors Regulation Authority and the Code of Conduct 2011

9.3 The Solicitors Regulation Authority (SRA) regulates legal services and most practitioners using this book will be working at firms regulated by the SRA. Practitioners should have access to the current version of the SRA Handbook.[1] Rather than lay down hard and fast rules which apply in all cases, the SRA uses 'outcomes-focused regulation'.

The 10 principles

9.4 The SRA has 10 mandatory principles which apply to all practitioners and all areas of work. In addition the SRA has a Code of Conduct, referred to as the 'SRA Code'. This sets out a series of mandatory 'outcomes'. These may be achieved in a number of ways. The Code provides guidance as to how these outcomes could be achieved, through 'indicative behaviours' (IBs). This means that if a firm or individual shows this behaviour it is an indication that they are acting in accordance with the Code. However, the list is not exhaustive and firms and individuals can show they are achieving the outcomes in other ways. The SRA stresses the importance of providing legal services in a way that meets the particular needs of individual clients. This is of special importance in the area of representation at tribunals.

9.5 The 10 mandatory principles are:

You must:

1. uphold the rule of law and the proper administration of justice;
2. act with integrity;
3. not allow your independence to be compromised;
4. act in the best interests of each client;
5. provide a proper standard of service to your clients;
6. behave in a way that maintains the trust the public places in you and in the provision of legal services;

1 *SRA Handbook*, Law Society Publishing (version 12) 2014.

7. comply with your legal and regulatory obligations and deal with your regulators and ombudsmen in an open, timely and co-operative manner;
8. run your business or carry out your role in the business effectively and in accordance with proper governance and sound financial and risk management principles;
9. run your business or carry out your role in the business in a way that encourages equality of opportunity and respect for diversity; and
10. protect client money and assets.

9.6 The Code itself is divided into chapters of which the relevant sections for the purpose of this book are:

- 1st section: you and your client
- 3rd section: you and your regulator
- 4th section: you and others.

9.7 Each section contains chapters explaining the outcomes which must be achieved and listing the indicative behaviours which suggest compliance with the Code.

9.8 The first section, 'You and your client' contains six chapters dealing with client care, equality and diversity, conflicts of interest, confidentiality and disclosure, your client and the court, and your client and introductions to third parties.

9.9 The client care chapter deals with providing a proper standard of service taking into account the needs of the particular client and includes provision of information and complaints management. All the outcomes are mandatory. Those of particular relevance are listed below:

Outcomes

9.10 You must achieve these outcomes:

O(1.1) you treat your clients fairly;

O(1.2) you provide services to your clients in a manner which protects their interests in their matter, subject to the proper administration of justice;

O(1.3) when deciding whether to act, or terminate your instructions, you comply with the law and the Code;

O(1.4) you have the resources, skills and procedures to carry out your clients' instructions;

O(1.5) the service you provide to clients is competent, delivered in a timely manner and takes account of your clients' needs and circumstances;

O(1.7) you inform clients whether and how the services you provide are regulated and how this affects the protections available to the client;

O(1.8) clients have the benefit of your compulsory professional indemnity insurance and you do not exclude or attempt to exclude liability below the minimum level of cover required by the SRA Indemnity Insurance Rules;

O(1.9) clients are informed in writing at the outset of their matter of their right to complain and how complaints can be made;

O(1.10) clients are informed in writing, both at the time of engagement and at the conclusion of your complaints procedure, of their right to complain to the Legal Ombudsman, the time frame for doing so and full details of how to contact the Legal Ombudsman;

O(1.11) clients' complaints are dealt with promptly, fairly, openly and effectively;

O(1.12) clients are in a position to make informed decisions about the services they need, how their matter will be handled and the options available to them;

O(1.16) you inform current clients if you discover any act or omission which could give rise to a claim by them against you.

Indicative behaviours

9.11 The following are the most relevant to this area of work:

Dealing with the client's matter

IB(1.1) agreeing an appropriate level of service with your client, for example the type and frequency of communications;

IB(1.2) explaining your responsibilities and those of the client;

IB(1.3) ensuring that the client is told, in writing, the name and status of the person(s) dealing with the matter and the name and status of the person responsible for its overall supervision;

IB(1.5) explaining any limitations or conditions on what you can do for the client, for example, because of the way the client's matter is funded;

IB(1.6) in taking instructions and during the course of the retainer, having proper regard to your client's mental capacity or other vulnerability, such as incapacity or duress;

IB(1.7) considering whether you should decline to act or cease to act because you cannot act in the client's best interests;

IB(1.10) if you have to cease acting for a client, explaining to the client their possible options for pursuing their matter;

IB(1.12) considering whether a conflict of interests has arisen or whether the client should be advised to obtain independent advice where the client notifies you of their intention to make a claim or if you discover an act or omission which might give rise to a claim;

Fee arrangements with your client

IB(1.18) where you are acting for a publicly funded client, explaining how their publicly funded status affects the costs;

IB(1.19) providing the information in a clear and accessible form which is appropriate to the needs and circumstances of the client;

Complaints handling

IB(1.22) having a written complaints procedure which:

(a) is brought to clients' attention at the outset of the matter;

(b) is easy for clients to use and understand, allowing for complaints to be made by any reasonable means;

(c) is responsive to the needs of individual clients, especially those who are vulnerable;

(d) enables complaints to be dealt with promptly and fairly, with decisions based on a sufficient investigation of the circumstances;

(e) provides for appropriate remedies; and

(f) does not involve any charges to clients for handling their complaints;

IB(1.23) providing the client with a copy of the firm's complaints procedure on request;

IB(1.24) in the event that a client makes a complaint, providing them with all necessary information concerning the handling of the complaint.

9.12 All firms should have their own client care letters, which can be used to evidence IBs 1–5. It is essential that the client care letter is examined critically to ensure it is comprehensible to detained clients, who may be vulnerable and whose ability to process complicated information may be impaired. Letters should use clear language and avoid jargon. Practitioners will be expected to satisfy themselves that the client has understood the information. This need not be onerous and may simply be a matter of checking on the next visit that the client has received the client care letter and asking if they have any questions. Some clients may need the letter read to them or summarised at the meeting. If you do this, then you should ensure you record it in your attendance note.

9.13 Complaints by mentally-disordered clients must be dealt with using the same skill and attention as with any other client. Consider whether your complaints procedure places any barriers to detained clients, for example requiring an excessive level of detail or requiring the complaints manager to be contacted in a particular way. The Law Society has produced guidance to clients in hospital about the methods of complaining about legal representatives, which includes an easyread version: see below paras 9.63–9.64.

9.14 The equality and diversity provisions in chapter 2 of the Code of Conduct are of particular importance in this area of work and apply in relation to age, disability, gender reassignment, marriage and civil partnership, pregnancy and maternity, race, religion or belief, sex and sexual orientation. The most relevant are listed below:

O(2.1) you do not discriminate unlawfully, or victimise or harass anyone, in the course of your professional dealings;

O(2.2) you provide services to clients in a way that respects diversity;

O(2.3) you make reasonable adjustments to ensure that disabled clients ... are not placed at a substantial disadvantage compared to those who are not disabled, and you do not pass on the costs of these adjustments to these disabled clients;

O(2.5) complaints of discrimination are dealt with promptly, fairly, openly, and effectively.

9.15 The following IBs are relevant:

IB(2.1) having a written equality and diversity policy which is appropriate to the size and nature of the firm and includes the following features:

(a) a commitment to the principles of equality and diversity and legislative requirements;

(b) a requirement that all employees and managers comply with the outcomes;

...

(f) details of how complaints and disciplinary issues are to be dealt with;

9.16 The firm's equality and diversity policy will cover all areas of law. Provision of mental health legal services in a way that takes into account the particular needs of the client would also be evidence that Outcomes 1–3 are being achieved.

9.17 Conflicts of interests are dealt with in chapter 3 of the Code of Conduct. Conflicts can arise between the practitioner and the client ('own interest conflict'); and between two or more current clients ('client conflict'). The Code provides that you can never act where there is a conflict, or a significant risk of conflict, between you and your client.

9.18 If there is a conflict, or a significant risk of a conflict, between two or more current clients ('client conflict'), then the Code provides you must not act for all or both of them except in very limited circumstances. The decision to act must be made in the best interests of the client. An important factor will be the relative benefits and risks to the clients of you acting for them. You must also consider how your duties of disclosure and confidentiality will be affected.

9.19 The SRA requires you to achieve all the listed outcomes:

Systems

O(3.1) you have effective systems and controls in place to enable you to identify and assess potential conflicts of interests;

O(3.2) your systems and controls for identifying own interest conflicts are appropriate to the size and complexity of the firm and the nature of the work undertaken, and enable you to assess all the relevant circumstances ...

O(3.3) your systems and controls for identifying client conflicts are appropriate to the size and complexity of the firm and the nature of the work undertaken, and enable you to assess all relevant circumstances, including whether:
(a) the clients' interests are different;
(b) your ability to give independent advice to the clients may be fettered;
(c) there is a need to negotiate between the clients;
(d) there is an imbalance in bargaining power between the clients; or
(e) any client is vulnerable;

Prohibition on acting in conflict situations

O(3.4) you do not act if there is an own interest conflict or a significant risk of an own interest conflict;

O(3.5) you do not act if there is a client conflict, or a significant risk of a client conflict, unless the circumstances set out in Outcomes 3.6 or 3.7 apply;

Exceptions where you may act, with appropriate safeguards, where there is a client conflict

O(3.6) where there is a client conflict and the clients have a substantially common interest in relation to a matter or a particular aspect of it, you only act if:
(a) you have explained the relevant issues and risks to the clients and you have a reasonable belief that they understand those issues and risks;
(b) all the clients have given informed consent in writing to you acting;
(c) you are satisfied that it is reasonable for you to act for all the clients and that it is in their best interests; and
(d) you are satisfied that the benefits to the clients of you doing so outweigh the risks;

O(3.7) where there is a client conflict and the clients *are* competing for the same objective, you only act if:

(a) you have explained the relevant issues and risks to the clients and you have a reasonable belief that they understand those issues and risks;
(b) the clients have confirmed in writing that they want you to act, in the knowledge that you act, or may act, for one or more other clients who are competing for the same objective;
(c) there is no other client conflict in relation to that matter;
(d) unless the clients specifically agree, no individual acts for, or is responsible for the supervision of work done for, more than one of the clients in that matter; and
(e) you are satisfied that it is reasonable for you to act for all the clients and that the benefits to the clients of you doing so outweigh the risks.

9.20 The relevant IBs are likely to be:

IB(3.2) declining to act for clients whose interests are in direct conflict, for example claimant and defendant in litigation;

IB(3.5) declining to act for clients under Outcome 3.6 (substantially common interest) or Outcome 3.7 (competing for the same objective) where the clients cannot be represented even-handedly, or will be prejudiced by lack of separate representation;

9.21 Some examples of where conflicts of interest can arise are considered in the 'case studies' at the end of this section.

9.22 Chapter 4 is about the protection of clients' confidential information and the disclosure of material information to clients. This is a complex area of practice, where difficult decisions may arise in tribunal work.

9.23 You, and all other members of your organisation, have a fundamental duty of confidentiality to your client. This duty continues after the case concludes and even after the death of the client. This is not the same as legal professional privilege which is absolute. You also have a duty to disclose to your client all information of which you are aware which is material to your client's case. Where the two duties conflict, then the duty of confidentiality takes precedence. You can disclose information about the client's affairs if this is required or permitted by law, or if the client consents.

9.24 You can only continue to act for a client to whom you cannot disclose all relevant information in very limited circumstances. The SRA expects you to achieve these outcomes:

O(4.1) you keep the affairs of clients confidential unless disclosure is required or permitted by law or the client consents;

O(4.2) any individual who is advising a client makes that client aware of all information material to that retainer of which the individual has personal knowledge;

O(4.3) you ensure that where your duty of confidentiality to one client comes into conflict with your duty of disclosure to another client, your duty of confidentiality takes precedence;

O(4.4) you do not act for A in a matter where A has an interest adverse to B, and B is a client for whom you hold confidential information which is material to A in that matter, unless the confidential information can be protected by the use of safeguards, and:

(a) you reasonably believe that A is aware of, and understands, the relevant issues and gives informed consent;

(b) either:

(i) B gives informed consent and you agree with B the safeguards to protect B's information; or

(ii) where this is not possible, you put in place effective safeguards including information barriers which comply with the common law; and

(c) it is reasonable in all the circumstances to act for A with such safeguards in place;

O(4.5) you have effective systems and controls in place to enable you to identify risks to client confidentiality and to mitigate those risks.

Indicative behaviours

Acting in the following way(s) may tend to show that you have achieved these outcomes and therefore complied with the Principles:

IB(4.1) your systems and controls for identifying risks to client confidentiality are appropriate to the size and complexity of the firm or in-house practice and the nature of the work undertaken, and enable you to assess all the relevant circumstances;

IB(4.2) you comply with the law in respect of your fiduciary duties in relation to confidentiality and disclosure;

...

IB(4.4) where you are an individual who has responsibility for acting for a client or supervising a client's matter, you disclose to the client all information material to the client's matter of which you are personally aware, except when:

(a) the client gives specific informed consent to non-disclosure or a different standard of disclosure arises;

(b) there is evidence that serious physical or mental injury will be caused to a person(s) if the information is disclosed to the client;

(c) legal restrictions effectively prohibit you from passing the information to the client, such as the provisions in the money-laundering and anti-terrorism legislation;
(d) it is obvious that privileged documents have been mistakenly disclosed to you;
(e) you come into possession of information relating to state security or intelligence matters to which the Official Secrets Act 1989 applies;

IB(4.5) not acting for A where B is a client for whom you hold confidential information which is material to A unless the confidential information can be protected.

9.25 The fifth chapter in this section deals with 'Your client and the court'. Tribunals are part of HM Courts & Tribunals Service and the requirements of the SRA apply to tribunals as well. The SRA requires you to achieve the following outcomes:

O(5.1) you do not attempt to deceive or knowingly or recklessly mislead the court;
O(5.2) you are not complicit in another person deceiving or misleading the court;
O(5.3) you comply with court orders which place obligations on you;
O(5.4) you do not place yourself in contempt of court;
O(5.5) where relevant, clients are informed of the circumstances in which your duties to the court outweigh your obligations to your client;
O(5.6) you comply with your duties to the court;
O(5.7) you ensure that evidence relating to sensitive issues is not misused;
O(5.8) you do not make or offer to make payments to witnesses dependent upon their evidence or the outcome of the case.

9.26 The indicative behaviours that may show that you have achieved these outcomes are:

IB(5.1) advising your clients to comply with court orders made against them, and advising them of the consequences of failing to comply;
IB(5.2) drawing the court's attention to relevant cases and statutory provisions, and any material procedural irregularity;
IB(5.3) ensuring child witness evidence is kept securely and not released to clients or third parties;
IB(5.4) immediately informing the court, with your client's consent, if during the course of proceedings you become aware that you have inadvertently misled the court, or ceasing to act if the client does not consent to you informing the court;

IB(5.5) refusing to continue acting for a client if you become aware they have committed perjury or misled the court, or attempted to mislead the court, in any material matter unless the client agrees to disclose the truth to the court;

IB(5.6) not appearing as an advocate, or acting in litigation, if it is clear that you, or anyone within your firm, will be called as a witness in the matter unless you are satisfied that this will not prejudice your independence as an advocate, or litigator, or the interests of your clients or the interests of justice.

Acting in the following way(s) may tend to show that you have not achieved these outcomes and therefore not complied with the Principles:

IB(5.7) constructing facts supporting your client's case or drafting any documents relating to any proceedings containing:
(a) any contention which you do not consider to be properly arguable; or
(b) any allegation of fraud, unless you are instructed to do so and you have material which you reasonably believe shows, on the face of it, a case of fraud;

IB(5.8) suggesting that any person is guilty of a crime, fraud or misconduct unless such allegations:
(a) go to a matter in issue which is material to your own client's case; and
(b) appear to you to be supported by reasonable grounds;

IB(5.9) calling a witness whose evidence you know is untrue;

IB(5.10) attempting to influence a witness, when taking a statement from that witness, with regard to the contents of their statement;

IB(5.11) tampering with evidence or seeking to persuade a witness to change their evidence;

IB(5.12) when acting as an advocate, naming in open court any third party whose character would thereby be called into question, unless it is necessary for the proper conduct of the case;

IB(5.13) when acting as an advocate, calling into question the character of a witness you have cross-examined unless the witness has had the opportunity to answer the allegations during cross-examination.

9.27 The question of what is 'properly arguable' is considered in *Buxton-Mill v Reeves*.[2] The issue is not its chances of success, or even whether it is bound to fail, but whether it can be properly articulated. The Law Society's Practice Note, which is discussed below, considers what this means in the context of a mental health tribunal. The Practice Note emphasises that there will be very few cases before the tribunal

2 [2010] EWCA Civ 122.

where to seek to argue for discharge in accordance with the patient's wishes will not be 'properly arguable' for this purpose. See also paras 9.53–9.54.

9.28 The second section of the Code deals with business management and is outside the scope of this book.

9.29 The third section 'You and your regulator' deals with the important issue of co-operation with the regulators and ombudsmen. The most relevant mandatory outcome for the purpose of this book is outcome 10.5: you report to the SRA promptly, serious misconduct by any person or firm authorised by the SRA, or any employee, manager or owner of any such firm (taking into account, where necessary, your duty of confidentiality to your client).

9.30 The fourth section: 'You and others', largely deals with ensuring lawyers do not take advantage of others and the most relevant outcome is:

O(11.1) you do not take unfair advantage of third parties in either your professional or personal capacity;

with the most relevant IBs being:

IB(11.4) ensuring that you do not communicate with another party when you are aware that the other party has retained a lawyer in a matter, except:
(a) to request the name and address of the other party's lawyer; or
(b) the other party's lawyer consents to you communicating with the client; or
(c) where there are exceptional circumstances;
...

Acting in the following way(s) may tend to show that you have not achieved these outcomes and therefore not complied with the Principles:

IB(11.7) taking unfair advantage of an opposing party's lack of legal knowledge where they have not instructed a lawyer;

IB(11.8) demanding anything for yourself or on behalf of your client, that is not legally recoverable, such as when you are instructed to collect a simple debt, demanding from the debtor the cost of the letter of claim since it cannot be said at that stage that such a cost is legally recoverable;

Case studies: using the Code at mental health tribunals

Case study 1

9.31 *You are asked to represent a detained patient where your firm also acts for the detaining authority.*

- This would represent a clear conflict where you would not be able to act in the best interests of each client (Principle 4) or without allowing your independence to be compromised (Principle 3).

Case study 2

9.32 *Your client applies to the tribunal. His mother who is the nearest relative seeks to discharge him from liability to detention using section 23(2)(a) of the Mental Health Act 1983. The RC blocks this (s25(1)) and the nearest relative appeals to the tribunal. The two hearings are consolidated. Both are parties (TPR 1) and can appoint a representative (TPR 11). Both are entitled to Controlled Legal Representation and the 2014 Contract Specification does not prohibit you from accepting instructions from the NR and patient (para 7.33).*

- Applying the Code to this scenario, the following issues arise. On the face of it both patient and NR may be seeking the same objective, eg discharge from detention. But you need to consider the risk of conflict developing which could compromise your independence (Principle 3) and make it difficult for you to act in the best interests of each client (Principle 4).
- The reasons for this include the vulnerability of the patient and the unequal bargaining power between the patient whose application may depend on the continued willingness of the NR to accommodate him or her (Outcome 3.3 (d) and (e)). You should also consider the risk of one party wishing you to keep certain information from the other, when this information might be material to the other client's case, so your duty of confidentiality would conflict with your duty to disclose material information to your client (Outcomes 4.1 and 4.2).

Case study 3

9.33 *You become aware through reports or reading clinical notes that one of your clients is in conflict with another, especially where there is an element of bullying. This is particularly difficult because you may be quite advanced in your preparation of both cases before the conflict comes to light. How do you decide which client to continue representing?*

- The nature of the Code is that it does not provide hard and fast answers, but requires you to demonstrate that you are achieving the relevant outcomes for the client. Here, you should consider your responsibility to act in the best interests of your clients (Principle 4) and the mandatory outcome of treating your client fairly (Outcome 1.1). You would also have to consider your responsibility not to allow your independence to be compromised (Principle 3). This might mean deciding to continue to act for the more vulnerable client, and making a referral to an alternative firm for the other client.
- In some cases you would have to withdraw from representing both clients, for example if you hold confidential information about client A which is relevant to the case of Client B and should therefore normally be disclosed to Client B. In this case your duty to protect A's confidentiality takes priority (Outcome 4.3).

Case study 4

9.34 *You receive a social circumstances report and see that the tribunal has made a direction under rule 14 that a piece of information in the report be disclosed to you but not to your client. If this has happened you must not disclose the information without having secured the agreement of the tribunal.*

- The relevant principle is Principle 1, and the relevant outcome you must achieve is Outcome 5.3. You have a duty to disclose material information to your client, but if you withhold such information, where legal restrictions prevent you from passing the information onto the client, this is an indicative behaviour (IB 4.4 (c)) likely to demonstrate that you have achieved the mandatory outcomes and are complying with the principles of the Code.
- The question of disclosure to the client is most likely to be considered as a preliminary issue at the tribunal but could also be considered in advance of the hearing, following written representations by you. This is considered in more detail at paras 11.115–11.118.

Case study 5

9.35 *You are seeking disclosure from a Trust or other body which holds information about your client, in the context of an application to the tribunal. Following dicta in* Dorset Healthcare NHS Foundation Trust v MH[3] *the Trust may agree to release information to you while seeking an undertaking that you do not disclose it to your client.*

3 [2009] UKUT 4 (AAC).

- The Upper Tribunal in that case concluded:

  > In most cases where there are confidential third-party documents, it should be possible for the responsible authority to disclose all such documents to the patient's solicitors subject to an undertaking from the solicitors not to disclose to the patient third-party documents specifically identified by the authority. The solicitors can then take a view as to whether the third-party rights override the rights of the patient, or vice versa. Where they consider the documents ought to be disclosed to the patient, then they must make an application to the tribunal for disclosure.

- This scenario raises different questions to the previous one, because in this case you are offered the choice of whether to accept material that you cannot pass to your client, when you do not know what it is and cannot assess the chances of successfully applying to the tribunal for permission to disclose it to your client.
- The relevant principles are Principle 1 (upholding the rule of law and administration of justice), Principle 3 (not allowing your independence to be compromised) and Principle 4 (acting in the best interests of your client). The Outcomes that you must achieve are: to treat your client fairly (Outcome 1.1) and making your client aware of all material information (Outcome 4.2). The only legal restriction preventing you from passing the information to the client is one to which you have agreed. Despite the comments in *Dorset Healthcare*, it might be prudent to make an application to the tribunal rather than give the undertaking. The only alternative would be to seek your client's consent to the undertaking being given, subject to his or her capacity to consent.

9.36 Other scenarios which can arise

1) *Your client discloses to you that he intends to inflict serious harm on another person.*
2) *You consider it necessary to prevent the client or a third party committing a criminal activity that you reasonably believe is likely to result in serious bodily injury.*
3) *The client is a child and discloses information which indicates ongoing sexual or other physical abuse but will not agree to disclosure by you.*
4) *The client discloses abuse of a child either by themselves or another adult but refuses to allow disclosure.*

The former version of the Solicitors Code of Conduct made a specific exception to the duty of confidentiality for the first three scenarios, under Rule 4.0. The solicitor was required to weigh up whether the threat to the client, another person or the child, is sufficiently serious to justify a breach of the duty of confidentiality.

There are now no specific exceptions in the Code save that you may disclose confidential information where permitted by law. Broadly, disclosure could be seen to be permitted by law where there is danger to a third party.

The former Code was silent on the issue of whether disclosure is justified in cases where a client discloses, for example, an intention to harm him- or herself. There is no professional guidance on how to manage such a situation save to seek advice from the SRA helpline.

The Law Society's Accreditation Scheme

9.37 The Law Society administers a number of panel schemes, the aim of which is to establish a list of practitioners with demonstrable skill and experience. The Law Society writes:

> An accreditation scheme is a group of legal practitioners whose expertise in a particular area of law has been tested, assessed and accredited by the Law Society or the Solicitors Regulation Authority. These schemes promote standards of excellence in the delivery of legal services.
>
> Accreditation schemes are also intended to help consumers identify solicitors and solicitors' employees who are competent and experienced in key areas of legal practice.
>
> Only practitioners who meet exacting requirements are permitted to join our accreditation schemes.
>
> When you see a professional accreditation scheme logo, you'll know that the practitioner's skills and knowledge have been rigorously and independently tested.

9.38 The relevant scheme for mental health work is the Mental Health Accreditation Scheme, referred to here as 'the scheme.' Originally known as the Law Society's Mental Health Review Tribunal Panel, the scheme in its original form included an undertaking that the member would not normally delegate work on tribunal cases but will carry out the work on each case personally. Scheme members now agree to follow a Code of Conduct which requires them not normally to delegate the preparation, supervision, conduct or presentation of the case but to deal with it personally. Where it is in the best interests of the client to instruct another advocate, or it is necessary to do so, panel members are to ensure that the advocate is also a scheme member or a barrister on the approved list for the member's firm who should themselves undertake not to delegate the work on the case. Scheme members also agree to abide by the Law Society's Practice Note (see below at paras 9.46–9.59).

9.39 Membership of the scheme has been a requirement for supervisors for the purpose of the Civil Contract with the Legal Aid Agency. Under the terms of the 2010 contract the ratio for supervisors to caseworkers was one to six. Firms therefore could have a department of six unqualified caseworkers headed by one panel member and a number of firms adopted this business model. This inevitably meant that the panel member would largely be engaged in supervision of cases, in breach of the Code of Conduct.

9.40 Over the next few years widespread concerns about the quality of representation began to be expressed by the Tribunal Judiciary and Trusts, through Mental Health Act Administrators and others. On 27 September 2012 after lobbying from practitioners, the Administration of Justice and Tribunals Council, the judiciary and the Law Society agreed to support a requirement in the next Civil Contract that all advocates at mental health tribunals should be accredited members of the scheme. This was followed by an announcement by the Legal Services Commission (LSC) that the next contract between what would then be the Legal Aid Agency and providers would contain a requirement that only panel members could represent at mental health tribunals. The 2014 Contract in force from August 2014 requires all tribunal advocates, apart from independent barristers, to be members of the scheme. The contract is discussed in more detail in chapter 10 on funding.

9.41 Membership of the scheme is open to admitted solicitors, members and fellows of the Chartered Institute of Legal Executives (CILEx), trainee solicitors and solicitors clerks and others, subject to the approval of the SRA. It is unusual in allowing non-solicitor members (although these must be employed by a solicitor) and this reflects the historical development of representation at tribunals and also the fact that the Tribunal Procedure Rules have always allowed patients to be represented by non-solicitors.

9.42 Current requirements include:

- attendance at a two-day course by an approved provider;
- a written application which includes case reports;
- an interview, which includes a multiple choice legal questionnaire and a case study; and
- a minimum CPD requirement.

9.43 Appointment is for an initial period of three years after which members must apply to be re-accredited. Applicants for both accreditation and re-accreditation must pay a fee. This is not refundable. Applicants must also obtain a disclosure from the Disclosure and Barring Service, for which a further fee is payable.

9.44 Members of the scheme:

- can use the Kitemark and the fact of panel membership in advertising;
- have their names on the Law Society's list which is advertised on the Law Society's website; and
- can be appointed under rule 11(4).

9.45 Information about the scheme can be found at: www.lawsociety.org.uk/accreditation/specialist-schemes/mental-health/.

The Law Society's Practice Note: Representation before mental health tribunals

9.46 The Law Society produces a variety of Practice Notes. These are introduced as follows:

> Practice notes are for our members and represent our view of good practice in a particular area. Following the advice in these practice notes will make it easier to account to oversight bodies for your actions.

9.47 The current version of the Law Society's Practice Note appears at Appendix D1. All representatives before the tribunal should ensure they are familiar with it. The Practice Note covers practical issues such as the routes through which practitioners may receive referrals and the roles of hospital and independent mental health advocates. It provides advice about communication issues, both face and in writing.

9.48 Section 4 of the Practice Note provides guidance on taking instructions. Section 4.1 deals with taking instructions from clients with capacity to instruct the solicitor. Section 4.2 provides guidance for cases where the solicitor considers that the patient who has asked to be represented does not have capacity to instruct them, and for cases where the solicitor is appointed by the tribunal under Tribunal Procedure Rules r11(7)(b) (ie the patient lacks capacity to appoint a representative but the tribunal considers that it is in the interests of justice for the patient to be represented).

9.49 In brief the guidance is as follows:

- The issues raised in tribunals are not usually complex and given clear information many clients will be able to provide capacitous instructions.
- A representative acting for a client with capacity to instruct him or her must act in accordance with the client's instructions even if these are inconsistent and counter to the client's best interests (though this may be evidence that the client lacks capacity).
- A representative may however refuse to put forward an argument that is not 'properly arguable'.[4]
- If the representative considers the client lacks capacity to instruct him or her then he or she can only continue to act if appointed by the tribunal or instructed by a properly authorised third party.
- The test for appointment under rule 11(7)(b) – ie whether the patient has capacity to appoint a representative – is not the same as whether the patient has capacity to litigate, although there is some overlap.
- A representative appointed by the tribunal is not in the same position as a litigation friend but has a heightened duty to identify and act in the client's interests. The representative does not 'take instructions' as he or she would from a client with capacity, but must instead identify the client's wishes and feelings. These should be given weight.
- The Law Society considers the client's right to a fair hearing to be paramount and that in most cases it will be appropriate to seek discharge of a client who wishes to be discharged even if the client lacks capacity to instruct the representative.
- Where the client cannot express their wishes the representative should ensure the tribunal receives all relevant material; should test the criteria for detention and remind the tribunal of the right to treatment in the least restrictive setting.

9.50 The Practice Note provides advice as to where it may be appropriate to seek to be discharged after appointment under rule 11(7)(b), eg where the client is so hostile to being represented that the client cannot participate in the proceedings.

9.51 It considers the questions of confidentiality and disclosure at section 5, and section 6 deals with good practice generally and provides details of other relevant guidance. Section 7 relates to

4 See *Buxton v Mills-Owen* [2010] EWCA Civ 122.

children and young people while section 8 signposts other sources of information.

9.52 In *YA v Central and North West London NHS Trust*[5] Charles J considered the role of the representative at tribunals. YA was detained under section 2 of the MHA 1983. Her RC told the tribunal that she lacked capacity to instruct a representative and a solicitor was appointed under rule 11(7)(b) very shortly before the hearing. At the hearing YA told the medical member and the solicitor she wished to represent herself. The hearing then commenced, without the solicitor having been told it had started, so by the time the solicitor entered the hearing room evidence was already being heard. The solicitor asked for clarification of YA's capacity as she considered the assessment to have been inadequate. There was a brief adjournment and the tribunal then directed the solicitor to remain in the hearing room in case YA needed advice. YA conducted the hearing herself and on appeal argued that she had been disadvantaged by this approach.

9.53 The Law Society and the Department of Health were joined as parties to YA's appeal and Charles J considered some of the Practice Note, which was still being developed at the time. Charles J reached the following conclusions:

- The system for appointments under rule 11(7) was generally working well and it was undesirable to introduce complications.
- Assessments of capacity should be made using the approach set out in the Mental Capacity Act 2005, including the presumption of capacity.
- Capacity to appoint a representative is not the same as capacity to conduct the proceedings oneself, but the difference is theoretical. This is because in order to decide whether to appoint a representative requires the patient to recognise whether he or she has the capacity to conduct the case without a representative. Thus, to have the capacity to appoint a representative it is not enough simply to be able to understand the role of the tribunal and of the representative.
- A representative appointed for a patient under rule 11(7)(b) must act in the patient's best interests, having regard to the relevant issues of law and fact in the case.

9.54 Charles J identified the following factors as relevant for the tribunal when deciding if it is in the best interests of a patient to be represented:

5 [2015] UKUT 0037 (AAC).

- The importance of an effective review of detention.
- The vulnerability of the patient, and the fact that their continued detention is at stake.
- The need for flexibility and speed.
- Whether the patient will be able to conduct the case effectively unrepresented (even if given assistance by the tribunal) and whether the tribunal will be fully informed of the competing factors in the case.
- The nature and degree of the patient's objections.
- The distress caused, and the resulting impact, if the patient's wishes were not followed.The likelihood that a legal representative will simply ask to be discharged if the appointment is made or continued.

9.55 Charles J recognised the importance of the rule 11(7) appointment as a safeguard to the patient's Article 5 rights. Representation of a patient who lacks capacity to conduct the proceedings against his or her wishes would not be contrary to Article 5(4) or Article 6 but departure from the patient's views or wishes should take place only when necessary.

9.56 He gave the following guidance to representatives appointed under rule 11(7)(b), where any of the following complicating factors arise:

a) the representative's views and the patient's views as to the patient's best interests diverge, and the patient lacks capacity to give instructions on relevant factors; or
b) the patient wants the representative to put forward an unarguable point; or
c) the patient does not want to be represented.

Even in these circumstances the need for an effective review of the patient's detention supports the continuation of the appointment. A representative appointed under rule 11(7)(b) should as far as possible act as if representing a patient with capacity to instruct him or her by reading the reports and seeking other relevant material, and discussing this with the patient. The representative should seek to ascertain the patient's wishes, feelings, beliefs and values. He or she should identify the areas where there is a disagreement between the patient and the legal representative and assess whether the patient has capacity to give instructions on all the relevant factors. If the patient has such capacity the representative must follow the instructions or seek discharge of his or her appointment.

9.57 Charles J continued:

> If the legal representative considers that the patient does not have or may not have capacity on all those issues, and the disagreements or other problems do not cause him to seek a discharge of his appointment, the legal representative should inform the patient and the tribunal that he intends to act as the patient's appointed representative in the following way:
>
> - he will provide the tribunal with an account of the patient's views, wishes, feelings, beliefs and values (including the fact but not the detail of any wish that the legal representative should act in a different way to the way in which he proposes to act, or should be discharged),
> - he will invite the tribunal to hear evidence from the patient and/or to allow the patient to address the tribunal (issues on competence to give evidence are in my view unlikely to arise but if they did they should be addressed before the tribunal),
> - he will draw the tribunal's attention to such matters and advance such arguments as he properly can in support of the patient's expressed views, wishes, feelings, beliefs and values, and
> - he will not advance any other arguments.

9.58 In such cases the tribunal should not delve into the reasons why the representative states he cannot make a particular argument. The Tribunal's role is to consider whether the representative should act or continue to act: the representative is responsible for deciding how he or she should act.

9.59 If there is no conflict between the legal representative and the patient, the legal representative still needs to decide whether the patient has capacity to instruct him or her in all relevant factors and act on capacitous instructions. But even if the patient lacks capacity the representative should advance 'all arguable points' to test the bases for detention in hospital.

Other codes of conduct

The Mental Health Lawyers' Association Code of Conduct

9.60 The Mental Health Lawyers' Association (MHLA) represents the majority of solicitors firms carrying out tribunal representation and is open to anyone who is a member of the Law Society's Mental Health Tribunal Panel or actively seeking membership. The Association is recognised as a Special Interest Group (SIG) by the Law Society and campaigns actively for improved standards in Mental Health work and for improvements to the legal aid regime in this area of work.

9.61 Its Code of Conduct can be found at www.mhla.co.uk/about/code-of-conduct. It gives practical advice about good behaviour on wards, seeking clients in an appropriate way, dispute resolution and appropriate dress and footwear.

Local Trusts Codes of Conduct

9.62 Faced with what they considered to be an increase in unacceptable behaviour by legal representatives many Trusts have implemented Codes of Conduct and will only admit legal representatives into their hospitals on these terms. These Codes generally cover issues such as referrals, gifts, behaviour towards clients and staff as well as access to information. Before visiting a new hospital ensure that you have checked the Code for the responsible Trust and ensure that you act in compliance with it. If you have concerns about the lawfulness of the requirements you may wish to seek advice from the Law Society or the Mental Health Lawyers' Association.

Complaints Guidance

9.63 A working group comprising representatives of the Tribunal Judiciary, the Law Society, the Mental Health Lawyers' Association, the Legal Aid Agency and various NHS Trusts worked together to prepare a written guide to detained patients and to hospital staff to ensure that complaints are properly directed. This guidance can be found at www.lawsociety.org.uk/accreditation/specialist-schemes/mental-health/, where a full version and an easyread version can be downloaded. Trusts have been asked to ensure that both versions are easily available to patients in hospitals.

9.64 In brief, clients with a complaint about the service they have received are advised to first complain to the firm. If they do not receive a response or are dissatisfied with the response they may complain to the Legal Ombudsman. Complaints about the professional conduct of a representative (which could be made by clients or members of hospital staff or the judiciary) will be dealt with the SRA or Bar Standards Board for solicitors and barristers respectively. In certain circumstances it will be appropriate to inform the Legal Aid Agency about concerns that a firm is failing to meet proper standards.

Peer Review Guidance

9.65 Peer review is a process used by the Legal Aid Agency to assess whether firms who have contracts to provide legally aided services are meeting proper standards in their areas of work. A randomly selected sample of files are examined by experienced 'peer reviewers' who assess the quality of the work. In April 2011 the Institute of Advanced Legal Studies published its third guide, entitled *Improving Your Quality: a guide to common issues identified during peer review*. The guide aimed to draw together some of the common areas of concern which peer reviewers had noted when assessing files. The most serious concerns related to failure to examine relevant section papers; failure to examine records; lack of evidence of written advice which was tailored to the client and their circumstances (in other words, over-reliance on standard letters); failure to consider the lawfulness of the tribunal decisions; acting where there is a conflict of interest; and failing to identify and discuss with the client the nearest relative. Peer review is limited to consideration of the evidence of work done disclosed by the file. However good the quality of oral advice and representation, a file will not score well on peer review unless this is backed up by written attendance notes and/or correspondence.

9.66 It is important to be familiar with the guidance which also provides useful tips about good case management. This includes setting standards such as seeing a section 2 client, or a client with an obviously urgent problem, within two days of contact; and ensuring that there is sufficiently frequent contact with the client to take instructions and inform them of progress. The guidance notes that some clients will need more frequent contact than others; for example those with a limited attention span; those with a significant impairment and those whose mental health fluctuates. It stresses that some information may need to be provided more than once for example in a visit (and recorded in an attendance note) and then followed up by correspondence. The guidance recognises that use of standard letters and information sheets can be useful but are likely to be confusing if they are not adequately tailored to the client's specific instructions.

9.67 The vital importance of thorough review of the client's medical records and cross-referring these to the statutory reports is recognised, as is the use of experts. The guidance recommends that consideration is given to attending section 117 planning meetings which are described as 'significant events'. The guidance emphasises the need to make onward referrals if the client has a problem in another area of law and gives suggestions as to how to evidence thorough preparation for the hearing.

The patient's perspective: mental health and disability awareness

9.68 A common theme running through the guidance of the various regulatory bodies is the need to communicate and provide advice in a way that meets the need of the unique individual client. This is expressed in the SRA's Principles 4 and 5 (see para 9.4 above) and the mandatory outcomes of treating the client fairly and providing services in a way that respects diversity. An awareness of how the client may be affected by mental disorder is central to this but is not always achieved.

9.69 In March 2011, the Care Quality Commission and the Administrative Justice and Tribunals Council published a report, *Patients' experiences of the First-tier Tribunal (Mental Health)* which examined the tribunal process from the patients' point of view, by carrying out interviews with 152 patients in 16 hospitals. The report refers to concern that the fixed fee scheme imposed by the then Legal Services Commission (LSC) was leading to a deterioration in the quality of legal advice in this area of law.

9.70 Most patients had no difficulty in finding a lawyer. The report noted a number of patients who accepted the recommendation of a particular lawyer by hospital staff. Patients met with their solicitor two or three times. Most appeared to be satisfied with their lawyers' performance though there were references to inadequate preparation and failure to follow instructions: for example one patient did not want to challenge their detention but their representative did. The report recommended that rather than hospital staff making specific referrals patients should be given a list of local solicitors who have legal aid contracts in mental health, particularly those who are members of the Law Society's Mental Health Tribunal Panel. The LSC was urged to accelerate its stated intention to require panel membership of all tribunal advocates. This is a new requirement: see para 10.22. Delay was a major cause of distress and frustration to patients, particularly when the reasons were unexplained.

9.71 The purpose of the pre-hearing examination by the Medical Member had not been explained to many patients and their experiences of it were mixed. Some found it stressful to have the examination on the same day as the hearing and as a result the report recommended that where possible it should take place a day or two before the hearing. The report recommended that the tribunal provide a leaflet about the medical member's visit including that his or her findings would be shared with the tribunal, as well as regular training for medical members. The pre-hearing examination is now voluntary and except for a section 2 patient must be requested. A leaflet is sent to patients who have been referred or who apply for a MHT.

9.72 Patients reported several problems with the hearing process. Some described feeling intimidated because the room was crowded. There are a number of comments that it was stressful for the patient to wait till the end of the hearing to speak, which led to the perception that the tribunal had already made up its mind by the time the patient spoke. Some felt they were not allowed to take part in the hearing and others complained about the use of long words and jargon. Some patients had to wait a long time to receive the reasons for the decision and many were very unclear about their rights to appeal. Further issues raised by patients and members of staff included a concern that patients with unusual conditions were at risk of injustice because the tribunal and their representative did not understand their condition adequately. It was suggested that deaf interpreters arranged by the Tribunals Service did not have enough expertise to interpret for patients with mental health problems or learning disabilities.

9.73 On 29 July 2013 the Legal Services Board, the Legal Services Consumer Panel and MENCAP published a report of research carried out by the Norah Fry Research Centre and the University of Bristol, called *What happens when people with learning disabilities need advice about the law?* It presented findings from interviews with 90 people with learning disabilities, and looked at their experiences in obtaining advice in a number of areas of law. The report found many barriers to access to justice for this group of people which included cost and lack of availability of appropriate specialists. There were examples of legal advisers taking care to explain things clearly, avoiding jargon, producing information in accessible formats and simply showing respect to learning disabled clients. However, some participants complained that legal advisers had failed to recognise the need explain things in terms that could be easily understood, and had come across as arrogant and unwilling to spend enough time with their client. The report found a need for guidance for the legal profession about good practice, such as producing easy to read materials about their services.

A patient's perspective: John's story

9.74 *We interviewed John, a patient in a medium secure unit who had been transferred from prison to hospital and had made two applications to the tribunal. He had a diagnosis of personality disorder. He had been successful in both applications. We asked about his experience of the tribunal. Here are some extracts from the interview which give a picture of what it felt like to go to the tribunal. John's tribunal was listed for an afternoon but eventually took several days, spread out over a period of weeks:*

How did it feel having the hearing spread out?

John It was terrible. I have a history of self-harm although I feel I have dealt with it. But had this happened the first time I am not sure I would be here today. I applied to the tribunal five years ago. I felt as though I was not ready. I was advised to withdraw and reapply and indeed I withdrew on two occasions. The real problem was not having reports from the Probation. My probation officer ... did not visit much so the reports were going on a lot of historical information. This was a big headache.

How was it having to withdraw?

John Not too bad because it was my decision. The solicitor said I did not have to but advised that if I did go ahead I would not get a successful outcome. I felt very anxious all the time and I kept wishing it would be over. It is trying to give a picture of your life to someone. It is very difficult to share some of these things. Having to meet the doctor the day before is difficult. It should be a longer period. You need time to reflect before and after. I could realise that some of the things I'd said weren't right. The first time the doctor came the day before the hearing. The last one was supposed to come a few days before but there had been a double booking. I had been expecting him the day before. I went to see my solicitor but then I got a message saying that I should be there and I didn't know about it. The medical man was also a bit irate and upset with the staff because of the double booking. I feel this amplifies your anxiety when it is too close. There should be a period to allow you to calm down and get prepared. As it was only half a day it left not very much time, so the hearing went over so many days and I felt very stressed. I was very fearful. But the judge engaged well and made me feel a bit more comfortable ... I felt they could empathise and see the problem and I was grateful for that. I had expected it to be more like a court.

What about your solicitor?

John I had the same solicitor throughout. He had dealt with the criminal case when I was transferred. He had spent a considerable amount of time going through my case and he knew the Panel and could tell me about them. This put me at my ease and the Panel explained procedures and what they would do. They asked if I wanted time out when I got a bit upset trying to explain something from my past. I felt that was helpful. The solicitor explained the law and visited often. I would have found it much harder if I didn't know as well but he knew my case in and out and he could discuss delicate issues. He gave me a good insight into what was going to happen and I had a good rapport.

I felt supported by the Panel too. Although I was questioned about a lot of things it wasn't as intrusive as I had thought. We had expected it to take one day but in fact it took a lot longer because there were several hurdles. The Panel listened to me intently ... They asked a lot of the questions I would have asked and that put me at ease but I did find it very stressful.

At the end of the day's hearing when it was all over I'd feel very anxious and unsettled, but I spoke to my solicitor and staff and the care co-ordinator and they reassured me. The Panel also reassured me in a way that wasn't demeaning. It was strange as being addressed as Mr X. So I asked them to call me John. I found that more relaxing ... The tribunal was trying to deal with me and humanised the situation and I was very impressed. It is good to have a solicitor who could help you but if you don't put your cards on the table and you are not honest you can get embroiled in things. It is important your solicitor is onboard. If you have a solicitor who is a stranger, it can go against you. If the solicitor doesn't know you well, how will the tribunal get the message. You need to feel you can trust the tribunal. If you word something right things may go your way, but if you withhold information things can go wrong.

What advice would you give someone starting off a career as a solicitor in this area?

John To listen. You have to be a good listener. You have to give the person the chance to start a paragraph, when they pause don't jump in. May be you can prompt them but don't put words in to their mouths. With all the reports the tribunal had highlighted them and they were very comprehensive. You have to be patient and listen to the tribunal and not make decisions straight away. It is no good going in angry. You will lose. That also goes for the solicitor too. ... I was annoyed by some bits of the report and I scribbled a note to give to my solicitor but I didn't even get the chance because they picked it up even then. I was very grateful for that and I was pleasantly surprised. I got a lot of support. I was commended for being open, honest and transparent. My solicitor said that that would help. If you want help don't hold back, put your cards on the table. At the end all the anger and emotion had gone and I felt like I had run a marathon. It is important to go in prepared. If I had not spent time going over everything, it might not have ended as well.

Was it a painful process?

John Yes, very. Having to sit still and listen to a report being read out is embarrassing and off-putting. It makes you feel very small and also is very personal. After the report was read out knowing it is being discussed you have to sit and listen and it is frustrating. You want to ask questions. I couldn't have done it myself. I know I can write things down and get my point across, but then the pressure is on and it is so great you can't think straight and you are more involved in the emotion than the facts ... The effect on me was that I lost sleep, I was very anxious on the day. Talking to my solicitor helped. I was aware of what was going to happen. I did a good job. It would have been better in one go but it turned out okay. Not being rushed on the tribunal is important. It is good if they can say to you 'Can you explain....' Rather than 'Tell us....'. it may be feel as though I was in capable hands. They didn't use over-bearing body language and there was eye contact. I don't think there was a single time when I felt patronised. I think if I had lost the tribunal I would still have said they were professional because they were honest.

What if your solicitor had known you less?

John I think from my personal demeanour I would have been more anxious; I would have been talking over people. As it was I was able to sit calmly, digest things; it made a big difference. I was able to address things properly and not start swearing. The solicitor told me 'don't get stressed, listen to what people say, pass me a note if you need and don't be impatient'. That advice was beneficial. If you know what you want that is not enough. You need to give the whole picture. I think dress is important.

I felt I should go in as I dress normally with T-shirt, slacks and be relaxed but then I decided to put on a long sleeved shirt and black trousers to show a sense of respect. I didn't want to look as though I was just turning up. Every day I was in the same sort of dress with shiny shoes. The solicitor should talk to clients about it. If you go in with a hoodie then that just gives the wrong message. The tribunal are going to say, is he here because he wants to get out or does he really want to change? I am not the same person I was 30 years ago. I have done something about it and I wanted to be recognised and I felt that the staff and tribunal have done that and shown some respect.

CHAPTER 10

Funding

continued

Introduction

10.1 This chapter deals with the funding of mental health cases. It draws on the *LAG Legal Aid Handbook* and we express our thanks to Vicky Ling and Simon Pugh for allowing use of the material. We are also grateful to Tam Gill for allowing us to use some of her material.

10.2 This chapter takes account of the provisions of the 2014 contract and the Legal Aid Agency's guidance, Contract Management – Mental Health Guidance, April 2014 v2.1.

10.3 The *LAG Legal Aid Handbook*[1] provides a detailed guide to the civil and criminal legal aid provisions. This chapter aims to summarise the key provisions as they apply to tribunal work. It does not provide a full guide to the provisions which relate to Legal Help generally, for which readers are referred to the *LAG Legal Aid Handbook*, and to www.legalaidhandbook.com, which provides regular updates.

10.4 For information about legal aid funding for mental capacity and Court of Protection work, readers are referred to LAG's *Court of Protection Handbook*[2] and to www.courtofprotectionhandbook.com which is regularly updated.

10.5 Practitioners will need to be familiar the following documentation, which is referred to in this chapter:

- Legal Aid, Sentencing and Punishment of Offenders Act 2012 Schedule 1
- Civil Legal Aid (Financial Resources and Payment for Services) Regulations 2013
- Civil Legal Aid (Merits Criteria) Regulations 2013
- 2014 Standard Civil Contract (with particular reference to the Mental Health Specification)
- Lord Chancellor's Guidance under section 4 of the Legal Aid, Sentencing and Punishment of Offenders Act 2012
- Contract Management – Mental Health Guidance April 2014
- Costs Assessment Guidance 2013
- Escape Cases Electronic Handbook July 2014.

Links to all these can be found at www.legalaidhandbook.com.

1 V Ling and S Pugh (eds) *LAG legal aid handbook 2013/14*, LAG (new edition due 2015).

2 A Ruck Keene, K Edwards, A Eldergill and S Miles, *Court of Protection Handbook*, LAG 2014.

The statutory background

10.6 Civil legal aid is regulated by the Legal Aid, Sentencing and Punishment of Offenders Act 2012 (LASPO). Civil legal aid, or as it is termed under the Act, 'civil legal services', is defined by LASPO as only that which is included in Schedule 1 of the Act. In contrast to the Access to Justice Act 1999, which provided that work was in scope unless specifically excluded by the Act, LASPO says that only work explicitly included in Schedule 1 is in scope.

10.7 LASPO s8 defines civil legal aid. It includes:

- providing advice as to how the law applies in particular circumstances;
- providing advice and assistance in relation to legal proceedings;
- providing advice and assistance in relation to the prevention settlement or resolution of legal disputes;
- providing advice and assistance in relation to the enforcement of decisions in legal proceedings or other decisions by which disputes are resolved.

10.8 Advice and assistance includes both representation and mediation and other dispute resolution.

10.9 LASPO s9 provides that only areas of law expressly listed in Schedule 1 are in scope and can be funded under legal aid. If work is not listed in Schedule 1, it will not be covered by legal aid and providers will not be paid for doing it.

10.10 LASPO s10 makes provision for what are known as 'exceptional cases'. Where cases not covered by the scope rules in Schedule 1 but certain conditions are satisfied, an application may be made to the Director to fund the case even though it is otherwise out of scope. Note that these cases should not be confused with Legal Help or CLR cases where costs exceed three times the fixed fee. Such cases were previously known as exceptional cases but are now called escape fee cases.

10.11 LASPO ss11 and 21 provide that legal aid will only be awarded if merits and financial criteria respectively are satisfied. Sections 25 and 26 create the statutory charge and give costs protection and section 27 enables the establishment of the mandatory telephone gateway. It is under these sections that the relevant regulations are made.

10.12 The Government sought by statutory instrument to impose an additional residence test. This was struck down as unlawful in *R (Public Law Project) v Secretary of State for Justice and Children's*

Commissioner.[3] This decision is subject to appeal at the time of writing. The proposed test would have affected some cases before the tribunal for example those subject to guardianship.

10.13 Schedule 1 to LASPO provides that the following areas of law are 'in scope':

- civil legal services in relation to matters arising under the Mental Health Act 1983;[4]
- civil legal services in relation to matters arising under the Mental Capacity Act 2005 (with exceptions, see paras 8.69–8.70 below);[5] and
- civil legal services provided in relation to the inherent jurisdiction of the High Court in relation to children and vulnerable adults.[6]

10.14 Regulations set out the detail of the scheme. Key Regulations are:

- Civil Legal Aid (Procedure) Regulations 2012
- Civil Legal Aid (Merits Criteria) Regulations 2013
- Civil Legal Aid (Financial Resources and Payment for Services) Regulations 2013
- Civil Legal Aid (Costs) Regulations 2013
- Civil Legal Aid (Remuneration) Regulations 2013
- Civil Legal Aid (Statutory Charge) Regulations 2013.

10.15 Regulations deal with the terms on which funding can be granted. They set out the detail of the various means and merits tests to be applied, how costs are dealt with through the statutory charge and cost protection, and not least, with the rate the practitioner is paid for doing the work.

10.16 The Lord Chancellor's Guidance[7] and the Procedure Regulations define the various levels of funding, set out who can apply the form of the application, together with appeal procedures against refusal.

The contract

10.17 The Standard Civil Contracts 2014 governs the relationship between the Legal Aid Agency (LAA) and individual mental health providers. The contract sets out the duties and responsibilities of providers,

3 [2014] EWHC 2365 (Admin).
4 LASPO Sch1 Part 1 para 5(1)(a).
5 LASPO Sch 1Part 1 para 5(1)(c).
6 LASPO Sch1 Part 1 para 9 (1).
7 https://www.gov.uk/funding-and-costs-assessment-for-civil-and-crime-matters.

together with any powers delegated. They also govern some of the detail of the operation of individual cases building on what is in the Regulations. Practitioners without a contract are not permitted to carry out legal aid work.

10.18 A contract consists of three main sections:

- **The standard terms** govern the relationship between the organisation and the LAA and Lord Chancellor and the obligations of the organisation.
- **The schedule** sets out the types of work the firm is permitted to do, and in the case of Legal Help and Controlled Legal Representation (CLR) the maximum numbers of matters the firm is allowed to start per year. It will also specify any additional requirements such as presence requirements. Breach of any provision of the schedule is a breach of contract subject to sanction.
- **The specification** deals with how you should conduct individual cases. The Mental Health Specification is at chapter 7 of the contract.

10.19 Other documents which are referred to in the contract, and which practitioners should follow or take account of (though not technically part of the contract) include:

- Specialist Quality Mark (or Lexcel if applicable);
- Equality and Diversity Guidance;
- Category Definitions 2014; and
- Independent Peer Review Process.

All of these documents are available on the LAA website now at www.gov.uk/government/organisations/legal-aid-agency.

10.20 The peer reviewer's guide contains useful guidance on the conduct of work and is considered in chapter 8, 'Becoming a tribunal representative'. The guide is available on the Legal Aid Agency website.

Definition of mental health work

10.21 The mental health category of law is defined by the category definitions:

- Cases under LASPO Sch 1 Pt 1 para 5 – services in relation to:
  - Mental Health Act 1983;
  - Mental Capacity Act 2005;
  - Repatriation of Prisoners Act 1984 Sch para 5(2);
  - cases involving the inherent jurisdiction of the High Court.

10.22 Mental health work is governed by the general provisions of the 2014 Standard Civil Contract, and by section 7 of the Specification. This sets out the requirements for mental health providers and includes the provision that all advocates before the mental health tribunal (MHT) other than self-employed counsel must be members of the Law Society's Mental Health Accreditation Scheme.[8] It appears that this is sometimes misunderstood to mean that it is acceptable for an advocate who is not accredited to conduct a tribunal, as long as the hearing fee is not then claimed. This is incorrect. The Specification requires the provider to ensure all advocates are accredited. Whether a provider does or does not claim for a particular hearing conducted by a non-accredited advocate is irrelevant. The provider will be in breach of contract in any event.

Practicalities

Who can do the work?

10.23 The 2010 Standard Civil Contract divided work in the mental health category into two types – standard work, and work in high security hospitals.[9] This division has been abolished and mental health contracts are let by procurement area, with each procurement area being based on a strategic health authority area.

10.24 To do any mental health work at all, providers must have a schedule authorisation for at least one procurement area.

Matter starts

10.25 Providers are allocated a certain number of matter starts at the start of the contract. Providers may use matter starts in any geographical area but must use 70 per cent of matter starts on clients physically located in the procurement area where they are situated.[10]

8 Standard Civil Contract 2014 Mental Health Specification para 7(6)b.

9 Broadmoor, Rampton, Ashworth – Standard Civil Contract 2010 Specification para 9.1.

10 Standard Civil Contract 2014 Mental Health Specification para 7.7.

Levels of funding

10.26 The following levels of funding apply to mental health work:[11]

- *Legal Help* – advice and assistance, but excluding representation before the tribunal;
- *Help at Court* – funding for representation for victims under the Domestic Violence, Crime and Victims Act 2004;
- *Controlled Legal Representation* (CLR) – representation before the tribunal;
- *Legal Representation* (certificate) – appeals to the Upper Tribunal and representation in the higher courts, including the Court of Protection.

Legal Help, Help at Court and CLR granted on the same case all form part of the same matter.

Standard fees

10.27 Mental health work is covered by standard fees (SF) for almost all controlled (ie non-certificate) work – the sole exception being Help at Court for Victims, considered at para 8.44.[12]

10.28 There are four fees:[13]

- the non-MHT fee, for all work that does not go to the tribunal;
- MHT fee level 1 – initial advice;
- MHT fee level 2 – negotiation and preparation once an application to the MHT has been made; and
- MHT fee level 3 – representation before the MHT, and follow-up work.

10.29 A fee may be claimed for each stage through which the matter passes. Any disbursements incurred are in addition to the fee, but where counsel is instructed, their fees are included in the graduated fee[14] and it is for the firm to negotiate with counsel which part of the fee it will pay to counsel and which part it will keep. In cases of unusual complexity firms can apply to the LAA for prior authority to pay a rate higher than that set for solicitors. This can not be retrospective.[15] Further fees are payable for adjourned/postponed/cancelled

11 Standard Civil Contract 2014 Mental Health Specification para 7.3.

12 Standard Civil Contract 2014 Mental Health Specification para 7.85.

13 Standard Civil Contract 2014 Mental Health Specification para 7.47.

14 Standard Civil Contract 2014 Mental Health Specification para 7.42.

15 Standard Civil Contract 2014 Mental Health Specification para 7.43.

hearings[16] and for travel to any hospital that the LAA has designated on their website as a remote hospital[17] (at the time of writing, none had been designated for the 2014 contract).

Escape Fees

10.30 Where the amount of a claim calculated at the relevant hourly rates (including counsel's time calculated on the same basis and including travel time but not disbursements[18]) is greater than three times the total fees payable, then the provider may apply for the case to be treated as an 'escape fee case' (formerly described as an exceptional claim). See paragraphs 7.79- 7.83 of the Specification.

Managing standard fees

10.31 The payment levels under the standard fee regime are low and it is exceptionally difficult to make this area of work profitable. For this reason interpretation of parts of the Specification – such as what is a new legal issue? – can be very important to the practitioner. It is essential to record very clearly on the file reasons why the practitioner takes a particular interpretation of the contract provisions in any given case. The LAA's own recent Contract Management Guidance suggests that if the practitioner does not find the answer in their guidance, they should contact the LAA's Mental Health Unit (MHU) for guidance, and this is sound advice. If the practitioner contacts the MHU for guidance then it is of course vital to make a clear record of who they speak to and exactly what is said. Ideally the guidance should be confirmed in an email, which can be copied and placed on the file.

Granting Legal Help

10.32 Legal Help in the mental health category may be granted if both the merits test and means test are satisfied.

10.33 Where the client's condition is such that he or she will not sign the application form, and there is no other person who could sign it on their behalf, a supervisor in the organisation can sign it on their

16 Standard Civil Contract 2014 Mental Health Specification para 7.70.

17 Standard Civil Contract 2014 Mental Health Specification para 7.74.

18 Standard Civil Contract 2014 Mental Health Specification para 7.79.

behalf.[19] The reasons should be noted on file. Note that the contract anticipates that this will be exceptional, and this is highlighted in the Contract Management Guidance. This does not include the situation where a client simply refuses to see the adviser and therefore the forms are not completed at all. In this case the adviser cannot make a claim (see Contract Management Guidance, section 2).

Means

10.34 The client must satisfy the means test to be eligible for Legal Help. This will require an assessment of both the client's income and capital. The practitioner will need to apply the Civil Legal Aid (Financial Resources and Payment for Services) Regulations 2013, which are amended periodically. The up to date limits can be found on the LAA's website where there is an eligibility calculator.

10.35 Unsurprisingly, detained clients often find it difficult to provide evidence of means. The Standard Civil Contract recognises that this will sometimes be impracticable and provides:

> 3.24 You may assess the prospective Client's means without the accompanying evidence where:
> (a) it is not practicable to obtain it before commencing the Controlled Work;
> (b) pre signature telephone advice is given; or
> (c) exceptionally, the personal circumstances of the Client (such as the Client's age, mental disability or homelessness) make it impracticable for the evidence to be supplied at any point in the case.
>
> 3.25 Unless paragraph 3.24(c) applies, you must require the Client to provide the evidence as soon as practicable. If satisfactory evidence of the Client's financial eligibility is not subsequently supplied, or if the evidence shows that the Client is not financially eligible, you may claim the work carried out as a Matter Start provided that:
> (a) you have acted reasonably in undertaking work before receiving satisfactory evidence of the Client's means;
> (b) you have acted reasonably in initially assessing financial eligibility on the information available;
> (c) you do not claim:
> (i) any disbursement; or
> (ii) if the Matter is remunerated at Hourly Rates, profit costs beyond those incurred in the period before it is practicable to obtain satisfactory evidence of the Client's means; and/or
> (d) you do not report time incurred beyond the period it was practicable to obtain satisfactory evidence of the Client's means.

19 Standard Civil Contract 2014 Mental Health Specification para 7.40.

10.36 If you are not able to obtain evidence of eligibility, then you must still carry out an assessment of means on the basis of the information that you have obtained from the client, and you must continue to seek evidence as best you can.[20] The LAA will expect to see 'a reasonable attempt at gaining evidence'.[21] This includes evidence of both income and capital.

10.37 However, where the client is a patient whose case is the subject of proceedings or contemplated proceedings before the MHT, no means test is required[22] – the client is automatically eligible.

10.38 The question as to whether the case is 'subject to proceedings or potential proceedings before the MHT' is therefore extremely important. The Contract Management Guidance issued by the LAA sets out conditions (at section 2) which include the following:

a) The client must be eligible to apply to the MHT (or the supplier could not have reasonably discovered either before or during the first attendance that the client was ineligible to apply); and
b) The advice given on the MHT application must satisfy the Sufficient Benefit test (ie, a reasonable private paying client of moderate means would pay for the legal advice and assistance); and
c) There must be a *reasonable expectation* on behalf of both the client *and* provider to pursue an application to the MHT[23] (notwithstanding where a client subsequently changes their mind and decide not to apply); and
d) The circumstances in which the means assessment was disapplied and reasons for doing so must be fully evidenced on file. This will include circumstances whereby having been specifically requested to attend upon the client to pursue an application to the MHT, the provider advises the client not to proceed; and
e) Where the client has capacity to do so, they must have instructed the provider to give Tribunal advice (in addition to instructing the substantive non-tribunal advice). Regardless of the client's capacity, the Sufficient Benefit test will always apply.

20 Contract Management Guidance April 2014 section 4, quoting Point of Principle 55.

21 Contract Management Guidance April 2014 section 2.

22 Civil Legal Aid (Financial Resources and Payment for Services) Regulations 2013 reg 5(1)(f); Standard Civil Contract 2014 Mental Health Specification para 7.15.

23 For example, decision to apply to MHT made at initial attendance or client says to provider 'I want a tribunal', 'I want to get out of hospital' or 'I am thinking about a tribunal application but want to discuss it' and the provider has a reasonable expectation at that time that such an application will be discussed and pursued. However, if a client says to provider 'I want to get out of hospital but I don't want a tribunal', the client's means must be assessed.

Merits

10.39 The merits test for granting legal help is often referred to as the 'Sufficient Benefit test.' It is set out in the Civil Legal Aid (Merits Criteria) Regulations.[24] Help may only be provided

> ... where there is likely to be sufficient benefit to the client, having regard to the circumstances of the matter, including the circumstances of the client, to justify the costs of the provision of legal help.

Granting CLR

10.40 Controlled Legal Representation (CLR) is granted by the practitioner's signature on a form already signed by the client (subject to the same provisions set out above for Legal Help where the client is unable or refuses to sign).[25] Since a grant of CLR is a requirement in any case that goes to the MHT (subject to merit, below), and therefore very much standard practice in most cases, it can become easy to overlook the necessity actually to sign the form and keep it on file. Practitioners may wish to consider incorporating a reminder into your file opening checklist.

Means

10.41 CLR for representation before the MHT is available without the need for a means test. This is the case whether the client is the patient or a nearest relative who has applied to the tribunal following a barring order under section 25 of the MHA 1983 (see para 2.236 and table 4 at para 5.11).[26]

Merits

10.42 The merits test applicable to CLR in the mental health category is set at a low threshold, given that the client's liberty is at stake. The test is that the Director (in practice, the practitioner) must be satisfied that it is reasonable in the particular circumstances of the case for CLR to be granted.[27]

24 Civil Legal Aid (Merits Criteria) Regulations 2013 reg 32(b).
25 Standard Civil Contract 2014 Mental Health Specification para 7.40.
26 Civil Legal Aid (Financial Resources and Payment for Services) Regulations 2013 reg 5(1)(j) and Standard Civil Contract 2014 Mental Health Specification para 7.34.
27 Civil Legal Aid (Merits Criteria) Regulations 2013 reg 51.

Conduct of the case

Non-MHT cases

10.43 All cases that do not concern an application or potential application to the MHT are deemed to be non-MHT cases and attract the non-MHT fee.[28] Only Legal Help is available.

10.44 Where you are acting for a victim, Help at Court for representation is available and claimed at hourly rates on top of the standard fee.[29] However, there will only be limited circumstances in which a victim will be given permission to attend tribunal proceedings and will only be entitled to representation is he or she is made a party.[30] See the Tribunal's Practice Guidance.[31] It is more likely that a victim would receive advice through Legal Help, subject to meeting the merits and means test.

10.45 Initial advice in a Mental Capacity Act case is a non-MHT matter,[32] including making an application for a certificate for representation before the Court of Protection.

MHT cases

10.46 MHT cases divide into three fee stages.

10.47 Stage 1 is funded by Legal Help and covers initial advice to the client, including a visit to the client and follow-up work up to, and including, making an application to the MHT.[33]

10.48 Once it becomes clear that the case is to be considered by the MHT, the provider should grant CLR[34] and continue work at stage 2, but can only go to stage 2 having passed through (and done at least 30 minutes of work at) stage 1.[35] This stage covers all work up to, but not including, the substantive hearing,[36] including preparation of the case generally and for the hearing, negotiation with third parties, attendance at managers' reviews and other meetings such as section

28 Standard Civil Contract 2014 Mental Health Specification para 7.56.
29 Standard Civil Contract 2014 Mental Health Specification para 7.85.
30 Tribunal Procedure Rules 11(1).
31 Practice Guidance in proceedings handling representations from victims in the First-tier Tribunal (Mental Health) available at www.judiciary.gov.uk
32 Standard Civil Contract 2014 Mental Health Specification para 7.29.
33 Standard Civil Contract 2014 Mental Health Specification para 7.63.
34 Standard Civil Contract 2014 Mental Health Specification para 7.36.
35 Standard Civil Contract 2014 Mental Health Specification para 7.66.
36 Standard Civil Contract 2014 Mental Health Specification para 7.65.

117 or Care Programme Approach (CPA) meetings[37] where appropriate,[38] as well as taking instructions from the client and instructing experts. The Contract requires the practitioner to consider at each stage whether it is necessary and/or appropriate to attend a Hospital Managers' Review, section 117 meeting or CPA meeting. The factors to be considered include the nature of the issues to be discussed at the meeting and whether legal advice and/or representations will be required.[39] It is suggested that this test is relatively easily satisfied and practitioners should also bear in mind the peer review guidance.[40] It is suggested there will be very few hospital managers' hearings where this test is not satisfied. It is however essential to document fully on the file *why* it is that this test is satisfied on the facts of a given case.

10.49 Stage 3 covers representation at the tribunal hearing,[41] including any adjourned/cancelled/postponed hearings (for which an additional fee is or may be payable[42]). Stage 3 also includes work done in applying to the tribunal for a review of its decision under the Tribunals, Courts and Enforcement Act 2007 s9, or applying for permission to appeal under section 11.[43]

10.50 Where the tribunal sets aside its decision, this forms part of stage 3 but the practitioner may claim an additional adjourned hearing fee.[44] However, where an appeal or review goes to the upper tribunal, they will need to apply for a certificate for representation at that stage.[45]

Separate matters

10.51 Each time a client becomes eligible to make an application to the tribunal they enter a 'period of eligibility'.[46] All work done for a client within a period of eligibility, on both MHT and non-MHT matters,

37 Standard Civil Contract 2014 Mental Health Specification para 7.67.
38 Standard Civil Contract 2014 Mental Health Specification para 7.68.
39 Standard Civil Contract 2014 Mental Health Specification para 7.68.
40 Improving Your Quality: Peer Review Guidance 2011 (Mental Health) section 13.
41 Standard Civil Contract 2014 Mental Health Specification para 7.69.
42 Standard Civil Contract 2014 Mental Health Specification para 7.70.
43 Standard Civil Contract 2014 Mental Health Specification para 7.86.
44 Standard Civil Contract 2014 Mental Health Specification para 7.86.
45 Standard Civil Contract 2014 Mental Health Specification para 7.90.
46 Standard Civil Contract 2014 Mental Health Specification paras 7.23, 7.57.

forms one matter start.[47] However, where more than one set of MHT proceedings are running concurrently during a period of eligibility, you may claim a fee for each.

10.52 When advising an informal patient (ie not detained) on a non-MHT matter, and the patient is then sectioned, you can open a separate matter to apply to the tribunal, even if the non-MHT matter continues.[48]

10.53 When dealing with a detained client, you must start a new matter for each of the following events (where work on a legal issue is required), even if you have an existing ongoing matter:[49]

- the client has an entitlement to a further MHT due to passage of time;
- there is a change in section type;
- the client is discharged from section;
- the client withdraws from the MHT, and within the same period of eligibility applies again.

However, note that communicating the decision of the MHT, advising the client about the decision and after-care is the same matter as the MHT.[50]

10.54 It will therefore be seen that much will turn on establishing that a new legal issue has arisen. The LAA's Contract Management Guidance suggests that a new legal issue 'should be considered to be a change or modification to the legal arguments used to advance the client's case'.[51] An example is given where a patient applies to the tribunal, withdraws and the 'a new legal issue emerges which triggers a further application to the MHT (for example a change in their presentation causes an MHT application to be a reasonable course of action once more)'. However, the LAA will not always treat a change in section type as a new legal issue. For example, patient B is detained under section 2. She applies to the tribunal. Before her hearing she is made subject to section 3. The hearing takes place within the section 3 period of eligibility and with the section 3 criteria. The LAA will treat this as the same legal issue (patient B is challenging her detention) and will expect it to be dealt with under the same matter start. But a separate matter start would be available for patient B if she makes an application against her detention under section 3. The

47 Standard Civil Contract 2014 Mental Health Specification para 7.20.
48 Standard Civil Contract 2014 Mental Health Specification para 7.21.
49 Standard Civil Contract 2010 Mental Health Specification para 7.23.
50 Standard Civil Contract 2014 Mental Health Specification para 7.24.
51 Contract Management Guidance section 3.

overall aim of these provisions is to prevent the LAA having to pay two sets of fees for the same application.

10.55 The Guidance recommends that providers seek the advice of the MHU in cases where the patient's status changes from section 3 to a CTO during the progress of the application. As set out above, any advice given should be carefully recorded together with the name of the person you spoken to.

10.56 When a patient who does not have a tribunal application pending is placed on a CTO, a new period of eligibility begins and creates a new legal issue. If the client is recalled, the guidance advises practitioners to refer to the comments about what may constitute a separate legal issue, as described above.[52]

10.57 Where a Mental Capacity Act matter is open, and then the client is sectioned or otherwise requires MHT advice, a separate MHT matter should be opened.[53]

'Rolling up'

10.58 Where the responsible clinician (RC) renews the patient's detention under section 20, and a managers' review is convened, work for this hearing 'rolls back' into the work for the pervious period of eligibility. For example, patient A is detained under section 3 and applies to the tribunal. He is represented and not discharged. His section is then renewed by his RC before it expires and the managers convene a review. Work carried out in connection with that review should be claimed as part of the work carried out for the first six months, because the RC's decision is taken during that first period.[54]

10.59 The Contract Management Guidance provides that a patient who is conditionally discharged is not a detained patient and the usual rolling up procedures do not apply. If a patient applies to the tribunal then this will be a new MHT matter. If the client is recalled and a referral is made to the tribunal then this will constitutes a new period of eligibility (as the client is now detained) and a new MHT matter start can be opened. See Specification para 9.60.

10.60 Automatic references to the tribunal are treated as separate matter starts.

52 Contract Management Guidance section 7.

53 Standard Civil Contract 2014 Mental Health Specification para 7.30.

54 Contract Management Guidance section 5.

10.61 If a nearest relative (NR) applies to the tribunal following a barring order under section 25, the NR is entitled to non-means tested CLR. Any advice given to the NR under legal help would form one matter with the representation at the tribunal and would be 'rolled up' with the fixed fee for the tribunal. The Contract Management Guidance states:[55]

> In some circumstances, a patient may wish to be represented at the Nearest Relative's MHT hearing. Funding for legal representation is available in these situations and is paid in accordance with the appropriate Mental Health Proceedings fees as a further separate matter (distinct from both the Nearest Relative's application and the patient's potential further application).
>
> Before undertaking such representation, due consideration should be given as to whether it is reasonably required in these cases. Specific attention should be paid to paragraph 9.35 of the Mental Health Specification and, further, the Sufficient Benefit Test of the Civil Legal Services (Merits) Regulations 2012. Considerations influencing the provider's decision to open a new matter will include the following:
>
> 1. Whether the patient is presenting a new and significant legal argument to the MHT which would not otherwise be advanced;
> 2. Whether there is a conflict of interest between the patient and Nearest Relative; and
> 3. Whether there are any other parties suitable and willing to provide assistance on behalf of the patient (such as an Advocate) should the need for specialist legal advice not be necessary.
>
> Where the client is the Nearest Relative who receives advice under legal help regarding their responsibilities and subsequently applies for a tribunal in their own right, then this should be treated as one matter with the Non-tribunal fee rolling up into the Mental Health Proceedings fees. On the other hand, where a provider is advising the patient and also a potential Nearest Relative (e.g. on delegation or displacement proceedings against the existing Nearest Relative), they may open two separate NMS for the two different clients.

10.62 It will therefore be seen that a provider can advise both the patient and nearest relative; however as set out in chapter 8 you must be alert to the potential for conflict that exists even if the NR is supportive to the patient. See the case study at para 7.32.

55 Contract Management Guidance section 6.

Disbursements

10.63 Practitioners can make a claim for payment on account of disbursements during the life of a case, but only where the matter has been open for at least six months and, if there has been a previous application for payment on account, at least six months have elapsed since that payment was made.[56]

10.64 There is no provision for obtaining prior authority for experts' fees. The maximum hourly rates payable are set out in the Remuneration Regulations.

Use of counsel

10.65 Practitioners may instruct counsel to represent clients before the tribunal. Where you instruct counsel, you will still only be entitled to the level 3 fee, and it is a matter for the practitioner to negotiate how much of that fee to pay to counsel. Counsel is not a disbursement.[57]

10.66 In unusually complex cases, practitioners can apply to the LAA to pay counsel at an hourly rate above the standard hourly rates in the contract.[58] The LAA will grant prior authority, specifying the hourly rate and the maximum costs limit if the case poses unusually complex evidential problems, or novel or difficult points of law. The LAA consider it highly unlikely that such issues will arise at MHT level.

Licensed work

10.67 An application for a determination in respect of licensed work to cover an appeal or review to the Upper Tribunal should not be made unless the MHT has determined whether to review its decision under TCEA 2007 s7.[59]

10.68 If a certificate is then granted then work reasonably carried out in applying to the MHT to review its decision (drafting grounds, submitting forms) will be deemed to be within the scope of the certificate even if it was carried out before the certificate was granted and

56 Standard Civil Contract 2014 Mental Health Specification para 7.49.
57 Standard Civil Contract 2014 Mental Health Specification para 7.41.
58 Standard Civil Contract 2014 Mental Health Specification para 7.42.
59 Standard Civil Contract 2014 Mental Health Specification para 7.90.

will be paid at the licensed rate work. The exception to this is when that work is already being claimed as part of the escape fee.

10.69 Licensed work in mental health cases includes applications for judicial review and representation in the county court on applications to displace the NR, as well as applications to the Court of Protection where the merits test for certificates is:[60]

- the standard criteria which apply to all civil legal aid work;[61]
- the Court of Protection has ordered, or is likely to order, an oral hearing; and
- it is necessary for the individual to be provided with full representation in the proceedings.

10.70 Representation is only generally available where the proceedings concern:

- right to life;
- liberty or physical safety;
- medical treatment;
- capacity to marry, enter a civil partnership or enter sexual relationships;
- right to family life.

10.71 Other matters are out of the scope of representation, and an exceptional funding application will be required.

Entitlement to further advice

10.72 The Legal Help form requires the client to certify that they have not previously received advice on the same matter, and where they have done so within the last six months, it requires the provider to explain why they took on the case. This is because there are specific rules in the contract to prevent the legal aid fund paying out twice for the same matter, and therefore providers must be able to demonstrate that the case meets one of the exceptions allowing you to do so.

10.73 In the case of controlled work a second matter start can only be opened on the same case as the original provider where:

a) at least six months has elapsed since there was a claim on the first matter; or

60 Civil Legal Aid (Merits Criteria) Regulations 2013 reg 52.

61 See the Civil Legal Aid (Merits Criteria) Regulations 2013 reg 39.

b) there has been a material development or change in the client's instructions and at least three months has elapsed since there was a claim on the first matter.[62]

10.74 Where you are relying on paragraphs 3.40 or 3.37(b) (material development or change) of the Specification, you should note that:

- Giving instructions following a failure to give instructions is not a change in instructions.
- A decision or response from any third party to any correspondence, application, appeal, review or other request made in the course of the original matter is not a material development.
- A change in the law that was anticipated in the original matter is not a material development.[63]

However, you can instead re-open the original matter and make a further claim (see chapter 4) in some circumstances.

10.75 A second provider, looking to take over a case, can only do so where:

a) there has been a material change in relevant circumstances since the initial decision to grant Legal Help; or
b) the client has reasonable cause to be dissatisfied with the first provider; or
c) the client has moved a distance away from the first provider and effective communication is not practicable; or
d) the first provider is not making a claim for the work and confirms that in writing.[64]

The contract requires you to make reasonable enquiries of the client as to whether there was previous advice.[65] Where there is a transfer, you must establish that there is good reason, and record that reason on the file.[66]

10.76 However, it is not sufficient for you to take the client's word as to the reasons for transfer. You must seek the client's authority to obtain the file from the previous provider, and must then request the file from the previous provider. You cannot start work on the case until you receive the file. Where the client refuses to give you authority, or where you obtain the file and discover that there is in fact no good reason for transfer, you may not make a claim for the case. The

62 Standard Civil Contract 2014 Specification para 3.36.
63 Standard Civil Contract 2014 Specification para 3.37(c).
64 Civil Legal Aid (Procedure) Regulations 2012 reg 23(4).
65 Standard Civil Contract 2014 Specification para 3.40.
66 Standard Civil Contract 2014 Specification para 3.42.

sole exception is where there is urgent work that is absolutely necessary to protect the client's position or meet a court deadline, in which case you can do the urgent work and claim for it, even if it transpires there was no good reason.[67]

Prison work for mentally disordered offenders

10.77 The LAA's Contract Management Guidance states:

> ... advice and assistance regarding sections 47 and 48 of the Mental Health Act (ie transfer of sentenced and unsentenced prisoners to hospital) can be carried out by providers with mental health schedule authorisation. This includes negotiation with and proceedings against prison authorities that may be required to secure the client's detention under these sections. However, care should be taken that the advice does not extend to prison law matters which should only be undertaken by crime providers, for example discussion of such matters before the Parole Board.[68]

67 Standard Civil Contract 2014 Specification para 3.43.

68 Contract Management Guidance section 10.

CHAPTER 11

Evidence gathering and preparation

continued

11.1 This chapter is about the steps you need to take to prepare the case effectively from the beginning. Given the restraints of legal aid you will not able to follow every step in every case but the following is the way that a case should be prepared in an ideal world.

Preparing to interview your client

11.2 The person you will see has had their liberty taken away from them against their will and often without having committed any offence. Imagine yourself being taken to a ward, told not to leave and to take medication when you feel there is nothing wrong with you. Even if you accept you may be ill, to have your autonomy taken away is of huge significance and this fact is often lost in the process. Mental health professionals and tribunals need to remember the enormity of the depriving a person of their liberty. It is up to you to remind them of this fact.

11.3 The courts have commented on the important nature of the tribunals decision:[1]

> The issues before mental health review tribunals are probably the most important issues decided by any tribunals. The tribunals make decisions as to the compulsory detention and treatment, and thus the liberty, of the individual.

11.4 As well as considering the position your client is in, remember the nature of your role. Your value to your client is as a legal representative. Your tasks are to ensure that the detention is legal and to advise your client on their case in legal terms. To do this you need to know the law, keep up with the developments, and importantly ensure that your client understands your role. You are not a friend, mental health professional or pastor – you are there to follow instructions and advise. Patients often feel patronised by those around them. If you make your role clear, and give clear advice, you are enabling them to take decisions in their case. It is their instructions on which you are acting, not on what you, or anybody else, thinks is best for them.

1 *R(KB and others) v (1) Mental Health Review Tribunal, (2) Secretary of State for Health* [2002] EWHC 639 (Admin), Stanley Burnton J at para 32.

Taking instructions on the first visit

11.5 When first meeting your client and taking instructions it will help to structure the interview if you use a checklist. Given the lack of money available for representation you need to get as much relevant information as possible within a reasonable time. Most representatives have some kind of checklist when they first see a client to ensure that the relevant information has been taken and the necessary forms have been filled out. This should have basic personal details such as name, date of birth, the section and when it started. The contact details should also be taken so that it is easy for you to contact your client. Most wards have a patient's telephone number as well as ward numbers and some patients are allowed their mobile telephones with them. Find out the name and contact details of the responsible clinician (RC), care co-ordinator, primary nurse and nearest relative (NR) if any. All these people are essential in preparing the case.

11.6 This is the first chance you have to start preparing the arguments you will run in the future. The basic question for any tribunal which should be in your mind at this stage is: is the patient's detention proportionate to the risks?

11.7 It is important for your client to have a chance to tell you about the circumstances of admission in their words, how and why they had been brought to hospital, and if they have been admitted before. You will also need to ascertain how many admissions, the length of the admissions, and the time between admissions. It maybe that this information comes later after the reports have been received and this should be cross-checked through the notes or with the Mental Health Act Administrator (MHAA), especially if your client does not remember the details.

11.8 Questions to ask your client:

- What do they want from the tribunal?
- If discharged where would they go?
- Do they have, or need, a community mental health team (CMHT)?
- Would they take medication and comply with treatment recommendations and why would they do this?
- If they would not do this is their objection reasonable?
- Have they suffered from side-effects from a particular medication; if so, would they agree to try another medication?
- Is a community treatment order relevant?

11.9 An important part of a case for discharge may be showing the tribunal that care can be provided outside a hospital setting. Establishing this is often based on arguments on what has happened in the past.

11.10 Common questions to ask would be:

- What community care package they were offered and whether they attended appointments and took medication and for how long?
- If your client defaulted on medication or appointments how often and for how long?
- What were the reasons for this?
- If they did stop medication how long was it before they were said to be getting unwell?
- Did they take any illicit drugs, was a drug test done on admission and was it positive and for what?
- Have they any previous convictions or allegations of harm to themselves or others and do they accept these?
- If so, what were the facts?
- Was anyone else involved in their admission, for example, a family member, neighbour, housing officer, or the police?
- Have there been any problems on the ward, eg, arguments with staff, allegations of inappropriate behaviour, bullying, taking of drugs or drinking etc?

11.11 You should explain to your client your role and the tribunal's role. Establish the parameters at the beginning of your contact. It may be that you are happy to pursue complaints on their behalf or it may be that you will represent them at the tribunal and refer to different services for different parts of their case. You are their contact with legal services and so if they have other needs it is important that you are able to either meet these needs yourself or refer to someone who can. If it is a complaint, there may be an advocacy service. If there are immigration matters, benefit matters or family matters it may be that someone else in your firm is the expert. It is important to recognise your limitations but not to limit your client by doing so.

11.12 It is important to ascertain whether the patient has any children and, if so, whether they are dependent. This is to ensure that if a referral to a family/childcare solicitor is necessary, it can be done quickly. It may be that if the client does have children, being back with them is the most important goal. The family court follows a very clear line which is that the welfare of the child is paramount. Not complying with the treating team's recommendations can jeopardise the patient's future as a parent. This may mean that despite the person's own belief that they are not unwell or do not need medication, they may have to balance that against their desire to be with their children. It is important that they get advice on this quickly especially if the child is very young.

11.13 The most important issue is what the client actually wants. If it is to leave hospital, do they want to apply for a tribunal in the hope they will achieve this? Do they want a hospital managers hearing?

11.14 Often your initial advice will clarify to your client what they do want. At some time it will be necessary to advise on the law and their chances of success if they want to have a tribunal or a hospital managers hearing. Remember the pre-hearing examinations in all cases but section 2 need to be requested or they are ordered by the tribunal of its own initiative. If the patient wants one, or you advise them to have one, then you should make the request to the tribunal 14 days before the hearing.[2]

The limits of the confidential relationship between you and your client

11.15 As you are the legal representative you are bound by legal professional privilege. This means that what your client tells you is confidential and you cannot repeat it without instructions to do so. Generally a patient who has been in the system for some time is used to having their most personal details discussed in great detail in reports or at ward rounds and so may be less concerned about this than clients in other fields.

11.16 However, it is very important that you understand your professional obligations about confidentiality and disclosure. Difficult ethical and practical dilemmas can arise in this area of work, for example if your client discloses to you the intention to harm themselves or someone else. This is discussed in detail in chapter 9 at para 9.36.

Advising your client

Avenues to discharge

11.16 How patients can be discharged is dealt with in chapters 2 and 3. Briefly, in an unrestricted case the avenues of discharge are:

2 Tribunal Procedure (First-tier Tribunal) (Health, Education and Social Care Chamber) Rules 2008 SI No 2699 r34 see also rule 39 hearing in the patient's absence. See also the guidance of HHJ Sycamore, 11 March 2014.

- the patient's RC who must keep the appropriateness of compulsory powers under review,[3]
- the hospital managers,
- the nearest relative,
- the tribunal.

11.17 For restricted patients the avenues to discharge are much more limited. If they are transferred prisoners the Parole Board has the final say. If they are serving a determinate sentence and their early date release is met then they revert to being like an unrestricted patient and the avenues open up. If they are subject to a hospital order with restrictions imposed by a criminal court the MHT or the MHCS are the only avenues of discharge.

11.18 For details of applications and referrals to the tribunal and for details as to applications and referrals to the hospital managers, see chapter 1.

The nearest relative

11.19 The NR is relevant to all patients except restricted patients and those detained under sections 35, 36 and 38. The patient needs to know the rights and powers of the NR as this includes the power to discharge.

11.20 The NR is defined by section 26 of the Mental Health Act 1983 which sets out the hierarchy of relatives entitled to be NR in order of preference. Many mental health professionals and legal representatives assume that the person who is the NR is the person who has the most to do with the patient. This is not necessarily the case and the list in section 26 is definitive. Having the list either included on your checklist or a copy of the section with you may help you identify the correct person.[4] The legislation has been amended to include civil partners and same, or opposite, sex couples living together in a relationship.

11.21 You need to explain the NR powers to your client and take instructions on whether the NR would be helpful to the case and whether you are instructed to contact them. Whether the NR is supportive or not, if they are involved it is important that you know their view. However, the NR must also know that you are under a duty to pass

3 Code of Practice para 32.18; Code of Practice for Wales para 12.27; see also chapter 2 at paras 2.17, 2.29, 2.36, 2.62, 2.79 and 2.117.

4 David Hewitt, *The Nearest Relative Handbook*, 2nd edition, Jessica Kingsley Publishers 2009: Seven steps to identifying the nearest relative.

on all information to your client and you should tell them this at the beginning of any conversation.

11.22 There are potential risks in agreeing to represent both the patient and the nearest relative. This is discussed in more detail in chapter 9 at para 9.32.

11.23 If your client is on a section 2 and they may be assessed for a section 3 and there is a chance the NR would object, then you should contact the NR if instructed to do so and ensure they make themselves known to the relevant social services authority so that they will be consulted by the approved mental health professional (AMHP) before a section 3 application is made. Ascertaining the appropriate person to give these details to may take some time and so ensuring the NR's contact details are in the notes at the front of the file is a good short term measure if they will take a part in the case. Ensure that the MHAA has these details.[5]

11.24 If there is no current allocated care co-ordinator there will usually be a CMHT team manager whom you can contact. So often the applications for section 3 are completed without contacting the NR; this would be more open to challenge if all the details were clearly known and recorded on the patient's hospital files.

11.25 If the patient does not want the NR involved, they have a right to say so if they have capacity and, if they lack capacity, if it would infringe their rights to private life under Article 8 to do so.[6] If this is the case you need to make the hospital aware. Ensure you tell the RC, the ward, the MHAA, the local social services authority and the tribunal of your client's position. Follow it up with telephone calls where possible. You can ask the tribunal to enter it on its computer system so that it is clear, and ask for the panel hearing the case to be informed. It is relevant as the NR will be told of the section in the following situations:

i) The managers of the hospital have to inform the NR of the admission under section 2 and their power to order discharge.[7]
ii) The NR will be contacted by the AMPH when making an application under section 3.[8]

5 See also table 1: the role of the NR at para 2.231.
6 For a discussion as to the exceptions to this following *TW v Enfield LBC* [2014] EWCA Civ 362, see chapter 2.
7 MHA 1983 s11(3).
8 MHA 1983 s11(4).

iii) When a patient is detained the managers have a duty to inform the NR of the provisions under which the patient is detained and their rights to order discharge.[9]

iv) If a patient applies for a tribunal the practice direction requests the hospital in the statement of information about the patient includes the patients NR details and if the patient has made a request that the NR is not consulted and the patient's capacity to make this decision.[10]

v) The tribunal will tell the NR if they have their details provided by the hospital and they have not been notified that the patient does not want them contacted.[11]

The decision on whether it is practicable to consult involves a balancing exercise between the patient's rights to respect for privacy (Article 8) and the right to liberty (Article 5). See *TW v Enfield LBC*, discussed in chapter 2.[12]

11.26 If the section has been completed, and the NR does not agree that the patient should be detained, they can write to the hospital to request discharge of the patient. The Code of Practice has an illustrative standard letter (at para 32.25). If the RC bars the discharge the hospital managers will consider whether the barring order should stand and you should represent your client at that hearing. If there is no evidence of dangerousness the hospital managers should consider discharge but this is not an inflexible rule and there may be circumstances when discharge is not appropriate.[13] This is discussed in more detail in chapter 2 at paras 2.31–2.42.

11.27 The NR can also apply for a MHT if the RC has made a barring order and in addition if they have been displaced by the County Court under section 29 of the Act.[14] The criteria to consider will be different in both those situations. This is considered further in chapter 2; also see table 1 at para 2.231 for details as to when the NR can apply to the tribunal. Note that the NR can make his or her own application to the tribunal for the discharge of a patient detained or placed under guardianship under section 37.

9 MHA 1983 s132.

10 Senior President's Practice Direction (FTT (HESC)): Statements and Reports in Mental Health Cases, 28 October 2013.

11 Tribunal Procedure (First-tier Tribunal) (Health, Education and Social Care Chamber) Rules 2008 SI No 2699 r33: Rule 16(c) in Wales.

12 [2014] EWCA Civ 362.

13 *R (SR) (by her litigation friend the Official Solicitor) v Huntercombe Maidenhead Hospital and others* [2005] EWHC 2361 (Admin).

14 MHA 1983 s66(1)(g)(ii).

11.28 You must bear in mind that a NR can only make an order for discharge once every six months and the six months runs from the date of the barring order and so timing is important for the making of the application.[15] The NR also runs the risk of an application to displace them being made by the AMHP, the patient, or another relative of the person residing with the patient before admission. The appropriate time to make such an application will depend on the circumstance of the case. In addition if they apply for discharge when the patient is detained under a section 2 they cannot apply to the tribunal.

11.29 If the patient objects to the person identified as NR then they can make an application to the county court to displace them and appoint someone else.

11.30 The NR is not a party to the proceedings before a tribunal unless they start the case by making an application.[16] This means they are not entitled to reports given to the tribunal but if notified have the right to attend to the extent that the tribunal considers proper.[17] The tribunal is always in charge of its own hearing and so can include or exclude the NR.

11.31 It has been held that a local authority should usually disclose local authority records to the NR to enable them to decide whether to exercise their legal rights under the Mental Health Act 1983.[18] However, the tribunal has no power to disclose reports or decisions unless the NR is a party.

11.32 If the NR is a party then they should receive the documents produced to the MHT,[19] may be represented, appear at the hearing and take such part as the tribunal thinks fit and proper which can include being heard, calling witnesses and cross-examination.[20] They should also receive a copy of the decision.[21]

11.33 As the NR is entitled to representation if they have made an application to the tribunal, it may be that you are asked to act for them as well as the patient. There are a number of risks which can arise

15 MHA 1983 s25(1)(b).

16 Tribunal Procedure (First-tier Tribunal) (Health, Education and Social Care Chamber) Rules 2008 SI No 2699 r1(3); rule 2(1) in Wales.

17 Rule 36 England; no equivalent rule in Wales but rule 16 envisages those notified attending and rule 25 gives the tribunal the power to permit or exclude witnesses.

18 *R v Plymouth City Council & C (Interested Party) ex p Ann Stevens* [2002] EWCA Civ 388.

19 Rule 32(3) England; rule 15 Wales.

20 Rule 36 England; rules 25 and 26 in Wales.

21 Rule 41 England; rule 28 Wales.

when seeking to fulfill professional obligations to both the patient and the nearest relative. (However, this is a matter of judgment and you may find that in some instances acting for both is appropriate. See chapter 9, para 9.32 for a discussion of the professional obligations and considerations that may arise.) If you are representing two parties and you discover a conflict between the two, then you may have knowledge of privileged information from both of the parties. In that case, it would probably be improper to continue to act for either in the proceedings.

Questions of capacity

11.34 You should satisfy yourself that your client has the capacity to instruct you to apply to the tribunal or hospital managers. 'The common law presumes that every person has capacity until the contrary is shown and the threshold for capacity is not a demanding one.'[22] This is reflected in MCA 2005 s1. The ability to give coherent instructions on complicated reports is not necessary. This is considered further in chapter 9 at para 9.46, in the discussion under the heading 'The Law Society's Practice Note'.

11.35 You should be aware of the power under section 67(1) for the Secretary of State to refer the case to a tribunal. If you are acting for an incapacitated patient, then you could request the Secretary of State make a section 67(1) referral or insist the hospital does so. See further discussion of the use of this power in chapter 5 at paras 5.17–5.22.

11.36 This power of the Secretary of State is also important to a section 2 patient who has missed the 14-day deadline in which to make an application.[23]

Checking the section papers

11.37 This is an essential task for all those representing detained patients and one that is surprisingly often overlooked. You should check to see if there is lawful authority to detain.

11.38 Always look at the original papers and follow the renewals through to ensure the section has been renewed appropriately and on time.

22 *R(MH) v Secretary of State for the Department of Health & others* [2005] UKHL 60 per Baroness Hale at para 26.

23 MHA 1983 s66(2)(a), also see *R (Modaresi) v Secretary of State for Health* [2013] UKSC 53, discussed in chapter 5 at para 5.12.

Remember the power given under section 15 to rectify mistakes on the papers within 14 days of the application; this power cannot rectify a fundamental error nor a renewal. In addition, CTO documentation cannot be rectified. See also chapter 2 at para 2.87. It may be that if your client has not been lawfully detained, compensation may be payable or they may secure immediate release either through court action or the agreement of the managers of the hospital.

11.39 In *TTM v Hackney LBC*[24] compensation was payable to the patient who had been unlawfully detained. However, see also *Bostridge v Oxleas NHS Foundation Trust*[25] where it was confirmed that for compensation to be paid for an illegal detention a proven loss was necessary. Once the false imprisonment has been accepted the burden is on the authority to show it made no difference. The judgment highlights the importance of liberty as enshrined in the Magna Carta. The importance of this principle can be lost when you are busy, struggling financially because of cuts in public funding and caught up in a case. However, it is essential to remember the fundamental concepts of liberty on which the law is founded and to ensure that those detaining have the lawful authority to do so.

11.40 There are checklists to use when going through section papers: see appendix E.

Application to the tribunal

11.41 Rule 32 of the Tribunal Procedure (First-tier Tribunal), (Health, Education and Social Care Chamber) Rules 2008 (the Rules) sets out the procedure for the making of an application to the tribunal. The application *must* be made in writing, signed by the applicant or someone authorised by the applicant and sent to the tribunal within time. There are standard forms available on the www.justice.gov.uk website to download. It may be helpful to take a blank form with you to see the patient so that they can sign it if they want at the first meeting.

11.42 If the patient is detained on a section 2 the application must be made within 14 days of admission. If your client fails to apply within this period then consider approaching the Secretary of State and request that they refer your client to the tribunal.

24 [2011] EWCA Civ 4. See para 2.46.
25 [2015] EWCA Civ 790.

11.43 Remember the nearest relative point which is highlighted on the application form.

11.44 The eligibility periods for other applications are set out in sections 66, 69 and 70 and 75 of the Act and set out in chapter 5 under the heading 'Routes to the tribunal' which includes table 4 setting out when the patient is eligible to apply.

Sending the application

11.45 When you send your application to the tribunal it is good practice to send a copy of it to the Mental Health Act Administrator as well. If you email or fax it you will know the time and date of receipt by the MHAA as other than in section 2 cases the responsible authority must send the documents with the tribunal within three weeks after *they* have received a copy of the application.[26] If it is sent by post it is difficult to know when they have received it.

11.46 On sending the application you should then diarise ahead three weeks from this date and chase the tribunal and the MHAA on the day. The tribunal should be issuing automatic directions for the filing of missing reports at this stage so check that this has been done. Diarise a week ahead and if no reports are forthcoming then an application for directions under rule 5(d) should be made. If you have secure email then send your directions application in a Word document with draft directions. This will allow the salaried judge or registrar to cut and paste your draft into a directions form; you are more likely to get the precise directions you want. In most cases you will not have anything particular you need addressed by the reports and it is better to see what is said by the professionals before asking for further directions for additional evidence to address specific issues. However, if you are aware of a particular problem, for example a reluctant local team with section 117 responsibility not co-operating in identifying accommodation, it may be useful to ask at this stage for this to be addressed. The judge or the registrar will not have read the reports, and so you should explain why you are asking for the directions you seek.

26 Tribunal Procedure (First-tier Tribunal), (Health, Education and Social Care Chamber) Rules 2008 r32(6); r15(5) in Wales.

The timing of an application

11.47 The hearing of an unrestricted application to the tribunal is usually booked to be heard about five to eight weeks after receipt of the application. If you do not get the reports within the statutory time period, you may not have time to take instructions from your client and if necessary instruct an expert and serve their report before the hearing takes place. Chasing the RA for reports is therefore an important part of your duty to your client.

11.48 In restricted cases the independent experts have limited availability and so the sooner you get the reports the earlier you can instruct them.

Once the tribunal have received the application and/or been notified that you are acting they will send you a Case Notification Letter and Directions.[27] This directs you to lodge an HQ1 with your availability for the hearing date.[28] On receipt of the reports, the tribunal will send them to you with a letter which you should read and respond to if need be.[29] For example, the hearing will have been listed for half a day unless you have said the hearing will take more time.

Access to the notes

11.49 At the same time as applying to the MHT you should write to the RC with a signed authority from your client giving you permission to access any information about them you request and that you require access to the notes. Your letter should say you are looking forward to the report and note the due date. Most trusts now have electronic records.

11.50 If you are appointed by the tribunal under rule 11(7) because your client lacks capacity to instruct a representative it may be that he or she lack capacity to give you permission to see their notes. In those circumstances you should ask the RC for permission on the basis that you are appointed by the tribunal to represent the best interests of the patient and to prepare the case you need to have access to this information. Frequently, when appointing a representative, the

27 This letter is currently being amended. Forms are available at: http://hmctsformfinder.justice.gov.uk/courtfinder.

28 This letter is currently being amended. Forms are available at: http://hmctsformfinder.justice.gov.uk/courtfinder.

29 This letter is currently being amended. Forms are available at: http://hmctsformfinder.justice.gov.uk/courtfinder.

tribunal will direct that the representative is given access to the notes (rule 5(d)).

11.51 Reading and analysing the notes can make the difference in winning or losing a case. Often it is from the notes that the strategy for the case emerges. For example it may be that taking cannabis has a great effect on your client's mental health and there is clear evidence that this is the case. In some cases however it seems that people can take cannabis whilst on medication and their mental health is not adversely affected. A thorough analysis of the notes should make this clear.

11.52 The tribunal will have the reports and in all section 2 cases and in some other cases where a pre-hearing examination has been directed or requested, the medical member's examination. They will not have the in-depth knowledge of the notes that you should have to make your case. If you do not get a satisfactory response from the Trust you can apply to the tribunal for access to medical records. However, it may first be appropriate to remind the RA of their duty to cooperate with the tribunal and help ensure a case is dealt with justly and fairly. By allowing you access to the notes the RA is fulfilling the duty to co-operate and is helping the tribunal deal with the case fairly and justly.[30] The Upper Tribunal gave detailed guidance in *Dorset Healthcare NHS Foundation Trust v MH*.[31] How much negotiating with the RA is possible will depend on how promptly they reply and the date of the hearing.

Considering after-care

11.53 The function and qualifications of the author of the social circumstances report will vary. For civil patients it is usually a care co-ordinator in the community, but for restricted or long term inpatients, it may well be a hospital staff member (eg a hospital ward social worker). Community care co-ordinators can be OTs, CPNs, or social workers. You may want to write to them depending on the issues in the case. If there is a real prospect of discharge a good tactic is to ask for a section 117/CPA meeting to be set up and ask for an invitation to the meeting. Many cases are won and lost on the availability of after-care and the more you can do to have this organised before the tribunal hearing, the higher your chances of achieving discharge will be.

30 Rule 2.

31 [2009] UKUT 4 (AAC).

> In general, in a case in which after-care is essential, and satisfaction of the discharge criteria depends on the availability of suitable after-care and accommodation, as in H's case, a tribunal should not direct immediate discharge at a time when no after-care arrangements are in place and there is no time for them to be put in place. The Tribunal should consider whether to exercise its power under section 72(3A) to recommend that the RMO should make a supervision application. If it considers that to be ... and there is uncertainty as to the putting in place of the after-care arrangements on which satisfaction of the discharge criteria depends, the tribunal should adjourn pursuant to rule 16 to enable them to be put in place, indicating their views and giving appropriate directions: cf *ex p Hall* [2000] 1 WLR 1323, per Kennedy LJ at 1352D.[32]

In many cases the availability of after-care will be integral to the decision of the tribunal as to whether the detaining authority has satisfied them that detention is necessary.

11.54 The problem with requesting that a section 117/CPA meeting is held is that as the law stands the there is no duty to hold such a CPA as the duty to provide after-care only arises on someone leaving hospital.[33]

11.55 However, in a restricted case where a deferred conditional discharge has been given Scott Baker LJ found that:

> (a) a health authority has the power to take preparatory steps before discharge of a patient;
>
> (b) it will normally be the case that, in the exercise of its discretionary power, an authority should give way to a tribunal decision, and should use reasonable endeavours to fulfill the conditions imposed by such a decision, in so far as they relate to medical care;
>
> (c) failure to use such endeavours, in the absence of strong reasons, would be likely to be an unlawful exercise of discretion.[34]

11.56 In your letter to the RC and to the social worker requesting the holding of a CPA/section 117 meeting you should say your client could be discharged by the tribunal and the panel will want to hear about after-care as it is integral to the decision to discharge that they have this information and therefore the section 117 meeting should be held. In addition the Code of Practice states at paragraph 27.8:[35]

32 *R(H) v Ashworth Hospital Authority and others* [2002] EWCA Civ 923 at para 69: Dyson J approved Stanley Burnton J in the High Court.

33 *R (B) v Camden LBC and others* [2005] EWHC 1366 QBD (Admin) per Stanley Burnton J para 57.

34 *R(W) v Doncaster* [2004] EWCA Civ 378, Scott Baker LJ.

35 See Code of Practice for Wales para 31.7; para 34.17 of the Code.

> ... the planning of after-care needs to start as soon as the patient is admitted to hospital.

11.57 The more likely the discharge of the patient by the tribunal the more the local authority and health authority should have used their best endeavours to arrange after-care for the patient. Otherwise an adjournment may be the only option. Many tribunals do take a robust attitude to after-care as so often it is integral to discharge.

Communicating with your client

11.58 Some clients are happy receiving correspondence and some are distressed by it. If correspondence distresses your client then a short letter with only basic information will suffice as long as you note the reasons for this on your file. If there is no such issue then you need to do the following:

1) confirm you are acting;
2) confirm you have applied to the tribunal and who you have told of this;
3) confirm the public funding position;
4) confirm in detail the instructions you have been given either by including a copy of the attendance note or writing the contents of the interview in the letter; and
5) confirm briefly what the section means to them and when and how it may end. (There are examples of standard letters in appendix D but below is some key information that you will wish to convey.)

Examples

Section 2

11.59 A social worker and two doctors will have decided that you should be in hospital for up to 28 days because they were concerned about a risk to your health or your safety or the protection of others. You are not able to leave the ward without your doctor giving you permission. Your doctor is able to treat you without your consent for your mental disorder.

Section 3

11.60 A social worker and two doctors will have decided that you should be in hospital for up to six months for treatment of a mental disorder because they were concerned about a risk to your health or your safety or the protection of others. This order can be renewed after six months but can also be discharged far earlier by your doctor, your nearest relative or the Mental Health Tribunal. Your doctor (RC) is able to treat you without your consent for your mental illness until you have been in hospital for three months and then another doctor must come and assess you. Unless that doctor agrees, you cannot continue to be treated although in practice it is unusual for the doctor to disagree with the RC.

Section 37

11.61 This section is imposed by the court on the basis that they were satisfied that you suffered from a mental disorder requiring treatment in hospital. It means you may have to stay in hospital for up to six months at first and then if the doctor thinks you need longer they can add another six months and then they can renew it yearly. However, you can also be discharged earlier by your doctor, your nearest relative or the Mental Health Tribunal. Your doctor (RC) is able to treat you without your consent for your mental illness until you have been in hospital for three months and then another doctor must come and assess you. Unless that doctor agrees, you cannot continue to be treated although in practice it is unusual for the doctor to disagree with the RC.

Sections 37/41

11.62 You were sentenced to a hospital order under section 37 along with an order restricting discharge section 41. The Crown Court would have had evidence from two doctors and a hospital must have agreed to take you. You now need to remain in hospital and the Mental Health Casework Section (MHCS) of the Ministry of Justice (MoJ) will be responsible for allowing you to leave the ward or the hospital grounds. They will do this on the advice of your RC if they agree with the recommendation. You can also be discharged by the tribunal either absolutely or with conditions which are like a license. Restriction orders (the section 41 part of your sentence) usually have no time limit. Your RC can treat you without your consent for your mental disorder until you have been in hospital for three months and then they would have to have another doctor come and assess you. Unless that doctor agrees you could not continue to be treated although it would be unusual for them to disagree with your RC.

Sections 47/49

11.63 After having been sentenced for an offence the Secretary of State for Justice has issued a warrant transferring you to hospital. The Ministry of Justice will be responsible for granting leave and allowing discharge (apart from a tribunal discharge). They will do this on the recommendation of your RC if they agree. If you have a fixed sentence (a number of years when you reach your early date of release (EDR)) your section then becomes a 'notional section 37' which means that the hospital can continue to keep you for a further six months and then renew the section for another six months and subsequent renewal periods of one year. At this stage the Ministry of Justice have no more say in your case. You can also be discharged by a tribunal to the community after your EDR has passed.

11.64 If you have been given a life sentence you will continue to be subject to the MoJ who can recall you to hospital after discharge. You will be able to apply to a tribunal who can recommend you are discharged. In addition they can recommend that you stay in hospital if you are not discharged rather than return to prison. You would then have your case heard by the Parole Board.[36]

11.65 Your clinical team can treat you without your consent for your mental disorder until you have been in hospital for three months and then another doctor must come and assess you. Unless that doctor agrees, you cannot continue to be treated although it would be unusual for them to disagree with your RC.

11.66 The next thing to do is to confirm the process that will now take place. For example:

- For a section 2 the process is that the tribunal will take place in seven days from the date the application is received by the tribunal. For section 3 and section 37 it will take about 5–8 weeks before a tribunal is convened and in a restricted case between 12 and 20 weeks.
- The tribunal will consist of a tribunal judge who will be a lawyer and in a restricted case a Crown Court judge, a recorder QC or a salaried judge.
- There will be a medical member and, if you are detained on a section 2 or if you have requested it, they will see you before the hearing hopefully a day or two before. They will also read the medical/nursing notes available. Whatever you tell them, and whatever they read, will be shared with all present before the tribunal.

36 See chapter 3 at para 3.18.

- There is also a specialist lay member who may be a social worker or psychiatric nurse or have some other relevant experience.
- The tribunal is completely independent of the hospital and will make an independent decision on the evidence it hears and read. If you want to speak to the tribunal without the clinical team present you can.
- The tribunal will introduce itself, explain the procedure and its independence. The tribunal will then report back on any interview you have had with their doctor so that you know what they have already heard. Usually the tribunal will announce the decision on the day and then you will receive written reasons after that (within three days for a section 2 and within seven days in every other case unless this time frame is extended[37]).

11.67 Then go on to explain the next steps:

- You will let the tribunal, RC, care co-ordinator and, in restricted cases, the Secretary of State know you are representing. You will apply to see the notes and you will discuss what you read. You expect to receive reports by the due date and if you do not there are steps that you can take to ensure that they are received and then you can take instructions on them.
- It may be after perusing the reports you will advise the client of a particular expert you should instruct and discuss it with them. For example if your client is suffering from autism you may look for an expert who is familiar with this. If your client is a forensic patient you would want to instruct someone with relevant expertise. Your expert witness should be at least as senior as the opposing witness. If you do instruct an expert and the client agrees with the expert's opinion that you can then disclose the report to the MHT and in a restricted case the Secretary of State if instructed to do so. If you do this the report will become part of the medical notes and the RC may read it before the MHT. It may be that you advise that the report maker should attend to give oral evidence. The types of report that would be useful will depend on the particular point that needs an opinion.

37 Rule 5(3)(a).

Further preparation for the hearing

Evidence gathering

The Responsible Authority Reports

11.68 Ensure you that have the reports in good time. A possible draft direction to send to the tribunal in the absence of reports is:

> The Responsible Authority shall lodge with the tribunal by day/month/year and time the clinical/nursing/social circumstances reports required under the rules and containing the information set out in the section (number) of the Senior President's Practice Direction.

11.69 You then need to diarise ahead to the date which the reports are directed.

11.70 What do you do if there is no response to a direction? It is questionable as to whether the First-tier Tribunal can issue a summons for a report that is not yet written. Rule 16(b) gives the tribunal the power to 'produce any documents in that person's possession or control'. If the report is not written then the document cannot be within the person's possession or control. However, rule 16(1)(b) also says the tribunal can order 'any person to answer any questions'.[38] Issuing the order has now been delegated to administrative staff and will say:

> 1. In accordance with rule 17(2) and the Senior President's Practice Direction in relation to Delegations of Functions to Staff and Registrars (10 June 2014), you are ordered to file a report that answers the questions arising from application of the Senior President's Practice Direction, Section , and to provide such answers in writing so that they are received by the tribunal no later than 4pm on: ________. If possible, please file the report by secure email.
>
> If you do not comply, the tribunal may exercise such powers, and impose such sanctions, as are provided for under the Rules, which may include, by summons, requiring you and/or any other person to attend personally as a witness before the tribunal, in order to provide the information and explain the default.

11.71 An order to answer questions or a summons needs to be made against a named person not just 'the RC' but Dr M, full address' as otherwise it is impossible to serve and enforce. You will need to supply their names, addresses, fax numbers and email to ensure service of the orders can take place.

38 This is being reviewed at the time of writing.

11.72 Enforcing these orders is difficult particularly given the short time scales in the tribunal from application to hearing. There is a power under rule 7 in England to refer any failure to comply with a rule, practice direction or a direction to the Upper Tribunal but this power would be used sparingly. In a case in SENDIST a witness who was not a party was fined £500.00 for not complying with a summons to attend the tribunal.[39]

Deciding on expert evidence

11.73 Generally it is important that you consider the worth that would be added to your case by instructing an independent expert. You have a duty to ensure that public funds are used wisely and the tribunal will usually know whether an expert has been instructed although they cannot make any inferences from the fact that they know an expert has visited.[40] The tribunal must make a decision on the evidence before them.

11.74 In terms of instructing an expert there are certain basic rules to follow. If the area is a specialist one, for example learning disability, make sure your expert is from the right area. Your expert must be as qualified or more qualified in the relevant area as the opposing expert. It is important not to instruct a registrar if the person giving evidence for the Responsible Authority is a consultant. Find out about their background. Most will have a short CV they can email to you.

11.75 Choose an expert that is good at giving oral evidence on the day. Some experts are extremely convincing in oral evidence and it is that expert that you want on your client's side.

11.76 You need to structure your written instructions and questions to your expert so that you get the answers to the issue that you need addressed. The experts you will be instructing will have different levels of knowledge of the law but you are the one with the legal knowledge and so it is your responsibility to set out the law.

11.77 Find out their available dates as soon as you can so you can factor this into the dates you offer the tribunal. You do not know at this stage whether you would be calling them to give evidence but if the case is set on a date when they are available then that will assist you in liaising with the tribunal and providing your dates on the HQ1. If you cannot do this it may mean that you need to apply for a postponement and if that is the case then you need to do it at the earliest

39 *CB v Suffolk County Council* [2010] UKUT 413 (AAC).

40 *MM v Nottinghamshire Healthcare NHS Trust* [2013] UKUT 0107 (AAC).

opportunity and provide the available dates with the postponement application. If you can agree these with the MHAA before the application is sent off that is an advantage but the tribunal will only be able to agree if there is a panel available.

11.78 Once you have received the draft report you should discuss it with the expert. If there is something that is not clear ask them to clarify and change the draft. At this stage you should be anticipating the arguments against your expert and if possible have them address these arguments before their report is finalised.

11.79 Make sure you discuss disclosure of the report with your client. It is up to you to advise them but you must act on instructions. Your expert may helpfully say that the patient may be discharged but that they do suffer from an illness. As a result your client may not want you to disclose the report as they do not agree they have ever been ill. You act on your client's instructions.

11.80 Once you have agreed the final report with the expert and if your client has agreed to disclose it send it to the tribunal and the MHAA. Make sure the MHAA knows to pass it to the RC and if not send it to the RC yourself. If the date has already been set on a day when your expert is not available try and agree another date and apply for a postponement. On rare occasions a report can stand on its own but in almost all cases the expert should be at the tribunal to give evidence and speak to their report. Otherwise the worth of their report is easily undermined.

Which expert to instruct?

An independent psychiatrist?

11.81 Once you have received the reports you can ascertain whether independent evidence will take you any further. In making this decision it is important to know what you are looking for from the report. It may be that in a restricted case you want a forensic psychiatrist to assess whether it is possible to manage your client's risk in the community. If you client is a sex offender looking for an expert who manages sex offenders in the community may be useful.

11.82 In specialist areas such as forensic work, personality disordered offenders or those with learning disabilities for example you need to ensure you have an expert with credibility in the field.

An independent psychologist?

11.83 You would usually be considering instructing a psychologist only in cases where psychological evidence is influential in diagnosis or treatment. For example, if your client suffers with autism or has a personality disorder. Psychological reports are usually expensive, and take some time. All the rules above equally apply to the instruction of a psychologist although they will be able to guide you in terms of the tests they carry out to come to their result.

11.84 Remember that a psychologist cannot diagnose and the psychiatrist may say that any psychological testing they do is only to inform a clinician who can diagnose. In cases where diagnosis is an issue you would usually have both an independent psychiatrist and a psychologist.

An independent social worker?

11.85 After-care is an extremely important part of preparing your case. If you can present the tribunal with a package of care that is workable you are more likely to succeed particularly if the package limits the risk that your client may pose to the community or themselves. In unrestricted cases in acute services this is sometimes more difficult as services can be overstretched and have fewer resources than those available to the forensic services.

11.86 If there are no plans then an independent social work report may help to identify placements. On occasions and depending on the hospital Trust it may be possible to have the hostel assess the person for a place as well. It is a matter of judgment for you in every case. If at all possible involving the authority in that search at an early stage will achieve a more favourable result for your client.

Importance of after-care information

11.87 There are some cases where involving the authority in the search is not possible. This may be because they are strongly opposing discharge. It is these cases where you will need the tribunal to help. The Senior President's Practice Direction[41] at paragraph 14 says that the social circumstances report must include the following information:

e) the housing or accommodation available to the patient if discharged;
f) the patient's financial position (including benefit entitlements);
g) any available opportunities for employment;

41 *The Senior President's Practice Direction: Statements and reports in mental health cases*, 28 October 2013 available from www.judiciary.gov.uk.

h) the patient's previous response to community support or section 117 after-care;
i) so far as is known, details of the care pathway and section 117 after-care to be made available to the patient, together with details of the proposed care plan;
j) the likely adequacy and effectiveness of the proposed care plan;
k) whether there are any issues as to funding the proposed care plan and, if so, the date by which those issues will be resolved.

11.88 If the report does not address this then you should apply for a direction that this information be included or talk to the author of the social circumstances report to ask them to give this information to you. Alternatively in an appropriate case you could ask the tribunal to hold a case management hearing before the day of the hearing to address this. This could be arranged as a telephone case management hearing which may facilitate the attendance of the parties. And finally if this information is not forthcoming then an application at the tribunal for an adjournment and directions may be the best way to proceed. In many cases a direction requiring the attendance of the person ultimately responsible for the funding decision such as the Clinical Director or Chief Executive of a Trust or the Director for Social Services produces the required result without a further hearing.

11.89 However, it is not essential that all information is available is every case. In *AM v West London Mental Health NHS Trust and Secretary of State for Justice*[42] the Upper Tribunal considered the RA's responsibility to provide a statement to the tribunal about after-care and the appeal was of the tribunal's refusal to adjourn in this case. The patient's argument was that without the information the tribunal could not come to a decision on the statutory criteria because what was available in the community was intrinsic to the decision. It was held that rule 32 and the relevant statutory guidance contained in the practice direction and the Code of Practice chapter 27.7 and 27.9[43] are set in the context of case management. Once the hearing starts it passes to a decision-making phase. It may be that the patient is not asking for discharge and therefore a discharge plan would not be appropriate. Rule 7 allows the tribunal to waive any failure to comply with any of the rules or statutory guidance.

42 [2012] UKUT 382 (AAC).

43 Paragraphs 33.11 and 33.12 in the new Code.

This case was appealed.[44] Although the appeal was dismissed Richards LJ recognised

> the need for great caution before reaching a conclusion that information about after-care could make no difference and is therefore unnecessary, given the importance attached to its provision, the fact that a patient depends on the authorities for its provision and also the need to ensure procedural fairness.[45]

However, he concluded that it must,

> as a matter of principle, be open to a Tribunal to conclude in the circumstances of a particular case that information or better information of after-care is incapable of affecting the decision, and that an adjournment to secure its provision could achieve nothing beyond additional expense and delay and would therefore be inappropriate.[46]

11.90 In intransigent cases another option is to look at the duties owed by the health authority or the director of social services under community care provisions and section 117 and consider whether judicial review proceedings are appropriate. If the only delay is finding suitable after-care this may help. Judicial review should only be used once all other avenues have been exhausted but is very effective if you have a clinical team supporting you and a recalcitrant funder. Explaining procedure and grounds for judicial review is beyond the remit of this text.[47]

Secretary of State's comments

11.91 In a restricted case it is really important to ensure that the Mental Health Casework Section (MHCS) has commented on the Responsible Authority's statement. Under rule 32(7) the MHCS should send any relevant information to the tribunal within two weeks of the Responsible Authority's statement.[48] In practice it often does this after the report from the RC and social worker but the duty under the rule does not arise until it has received the relevant authorities' statement which is made up of all the reports.

11.92 In restricted cases where your client is still detained, the Secretary of State should send a statement of further relevant informa-

44 *AM v West London MH NHS Trust and Secretary of State for Justice* [2013] EWCA Civ 1010.

45 Para 9.

46 Para 9.

47 Readers are referred to Manning, Brown and Salmon *Judicial Review Proceedings*, 3rd edition, LAG, 2013.

48 See rule 15 Wales.

tion within three weeks of receiving the reports from the RA. If the patient has been recalled from the community then the time limit for further relevant information is two weeks after receiving reports.[49] For a conditionally discharged patient applying the Secretary of State must tell the tribunal the names and addresses of the RC and Social Supervisor. The tribunal then informs them and they need to send reports within three weeks after being notified.[50]

11.93 The MHCS also sends in its observations on the reports lodged with the tribunal and serves on them within two weeks of receiving reports for a conditionally discharged patient who has been recalled or within three weeks in all other cases.[51] They have agreed in the protocol between the MHCS and the MHT in England that, despite the time limits in the rules, the MHCS will, in most cases, endeavour to have the comments with the tribunal as long as it has five working days before the tribunal takes place:

> 2.14 A key determining factor will be the amount of time the Ministry of Justice has to consider the late report before the date of the hearing. Where the Ministry of Justice has at least 5 working days in which to consider the late Responsible Authority statement it will use all reasonable endeavours to provide a response.[52]

11.94 There is no need for the tribunal to have comments on supplementary reports. The protocol addresses what statement the MHCS will lodge and says that it will produce the original statement but not comment on supplementary reports:

> 2.17 There is no obligation under the Rules on the Ministry of Justice to comment on each supplementary report. Consequently a Tribunal may proceed in the absence of Ministry of Justice comments on supplementary reports and documents, as long as the Tribunal is satisfied that they have been sent to the Ministry of Justice. The Ministry of Justice accepts that an electronically generated acknowledgment of any report sent to the dedicated Tribunal communication email address or a fax receipt confirmation will constitute sufficient evidence of receipt by the Secretary of State for Justice.[53]

49 Rule 32(7A).

50 Rule 32(4); f or Wales see r15.

51 Rule 32(7A) England: r15(6) Wales.

52 Ministry of Justice – Tribunal Service, Mental Health Guidance, April 2009: www.mentalhealthlaw.co.uk/ministry-of-justice-involvement-in-restricted-cases/ (currently under revision). See appendix C.

53 Ministry of Justice – Tribunal Service, Mental Health Guidance, April 2009: www.mentalhealthlaw.co.uk/ministry-of-justice-involvement-in-restricted-cases/ (currently under revision).

11.95 This protocol also addresses no notice evidence. It may be that the evidence changes at the hearing and the oral evidence given by the clinical team supports conditional discharge when it did not in the written evidence. It is important to keep abreast of the changing opinions for many reasons but one of these is to ensure that the RC has told the MHCS of their change in evidence and that the MHCS know of this change. This may be through an addendum tribunal report or by letter or its periodic reports. If the tribunal can be shown that the MHCS know about the change, know about the tribunal and has not provided any supplementary comments or representation then you will be able to proceed. If you are representing in a case where you know that the RC will recommend discharge when particular hurdles are jumped it would be useful to encourage the RC to say that in a list in the report. So, for example, a report may read 'If Mr ____ has had a successful overnight leave I will be supporting conditional discharge at the tribunal hearing.' You will then be able to demonstrate to the tribunal that these objectives have been reached.

11.96 The provision on no notice evidence in the protocol says:

> **No notice evidence**
>
> 2.20 The approach to 'no notice' oral evidence which directly contradicts the written evidence previously presented e.g. the Responsible Clinician now supporting discharge counter to his/her previous written reports is a matter for the exercise of judicial discretion. The Tribunal will consider each case on its facts bearing in mind the overriding objective, relevant case law and the power to set aside decisions contained in rule 45.

11.97 One of the major hurdles in a tribunal for a detained restricted patient is whether the patient has had adequate leave. Even if the clinical team supports a conditional discharge unless the requisite leave has been taken the tribunal is unlikely to discharge. Even if the discharge is to be deferred, the current law is that a patient cannot be given a deferred conditional discharge if they are not ready to go on that day if the conditions could be fulfilled. The tribunal will want to know that the patient has been tested out on leave. If the leave is just a practical step necessary for the hostel to accept the patient, and the RC would be happy with the patient leaving that day, it may be that the tribunal would grant a discharge, but this needs to be carefully planned all the way from application to the tribunal. The timing of a tribunal is important. The MHCS has issued guidance on leave applications and it is important to be aware of this and help the RC if that is necessary.

11.98 You should be aware of the MoJ guidance for those working with mentally disordered offenders and this can be accessed at www.justice.gov.uk/offenders/types-of-offender/mentally-disordered-offenders.

Victims

11.99 This is a developing area of jurisprudence and it may be likely given the current primary legislation that victims will have a greater role in tribunals than they have in the past. The Domestic Violence, Crime and Victims Act (DVCA) 2004 gives rights to the victims of a violent or sexual offence. The definition of victim includes the family of a deceased or incapacitated victim or anyone representing the wishes of the victim.[54] Patients who are convicted and sentenced on or after 1 July 2005 of a violent or sexual offence and who are sentenced to a hospital order with restriction or convicted of the relevant offence and given a sentence of imprisonment of 12 months or more and then transferred to a hospital are covered by the statutory scheme. Unrestricted cases were included in the scheme if sentenced on or after 3 November 2008.

11.100 The Chamber President issued guidance on this in July 2011 which can be found at www.justice.gov.uk/tribunals/mental-health under 'forms and leaflets' and is reproduced at appendix C.

11.101 The local Probation Board where the patient was sentenced has a duty to take all reasonable steps to ascertain who the victim is and to let them know of their right to make representations and receive information. They appoint a victim liaison officer (VLO) to do the actual liaising with the victim and the tribunal.

11.102 Increasingly victims are sending in written representations and applying to attend hearings. The representations are limited to whether in the event of discharge the patient should be subject to conditions. However, in theory this could include presenting evidence to the tribunal of the distress caused by the offence to make a case as to why an exclusion zone would be relevant. Once a decision has been made the tribunal has a duty to tell the VLO all of the conditions to which the patient will be subject and the VLO then tells the victim any condition relevant to contact with the victim.

11.103 In unrestricted cases the responsibility for contact with the victim lies with the hospital managers. The purpose of making representations as to conditions is limited in these cases as the tribunal cannot discharge a patient with conditions. The only thing a tribunal could

54 DVCA Act 2004 ss35–45 and Schedule 6 to the MHA 2007.

do is recommend a CTO and record the evidence of the victim on conditions. The tribunal cannot make or vary these conditions unlike in a restricted case the victim has little ability to make any difference to the outcome.

11.104 The victim, having been informed of the tribunal, is entitled to make an application to attend.[55] However, the guidance of the Chamber President in England says that '... The victim will have to demonstrate that the opportunity to make written representations is insufficient and that he or she needs an opportunity to be heard in relation to relevant matters'.

11.105 In non-statutory cases the tribunal only has contact with the victim where the victim has contacted it. The tribunal will receive any representations the victim wishes to make and consider any application for attendance. The judge seized of the case has the discretion about what to disclose to the victim and should do this in the decision. The victim will be informed of the date and time but will not be given any information about the address of the patient unless the application to attend is successful and there is no danger to the patient that his or her whereabouts is known.

Case management directions: using the Tribunal Rules

11.106 It is essential to be familiar with The Tribunal Procedure (First-tier Tribunal) (Health, Education and Social Care Chamber) Rules 2008[56] ('The Rules') or the Mental Health Review Tribunal for Wales Rules 2008.

11.107 When dealing with the tribunal and making applications for case management directions start by considering rule 2[57] and the overriding objective of dealing with cases fairly and justly. This is the most important rule to know when making applications for case management directions and referring to it in your applications will be essential. Every decision taken under the rules must be taken with it in mind.

55 Rule 33(e) England; Wales r26.

56 SI No 2699.

57 Rule 3 in Wales.

11.108 Rule 2(2) gives a non-exhaustive list of considerations and of those (a) and (c) may be useful from a representative's point of view.[58] Rule 2(2)(a) could be used to postpone a hearing where, for example, it may not have to proceed if an agreement is reached between the patient and the clinicians. Rule 2(2)(c) says that dealing justly and fairly with a case also includes ensuring so far as is practicable that the parties are able to participate fully in the proceedings. This may help in an application for an adjournment/postponement for an independent report. It may also help, for example, when your client does not attend if they are on a CTO and you expected them or where your client wants you to attend and not another representative. Remember that avoiding delay is only one of these five considerations and even that is tempered with 'avoiding delay so far as compatible with proper consideration of the issues'. [59]

11.109 Rule 2(2)(e) is helpful if the tribunal or the RA is delaying the hearing because someone cannot attend. However, delay must be avoided so far as is compatible with proper consideration of the issues. If you are making the application, you may want to say that the patient recognises the delay but wants the adjournment. Delay has the greatest effect on the patient and the right to a speedy hearing protected by Article 5(4) ECHR is to protect them. The tribunal does not like to adjourn matters as the administrative burden of rearranging the case is great. You will therefore have to put your case robustly with reference to the rules and the overriding objective and, if you can apply with another agreed date, this will help the chances your application will be granted.

11.110 The tribunal discourages applications for adjournments and has reduced significantly the number in recent years. However, each decision must be made on the particular facts of the case taking into account the overriding objective. It would be difficult for the tribunal to refuse to agree a postponement to get independent evidence, or to allow witnesses to attend the tribunal, as long as the application is explained.

11.111 Rule 5 gives the tribunal wide case management powers. One of these commonly used in England is the consolidation of references and applications under rule 5(3)(b) so that they are heard together.[60]

58 In the Welsh Rules the considerations are the same except the first of the considerations in the English rules dealing with the importance of the case, the complexity of the issues and the resources of the parties is omitted.

59 One of the four in Wales.

60 In Wales rule 5(1) gives the tribunal the power to give directions at any time but the power to consolidate or hear together is not expressly provided for.

It is better to avoid a situation where you wish to withdraw and application that has been consolidated by the tribunal but if you do then it would be wise to argue why the tribunal should consent to the application under rule 17. The practice of allowing the patient to withdraw their applications can vary. However, as long as you give a legitimate reason then the application should be granted. In *KF v Birmingham and Solihull Mental Health Foundation Trust*[61] the court considered the right to withdraw and said the consent of the tribunal was a judicial decision which would depend on the circumstances of the case. They identified the danger of an unduly broad approach which may mean a patient is deprived of what would otherwise be a legitimate opportunity to question their detention.

An application to withdraw has been considered in a recent case of *AMA v Greater Manchester West Mental Health NHS Foundation Trust and others*.[62] This case concerned the lawfulness of a decision by a tribunal to accept the application to withdraw by the patient's mother. She had been appointed his deputy to make personal welfare decisions by an order of the Court of Protection. AMA had appointed his own solicitor who submitted that the case should proceed as AMA was arguing that he would stay in hospital informally. The court held that unless the order of the Court of Protection expressly provides that the deputy should act as a representative in proceedings under the MHA 1983, the general powers should not be relied upon by the deputy to appoint themselves as a representative and the tribunal should not have accepted the application (para 50). Charles J said:

> 36. Rule 17 provides that no notice of withdrawal will take effect unless the Tribunal consents to it. It is clear that this is intended to and does provide a safeguard for the patient as it means that such consent should not be given unless the FtT is itself satisfied that a review of a detention by an independent tribunal is not then necessary. ...
>
> 37. It follows in my view that:
>
> i) the FtT must always ask for and consider who made the application to withdraw, how it was made, and perhaps most importantly the reasons for it and thus the continuation of a detention,
>
> ii) the FtT must always make its own mind up on whether it should agree to it or conduct a review of the detention and give reasons for its decision, and
>
> iii) if it is in doubt it should refuse consent and as a consequence carry out the review itself.

61 [2010] UKUT 185 (AAC).

62 [2015] UKUT 36 (AAC).

> In effect the decision to give consent has to be based on a conclusion of the tribunal that continued detention under the MHA is justified for the reasons founding the application to withdraw (or other reasons).

Both cases recognise the tribunal's power to consent to an application to withdraw is to protect the patient.

The Code of Practice at para 12.24 says, 'The tribunal is not bound to agree, especially if the withdrawal is merely tactical or is sought within 48 hours of the hearing'. Clearly the tribunal is not bound to agree to an application but in considering this decision they will need to consider that the purpose of the tribunals consent is to protect the patient as explained in the case above.

11.112 Rule 5[63] also gives the tribunal the power to postpone hearings,[64] direct documents be provided and to hold a hearing to consider any matter including a case management matter. It may be useful in a complex case which involves a victim or evidence from MAPPA to apply for this to be dealt with in a pre-hearing. Rule 5 also gives the power to the tribunal to extend the time limits under the rules.

11.113 Rule 7[65] allows the tribunal to enforce or waive the Rules or Practice Guidance. This was discussed above at para 11.89 in terms of refusing to adjourn a case despite not having the information required by the practice direction.[66]

11.114 Rule 11(7)[67] allows the tribunal to appoint a representative where the patient wishes them to, does not wish to conduct their own case or where the patient does not have capacity to instruct a solicitor and it is in the interests of justice for them to be represented. The tribunal has a policy that if they are appointing it will be a representative who is on the law society panel of mental health representatives. This policy is now supported in practice by the fact that legal aid funding for representation is only open to those who are on the panel.[68] If you are contacted by the MHAA or a ward to represent a patient and are of the view they lack capacity then you should apply to be appointed under this rule. The tribunal also contacts solicitors to

63 Rule 5 in Wales.

64 The power to postpone or adjourn hearings is contained in a separate rule in the Welsh Rules at rule 21.

65 In Wales rule 7 and it is an irregularity from a failure to comply with and provision of the rules or a direction.

66 *AM v West London MH NHS Trust and Secretary of State for Justice* [2012] UKUT 382 (AAC).

67 Rule 13(5) in Wales.

68 Barristers are exempt from this requirement. See para 10.22.

represent when they are informed that the patient lacks capacity to instruct a representative or when they have been asked by the patient to appoint a representative.[69]

11.115 Withholding information is dealt with in rule 14.[70] The test was changed in the new Rules and the bar for not disclosing information set higher. The test is twofold. For the tribunal to withhold information they must find that the information if disclosed would be likely to cause that person or some other person serious harm; and having regard to the interests of justice, that it is proportionate to give such a direction. The question that needs to be asked even if there is evidence of serious harm is can the patient to make an effective challenge to the decision to continue to detain him if the information withheld?[71]

11.116 It is difficult to deal with these applications as they nearly always arise on the day of the hearing. The practice on whether you tell your client about the application varies. In theory the tribunal could direct that you cannot tell your client that the information exists. However, this would be extremely unusual and would only happen if telling the patient would inevitably identify the person at risk or the information to be withheld. It would be usual practice to tell your client that there is information withheld and that you will apply for disclosure of that information. There is usually an interim order made before the day withholding the information. The information withheld may not be in a report but in the notes and the tribunal has the power under this rule to withhold that as well.

11.117 As it is the duty of the parties to cooperate you should talk to the report writer to see if disclosure can be agreed if you have time. You will need to inform the tribunal that you apply for the disclosure and the tribunal will hear from the report writer and perhaps the other witnesses on why it should not be disclosed. You will have the opportunity to cross-examine them. You should then make your submissions based on rule 14[72] the overriding objective and the patient's right to be able to put their case before the tribunal. Relevant matters will include what is the basis of the patient's application and whether there is a real risk of serious harm proven by past history or current

69 In *YA v Central and North West London NHS Trust* [2015] UKUT 0037 (AAC) the Upper Tribunal considered the role of the representative at tribunals and this is fully discussed at para 9.52 above.

70 Rule 17 in Wales.

71 *RM v St Andrew's Healthcare* [2010] UKUT 119 (AAC).

72 Rule 16 in Wales.

threats. This issue and the guidance given in case-law including the *Dorset Healthcare* case are discussed in chapter 9, at para 9.35.

11.118 One common situation would be that the patient says they can return home but their relative has said they are not prepared to have them and are afraid of them knowing this. In this case it would be difficult for the patient to put their case and disclosure would depend on the likelihood of serious harm resulting from the disclosure. Any history of violence would be relevant to the tribunal's assessment.

The medical member's role and preliminary examinations

11.119 Before the change in rule 34 which took effect in April of 2014 all patients were examined by a medical member before the hearing. Rule 20 of the Welsh Rules did not change and so this remains the case in Wales. Since the change in England the only patients who will now be automatically examined by the medical member are those on section 2 or who applied whilst under section 2.[73] All other patients who want a pre-hearing examination (PHE) will have to ask the tribunal not less than 14 days before the hearing. Those who lack capacity should have a solicitor appointed before this time and then those representing can decide whether to ask for a PHE within the relevant time-limits. The tribunal could also direct a PHE of their own volition but this would be unusual.

11.120 Rule 34 should be read in conjunction with rule 39 which deals with the absent patient. In this situation the tribunal may not proceed unless they are satisfied that the patient has decided not to attend the hearing, is unable to attend the hearing for reasons of ill health as long as a PHE has been carried out unless this is impracticable or unnecessary or contrary to the interests of justice.

11.121 The Chamber President has issued guidance on medical examinations.[74] If the patient does not attend the hearing or the PHE then the tribunal are advised not to look at the notes. This is most likely to happen if the patient is on a CTO and/or referred to the tribunal. You need to be aware of this if you are representing them and if there are notes to which you wish to refer then the guidance says that if there are salient parts of the notes it is for the parties to bring this to the attention of the tribunal and lodge any part of the notes that they wish to bring to the tribunal's attention.

73 Rule 34.

74 See appendix B2.

When would you ask for a PHE?

11.122 This is a decision you will have to take with your client in every case and every case is different. If your client would present well with the tribunal medical member you may well advise them to ask for a PHE. It may help clarify the issues to be decided as your client will have had their mental state examined and will tell the medical member what they are seeking from the tribunal. It will also ensure that the medical member has access to the recent notes which if these are salient to your case is another matter to consider. This will also help you get access to the notes if this is difficult as it would be unfair for the tribunal to have seen information that you have not. Some patients say that the chance to speak to the medical member before the tribunal is important as it is the time they feel most heard and so in those cases they may instruct you to ask for a PHE. Some client's feel very nervous of the medical member and so will not want to see them. It will usually make the hearing shorter if there has been a PHE as this will mean that the medical member does not seek to elicit symptoms of illness within the hearing itself as they will have done this before the hearing and passed on their preliminary views to the other members of the panel.

How do you ask for a PHE?

11.123 You must send in your request on a T129.[75] If it arrives in a letter it will not be seen by the administrative office and not acted upon. If you are instructed within the two weeks before a hearing then you should still make the application if it is appropriate to make one. You should explain why you are making the application and why it is in accordance with the overriding objective in rule 2 that one should be ordered. You may refer to rule 2(2)(c) ensuring participation in the hearing and/or rule 2(2)(d) using the special expertise of the tribunal effectively and there may be other relevant grounds particular to your case. You must explain the reason you did not apply within the relevant time limits.

MAPPA

11.124 MAPPA stands for the Multi-Agency Public Protection Arrangements. It is essentially for coordinated management of offenders in

75 This form is currently being amended. Forms are available at: http://hmctsformfinder.justice.gov.uk/courtfinder.

the community who pose a serious risk and places duties of cooperation on those responsible for management of offenders. Those involved are probation, the prison service and the police. For mentally disordered offenders social supervisors and clinicians have a duty to cooperate. The MAPP arrangements have their origin in the Criminal Justice Act 2000 and 2003.

11.125 They grade offenders in whom they have an interest into 3 levels. Level one is the lowest level and someone at this level would be managed normally with some liaison but would not generate their own meeting. If an offender is managed at level 2 this means that a meeting or meetings will be held where the management of the offender will be discussed. The offenders considered most dangerous will be managed at level 3. These offenders are sometimes called the 'critical few'. The management of these offenders will be more robust and more senior people will be involved in the discussions with greater resources applied. The offender for example may be subject to surveillance.

11.126 The way to manage MAPP evidence at a tribunal is to ensure you know as much as possible about their involvement. Knowing the level is important. If your client is managed at level one you can submit that this means that the perceived risk from him/her is relatively low. If your client is level 2 or above then positively used it can bolster the proposition that there is an extra risk management tool in place on top of the management of the CMHT and so the risk of reoffending is less likely.

11.127 MAPP reports are often much more weighty in the tribunal's mind in the absence of the witness. The witnesses can be unfamiliar with mental health and so they are more real and fallible in person. Their oral evidence may well add a different perspective that what is written in the report. For instance it may transpire on cross-examination the evidence base is not strong or the risks assessments relied upon are static and have not allowed for the reduction in risk brought about by therapy completed in a mental health setting. It does not always serve your client to object to MAPP attending to give evidence but you need to consider making submissions about how much of the other evidence in the tribunal they should hear. They will take the information back and share it with other agencies.

11.128 What is difficult about MAPP is that they may bring much unverified information to the tribunal gained from other agencies. The offender has no right to attend meetings where they are discussed. They have no right to find out where the information given by MAPPA has come from and therefore the ability to effectively challenge the information is limited. Whether there is a right to more than the executive summary as MAPP say is a moot point but without further litigation this is as much as you are likely to get unless there is more in the reports of the Responsible Authority. At the very least it is important to point out the inability of your client to challenge this evidence or test its reliability.

11.129 The Senior President's Practice Direction of 28 October 2013 sets out how MAPPA information should come before the tribunal. Paragraph 14(r) says that the Social Circumstances Report should say 'whether the patient is known to any MAPPA meeting or agency' the level, the name of the chair of the meeting and the name of the representative of the lead agency. Para (s) says that if a MAPPA meeting wants to produce evidence to the tribunal of their view this should be attached to the social circumstances report. The same applies to community patients,[76] guardianship patients[77] and those patients who are conditionally discharged.[78]

11.130 For more information and a copy of the annual report see www.londonprobation.org.uk/what_we_do/public_protection_mappa.aspx.

76 Para 19(s) and (t).
77 Para 24(t) and (u).
78 Para 30(t) and (u).

CHAPTER 12

The process before the hearing

Making an application

Making an application and fixing a date

12.1 Once the tribunal has received the application and/or been notified that you are acting, it will send you a Case Notification Letter and Directions for all for all applications and references except applications for patients detained under section 2. This directs you to lodge an HQ1 with your availability for the hearing date. If you do not lodge this within time the tribunal will assume you agree and impose a date upon you. If the date is one on which you are not available and you have not complied with this process, you may find it more difficult to have a postponement application granted. Once the tribunal receive the medical report it will send you a request to lodge an HQ2, which is a self-explanatory form in which you fill in details of the case, for example, an estimate of the time the hearing will take.[1] Therefore if you are instructed after an application is made you will have less time.

Making pre-hearing applications

12.2 If you need make a pre-hearing application, it is useful to understand how this is done. The form is a CMR1 and is available on the website.[2] The application is decided by a *Registrar* or one of the salaried judges. The only information available to either is the information that you provide and any information that may be on the computer system. The information on the computer system includes the name of the patient, contact details of the parties, the date of the application/referral, the date of the detention and the date of hearing and the panel sitting. It will also include notes of when things happen for example when the case notification was sent out, or when reports were received, and may include cut and pasted directions or a note that a previous application has been made. The person perusing the application will not have reports nor know your client or any of the parties or circumstances of the case. There is not time to read reports.

12.3 In England, if you have secure email, this should be used to send the application so that the registrar or judge can cut and paste the directions. The Criminal Justice Secure Email Network (CJSM) is

1 These forms are currently being amended. Forms are available at: http://hmctsformfinder.justice.gov.uk/courtfinder.

2 This is the English procedure.

free and the system used by the tribunal to communicate with its stakeholders.[3] It is advisable to set up a secure account. In Wales, applications are made in correspondence with the tribunal and no separate forms are necessary.

An application for late reports

12.4 The responsible authority is notified of the application and the time for reports. If the reports do not arrive on time automatic directions will be sent. When the reports are received they are sent to the parties and the panel if one has been booked. If the hospital has identified a nearest relative in the Section B statement then the nearest relative will be noted and told of the hearing date. If your client does not want the nearest relative (NR) notified then the administrative office should be told this. For more information on this see chapter 9.

12.5 Restricted cases are currently case managed more than unrestricted cases. There is no real capacity to manage all cases closely and that is why it is important that you assist. Where reports are missing or directions need to be made you must apply.

12.6 One example of the reasons for the directions and the draft directions is:

> The application was made on day/month/year. We served the RA with the application by email/fax that same day and so the reports were due on the day/month/year. If the reports are any later the hearing will be delayed as we will need to take instructions on the reports and consider whether we need independent evidence on the basis of the evidence in the reports and further prepare our client's case. The RA is failing in its duty to cooperate with the tribunal and comply with the tribunal rules.
>
> We request the tribunal makes the following direction:
>
> 1. The Responsible Authority, shall provide the outstanding clinical / nursing / social circumstances reports to be in the form required by the Senior Presidents Practice Direction to the Tribunal Office and served on the solicitors representing and the Mental Health Casework Section by no later than 4pm on day/month/year.

An application to postpone for expert evidence

12.7 The following is an example of an application to postpone a hearing for independent evidence to be sought.

3 www.cjsm.net/.

Mr J is applying for discharge from his section 3. We received the reports of the responsible authority on Wednesday last week and have only had the opportunity to see Mr J and take his instructions today. He disagrees with the evidence of the responsible clinician that he needs to remain detained in hospital and wishes to instruct an independent psychiatrist to prepare a report on his behalf which will address, in particular, whether he can be managed in the community. We have identified the appropriate expert who can complete a report within four weeks of today's date.

We rely on the overriding objective in Rule 2[4] which includes encouraging the effective participation of the patient in the hearing. We also say that the patient has asked for the delay to his hearing and so delay is not an issue in this case and in any event is in accordance with the proper consideration of the issues. We therefore request the tribunal postpone the hearing of this case.

We would also ask the tribunal to make the following directions:

1. Those representing Mr J shall serve the tribunal and the parties with any independent evidence on which they intend to rely no later than 4pm on day/month/year.
2. If such evidence is served the expert for the patient and the RC shall decide the matters of agreement and dispute and lodge an agreed statement by 4pm on day/month/year one week later.
3. The hearing shall be listed for hearing on a date no later than (two weeks after that) with agreement of the parties.
4. Those representing the patient shall prepare an indexed and paginated bundle of the evidence, such bundle and 3 copies to be filed at the tribunal offices and one copy served on the Responsible Authority by 4pm on (one week before the hearing).
5. Both parties shall lodge an HQ1 with available dates in the listing window above.
6. Liberty to all parties to apply to the tribunal for further directions.

An application to postpone due to your unavailability

12.8 If you want the hearing postponed, you must explain your unavailability. Any application must be on the instruction of your client. For example:

I have instructions from Mr J to apply for a postponement of his hearing so that I can represent him on the day. I have known him for 10 years and he finds tribunals particularly stressful. He realises here will be a delay getting a new date but is clear that he wants me personally to represent him. I am in another tribunal hearing on that day. In

4 Tribunal Procedure (First-tier Tribunal) (Health, Education and Social Care Chamber) Rules 2008. Rule 3 in Wales.

> order to ensure my client can effectively participate in the hearing in accordance with the overriding objective I request the tribunal postpones the hearing and lists it for the date agreed.
>
> In addition I have liaised with the RA and confirm that on day/month/year at am/pm all witnesses would be available to attend.

The fuller and clearer your application the more likely you are to succeed.

Telephone case management

12.9 If your case is complex it can be useful to have a telephone case management hearing before the case convenes. A common problem when a patient is placed in medium security or out of area is engaging the local team in the discharge process. It may be that a pre hearing telephone conference is warranted with a salaried judge who may then sit on the case or at least make the initial decisions. This can be helpful to avoid adjournments. For example specific directions could be made against the local services for reports and/or attendance at the hearing. To request this you would make an application to the tribunal and ask for it to be considered by a salaried judge.

Preparing the case

Skeleton arguments

12.10 Skeleton arguments should be lodged when there is a human rights issue which requires legal analysis and reference to case-law. Skeleton arguments should only be used in a case where there is a complex legal issue to be decided and the tribunal needs to be aware of the case-law around the issue. In a fact finding tribunal though a skeleton argument can tie you into an argument which may change before the tribunal and so they should be used with care.

Preparing for the hearing

12.11 The day before you represent your client at the tribunal you will have all the evidence together. It is a useful exercise to sit down and read the evidence, putting yourself in the position of the tribunal as if you were doing so for the first time. What jumps out at you? What needs explaining? The tribunal will be looking at risk issues in particular. How long ago were the incidents of risk and why are they now manageable? What has changed?

12.12 It is also useful to do a chronology. This gives you an overview of your client's history and you can ascertain how long your client has been in the community and how long in hospital. Include admissions – voluntary and on section, dates of discharge, times spent in the community on leave and discharged, dates of offences and dates of incidents where there has been risk to the patient. Keep this as a separate sheet that you can refer to during the hearing so when the tribunal ask questions in the hearing you will have the answers at your fingertips. Some strategies for arguments to present are dealt with in chapter 13.

Preparing your client for the hearing

12.13 The day of the hearing will be stressful for your client. It may be that they see the medical member of the tribunal (although currently this should not happen unless your client is on a section 2 or a CTO), their own clinical team and the tribunal. Be aware of this stress and do what you can to ameliorate it. Try not to take your client's instructions on this day although sometimes that would be unavoidable particularly in a section 2 case. It should never be the case in a restricted case and rarely in other cases because the reports should have been with you for some time before the hearing. It is important how your client presents to the tribunal as for two, if not three, of the members this is the only time it will see them.

12.14 If your client tells you they have no mental disorder and that is what they want to tell the tribunal, then that is what your instructions are, even if the evidence of a mental disorder is compelling. If your client lacks capacity to appoint a representative and you have been appointed under Rule 11(7) then you must ascertain your client's wishes and give great weight to these. See chapter 9 for more discussion about how to approach this.

12.15 You can advise your client to make a primary submission and then a submission in the alternative. For example, if your first submission is that your client has no mental illness your second could be that if the tribunal do not accept this then submit that the loss of liberty is not proportionate to the risks posed. Use the evidence that support this case in your submissions.

12.16 As an advocate you must advise your client on the likely outcome of the hearing. In all areas of law this is an essential part of the advice you must give them. The fact that your client has a mental disorder does not mean that they are not entitled to this advice. It is important to manage their expectations as otherwise they have unrealistic hopes which may be dashed. There are many ways to do this and it can be done sensitively. For example, 'This tribunal is really important and I will help you present your case in the best possible light. It may be that the tribunal does discharge you but what it will be looking at is ... If the tribunal does not discharge you this time you will be able to reapply after .../apply to the hospital managers.'

12.17 If there are relatives who want to come to the tribunal consider how you would like them to give evidence. It may be that they oppose discharge when your client wants to be discharged and in that case they are not your witnesses and the tribunal can hear evidence if it wishes. You will then have the opportunity to cross-examine them later. Remember the importance of being polite to all witnesses. If you know your client's relatives will not support discharge you could explain to the patient that it may not be a good idea for them to be present at the hearing.

12.18 Some clients will not want to attend the tribunal. There are ways the hearings can be made easier for them, for example, speaking first and then leaving. They should be aware that it may affect the outcome but if they do not want to attend, then it is also important to respect their wishes.

Tips for advocacy at the hearing

12.19 The most important things to remember as an advocate is you are trying to convince the decision-makers. In your case it is the three members of the tribunal. Even if you are well prepared, if you see the tribunal as an opponent and are antagonistic, you will not serve your client's case.

12.20 Taking a careful note and being confident in your advocacy is important. If the panel does something you think is unnecessary or legally wrong either make legal submissions on it or politely point it out.

12.21 If you want to make submissions upon which, if the decision goes against your client, you wish to appeal, you must make sure that you do this in the hearing. Otherwise on review, or in the Upper Tribunal, you risk being unable to put the argument as it was not put to the first-tier tribunal.

12.22 The tribunal will make the decision and it is up to you to convince them that the decision your client wants is the right one. Listen to what the panel says and what its theory of the case seems to be and try to incorporate this into your submissions. Any violence on the ward, in the community or any particular vulnerability will be at the forefront of the panel's mind and that is what you must deal with in the case. It is easy to forget this if you have built a relationship with your client over some time and the offence has faded into the background for you. It will not have faded for the tribunal.

12.23 Your first duty as an advocate is to the court. This is enshrined in section 188 of the Legal Services Act 2007 and in the code of conduct for solicitors and barristers. This duty overrides all other duties including those to your client. See chapter 7 for a full discussion of this. If you are making submissions on law, and you know of an authority that goes against you, it must be put to the tribunal in submissions and you must try to distinguish it. You must not knowingly let your client lie to the tribunal. If your client says, 'I will tell the tribunal that I will agree to see my community team but as soon as I am out I am moving and will not be found' you cannot let them say this knowing it to be untrue. You advise your client of this and then they need to decide whether to tell the truth or instruct another representative. The more common situation is if you are told by your client that they will accept treatment and you doubt this. In this situation you can still continue to act. You are bound by your instructions and it is not up to you to determine the facts. That is for the tribunal. However, it may be that your client has previously left hospital and ceased taking medication so you need to have the tribunal think about what has changed and why it would be different this time.

12.24 The tribunal is to a significant extent inquisitorial, not adversarial, in nature.[5] There are few rules of evidence and the tribunal can listen to any evidence they decide is relevant.[6] Being unnecessarily combative is not good strategy. When witnesses are impolite to you, your greatest weapon is to be polite back. This does not mean letting then off the hook. Explain this to your client who may want you to act like a lawyer from the television who reduces the witness to tears. This is just a TV programme and reducing any witness to tears is not a good

5 *R (Ashworth Hospital Authority) v Ealing, Hammersmith and Hounslow Health Authority* [2001] EWHC 901 (Admin) at para 16, 'The procedure of a Mental Health Review Tribunal is to a significant extent inquisitorial. Rule 11 of the Mental Health Review Tribunal Rules 1983 ... requires the medical member of the tribunal to examine the patient and to form an opinion of his mental condition ...' Given the medical members examination has been changed in many cases the inquisitorial nature of the tribunal may be more nuanced.

6 There are principles which apply to the use of evidence, eg the comments of Munby J in *R (DJ) v MHRT* [2005] EWHC 587 (Admin) on hearsay evidence and the weight to be given to it.

idea. If your client understands this they will feel more involved in their own case and understand your tactics.

12.25 You may know a lot of information about your client as you may have acted for them for some time. Remember that the tribunal only knows what is in the reports and what it may have been told by the medical member and heard in oral evidence. The tribunal will not have the empathy with your client that you may have. If there is important evidence that does not appear in the reports, it is for you to ensure that is before the tribunal. The most recent Practice Direction emphasises that this is the task of the representative and suggests that the best way to achieve this is to prepare an extract of evidence.[7]

12.26 Do not repeat evidence. If the evidence is there in a form that suits you then leave it as it is and make a submission at the end. For example, frequently the question about how well leave is going elucidates a response from the witness which is worse that the evidence in writing. Going over evidence already before the tribunal will just irritate the panel and, importantly, the more you explore it with a responsible clinician (RC) who wants detention upheld, the more they will explain their position and the more influence their view will have on the tribunal. If the reports say Ms S has been compliant with treatment since her admission, leave it as it is and make a submission on it at the end. Before you ask a question, know where you are going with it. Fishing expeditions in tribunals are usually not a good idea because generally the RA witnesses will make their case more strongly.

12.27 A properly prepared case is the way to win. The notes often hold the evidence which will help. For example, the RC says Mr C keeps smoking cannabis which is bad for him. You go through the notes, analyse what happens after he has smoked cannabis and, if his mental state is not deteriorating and this is clear from the notes, use this before the tribunal. You couch it in terms of an understanding that research shows illicit substances generally have a bad effect on a person's mental illness but in this case the evidence does not bear this out. Do check the evidence in the community as well as sometimes the effect can be linked to the amount of substance consumed.

12.28 Preparing your case means developing a theory. This means working out what your argument will be, ensuring the evidence is there to support your theory, and making clear submissions on it. So for example, if your argument will be that your client is much more compliant than is said in the reports, make sure the evidence

7 See Practice Direction and Guidance: Medical Examinations.

is there. Check how many appointments they attended in the community, how they took medication, and whether the evidence shows they did. If your client was treated by depot injection, whether they were late for the appointments and whether the real date of discharge from hospital was earlier than stated as they were on section 17 leave for two months before. How quick was the deterioration and how high the risks before admission? All of this evidence will help you formulate the questions you need to ask of the professional witnesses present.

12.29 However, particularly in mental health cases, the oral evidence may differ from what you had prepared. Do not be tied to your theory if it becomes untenable. The difference between a competent advocate and a good advocate is the ability to change the theory as the evidence unfolds. You must have a clear sense of what you are hoping for and what is potentially achievable. Your advice on the evidence and chances of success should not only inform your strategy but if explained to your client should have an effect on their instructions so that they are realistic about the outcome.

12.30 Your job at the end is to sum up the case by directing the tribunal to relevant law, including case-law, and explaining the theory of the case you want them to accept. You can refer to the evidence heard but do not just repeat it.

12.31 Do not state as a fact evidence which is in dispute. If the client says in answer to your question 'I will take my treatment' and in answer to the medical member 'If I have a choice I will not' do not say at the end 'my client says he will take medication' because this is not all of the evidence. That is why you need to carefully listen. This will only serve to highlight the inconsistency.

12.32 You should make sure you know the relevant law and are able to relate cases to your submissions. The case-law of the Upper Tribunal is available on their website and is accessible to all. The other tool the MHT panel will turn to is the *Mental Health Act Manual*[8] which is issued to all legal members and so you need to rely on this resource. *Legal Action*[9] has regular mental health law updates which helpfully summarise cases. Mental Health Law Online is also useful. If relying on any source, take the panel to the place in the text you are relying on and bring copies. Anticipate the legal problems and ensure you have an answer, or at least the material on which the tribunal can

8 Richard Jones, *Mental Health Act Manual*, Sweet and Maxwell, 17th edition, 2014.

9 www.lag.org.uk/magazine/.

make a decision before you get to the tribunal. In a restricted case this will include having draft conditions if you are seeking a conditional discharge.

Conditions usually cover where the patient is to live on leaving hospital and attending appointments for treatment and with the community team. They can cover abstinence from substances and requirement to submit to random drug tests and exclusion zones to safeguard victims among other things. An example of conditions set by a tribunal would be:

1. Mr ... shall live in 24-hour supported accommodation agreed by his RC and social supervisor.
2. Mr ... shall attend appointments and follow treatment recommendations of his RC and social supervisor.
3. Mr ... shall not take substances, either legal or illicit, and shall submit to random drug testing by his community team.
4. Mr ... shall not enter the postcode ... as set out on the attached map.

12.33 The ultimate decision for the tribunal is this. Is denying the patient their right to liberty proportionate to the risks posed? It is this question you need the tribunal to consider and the question to which you should address your mind in preparation and delivery of your client's case.

12.34 Many advocates run out of steam when it gets to the submissions. If you need 10 minutes to get your submissions prepared ask for the time. They are very important both for the decision on the day and for setting up any appeal that you may take. The tribunal must address your submissions in its decision.

12.35 It is useful to remind the tribunal that the decision it makes in the case of a detained individual is an extremely important one.

> The issues before Mental Health Review Tribunals are probably the most important issues decided by any tribunals. The Tribunals make decisions as to the compulsory detention and treatment, and thus the liberty, of the individual. A wrong decision may lead on the one hand to the unnecessary detention of a patient, and, at the other extreme, to the release of a patient who is a danger to himself and may present a risk to the public.[10]

10 *R (KB and others) v Mental Health Review Tribunal and the Secretary of State for Health* [2002] EWHC 639 (Admin) per Stanley Burnton J at para 32.

CHAPTER 13

The hearing

The tribunal panel

13.1 The tribunal panel is made up of three people. The judge is legally qualified and chairs the hearing. There is also a psychiatrist and a specialist member. The specialist member may come from a variety of backgrounds but usually have substantial experience of a related area. They could be a retired member of the police, a psychologist, a social worker or nurse or have worked as a manager in the NHS or social services. The psychiatrist will also be from different areas of specialism, for example old age psychiatry or forensic psychiatry.

13.2 The judge sits in the middle with the psychiatrist to their right and the specialist member to their left. The witnesses are usually arranged from right to left: the Responsible Authority (RA)'s psychiatrist, representative, patient, nurse or nearest relative, and social worker. This may vary depending on the shape of the room and the witnesses attending. The tribunal relies on the hospital to provide rooms and so are subject to what is available. When seeing a client who has not had a tribunal before it is useful to draw a diagram of this so that they know what to expect and leave it with them.

The hearing process

13.3 The introductory process differs with different judges. The judge will introduce the panel, explain the procedure, the privacy of the hearing, highlight the independence of the tribunal from the hospital and usually whether the decision will be announced on the day. There is no compulsion to announce the decision but it is usual practice to do so. Rule 41[1] of the Tribunal Procedure Rules (HESC) provides that the tribunal may announce the decision orally at the hearing. How much the judge says will depend on the individual judge. Some will just give the decision without reasons but many may outline their reasons then and there.

13.4 After the introduction the judge will report back what they have heard from the medical member of the interview with the patient before the hearing, if there has been a pre-hearing examination (PHE), see above at paras 11.119–11.123. It is lawful for the medical member to reach a provisional opinion of the patient's mental

1 The Tribunal Procedure (First-tier Tribunal) (Health, Education And Social Care Chamber) Rules 2008 SI No 2699; Rule 28 of the Mental Health Review Tribunal for Wales Rules 2008.

condition at this stage as long as it is a preliminary view. It can be a view on the ultimate issue of the need for detention.[2] Unless the matter is a section 2 or a CTO the patient will probably have been seen by the medical member on a different day if they have requested a PHE.

13.5 The judge may also seek clarification on the application the patient is making, if any, before the tribunal that day and an agreement on the order in which they will hear from the witnesses. For example, if the patient is seeking a recommendation for a CTO only, say so. The tribunal has wide powers to control the hearing under the Rules. When applying the rules controlling the hearing the tribunal must consider the overriding objective of justice and fairness and in particular avoiding unnecessary formality and seeking flexibility in the proceedings.[3] If a witness is being disruptive and preventing the hearing from proceeding the tribunal can exclude the witness but this is quite rare.[4] They can also exclude a witness if the presence of that witness is likely to prevent another person giving evidence and to ensure information that should be private is kept private.[5] If a person is notified of the hearing as the tribunal was of the opinion that he or she should be given the opportunity of being heard (eg the victim of any offence) that person has a right to attend the hearing.[6] What part they take in the hearing, when they are able to speak to the tribunal, and in the presence of whom, is up to the tribunal considering the facts of the particular case and applying the rules discussed above.

13.6 In terms of the order of the proceedings the patient should have given instructions on whether they want to speak first or after the professional evidence before the hearing begins. It is sometimes useful if the patient speaks first as it may be hard for them to remain through the whole hearing given they may disagree and be distressed by what is said. It is also sometimes useful to clarify the issues and so the first person the tribunal hears from is the patient and the whole case of the RA is not embedded in the minds of the panel before you begin. This tactic is useful when a client is not very well but also when they are and will be good witnesses. A report prepared jointly by the Care Quality Commission and the Administrative Justice and

2 *R (RD) v Mental Health Review Tribunal and Secretary of State for the Home Department* [2007] EWHC 781 (Admin).

3 Rule 2(b) England; r3(a) Wales.

4 Rule 38(4) England; r25(4) Wales.

5 Rule 38(4) (a)–(d) England; r25(4)–(5) Wales.

6 Rules 33 and 36 England; rr16 and 26 Wales.

Tribunals Council reported that a significant number of patients felt they had not been listened to.[7] Having the patient talk first and then be given an opportunity to speak at the end can ensure that they feel they are heard.

13.7 However, it is probably more common for the professional witnesses to go first. Some judges may remind the patient that they can give evidence in the absence of others if they choose but it would be rare that a client would be advised to do this. Many applications are made on the basis that the patient will cooperate with the community team and if they will not give evidence in front of them this may undermine the argument.

13.8 Preliminary matters may arise about disclosure of evidence to the patient. This is discussed at paras 11.115–11.118.

13.9 The tribunal need to be satisfied of the criteria in section 72, 73 or 74 of the MHA 1983, which places some burden on the Responsible Authority.[8] This standard of proof is a civil one and not a 'beyond reasonable doubt' standard as in criminal proceedings.[9] The tribunal is a finder of facts and can come to a different conclusion on the evidence than all witnesses in front of it as long as it adequately explains why it has come to that conclusion. See *RH v South London and Maudsley NHS Foundation Trust* where the evidence of the RA and an independent psychiatrist supported absolute discharge but the tribunal came to a different conclusion and explained adequately why it had done so.[10]

13.10 In addition, the rules of evidence that would apply in civil courts do no apply to the tribunal.[11] This means the panel can admit, and give appropriate weight to, hearsay evidence (ie, evidence that the witness has only heard about but not witnessed themselves) and hear from any witnesses it finds could give relevant evidence. There will always be a significant amount of hearsay evidence in tribunal reports and oral evidence. If the evidence of the responsible clinician (RC) is not convincing the tribunal can explore other evidence and it would not be open to a representative to say that the RA has not proved their case and therefore the patient should be discharged as you might in

7 *Patients' experiences of the First-tier Tribunal (Mental Health)*, AJTC/CQC March 2011, page 6. Available at http://ajtc.justice.gov.uk/.

8 See rule 10.

9 *R(DJ) v Mental Health Review Tribunal* [2005] EWHC 587 (Admin) and approved in the Court of Appeal [2005] EWCA Civ 1605.

10 *RH v South London and Maudsley NHS Foundation Trust* [2010] UKUT 32 (AAC)

11 Rule 15 England; r18 Wales.

a criminal trial.[12] Hearsay evidence in the mental health tribunal was dealt with by Munby J, as he then was, in the High Court and his comments were endorsed in the Court of Appeal.[13] He provided useful guidance for advocates and tribunals when he said:

> If the tribunal is relying upon hearsay evidence it must take into account that it is hearsay and must have regard to the particular dangers involved in relying upon second, third or fourth hand hearsay. The Tribunal must be appropriately cautious or relying upon assertions as to past events which are not securely recorded in contemporaneous notes, particularly of the only evidence is hearsay. The Tribunal must be alert to the well-known problem that constant repetition in 'official' reports or statements may, in the 'official' mind, turn into established fact something which rigorous forensic investigation shows is in truth nothing more than 'institutional folk law' with no secure foundation in either recorded or provable fact. The Tribunal must guard against too quickly jumping to conclusions adverse to the patient in relation to past events where the only direct evidence is that of the patient himself, particularly where there is no clear account in contemporaneous notes of what is alleged to have happened. ... and if the incident is really fundamental to its decision, it must bear in mind that fairness may require the patient to be given the opportunity to cross-examine the relevant witness if their evidence is to be relied on at all.

13.11 If a party fails to attend the hearing the tribunal may proceed if they know that the person knows about the hearing or that reasonable steps have been taken to notify them of the hearing and it is in the interests of justice to proceed.[14]

The reason for representation

13.12 The role of the representative before the tribunal is that of a legal advocate. The aim of an advocate is to convince the panel that the interpretation of the evidence put forward by the patient is the interpretation that they should accept. An advocate should not be the tribunal's adversary as if this is the case the tribunal panel will become alienated and more difficult to persuade.

13.13 Being organised greatly assists an advocate. A hearing folder with dividers and tabs which aid access to parts of the reports challenged, or parts of the reports relied upon, enables a representative to access

12 Jeremy Cooper, 'The burden and the standard of proof?' *Tribunals*, Spring 2008. Available at www.judiciary.gov.uk.

13 *R(DJ) v Mental Health Review Tribunal* [2005] EWHC 587 (Admin) and approved in the Court of Appeal [2005] EWCA Civ 1605.

14 Rules 39 and 34 England; rr20 and 27 Wales.

quickly the evidence needed for the question or submission facilitates the advocacy. When referring to the report the tribunal and the witness should be taken to the page and paragraph.

13.14 Questioning an expert is a very difficult skill to perfect as the expert will know more about their area of expertise than any advocate. In the mental health context a psychiatrist will know more about psychiatry than any advocate before them could know. Any advantage an advocate may have will come from thorough knowledge of the client's notes and reports and, through this preparation, being able to challenge the facts which form the evidence for the opinion. It is important to use questions to establish facts as it is much more difficult to challenge the RC's opinion. For example an argument for the release of a patient who is inevitably going to relapse could be based on the fact that in the past it has taken over a year for the relapse to occur. [15] You will only know this by knowing the history. Therefore the questions should focus on establishing the facts that have gone before. Once they are established the next step is not to make a submission to the RC but to the tribunal. It will not help to ask the doctor why he is not discharging the patient given the length of time it takes for the patient's mental health to deteriorate as they will be able to set out at length their reasons why. The case-law is clear on deterioration in the near future particularly when the risks are low.[16] Establish the facts and leave the determination to the tribunal on the submissions you make. Unless there is strong expert evidence against the RC a case will not usually be won on medical knowledge except if this comes from the panel itself or an independent expert.

A case plan

13.15 Advocates should have a case plan. Preparing a chronology is a first step so that the patient's care is seen longitudinally and in perspective. It may be that a patient has had one admission a year for 10 years but that the admissions are short and the recovery fast. Or your argument may be that the patient will take medication in the community. Careful reading of the notes may clarify that although the patient does stop taking medication they have taken medication for much longer periods of time than they have not. Having evidence of this from the community notes will be invaluable. It is often the case the

15 *CM v Derbyshire Healthcare NHS Foundation Trust and Secretary of State for Justice* [2011] UKUT 129 (AAC).

16 *CM v Derbyshire Healthcare NHS Foundation Trust and Secretary of State for Justice* [2011] UKUT 129 (AAC).

inpatient RC does not treat the patient in the community and therefore a representative has the opportunity to know much more than the witness before the tribunal. Cross-examination of the RC on how many times the patient did attend for the depot and keep appointments may make inroads into a report that relies on non-compliance with treatment and disengagement with their mental health team. It may be that the patient was taking medication and seeing their team until two weeks before the admission and they had been taking medication and seeing their team at all other times. Using this argument you will also need to look at why they stopped and, once they did, how long it took for them to relapse. In addition, what happened when they did relapse and why it would not happen now or why it takes some time to happen? Even if the patient may relapse the next question should be what happens when the relapse occurs, and how great are the risks to them or the public on relapse? Follow your plan by asking the appropriate questions.

13.16 The tribunal is generally reluctant to adjourn but every case needs to be considered on its own facts and in light of the overriding objective of justice and fairness.[17] The Upper Tribunal has been clear that there can be no policy of refusing adjournments and all cases must be decided on their own merits and in accordance with the overriding objective of fairness and justice.[18]

Questions to ask when preparing a case

13.17 Below are some common scenarios which occur and questions to ask yourself when preparing your theory of the case. All cases are different but there are common themes and this is an attempt to identify them so that you can begin to develop the arguments on the facts that face you. In any case the starting point to put to a tribunal is that detention should be the last resort. In general a representative should never ask a question that they do not know the answer to.

1. Patients who will inevitably relapse with a long psychiatric history

- Why does the patient relapse?
- If it is because they do not take medication how long does it take them to deteriorate? In a case where a patient on a restriction order had a chaotic lifestyle he was recalled to hospital because his team were concerned that his chaotic lifestyle would lead him

17 Rule 2 England; r21 Wales.

18 *RC v NHS Islington and others* [2013] UKUT 167 (AAC).

to relapse. He had not relapsed for many years and it took some time for a relapse to occur. The UT held '*there was no real evidence to support its view that non-compliance with medication and the risk of consequent relapse in the near future would probably occur*'.[19]

- Why did they stop medication?
- What type of medication are they on? Compliance with a depot injection is easier to monitor. Does it take longer to relapse on depot medication? How often do they have to take the depot? If only once a month is it more likely they will comply?
- What are the signs of deterioration?
- How long is the recovery?
- Once well how long are the periods of remission?
- Can the signs of deterioration (relapse indicators) be picked up by the patient or their care team/family/friends? Does the CMHT visit regularly? Are they in contact with anyone regularly? Does the patient present to anyone?
- What happens when the patient does deteriorate? Is the risk to their own health or safety or the protection of others?
- Is detention a proportionate response to the risks?
- Is detention the least restrictive alternative? Could care be provided in the community? Is there a Home Treatment Team who could visit daily for a limited period?
- Is the risk different now? Has something changed?
- Are the symptoms distressing?
- Do the symptoms interfere with the patient's daily living/social functioning?
- How much better can they get?

2. Patients who will inevitably use illicit substances

- Analyse the effect of drugs on the patient's mental state from the notes. Look at the times when the patient is known to have taken drugs and the days subsequent to analyse the effect on the patient's mental state.
- Some patients can take illicit drugs whilst on medication with little effect on their mental state as the medication works to protect relapse even with substances. Some patients only need a small amount of cannabis to relapse.

19 *CM v Derbyshire Healthcare NHS Foundation Trust and Secretary of State for Justice* [2011] UKUT 129 (AAC).

- If drug taking is inevitable and causes relapse what are the risks on relapse? Can they be managed in the community? Can the relapse be picked up at an early stage?
- Is the patient taking drugs in hospital in any event?
- The use of drugs in itself is not a ground for detention unless it affects the patient's mental state.[20]
- Can the use of medication ameliorate the effect of substances?

3. Patients who are acutely unwell

- Does the patient accept they are unwell?
- Would they leave the ward?
- Are they impulsive?
- Are they consenting to treatment?

4. Patients who are currently well

- Do they accept their illness?
- Would they take their medication even if they do not believe it helps to avoid another admission?
- Would they keep in contact with the CMHT?
- How long would a relapse take?
- How long does the recovery take?
- How long does recovery last?
- Could further relapse be picked up by the patient /others?
- What are the risks on relapse?
- In a restricted case would the conditions be enough to mange any risk?
- Could the risks be managed by a CTO?

5. The first admission

- Is this the first episode of illness?
- If so, there is no evidence that it will happen again.
- How long were there signs of deterioration apparent?
- If there has been some time when the illness has been developing what interventions were tried?
- Will the discharge plan be different from what was tried before admission?
- What are the risks of relapse?
- Rapidity of relapse or relapse cannot be relied upon without history.
- Why are things different now than before admission?

20 MHA 1983 s1(3).

- Could community treatment work?
- Is it better to leave hospital as soon as possible for therapeutic relationships?
- Is there an early intervention team with more resources available to the patient?

6. Patients with a learning disability

- A patient suffering with a learning disability also needs to be exhibiting seriously irresponsible or abnormally aggressive behaviour along with the learning disability to be detained under the Act.
- What is the behaviour?
- The behaviour needs to be *seriously* irresponsible
- Is the behaviour within a cultural/social context? Even if unwise it may not be seriously irresponsible.

7. Patients on a CTO

- The main argument on a CTO relates to the necessity of the RC's power of recall. Is there another way, a relative, informal admission?
- Is the CTO just being used to enforce treatment and is therefore treatment in the community by another route?
- Is the patient a revolving door patient at whom the CTO was aimed?
- Does the patient agree to treatment in any event?
- Why is a quick admission essential?
- What are the risks on relapse?
- Has the power of recall been used?

8. Restricted patients

- Can the risks be managed in the community with conditions and the power of recall?
- Look for risk assessment tools. In restricted inpatient wards every patient will probably have been assessed using the HCR-20. This is a risk assessment tool which looks at 20 items. There are static factors that cannot be changed, eg previous violence; dynamic factors which are clinical items which can change eg active symptoms of a major mental illness; and risk management items which include feasibility of plans and exposure to destabilizers. Any assessment using the HCR-20 includes an interview, review of the file, interviews with appropriate others such as probation officers, psychologists and family. If using a psychiatric expert then they should comment on the HCR-20.

- The power of recall can be exercised when there is a risk of deterioration rather than having to wait for a deterioration to occur.
- Forensic teams generally have less patients on their case load and so are able to offer greater support (although some boroughs and counties now have no forensic teams).
- Forensic patients usually go into 24-hour supported care first, which enables better monitoring.
- If possible present a care plan as an alternative to hospital, eg, a social work report with suggestions of placements and if possible a hostel who has assessed the patient.
- In general the more unescorted leave the patient has had before the hearing the better.
- The patient has to understand disclosure to the clinical team, eg, if the past offence is rap,e any future relationship would have to be disclosed.
- The past is the best predictor of the future so there must be a change in circumstances, eg, the patient was not managed by a forensic team, lived independently had not completed the treatment etc.
- Does the patient understand their relapse indicators and what would they do if they began to relapse?
- If seeking a DCD check with the RC whether any leave to a hostel is familiarisation leave or testing? If the leave is for testing the patient's readiness for discharge then that may mean that the patient is not ready for discharge. However, if it is just a hostel requirement to familiarise the patient with the hostel, rules and other residents then they may be ready.
- This is a useful quote for submissions to the tribunal in a restricted case and for formulating the case plan:

  > ... the conditional discharge regime, properly used, is of great benefit to patients and the public, and conducive to the Convention object of restricting the curtailment of personal liberty to the maximum, because it enables tribunals to ensure that restricted patients compulsorily detained in hospital represent the hard core of those who suffer from mental illness, are a risk to themselves or others and cannot be effectively treated and supervised otherwise than in hospital. If there is a possibility of treating and supervising a patient in the community, the imposition of conditions permits that possibility to be explored and, it may be, tried.[21]

- Are there additional safeguards, eg MAPPA, conditions of licence, probation input, exclusion zones?

21 *R v Secretary of State for the Home Department ex p IH* [2003] UKHL 59 para 26.

- In addition, the same questions set out above apply to preparing the case of a restricted patient. Usually the risks of harm are greater but there are additional risk management tools of conditions and recall.

9. Patients with personality disorder

- Personality disorder (PD) cases are usually restricted cases or cases where the patient has done something dangerous but not been convicted. They can also be those with emotional instability who self-harm and these patients are often not restricted.
- The focus in these cases will be on psychological treatment and management of risk.
- What treatment has been completed?
- Is the risk increased by a return to illicit substances?
- Is the patient able to be trusted? Is there evidence of failures in supervision such as breach of bail, absconding etc? This is very important in personality disorder cases as there is no easy treatment.
- Will the patient work with a clinical team in the community openly? If they are not trustworthy is there another way to manage the risks? For example, if the risk is increased by return to illicit drugs will random urine drug screens help? Could a 24-hour hostel manage the risks with supervision?
- What are the reports of the psychology groups?
- In cases where the risk is to others, it is useful to remember that the offending behaviour and the details of this behaviour will be in the tribunals mind. They have no relationship with the patient and most reports start off with a description in graphic detail of the offending. The Statement of the Secretary of State will also have a description. This is a hurdle that needs to be overcome. There is often no debate about the seriousness of the offence but the question for the tribunal is not this but whether the risk to others can be managed in the community with conditions.
- The circumstances around offending will lead to an analysis of the risk factors for future offending. Any change in those circumstances may lead to a decrease in risk.
- Use the analysis to look at what has changed from the time the offence was committed and the time of the tribunal.
- Both considering independent psychiatric and psychological reports is necessary but independent experts need to be good both in writing and in front of the tribunal and have some seniority in their field.

- Personality disorder cases are nearly always focused on management of risk. Breaking down the risk can be helpful.
- Is the risk encapsulated in any way, eg, partners in intimate relationships.
- Look for psychopathy scores from a PCL-R (psychopathy checklist revised) or PCL-SV (psychopathy checklist short version). In general a person with a high psychopathy score is seen as more likely to reoffend. There is lots of research around this and some research that suggests these tests are less reliable that previously thought to be. Perhaps signpost some of the research? An expert report is the best way to have this evidence considered and they will know about the research. An advocate using expert research for cross-examination is difficult as there will always be another paper. An expert using the evidence will be much more effective given their professional expertise.
- There will be other risk assessment tools which will try to quantify a risk of reoffending for example the HCR-20, or OASys which will apply to most patients and there are specific tools for example the sex offenders like the MATRIX or the VRAG (which includes a PCL score as one of the factors in assessing the risk) for violent offenders. Some of these assessments will contain static factors which will not be able to be changed such as the offence and dynamic factors that can change such as response to treatment and insight. Your expert will be able to deal with these tools and their interpretation.
- Medical treatment is defined widely in the MHA 1983[22] as '... medical treatment includes nursing, psychological intervention and specialist mental health habilitation, rehabilitation and care ...' and in s145(4) 'Any reference in this Act to medical treatment, in relation to mental disorder, shall be construed as a reference to medical treatment, the purpose of which is to alleviate or prevent a worsening of the disorder of one or more of its manifestations'. However, these provisions only define treatment not the circumstances in whether it is available and appropriate.[23]
- The Code of Practice deals with appropriate medical treatment and at para 23.9 it says 'this medical treatment must be appropriate, taking into account the nature and degree of the persons

22 MHA 1983 s145.

23 *MD v Nottinghamshire Health Care NHS Trust* [2010] UKUT 59 (AAC), Judge Jacobs at para 15 '[These] provisions only define medical treatment. They do not define the circumstances where the treatment is either available or appropriate...'.

mental disorder ...'.[24] Chapter 21 deals with those who are suffering from a personality disorder and says at para 21.8 'What constitutes appropriate medical treatment for a particular patient with a personality disorder will depend very much on the individual circumstances. First and foremost that calls for a clinical judgment by the clinicians responsible for their assessment and treatment'.

- There is no definition of what is available or appropriate and this is a matter of fact and judgment of the tribunal which is an expert body.[25] A useful structure of questions was suggested in the Upper Tribunal to determine whether in fact the detention was containment.[26] At paragraph 33, Upper Tribunal Judge Jacobs says, '... The solution lies in the tribunal's duty to ensure that the conditions for continued detention are satisfied. The tribunal must investigate behind assertions, generalisations and standard phrases. By focusing on specific questions, it will ensure that it makes an individualised assessment for the particular patient. What precisely is the treatment that can be provided? What discernible benefit may it have on this patient? Is that benefit related to the patient's mental disorder or to some unrelated problem? Is the patient truly resistant to engagement? ...' These questions are useful to put to your expert to answer so that in submissions you can explain this to the tribunal.

10. Patients without after-care

- All patients who have been on treatment sections of the MHA 1983 are entitled to section 117 after-care.
- The argument may be that with after-care the patient can be managed in the community and therefore the detention in hospital is no longer appropriate.
- There is no duty for the local authority to monitor inpatients to see whether an after-care package could be provided[27] and so if a representative thinks this is the case contacting the local authority

24 See paras 23.7–23.21 of the Code for the appropriate medical treatment test and its application.

25 *MD v Nottinghamshire Health Care NHS Trust* para 48: 'I have not given a definition of either "available" or "appropriate". Nor have I drawn the boundary between containment and treatment. Those are matters of fact and judgment for the tribunal. It is an expert body and it has to use that expertise to make its findings and exercise its own judgment ...'.

26 *DL-H v Devon Partnership NHS Trust v Secretary of State for Justice* [2010] UKUT 102 (AAC).

27 *R (B) v Camden LBC* [2005] EWHC 1366 (Admin).

or applying to the tribunal for a direction for a care plan are useful ways to begin the after-care planning process.

- In a restricted case, once a deferred conditional discharge has been made, the local authority and health authority have to use reasonable endeavours to provide after-care to the patient once they know of the decision, but the duty to provide after-care only arises on discharge. It is important that the representative lets them know if they do not. They may leave before the decision is announced and the MHAA may not send them a copy.
- In an unrestricted case it may be appropriate to make an application to adjourn if the evidence shows that with an after-care plan the patient could be discharged but the tribunal needs more information about what the after-care would entail.[28]
- Chapter 33 of the Code deals with after-care and says that the planning for after-care needs to begin happening on admission.[29]

28 *R (H) v Ashworth Hospital Authority* [2000] EWCA Civ 923.

29 Code of Practice para 33.10; para 31.7 in the Code of Practice for Wales.

CHAPTER 14

Appeals

Receiving the decision

14.1 Once a decision has been made by the First-tier Tribunal (FTT) written reasons must be provided within seven days or within three days on a section 2.[1] The FTT can extend or shorten the time for delivery of the decision[2] but this is unusual and would only happen in a complicated case or where there was a specific reason to extend time.

Deciding on whether to appeal

14.2 The right to appeal should be considered every time a decision is received. The representative needs to discuss the decision with the client to decide whether there are any grounds to appeal. There must be an error of law in the decision to make an appeal and the client must want to appeal the decision. Not agreeing with the decision is not enough. The facts have been found by the FTT, and the Upper Tribunal (UT) will not interfere unless they are so irrational that no tribunal could have reasonably reached the same decision. This is very rare.

14.3 In 2012 there were approximately 75 applications in England. 18 of these were overturned by the FTT. The most common reason for an application was that the tribunal's reasons were inadequate.[3]

14.4 Once the parties receive a decision they then have 28 days from the time it was sent by the tribunal to apply for permission to appeal.[4] This time can also be extended if there is an adequate reason for the delay.[5] As with all the rules and decision to extend time would happen with the overriding objective in mind.[6]

14.5 Careful reading of the decision is crucial when deciding whether it is lawful and whether there are any grounds on which to appeal. In addition to reading the decision, and making the assessment of lawfulness, advise your client the possible outcomes of any appeal and the chances of success. In England the FTT must first decide whether to review the decision and if not whether they will grant

1 Tribunal Procedure (First-tier Tribunal) (Health, Education and Social Care Chamber) Rules 2008 SI No 2699 rule 41.

2 Rule 5(3)(a).

3 A recent clear decision on reasons is *HK v Llanarth Court Hospital* [2014] UKUT 410 (AAC) paras 10–16.

4 Rule 46. The UT Rules r21(3)(b) say a month.

5 Rule 5(3)(a).

6 Rule 2.

permission to appeal. In Wales the application is only for permission to appeal and the FTT has no power to review the decision or take any action to set it aside.[7] If an application to review in England is successful the most likely outcome is a rehearing.

14.6 A successful application for review and permission to appeal would only in exceptionally rare circumstances result in the release of a patient who is still detained. This has not happened since the new system has been in place. So far the Upper Tribunal has only substituted their decision for that of the FTT in the case of *AH*[8] when allowing a public hearing. It may be that if this is the only possible outcome, and the likelihood of success in front of the FTT is low, your client will not want to pursue this. It may be that they have another right to an application in any event and want to proceed in that way.

The funding position is discussed at paras 10.67–10.68.

The relevant Rules in the First-tier Tribunal

14.7 Rule 44 of the English Rules[9] is a slip rule which allows the correction of a clerical mistake or accidental slip or omission. So, for example, if the date if birth of the patient is wrong or the date on which the tribunal sat is wrong then the judge can change these details.[10] You should notify the tribunal who will then get the judge to address the mistake and the corrected decisions will be sent out to the parties.

14.8 Rule 45 gives the tribunal the power to set aside decisions on the basis of procedural irregularity. This must be in the interests of justice[11] and one of the conditions set out in the rule must also be satisfied. They are that: a document had not been sent or received by a party[12] or the tribunal,[13] or a party or their representative was not at the

7 Mental Health Review Tribunal for Wales Rules 2008.

8 *AH v West London Mental Health NHS Trust* [2011] UKUT 74 (AAC).

9 Tribunal Procedure (First-tier Tribunal) (Health, Education and Social Care Chamber) Rules 2008 SI No 2699.

10 This power has now been given to the tribunal staff, *see Practice Statement: Delegation of Functions to Staff on or after 10 June 2014.*

11 Tribunal Procedure (First-tier Tribunal) (Health, Education and Social Care Chamber) Rules 2008 SI No 2699 rule 45(1).

12 Rule 45(2)(a).

13 Rule 45(2)(b).

hearing,[14] or there was some other irregularity in the proceedings.[15] For example, if the nearest relative had written a letter to the tribunal and the patient's representative did not receive a copy of this then the FTT could set aside the decision.

14.9 An application for permission to appeal has to be considered by the FTT as a first step. The FTT on receipt of the application must consider whether it should review the decision if it believes there has been an error of law.[16] The FTT should only review a decision where the error is clear and unarguable. If there is an arguable case the FTT should grant permission to appeal and the Upper Tribunal should consider the arguments.[17] If a decision is reviewed and set aside without all the parties having been able to make representations then the party can apply for the action to be set aside and reviewed again.[18]

14.10 Reviews are undertaken by the FTT in response to an application or on its own initiative.[19] If it does review a decision it can correct accidental errors,[20] amend reasons given for a decision[21] or set aside a decision.[22]

14.11 The review process and the Upper Tribunal took the place of the past system where the only avenue for an appeal from the FTT was an application for judicial review to the High Court. This was a complicated process and often slow. The idea behind the current system is that it allows quick access to justice for those challenging the decision of the First-tier Tribunal. Therefore in most cases the FTT does not ask the other parties to the proceedings for their views so that a decision is made quickly and if the result is a rehearing it can be expedited. In some cases the judge reviewing the decision will ask for submissions from the other side. If this does not happen, and your client is unhappy with the result, you can lodge your submissions after the decision. The FTT then looks at the original decision again in light of your submissions. The FTT cannot review its own review decision and this was made clear in the Upper Tribunal in *R (RB) v First-Tier Tribunal (Review)*.[23] The review decision is excluded from

14 Rule 45(2)(c).
15 Rule 45(2)(d).
16 Rule 47(1).
17 *R (RB) v First-Tier Tribunal (Review)* [2010] UKUT 160 (AAC).
18 Rule 49(3).
19 TCEA 2007 s9.
20 TCEA 2007 s9(4)(a).
21 TCEA 2007 s9(4)(b).
22 TCEA 2007 s9(4)(c).
23 [2010] UKUT 160 (AAC).

decisions that can be reviewed by section 11(5)(d)(i) and (iii) of the Tribunals, Courts and Enforcement Act 2007 so that there was no right of appeal under section 11(1). It could therefore not itself be reviewed (other than to correct accidental errors in the decision or in a record of the decision).[24] While the review decision itself is not reviewed as it is excluded the action of the judge reviewing can be set aside. [25]

14.12 For example, the RA applies for permission to appeal against a decision of the FTT to discharge the patient which is deferred for three weeks as they say the reasons are inadequate. The patient does not know of the appeal and is happy with the decision. The FTT judge sets aside the decision and remits it for rehearing. You are served with the decision and want the FTT to reconsider. You lodge your submissions and ask that the original decision be looked at in light of the submissions. The FTT judge can set aside the action setting aside the decision in light of your submissions.

14.13 In addition, the review decision may be amenable to judicial review in the Upper Tribunal.[26] If the applicant is seeking a declaration of incompatibility with the Human Rights Act 1998 then this is not within the jurisdiction of the Upper Tribunal but would be within the jurisdiction of the High Court. Any application to the Upper Tribunal for permission for judicial review must be made promptly and no later than three months after the date of the decision reflecting the judicial review jurisdiction in the High Court.[27] If the reasons were sent so that the time limit had expired, the time limit can be extended. The information the Upper Tribunal requires is the same with an application for permission to appeal, namely the name and address of the applicant, respondent and other possible interested parties, the name and address of the representative, an address for service, the details of the decision challenged, the application for permission the outcome the applicant is seeking and the facts and grounds upon which they rely along with relevant documentation including the decision.[28] If you are seeking an extension of time to apply then it is necessary to make this application at the same time.[29]

24 TCEA 2007 s9.

25 Rule 49(3).

26 TCEA 2007 ss15–18 and *Practice Direction (Upper Tribunal: Judicial Review Jurisdiction)* (2009) 1 WLR 327.

27 UT Rules r28.

28 UT Rules r28(4) (5) and (6).

29 UT Rules r28(7).

14.14 The forms are available from the government website.[30] If the matter is urgent alert the tribunal. The FTT have very good contact with the Upper Tribunal and can expedite applications so that the Upper Tribunal hears the case very quickly. For example, in *RM v St Andrew's Healthcare,* a decision on disclosure, the Upper Tribunal first became aware of the application by email on 14 April 2010 and was heard on 22 April 2010 and the written decision was dated 23 April 2010.[31]

The practical procedure on receipt of an application for permission to appeal in the First-tier Tribunal

14.15 The current procedure is that salaried judges are allocated applications in alphabetical order. Although there is no time limit in the Act or in the Rules to decide the reviews the intention is to have a decision within two weeks of it being allocated. This means the quicker it gets to the salaried judge the better and so chasing the tribunal is worthwhile. Whatever the decision, it should be sent to the parties and it will also be sent to the tribunal who made the decision.

Some suggestions of what to look for when looking at a decision

Inadequate reasons

14.16 The most common applications for appeal made to the tribunal are on the grounds that the reasons in the decision are inadequate. There is much case-law around this but the principles are well established. Written reasons must be 'adequate and intelligible and must grapple with the important issues raised'.[32] The reasons must inform the parties and any court to which the parties appeal of the reasons why the decisions was reached:

> ... if the appellate process is to work satisfactorily, the judgment must enable the appellate court to understand why the judge reached his decision. This does not mean that every factor which weighed with the judge in his appraisal of the evidence has to be identified and explained. But the issues the resolution of which was vital to the judge's conclusions should be identified and the manner in which

30 www.gov.uk/administrative-appeals-tribunal/overview.

31 [2010] UKUT 119 (AAC).

32 *R v MHRT ex p Pickering* [1986] 1 All ER 99.

> he resolved then explained. It is not possible to provide a template for this process. It does require the judge to identify and record those matters which were critical to the decision ...The essential requirement is that the terms of the judgment should enable the parties and any appellate tribunal to analyse the reasoning that was essential to the judge's decision.[33]

14.17 The Upper Tribunal said that '... what the [First-tier] Tribunal says should enable the parties and any appellate Tribunal readily to analyse the reasoning that was essential to the decision. The Tribunal should provide an explanation as to why it has accepted the evidence of one expert and rejected that of another'.[34]

14.18 In *MS v NE London F Trust*[35] the process was described as follows:

> The reasons should show the decision was justified in law. They should: state what facts the tribunal found; explain how and why the tribunal found them; show how the tribunal applied the law to those facts.

14.19 The tribunal must explain why it preferred one part of the evidence over another. It must apply the law to the facts. The tribunal must engage in the arguments before it, address the submissions put to it and come to a decision. It is not enough to set out the facts and then rely on the statutory criteria. There needs to be an analysis and that analysis needs to be rational.

14.20 Check that the tribunal has been through the statutory criteria and found on all three limbs of section 72 by providing the evidence heard for all three. Look for the reasons why each limb is satisfied. Think of whether nature is made out. For example, did it address the evidence that the patient's illness would relapse in the near future if discharged?[36]

14.21 If a tribunal preferred the evidence of the RC, check the reason why. In *AC, Partnership in Care Ltd v Secretary of State for Justice*, Jacobs J said:

> It said that the responsible clinician had more experience of Mr C than did Dr Kahtan. That is not of itself a reason for preferring evidence. It

33 In *R (H) v Ashworth Hospital Authority* [2003] 1 WLR 127 Dyson LJ cited with approval a passage from the judgment of Lord Phillips MR in *English v Emery Reimbold & Strick Ltd* (Practice Note) [2002] 1 WLR 2409.

34 *BB v South London & Maudsley NHS Trust and the Ministry of Justice* [2009] UKUT 157 per Judge Jacobs.

35 [2013] UKUT 92 (AAC).

36 *CM v Derbyshire Healthcare NHS Foundation Trust and Secretary of State for Justice* [2011] UKUT 129 (AAC).

is the background to almost every case and it does not always follow that greater knowledge means greater insight.[37]

14.22 Although the unanimity of the professional evidence can be taken into account by the tribunal it is not only that everyone says the same thing that is important particularly given that reports can be almost identical due to the fact that sections can be cut and pasted from electronic notes. It is not enough to rely on the fact that the evidence is anonymous without giving reasons as to why the unanimous evidence satisfies the tribunal on the statutory criteria:

> The weight to be given to expert evidence is not, or at least not always, and never only, a function of how many people say the same thing.[38]

14.23 When a submission is put to the tribunal they must address it in their reasons. Therefore a decision of the FTT was overturned on this basis despite the decision being complimented by the Upper Tribunal. The one flaw that meant the decision must be set aside was that the submission from counsel had not been specifically addressed:

> The presiding judge set out the tribunal's reasoning methodically. My concern is with what she did not say. She did not expressly refer to [the Appellant's] argument on the MCA ...[39]

An appeal to the Upper Tribunal

14.24 The application for permission to appeal can be granted in the FTT. If it is not, and you are instructed to continue, you can apply for permission directly to the Upper Tribunal within one month of the date of the letter from the FTT informing you of the decision.[40] You can ask the Upper Tribunal for an oral hearing but it will be up to them whether they decided the matter on the papers or not. They do have to take the parties views into account.[41] The forms are available at www.justice.gov.uk under 'Tribunals', click on 'A-2'.

14.25 The application must state the name and address of the appellant, their representative, an address for service, details of the decision and the written decision challenged the grounds on which you will rely.[42]

37 [2012] UKUT 450 (AAC) para 11.

38 *R(H) v Ashworth* [2002] EWCA Civ 923.

39 *DN v Northumberland Tyne and Wear NHS Foundation Trust* [2011] UKUT 327 (AAC).

40 The Tribunal Procedure (Upper Tribunal) Rules 2008 rule 21(b).

41 UT Rules r34(1) and (2).

42 UT Rules r21(4).

You need to include the original decision of the FTT, the review decision declining or giving permission to appeal.[43] If you are asking for an extension of time in which to lodge the appeal you must say why at this stage.[44] You must also enclose a copy of the legal aid certificate. You can apply at this stage for an oral hearing and you must say why an oral hearing is necessary.[45] The form is self explanatory.

14.26 If the Upper Tribunal does not grant permission to appeal then they will tell you, the appellant, and would normally inform the other parties. If permission is granted then a written notice is sent to all parties which includes the application and the reasons permission was given. If all parties agree the appeal can be determined without any further response.[46] This can make the process much quicker. If the application for permission to appeal is determined on the papers, and permission is refused or granted on limited grounds, the appellant may apply for the decision to be reconsidered at a hearing but this must be done within 14 days of the date on which the Upper Tribunal sent written notice of the decision.[47]

14.27 If permission to appeal is not granted by the Upper Tribunal this decision is an excluded decision under section 11 of the TCEA 2007 and so the Upper Tribunal has no power to review this even if they thought it was wrong. However, the decision may be amenable to judicial review if (a) the proposed appeal would raise some important point of principle or practice, or (b) there is some other compelling reason for the court to hear the appeal.[48]

14.28 If permission was granted by the FTT then you must send a notice of appeal to the Upper Tribunal within one month after the date permission was given.[49] If permission was granted by the Upper Tribunal then the application is usually treated as the notice of appeal. Any extra documentation arising from the permission application should be sent to the Upper Tribunal.[50]

14.29 Once permission is granted the respondent has one month from the date on which they were sent to notice of permission. The response must be in writing and essentially it must contain the same type of information as the application. Rule 24 requires that the response

43 UT Rules r21(5).
44 UT Rules r21(6).
45 UT Rules r34.
46 UT Rules r22.
47 UT Rules r22(4) and (5).
48 *R (Cart) v The Upper Tribunal* [2011] UKSC 28.
49 UT Rules r23(2).
50 UT Rules r23(3) and (4).

must have details of the name and address of the respondent and their representative, an address for service, the grounds on which they rely and whether they want a hearing and why.[51] If they are late they can request an extension of time and explain the reasons why it is necessary. All of these documents will be sent to the appellant and each other party. Rule 25 gives the appellant one month to reply.

14.30 The Upper Tribunal can review its own decisions and can do the same as the FTT can do to its own decisions. It can set aside a decision for procedural irregularity and remake the relevant part of the decision.[52] It can also review the decision and take no action, or review the decision and give permission to appeal to the Court of Appeal on the grounds that the decision overlooked a legislative provision or binding authority which could have a material effect or a later decision was made which may have an effect on the decision of the Upper Tribunal.[53]

Judicial review

14.31 Judicial review is a court's review of the decision, action or failure to act of a public body. It addresses the process of the decision-making or the action rather than the merits of the decision.[54]

14.32 The Upper Tribunal can hear applications for judicial review and applications lodged in the High Court can be transferred to the Upper Tribunal.[55] The Upper Tribunal's jurisdiction for judicial review is set out in section 15–19 of the Tribunal Courts and Enforcement Act 2007. The Upper Tribunal has the power to make certain orders if the conditions in section 18 are met. They are that: the application seeks the relief the Upper Tribunal can give under section 15 or an award under section 16; the application does not call into question anything done by the Crown Court; and the judge sitting is either a High Court Judge, a judge of the Court of Appeal or a judge authorised to sit on judicial review applications. Condition 3 allows for a practice direction to set out what judicial review should be dealt with by the Upper Tribunal.

51 UT Rules r24(3).

52 UT Rules r43(1).

53 UT Rules r45.

54 For full guidance on judicial review see Jonathan Manning, Sarah Salmon and Robert Brown, *Judicial Review Proceedings: a practitioner's guide*, LAG 2013.

55 TCEA 2007 ss15–18.

14.33 If all the conditions in section 18 are fulfilled the High Court must transfer the action to the Upper Tribunal. The High Court may authorise the transfer if condition 3 is not met following *the Practice Direction (Upper Tribunal: Judicial Review Jurisdiction)*.[56] This is where there is no right to appeal the decision of the First-tier Tribunal to the Upper Tribunal and the decision is not excluded by section 11(5) (b), (c) or (f). This could be, for example, a review decision of the First-tier Tribunal as although it is not amenable to appeal it may be amenable to judicial review. The Upper Tribunal cannot deal with judicial reviews that seek a declaration of incompatibility with the Human Rights Act 1998, cannot determine an application of habeas corpus, nor does it have any jurisdiction over managers' decisions under section 23 of the Mental Health Act 1983.

14.34 When exercising its judicial review jurisdiction, like the High Court, the remedy is discretionary and even if the action was unlawful the tribunal may exercise its discretion and not grant relief.

The practical workings of the Upper Tribunal

14.35 When an application for permission to appeal, an appeal or an application for judicial review is lodged with the tribunal, it is sent to the specialist mental health registrars. There is a checklist that they apply which looks at the urgency of the case and whether there is any outstanding action that needs to happen in the First-tier Tribunal. It is useful, if the appeal is an interlocutory one, to highlight that so the appropriate urgency can be give to it. There is a lead mental health judge who liaises closely with the registrars to determine the urgency of the matter. The Upper Tribunal does not have to ask for submissions from the other parties to the appeal. In fact in mental health appeals getting parties other than the patient to be represented in proceedings has been difficult.

After the Upper Tribunal

14.36 Once permission has been granted to appeal to the Upper Tribunal counsel or a solicitor with higher rights of audience will be involved. If you are unsuccessful in the Upper Tribunal they will be able to advise you on appealing to the Court of Appeal. The decision to pursue an appeal to the Court of Appeal, and the procedure, is beyond the remit of this book.

56 (2009) 1 WLR 327.

PART 3

Understanding mental disorder

CHAPTER 15

Understanding mental disorder

continued

Definition of mental disorder

Legal definition

15.1 Mental disorder is defined for the purposes of the Mental Health Act 1983 as 'any disorder or disability of the mind'. This is a very broad and non-specific definition and the Code of Practice to the Act provides guidance regarding how this definition is to be considered and applied emphasising that the identification of mental disorder is based on a clinical process where 'relevant professionals should determine whether a patient has a disorder or disability of the mind in accordance with good clinical practice and accepted standards of what constitutes such a disorder or disability'.

Clinical definition

15.2 It is problematic to give a clinical definition of 'mental disorder' when there is much debate amongst the psychiatric profession. A typical definition of mental disorder states 'any mental or bodily condition marked primarily by sufficient disorganisation of personality, mind, and emotions as to seriously impair the normal psychological functioning sufficient to cause an individual significant/excessive distress leading to an impairment of their ability to function in life, and/or significantly increases their risk of death, pain, disability'. Although this type of definition holds initial face validity two aspects of the definition results in major controversy in trying to utilise the definition to develop criteria for the clinical identification of mental disorder.

15.3 First, it is problematic to determine when the experience of the individual lies 'outside' or 'beyond the normal' experience without an accepted definition of what constitutes normal. Particularly as there is substantial variability in terms of what is accepted as a normal psychological experience across different cultures and societies.

15.4 The second aspect that results in difficulty and debate is that the 'experiences lead to distress and/or dysfunction'. Again major debate results when attempt is made to set a measure or baseline for 'significant or excessive'. This leads to additional 'criteria' being set for a mental disorder to be present such that the symptoms must be more than an expected response to a particular event (eg, normal grief after the loss of a loved one evolving into an abnormal state).

Mental illness v mental well-being

15.5 An alternative approach to the difficulties in defining a definition of mental disorder has been the evolution of the concept of 'mental well-being' or 'mental health'. This approach recognises that a sense of mental well-being extends beyond the simple absence of mental disorder to embrace a holistic balance of factors and fundamentally recognises the importance of every individual's connection to family friends and society. To illustrate this, an individual may describe themselves as 'unhappy and dissatisfied with their life' with few friends, poor living circumstances and unfulfilling job and no prospect for change. This constellation of circumstances may negatively impact on their sense of mental well-being and the individual may describe themselves as 'depressed' and seek psychiatric or psychological help. Such an individual may well experience a significant level of personal distress which may result in difficulties or impairment of their ability to function. However, this individual could not be described as having a mental disorder in the sense of the presence of a mental illness.

Identification of mental disorder relevant to the Mental Health Act 1983

15.6 Although there are clearly difficulties and debate regarding the definition of mental disorder, in everyday clinical practice the presence of an identifiable psychiatric condition is equated with the presence of mental disorder within the meaning of the Mental Health Act 1983. It is important to note that the Code of Practice to the Act sets down a number of important principles in relation to this issue within section 3:

> 3.4 The fact that someone has a mental disorder is never sufficient grounds for any compulsory measure to be taken under the Act. Compulsory measures are permitted only where specific criteria about the potential consequences of a person's mental disorder are met. There are many forms of mental disorder which are unlikely ever to call for compulsory measures.
>
> 3.5 Care must always be taken to avoid diagnosing, or failing to diagnose, mental disorder on the basis of preconceptions about people or failure to appreciate cultural and social differences. What may be indicative of mental disorder in one person, given their background and individual circumstances, may be nothing of the sort in another person.

> 3.6 Difference should not be confused with disorder. No-one may be considered to be mentally disordered solely because of their political, religious or cultural beliefs, values or opinions, unless there are proper clinical grounds to believe that they are the symptoms or manifestations of a disability or disorder of the mind. The same is true of a person's involvement, or likely involvement, in illegal, anti-social or 'immoral' behaviour. Beliefs, behaviours or actions which do not result from a disorder or disability of the mind are not a basis for compulsory measures under the Act, even if they appear unusual or cause other people alarm, distress or danger.

Psychiatric diagnostic systems

15.7 In clinical practice making a diagnosis can be defined as the process of identifying a disorder from the presence of its symptoms (what a patient complains of) and its signs (features recognised on observation). The process of classification of psychiatric disorders into diagnostic systems attempts to provide an order and structure into the great diversity of the psychiatric diagnoses and psychiatric phenomena seen in clinical practice. The fundamental purpose of this classification to identify groups or clusters of individuals who share a common clinical presentation so that a suitable treatment can be planned and the likely outcome (prognosis) predicted.

15.8 In many aspects of physical medicine the process of disease classification is based on an understanding of the aetiology – cause or origin – of the condition. The development of a specific aetiology for a disease results from scientific research and has the potential for the development of an aetiologically specific and effective treatment. Developments in medicine that have, for example, identified that malaria is a mosquito-borne infectious disease caused by the introduction of a micro-organism of the genus *Plasmodium* from the bite of an infected female mosquito. Based on this understanding of the aetiology of malaria, anti-malarial drugs have been developed which are effective in killing the plasmodium at different stages in the life cycle that have the potential to prevent the disorder occurring as well as offering a treatment when infection has occurred.

15.9 In contrast, the majority of diagnoses in psychiatry cannot be based on the aetiology of the condition as the cause or origins of the disorder are not yet understood. Diagnosis is therefore based on a 'syndromal approach' where an 'accepted' cluster of symptoms and signs are used to identify a specific disorder.

15.10 To a large extent this reliance on syndromal diagnoses, which cannot be confirmed by specific aetiologically-based tests, accounts for the diagnostic disagreement that not uncommonly occurs between two psychiatrists examining the same patient. It is important that a tribunal is not 'distracted' by this element of clinical debate. The requirement of the Act is for the demonstration of mental disorder as described above and liability to detention is not dependent on the presence of a specific diagnosis. Moreover, as noted is section 3.4 of the Code of Practice (reproduced above) the positive diagnosis of a specific disorder is *not in itself* a sufficient basis for detention.

15.11 Over the last 50 years it has been increasingly recognised that it is important for there to be consensus amongst clinicians regarding the categorisation of symptoms and signs into a psychiatric classificatory system. Clearly agreement as to the symptoms and signs which constitute a particular diagnosis is of benefit both in terms of clinical practice and in the research into psychiatric conditions, including the development of drug treatments. However, it is important to recognise the criticisms of this approach:

- Uncertainty regarding the validity of the categories as identifying distinct entities.
- Classification is dependent on the adequacy of the definitions and the extent to which these definitions are capable of being reliably applied.
- Growing recognition that many psychiatric conditions do not fall neatly within the current set of categories.

15.12 There are two classificatory systems in widespread use within psychiatry in England both in terms of clinical use and upon which national clinical guidelines are produced by the National Institute for Health and Care Excellence (NICE).

International Classification of Diseases

15.13 The International Classification of Diseases (ICD) is the standard diagnostic tool for epidemiology, health management and clinical purposes and is published by the World Health Organization. It is used to classify all forms of disease and other health problems recorded on many types of health records including death certificates and provides the basis for the compilation of national mortality and morbidity statistics by World Health Organization Member States.

15.14 ICD-10 was endorsed by the Forty-Third World Health Assembly in May 1990 and came into use in WHO member states from 1994. An updated version was introduced in 2010 and the 11th revision of the classification is likely to be available in 2017.

15.15 Chapter 5 of ICD-10 gives the classification and clinical guidelines for 'Classification of Mental and Behavioural Disorders' and represents the collaborative work of a large number of psychiatrists drawn from across all WHO member states.

15.16 This 'chapter' of ICD is available in hardcopy and is a very useful resource. An electronic version can be accessed at www.who.int/classifications/icd/en/bluebook.pdf. Each section contains a 2–3 page description of the condition described in detail within the section and forms a very useful reference document to facilitate a basic understanding of the disorder.

Diagnostic and Statistical Manual

15.17 The fifth edition of the Diagnostic and Statistical Manual (DSM5) was published in 2013 by the American Psychiatric Association (APA) in the United States where the DSM system serves as the authority for the diagnosis of psychiatric disorders. In the USA, treatment recommendations, as well as payment by health care providers, are often determined by DSM classifications. The American Psychiatric Association emphasise that professionals from the mental health and medical communities, patients and their families, and members of the public have worked for 10 years to produce this new revision.

DSM5 is available in hardcopy and the APA website[1] has a series of leaflets available which are linked to the diagnostic categories within DSM5 which contain short descriptions of the conditions.

ICD-10 versus DSM5

15.18 A discussion of the differences, advantages and disadvantages of the two major classificatory systems is beyond the remit of this chapter. Although there has been substantial effort expended by the psychiatric community to ensure the compatibility of the two systems there remain clear differences both in the diagnostic criteria for individual condition such as schizophrenia and the inclusion of defined psychiatric conditions that are coded in one classification system but not in the other. From the perspective of the tribunal what is important is that any diagnosis advanced as part of the evidence of mental disorder is based on the use of a recognised system of classification of mental disorders. This has a direct bearing on section 8 of the Code of Practice 'Relevant professionals should determine whether a patient has

1 www.psychiatry.org.

a disorder or disability of the mind in accordance with good clinical practice and accepted standards of what constitutes such a disorder or disability'.

How a psychiatric diagnosis is made

15.19 The validity of a particular psychiatric diagnosis for an individual is clearly dependent on the quantity and quality of the information upon which the diagnosis has been made. Interviews with the individual patient undertaken by a full range of professionals including psychiatrist, psychiatric nurse, occupational therapist, and social worker and support workers all have the potential to contribute information that is relevant to the formulation of a clinical diagnosis. It is important to recognise that an individual with a psychiatric disorder will have a variable level of motivation to disclose information to an interviewer and there may be significant variation in terms of what information the individual patient is willing to disclose to different members of the multi-disciplinary team. It is also important to note that an individual patient's ability to articulate or describe their inner world and thoughts may well be limited if they are actively experiencing some psychiatric phenomena. For example an individual who is very paranoid and fears that there is a conspiracy directed by doctors against them is unlikely to be willing or able to describe their inner thoughts to a doctor but may be more willing to talk to a support worker. This is one of the reasons that psychiatric services are built around a multi-disciplinary team approach.

15.20 Information from a collateral informant who knows the individual also has the potential to contribute information that is fundamental to the diagnostic process. This information is important as a source of additional data to confirm or clarify information taken directly from the individual patient. A second key aspect of collateral information is to provide descriptions of changes in the individual from their 'normal' behaviour, personality and function that may not be recognised by the individual themself.

15.21 This collection of information is usually organised into headings and described as the 'psychiatric history':

- present problem/condition;
- history of the present problem/condition
- personal history of the individual;
- family history;
- past illness and treatments (physical and psychiatric);

- personality;
- history of substance mis-use;
- present social situation.

Mental state examination

15.22 In addition to gathering information from the individual patient and collateral information it is standard practice to conduct a Mental State Examination. This is a process analogous to the physical examination of a patient under investigation for a physical health disorder. The Mental State Examination is primarily concerned with the individual patient's symptoms, signs and behaviour at the *time that the examination is undertaken*. The Mental State Examination makes a detailed assessment of any symptoms disclosed by the individual patient during the information gathering exercise described above. In addition, during the conduct of the Mental State (or Status) Examination the psychiatrist makes a systematic inquiry into other aspects of the individual patients current psychosocial and behavioural functioning.

15.23 The term 'degree' in the context of the criteria for detention under the Mental Health Act 1983 relates to the 'current manifestations' of the mental disorder and therefore the information that forms the Mental State Examination has a direct relevance to the assessment of the extent to which the individual's current presentation meets the criteria of degree. For this reason it is a matter of good practice that the responsible clinician (RC)/approved clinician (AC) findings on the individual's Mental State Examination that are documented within the tribunal report may require to be updated if the report is dated significantly in advance of the timing of the tribunal. In addition, the finding on a Mental State Examination form an important component of the medical member's preliminary examination conducted on behalf of the tribunal at a time close to the hearing of the tribunal.

Key psychiatric conditions

15.24 Possible psychiatric diagnoses described in ICD-10 number in the hundreds. However, in common practice within the tribunal a number of conditions occur with a greater frequency. It should be recognised that part of the role of the medical member of the tribunal is to assist non-medical members of the tribunal in their understanding of psychiatric disorders in general terms in addition to their contribution as a member of the tribunal. It is important to show a willingness to ask questions seeking factual knowledge of the tribunal medical member who will be a consultant psychiatrist with at least five years' experience of practising as a consultant in addition to the years spent in psychiatric training.

15.25 This list of conditions is not an exhaustive or comprehensive list but does include the most commonly encountered psychiatric disorders in tribunals:

- mood disorders, such as depression and bipolar disorder;
- schizophrenia and delusional disorders;
- organic mental disorders such as dementia and delirium;
- personality disorders;
- learning disabilities.

Mood disorders, such as depression and bipolar disorder

Depression

15.26 The symptom of a depressed mood is a common component of many psychiatric disorders (eg dementia and anxiety disorders) and is also a common accompaniment to a number of physical illnesses (eg hepatitis and brucellosis). However, low or depressed mood may also occur as a primary component of a depressive illness.

Clinical features of a depressive illness

15.27 **Core symptoms**

- depressed mood;
- anhedonia – loss of interest and enjoyment;
- anergia – reduced energy levels leading to increased fatigability and reduction in physical activity levels.

15.28 **Additional symptoms**

- reduced concentration and attention which may manifest as a deterioration in memory functioning;
- reduced self-esteem and self-confidence leading to a withdrawal from occupational and daily living activities;
- ideas of guilt and unworthiness;
- bleak and pessimistic views of the future;
- ideas or acts of self-harm or suicide;
- disturbed appetite and sleep pattern.

15.29 The patient's experience of the lowered mood is one akin to that of misery, although it is often described by patients once they have recovered as being different from ordinary sadness. The lowered mood is very consistent and shows little variation from day to day and is unresponsive to circumstances. There may also be the development of a characteristic pattern of diurnal variation as the day progresses.

Severity of depressive illness

15.30 The differentiation between mild, moderate and severe depressive illness depends upon a clinical judgment taking into account the number, type and severity of the symptoms present.

Mild depressive illnesses

15.31 To make a diagnosis of mild depression, the core symptoms of depression must be present together with at least two of the additional symptoms (listed above). None of the symptoms should be present to an intense degree and there is a minimum duration of about two weeks. The patient is usually distressed and experiencing some difficulties with occupational or social activities but has not ceased to function in these areas.

Moderate depressive illness

15.32 For moderate depressive illness, in addition to the core symptoms, there will be three to four of the additional symptoms. To fulfill criteria for a moderate depressive illness either several of the symptoms are present to a marked degree or there will be a particularly wide variety of symptoms present overall. The patient will be having considerable difficulties in sustaining their normal occupational and social activities and may additionally have problems with more basic activities of daily living.

Severe depressive illness

15.33 In addition to the core symptoms the patient with severe depressive illness has a wide range of the additional symptoms of depression which are present to a significant degree of intensity. The patient is unlikely to be able to continue with occupational, social or basic activities of daily living. Marked agitation or retardation is usually present. In the most severe episodes of illness the patient will also develop psychotic symptoms, delusions (abnormal ideas commonly involving sin, poverty, guilt or impending disasters for which the patient takes personal responsibility) and hallucinations (the experience of hearing, seeing or smelling things that are not real, often of an unpleasant nature related to the abnormal ideas, eg smelling rotting flesh or hearing accusatory voices).

Treatment approaches in depression

15.34 The key elements of the assessment, treatment and management of depression are described in the NICE guidance *Depression in adults: the treatment and management of depression in adults.*[2] This clinical guidance is based on the use of the 'stepped-care model' which provides a framework in which to organise the provision of services, and supports patients, carers and practitioners in identifying the most effective interventions. In stepped care the least intrusive, most effective intervention is provided first; if a person does not benefit from the intervention initially offered, or declines an intervention, it is recommended that they should be offered an appropriate intervention from the next step. The different elements of treatment approaches are summarised in the table opposite. Very detailed guidance is also provided regarding the use of both anti-depressant medication and the provision of psychological therapeutic interventions.

2 CG90, published in October 2009. Available at www.nice.org.uk/guidance/cg90.

Table 6

Focus of the intervention	Nature of the intervention
STEP 4: Severe and complex[a] depression; risk to life; severe self-neglect	Medication, high-intensity psychological interventions, electroconvulsive therapy, crisis service, combined treatments, multi-professional and inpatient care
STEP 3: Persistent sub-threshold depressive symptoms or mild to moderate depression with inadequate response to initial interventions; moderate and severe depression	Medication, high-intensity psychological interventions, combined treatments, collaborative care[b] and referral for further assessment and interventions
STEP 2: Persistent sub-threshold depressive symptoms; mild to moderate depression	Low-intensity psychosocial interventions, psychological interventions, medication and referral for further assessment and interventions
STEP 1: All known and suspected presentations of depression	Assessment, support, psycho-education, active monitoring and referral for further assessment and interventions

[a] Complex depression includes depression that shows an inadequate response to multiple treatments, is complicated by psychotic symptoms, and/or is associated with significant psychiatric comorbidity or psychosocial factors.
[b] Only for depression where the person also has a chronic physical health problem and associated functional impairment.

Anti-depressant drugs

15.35 Emphasis is given within the NICE guidance to a discussion of the use of anti-depressant medication covering:

- the choice of anti-depressant, including any anticipated adverse events, for example side effects and discontinuation symptoms and potential interactions with concomitant medication or physical health problems; and
- the patient's perception of the efficacy and tolerability of any anti-depressants they have previously taken.

15.36 It is important to support the patient to understand:

- the gradual development of the full anti-depressant effect;
- the importance of taking medication as prescribed and the need to continue treatment after remission;
- potential side effects;
- the potential for interactions with other medications;
- the risk and nature of discontinuation symptoms with all anti-depressants, particularly with drugs with a shorter half-life (such

as paroxetine and venlafaxine), and how these symptoms can be minimised; and
- the fact that addiction does not occur with anti-depressants.

Psychological interventions

15.37 For all high-intensity psychological interventions, the duration of treatment should normally be within the limits indicated within the NICE guidelines. As the aim of treatment is to obtain significant improvement or remission the duration of treatment may be:
- reduced if remission has been achieved; or
- increased if progress is being made, and there is agreement between the practitioner and the person with depression that further sessions would be beneficial (for example, if there is a comorbid personality disorder or significant psychosocial factors that impact on the person's ability to benefit from treatment).

15.38 There is a wide range of different types of psychological therapies available and which have proven efficacy in depression. For an individual patient what is provided often reflects both availability of suitably qualified therapists and individual patient choice over the type and acceptability of a particular psychological therapy. For example, some patients engage more with a talking based psychological approach; other patients find a more behavioural or activity based psychological approach more acceptable.

Bipolar disorder

15.39 Bipolar disorder is a mental illness where the fundamental disturbance is a change in mood to depression or to elation and a commensurate shift in energy, thinking, and behaviour. The degree and frequency of these mood fluctuations are more than just the ordinary and transitory experience of a good or bad mood, the cycles of bipolar disorder last for days, weeks, or months. Unlike ordinary mood swings, the mood changes experienced in bipolar disorder are so intense that they interfere with an individual's ability to function.

15.40 The diagnostic criteria for bipolar disorder are given in the International Classification of Disease (ICD-10) established by the World Health Organization:

> This disorder is characterized by repeated (ie at least two) episodes in which the patient's mood and activity levels are significantly

disturbed, this disturbance consisting on some occasions of an elevation of mood and increased energy and activity (mania or hypomania) and on others of a lowering of mood and decreased energy and activity (depression).

15.41 There are several patterns of bipolar disorder recognised.

Bipolar I

15.42 There has been at least one high or manic episode, which has lasted for longer than one week. Some individuals with Bipolar I will have only manic episodes, although most will also have periods of depression. Untreated, manic episodes generally last three to six months. Depressive episodes last longer, usually six to 12 months without treatment.

Bipolar II

15.43 There has been more than one episode of severe depression, but only mild manic episodes – these are called 'hypomania'.

Rapid cycling

15.44 More than four mood swings happen in a 12-month period. This affects around 1 in 10 people with bipolar disorder, and can happen with both types I and II.

Cyclothymia

15.45 The mood swings are not as severe as those in full bipolar disorder, but can be longer. This can develop into full bipolar disorder.

15.46 The individual patient's experience of depression and mania is variable and coloured by their lifetime events and also recent circumstances. However, in bipolar disorder the experience of depression and elation significantly exceed the normal experience and critically additionally impede the individual's ability to function and 'cope' with life's difficulties.

15.47 Characteristic disturbances are recognised in the domains of:

- emotional experiences;
- thinking ability;
- physical symptoms; and
- behaviour.

Table 7

Depression	Mania
Emotional experience	
Persistent feeling of unhappiness	Feeling of being very happy and excited
Feeling of wanting to burst into tears for no reason	Irritated with other people who don't share your current optimistic outlook and feeling more important than usual
Losing interest in things	
Being unable to enjoy previously pleasurably activities	
Feelings of restlessness and agitation	
Loss of self-confidence	
Feelings of being useless, inadequate and hopeless	
Feeling more irritable than usual	
Thinking of suicide	
Thinking ability	
Can't think positively or hopefully	Full of new and exciting ideas
Finding it hard to make even simple decisions	Moving quickly from one idea to another
Difficulties in concentration	
Physical symptoms	
Loss of appetite and loss of weight	Full of energy
Difficulty in getting to sleep	Unwilling to sleep
Waking earlier than usual	More than usually interested in sex
Feeling extremely tired	
Constipation	
Loss of interest in sex	
Behaviour	
Difficulty in starting or completing things even everyday activities	Making plans that are grandiose and unrealistic
Crying a lot or feeling like wanting to cry but not being able to	Very active and moving around very quickly
Avoiding contact with other people	Behaving out of character
	Talking very quickly to the extent that others find it hard to understand what you are talking about
	Making odd decisions on the spur of the moment
	Recklessly spending money
	Over familiar or excessively critical in the company of other people
	Less inhibited than usual

15.48 The symptoms of depression and mania are summarised in table 7 opposite.

Psychotic symptoms

15.49 In addition in both manic and depressive episodes the distortions in thinking may amount to the experience of psychotic symptoms.

15.50 In a manic episode patients generally hold over-positive views about themselves and their abilities which develop into grandiose delusions, for example believing that they are on an important mission or that they have special powers and abilities.

15.51 By contrast in a depressive episode patients beliefs tend to be negative and commonly take the form of delusional beliefs of guilt or of being worthless or even the belief that they do not deserve to exist.

15.52 In addition to these abnormalities of thinking patients may also experience hallucinations, ie describing the experience of hearing, smelling, feeling or seeing something, when there isn't anything (or anybody) there to account for it.

Medication and bipolar disorder

15.53 Drug treatments are used in two specific ways in the management of bipolar disorder:

- to prevent episodes of depression or mania;
- to treat an episode of depression or mania.

Preventing episodes

15.54 The drugs used are often referred to as mood stabilisers and include lithium and some drugs also used as anti-epileptics such as carbamazepine, sodium valproate and lamotrigine. Guidance from NICE is given:

- Valproate should not be prescribed routinely for women of child-bearing potential. If no effective alternative to valproate can be identified, adequate contraception should be used, and the risks of taking valproate during pregnancy should be explained.
- Lithium, olanzapine or valproate should be considered for long-term treatment of bipolar disorder. The choice should depend on:
  - response to previous treatments;
  - the relative risk, and known precipitants, of manic versus depressive relapse;

   – physical risk factors, particularly renal disease, obesity and diabetes;
   – the patient's preference and history of adherence;
   – gender (valproate should not be prescribed for women of child-bearing potential);
   – a brief assessment of cognitive state (such as the mini-Mental State Examination) if indicated.
- If the patient has frequent relapses, or symptoms continue to cause functional impairment, switching to an alternative monotherapy or adding a second prophylactic agent (lithium, olanzapine, and valproate) should be considered. Clinical state, side effects and, where relevant, blood levels should be monitored closely. Possible combinations are lithium with valproate, lithium with olanzapine, and valproate with olanzapine. The reasons for the choice and the discussion with the patient of the potential benefits and risks should be documented.
- If a trial of a combination of prophylactic agents proves ineffective, the following should be considered:
   – consulting with, or referring the patient to, a clinician with expertise in the drug treatment of bipolar disorder;
   – prescribing lamotrigine (especially if the patient has bipolar II disorder) or carbamazepine.

15.55 Psychological treatments are also recognised to be important contributors to the maintenance of the patient's well-being. The Royal College of Psychiatry information on bipolar disorder notes that psychological treatment should comprise 'around 16 one-hour sessions over a period of six to nine months and should include;

- psycho education – to increase knowledge about the signs and symptoms of bipolar disorder;
- mood monitoring – helps the individual identify early warning signs of a mood swing;
- mood strategies – to help stop a mood swing developing into a full-blown manic or depressive episode;
- assistance/guidance to develop general coping skills;
- cognitive behavioral therapy (CBT) for depression.

Treatment of acute episodes

Depressive episodes

15.56 Anti-depressant medication is usually prescribed in addition to the patient's regular mood stabiliser. The most commonly used are the

'SSRI' (selective serotonin re-uptake inhibitor) anti-depressants. These effect the action of a chemical in the brain called serotonin, and research indicates that they are less likely than other kinds of anti-depressant medication to precipitate a 're-bound' manic episode.

Mania and mixed depressive episodes

15.57 Any anti-depressant should be stopped. A mood stabiliser or anti-psychotic medication can be used, either alone or together. The older anti-psychotics (eg chlorpromazine, haloperidol) have some unpleasant side-effects such as stiffness, shakiness and muscle spasms. Some of the newer drugs (eg risperidone, olanzapine) can improve manic symptoms without these short-term unpleasant side-effects.

Schizophrenia

Symptoms, presentation and patterns

15.58 Schizophrenia is a diagnostic term for a major mental disorder that is characterised by an alteration in an individual's perception, thoughts, affect and behaviour. The constellation and pattern of symptoms experienced by an individual varies and is influenced by their individual personal circumstances and the presence of any co-morbid conditions, particularly the misuse of psychoactive substances.

15.59 Typically, the problems of schizophrenia are preceded by a 'prodromal' period. This is often characterised by some deterioration in personal functioning. Difficulties may include memory and concentration problems, social withdrawal, unusual and uncharacteristic behaviour, disturbed communication and affect, bizarre ideas and perceptual experiences, poor personal hygiene, and reduced interest in and motivation for day-to-day activities. Relatives and friends frequently report that the person with schizophrenia has changed 'in themselves'.

15.60 The prodromal period is typically followed by an acute phase marked by characteristic positive symptoms of hallucinations, delusions, and behavioural disturbances, such as agitation and distress.

15.61 The prognosis for an individual after an initial episode varies. Research studies have indicated that, after an initial episode approximately 20 per cent of individuals will recover fully. Approximately 30 per cent individuals will have a pattern of relapse and recovery. Individual recurrences of illness may be provoked by stress, social adversity and isolation.

Diagnosis

15.62 The International Classification of Disease (ICD-10)[3] sets down the following diagnostic guidelines for schizophrenia:

a) thought echo, thought insertion or withdrawal, and thought broadcasting;
b) delusions of control, influence, or passivity, clearly referred to body or limb movements or specific thoughts, actions or sensation; delusional perception;
c) hallucinatory voices giving a running commentary on the patient's behaviour, or discussing the patient amongst themselves, or other types of hallucinatory voices coming from some part of the body;
d) persistent delusions of other kinds that are culturally inappropriate and completely impossible, such as religious or political identity, or superhuman powers and abilities (eg being able to control the weather or being in communication with aliens from another world);
e) persistent hallucinations in any modality, when accompanied either by fleeting or half-formed delusions without clear affective content, or by persistent over-valued ideas, or when occurring every day for weeks or months on end;
f) breaks or interpolations in the train of thought, resulting in incoherence or irrelevant speech, or neologisms;
g) catatonic behaviour, such as excitement, posturing or waxy flexibility, negativism, mutism and stupor;
h) 'negative' symptoms such as marked apathy, paucity of speech, and blunting or incongruity of emotional responses, usually resulting in social withdrawal and lowering of social performance; it must be clear that these are not due to depression or to neuroleptic medication;
i) a significant and consistent change in overall quality of some aspects of personal behaviour, manifest as loss of interest, aimlessness, idleness, a self-absorbed attitude, and social withdrawal.

15.63 The normal requirement for a diagnosis of schizophrenia is that a minimum of one very clear symptom (and usually two or more if less clear-cut) belonging to any one of the groups listed as (a) to (d) above, or symptoms from at least two of the groups referred to as (e) to (h), should have been clearly present for most of the time *during a period of one month or more.*

3 World Health Organization: see www.who.int/classifications/icd/en/.

Treatment and management of schizophrenia in the NHS

Pharmacological treatment

15.64 Anti-psychotic medicines are the primary treatments for schizophrenia. There is well-established evidence for their efficacy in both the treatment of acute psychotic episodes and relapse prevention over time.

15.65 Conventional or typical anti-psychotic agents (more recently called first-generation anti-psychotics) are associated with a high incidence and broad range of side effects including lethargy, sedation, weight gain and sexual dysfunction. Movement disorders, such as Parkinsonism, akathisia and dystonia are common and can be disabling and distressing. A serious long-term side effect is tardive dyskinesia, which develops in around 20 per cent of people

15.66 These difficulties have led to the development of a newer range of anti-psychotic drugs second-generation ('atypical') anti-psychotics which have been noted to have a lower liability for acute side effects and tardive dyskinesia. However, they have a different side effect profile which includes weight gain and other metabolic problems that may increase the risk of type-2 diabetes and cardiovascular disease.

15.67 For individuals who have not responded to first line treatment with these drugs, one anti-psychotic drug, clozapine, has a specific licence for the treatment of resistant schizophrenia.

Psychological and psychosocial interventions

15.68 The use of specific psychological and psycho-social methods to help people with schizophrenia is relatively recent and a wide range of different psychological interventions have been implemented.

15.69 Cognitive behavioural therapy approaches were initially focused on the reduction of psychotic symptoms but have more recently broadened in scope to include work with emotional problems and functioning.

15.70 Cognitive remediation therapy developed in the 1980s and 1990s, and is focused on training in cognitive functions, such as learning, planning, attention or memory.

15.71 Adherence therapy was introduced in the mid-1990s with the specific goal of enhancing compliance with medication.

Dementia

15.72 Dementia is the diagnostic term used to describe a condition which is characterised by the gradual loss of mental abilities such as thinking, remembering, and reasoning. Dementia is further defined as being *chronic, progressive and irreversible* indicating that the symptoms evolve and increase in severity over time and that currently there is no cure available.

15.73 Common symptoms that are seen in the earliest stages of many forms of dementia are:

Personality changes

- frustration, anger, and irritability;
- emotional lability, unstable moods;
- paranoia, suspicion, and jealously;
- insensitivity to others;
- flat emotional responses;
- loss of inhibitions;
- fear of being alone.

Loss of problem-solving skills

- inability to do familiar tasks;
- inability to make connections;
- inability to make decisions;
- inability to initiate or complete a project.

Communication problems

- problems finding words;
- inability to follow a conversation;
- repeating the question.

Disorientation

- loss of a sense of time;
- getting lost in familiar areas;
- not recognising people.

New and unfamiliar behaviours

- neglect of self or property;
- hoarding.

15.74 There are over 70 different types of dementia described but whatever the cause the final pathological process is that symptoms develop as a consequence of neurodegeneration (loss of brain cells). The most common causes of dementia are Alzheimer's disease, vascular dementia and Dementia with Lewy Bodies. Together these three types of dementia account for between 70–80 per cent of all cases. There are important differences between the different types of dementia, most notably in the pattern of illness and response of symptoms to different groups of drugs.

15.75 In addition to the deterioration in the patient's cognitive abilities, it is widely recognised that the majority of patients also experience other psychiatric symptoms which are often collectively termed the 'behavioural and psychological' symptoms of Alzheimer's disease.

Behavioural symptoms

15.76 These are usually identified on the basis of observations made of the patient's behaviour and includes physical aggression, screaming, restlessness, agitation, wandering, culturally inappropriate behaviours, sexual disinhibition, hoarding, cursing and shadowing (constant following or asking after another individual).

Psychological symptoms

15.77 These symptoms are assessed on the basis of interviews with the patient and their relatives; and include anxiety, depressed mood, hallucinations and delusions.

Learning disability

15.78 Learning disability is a diagnostic term used in a very specific way in the United Kingdom. It is relevant to note that the term does not represent a single disease entity but represents a syndromal description identifying a group of individuals who share key characteristics. Within the group of individuals so defined there are a number of very specific aetiologically distinct sub-groups, such as those with Down's Syndrome or other genetically determined causes of learning disability. However, for the majority of individual who fulfil the criteria for learning disability the aetiology (cause) of the disorder is not known.

15.79 The International Classification of Diseases (ICD-10)[4] section on mental and behavioural disorders defines learning disability as

> a condition of arrested or incomplete development of the mind, which is especially characterized by impairment of skills manifest during the developmental period, which contribute to the overall level of intelligence, ie cognitive, language, motor and social abilities.

15.80 It is noted that whilst learning disability can occur with or without any other mental or physical disorder, many studies indicate that the prevalence of mental disorders are three to four times greater in this population than in the general population.

15.81 At a basic level, three criteria are regarded as requiring to be met before learning disability can be identified:

- intellectual impairment;
- social or adaptive dysfunction;
- early onset.

Intellectual impairment

15.82 Intelligence is not a unitary concept but is comprised of a large number of different but specific cognitive skills. These include:

- attention;
- concentration;
- orientation;
- memory;
- use of language;
- perception;
- praxis (performance of manual tasks);
- visio-spatial skills;
- arithmetic skills.

15.83 Neuropsychological studies completed over the last 20 years have sought to establish which areas of the brain are necessary for an individual to perform the different cognitive tasks. In addition research has established rating scales to quantify an individual's performance of the different cognitive tasks. In general these skills develop to a similar level in an individual and together contribute to what is collectively referred to as an individual's 'intelligence'.

15.84 Executive function relates to the mental capability to use/integrate these basic cognitive skills in order to undertake more complex thinking tasks including:

4 World Health Organization: see www.who.int/classifications/icd/en/.

- understanding complex ideas;
- adapting effectively to the environment;
- learning from experience;
- engaging in reasoning;
- solving problems; and
- thinking in the abstract.

15.85 Measurement of the extent of impairment in intellectual functioning is often carried out through the use of psychometric tests. These comprise batteries of tests of the cognitive skills that are the substrate of intelligence the results of which are combined together to give an Intelligence Quotient – IQ. The most commonly used test is the Wechsler Adult Intelligence Scale which is comprised of 14 tests the results of which are combined to give an IQ-score. The test has been standardised in the general population such that the mean score is an IQ of 100 and the standard deviation is 15. An IQ score of lying less than 2 standard deviations from the mean, ie less than 70 is taken to be indicative of a significant degree of intellectual impairment.

Social or adaptive dysfunction

15.86 The second criteria for the diagnosis of learning disability stated in ICD-10 is the requirement that:

> For a definite diagnosis, there should be a reduced level of intellectual functioning resulting in diminished ability to adapt to the daily demands of the normal social environment.

15.87 The concept of adaptive/social functioning is very broad and relates to an individual's performance in coping on a day-to-day basis, ie relates to what an individual person actually does. The types of functions that are included are: communication, self-care, home living, social/interpersonal skills, and use of community resources, self-direction, functional academic skills, work, leisure, health and safety. Thus the range of activities is very extensive and in part performance of these skills depends on differential social and cultural expectations.

15.88 For a diagnosis of learning disability it is expected that an individual requires significant assistance:

- to provide for his/her own survival (eating and drinking needs and to keep himself/herself clean, warm and clothed), and/or
- with his/her social/community adaptation (eg social problem solving and social reasoning).

15.89 The degree of assistance required may vary in terms of intensity (eg physical or verbal prompting) and frequency (eg daily or less often than daily), but the required assistance should always be outside the range of that expected within the individual's particular culture/community.

15.90 Despite the difficulties in defining adaptive/social functioning, there exists a variety of scales purporting to measure it. These are usually completed by direct observation and/or in conjunction with at least one informant who knows the person well (for example, a parent, carer or friend). Commonly used scales include the Hampshire Assessment for Living with Others (HALO) and the Adaptive Behaviour Scale (ABS).

Early onset

15.91 For a person to be considered to have a learning disability, significant impairments of intellectual and adaptive/social functioning must have been acquired during the developmental period. In general this is taken as before the age of 18 years.

15.92 Age of onset before adulthood may be demonstrated by historical evidence from medical records (eg delayed attainment of developmental milestones), educational records such as a Statement of Educational Need, or records of previous use of specialist health and social services.

Personality disorder

15.93 The diagnostic term Personality Disorder is defined within ICD-10[5] as:

> ... deeply ingrained and enduring behaviour patterns, manifesting themselves as inflexible responses to a broad range of personal and social situations. They represent either extreme or significant deviations from the way the average individual in a given culture perceives, thinks, feels and particularly relates to others. Such behaviour patterns tend to be stable and to encompass multiple domains of behaviour and psychological functioning. They are frequently, but not always, associated with various degrees of subjective distress and problems in social functioning and performance.

15.94 There are various different types of personality disorders but all of them share the following features:

5 World Health Organization: see www.who.int/classifications/icd/en/.

- Most often the first signs of a personality disorder appear in late childhood or adolescence and continue during adulthood.
- Personality disorders in children or adolescence are sometimes described as conduct disorders. However most conduct disorders in children do not necessarily lead to personality disorders in adults.
- An individual with a personality disorder holds attitudes and behaves in ways that can cause considerable problems for themselves and others. For example the way they perceive the world; the way they think; the way they relate to other people; the way they do or do not get upset.
- An individual diagnosed with personality disorder may be inflexible in that they may have a narrow range of attitudes, behaviours and coping mechanisms.
- These ways of behaving are long standing.

15.95 Other key points:

- Most people diagnosed with a personality disorder fit the criteria for at least two different types of personality disorder.
- Most people diagnosed with a personality disorder are not dangerous.
- Dangerousness is most often but not exclusively associated with anti-social or psychopathic disorder.
- An individual diagnosed as borderline or paranoid personality disorder may be at higher risk of self-harm and/or suicide than other people.
- Individuals with a personality disorder have multiple needs and vulnerabilities.

15.96 It is generally considered helpful both at a diagnostic level and in terms of identifying suitable treatments to consider the personality disorders as falling into three clusters.

15.97 **Cluster A – 'Suspicious' includes:**

Paranoid	Characterised by dominant feeling of suspicion, sensitive to rejection and tendency to hold grudges.
Schizoid	Characterised by difficulties with relationships, individuals avoid contact with other people and prefer their own company. A complex and rich fantasy world often develops over time.
Schizotypal	Characterised by individuals who have odd ideas and difficulties with thinking. Often seen by other people as eccentric.

15.98 **Cluster B – 'Emotional and impulsive' includes:**

Antisocial	Characterised by lack of care regarding the feelings of others, easily frustrated, aggression often occurring. Tendency to act without thinking, lack guilt and difficulties learning from experience to modify behaviour.
Borderline, or emotionally unstable	Characterised by action without thinking, difficulties with emotional control and feelings of emptiness. Low self-esteem and self-harm common.
Histrionic	Characterised by tendency to over-dramatise events and to be self-centred. Emotional responses tend to be strong but short lived. Individuals often worry a lot about their appearance and crave excitement.
Narcissistic	Central feature is of feelings of importance and dreams of success, power and status. Individuals crave attention but demonstrate a tendency to exploit others.

15.99 **Cluster C – 'Anxious' includes:**

Obsessive-Compulsive (aka Anankastic)	Characterised by perfectionistic approach with substantial worry about detail and rigid responses to difficulties. Individuals often very cautious and find it hard to make decisions and are sensitive to criticism and may have obsessional thoughts and behaviours.
Avoidant (aka anxious/avoidant)	Characterised by pervasive sense of anxiety and tension, with feelings of insecurity and inferiority.
Dependent	Individuals rely on others to make decisions and do what others want even in relation to common place or everyday decisions.

Treatments and self-management strategies

15.100 Personality disorders are difficult to treat because they involve life-long, pervasive attitudes and behaviours and because individuals with personality disorders often have other mental health problems. When a treatment is seen to fail it is often the patient who is 'blamed' for not fitting the programme rather than recognition that the treatment paradigm is inappropriate for that particular patient.

Medication (pharmacological treatments)

Anti-psychotic drugs

15.101 Anti-psychotic drugs (usually at a low dose):

- Can reduce the suspiciousness of the three clusters a personality disorders (paranoid, schizoid and schizotypal).

- Can help with borderline personality disorder if individual feels paranoid, or is hearing noises or voices.

Anti-depressants

15.102 Anti-depressants:

- Can help with the mood and emotional difficulties that individuals with cluster B personality disorders (antisocial or dissocial, borderline or emotionally unstable, histrionic, and narcissistic) have.
- Some of the selective serotonin re-uptake inhibitor anti-depressant s (SSRIs) can help people to be less impulsive and aggressive in borderline and antisocial personality disorders.
- Can reduce anxiety in cluster C personality disorders (obsessive-compulsive, avoidant and dependent).

Mood stabilisers

15.103 Medication such as lithium, carbamazepine, and sodium valproate can also reduce impulsiveness and aggression.

Psychodynamic treatment

15.104 This type of treatment emphasises personality structure and development. It aims to provide insight for individuals allowing them to understand their feelings and to find better coping mechanisms. This approach has had limited success and is likely to be less successful for those with addiction and/or antisocial personality disorder.

Cognitive and behavioural therapy

15.105 Cognitive and behavioural therapies cover a wide range of treatments such as cognitive therapy, dialectical behaviour therapy, interpersonal psychotherapy and cognitive analytic therapy. Most cognitive behavioural approaches address specific aspects of thoughts, feelings, behaviour or attitude, and do not claim to treat the entire personality disorder of the person.

Antisocial personality disorder

15.106 NICE has provided guidance for the diagnosis and treatment of Antisocial Personality Disorder (January 2009). This guidance uses the term Antisocial Personality Disorder noting that the equivalent term within the International Classification of Disease would be Dissocial

Personality Disorder. In setting out the basis for the diagnosis the guidance notes in section 2.2.1:[6]

> **2.2.1 Symptoms, presentation and pattern of disorder**
> The diagnostic system DSM-IV (the preferred diagnostic system for this guideline – see section 2.2.2) characterizes antisocial personality disorder as a pervasive pattern of disregard for and violation of the rights of others that has been occurring in the individual since the age of 15 years, as indicated by three (or more) of seven criteria, namely: a failure to conform to social norms; irresponsibility; deceitfulness; indifference to the welfare of others; recklessness; a failure to plan ahead; and irritability and aggressiveness (APA, 1994).

15.107 In relation to the difference of emphasis between the two classificatory systems the guidance notes in section 2.2.2:[7]

> **2.2.2 ICD-10**
> In ICD-10, the term used is dissocial personality disorder, rather than antisocial personality disorder. In summary, its criteria focus more than DSM-IV on interpersonal deficits (for example, incapacity to experience guilt, a very low tolerance of frustration, proneness to blame others, and so on) and less on antisocial behaviour *per se*. It does not require symptoms of conduct disorder in childhood. This definition of dissocial personality disorder has been criticised for including features of aggressive/sadistic personality disorder that cannot be accommodated elsewhere in ICD-10 (Millon & Davis, 1996).

6 www.nice.org.uk/guidance/cg77/resources/cg77-antisocial-personality-disorder-full-guideline3 at page 17.

7 www.nice.org.uk/guidance/cg77/resources/cg77-antisocial-personality-disorder-full-guideline3 at page 19.

PART 4

Top ten cases

CHAPTER 16

Top ten cases

1. R v London South and South West Region Mental Health Review Tribunal ex p Moyle (1999) QBD
2. CM v Derbyshire Healthcare NHS Foundation Trust and Secretary of State for Justice [2011] UKUT 129 (AAC)
3. R v Secretary of State for the Home Department and another ex p IH [2003] UKHL 59
4. R (AN) v Mental Health Review Tribunal (Northern Region) and others [2005] EWCA Civ 1605
5. RM v St Andrew's Healthcare [2010] UKUT 119 (AAC)
6. GA v Betsi Cadwaladrv University Local Health Board [2013] UKUT 280 (AAC)
7. AM v South London and Maudsley NHS Foundation Trust and the Secretary of State for Health [2013] UKUT 365 (AAC)
8. BB v South London and Maudsley NHS Trust and the Ministry of Justice [2009] UKUT 157 (AAC)
9. TW v Enfield Borough Council [2014] EWCA Civ 362
10. MH v United Kingdom (App No 11577/06) (2013) ECHR 1008

16.1 This is a list of the cases both old and new which are useful when practising mental health law. All but one of these cases are confined to the tribunal setting but case 10 addresses the procedure before the section is applied for. There are many more important cases but hopefully these will act as a guide and signpost other cases which may be useful.

1 R v London South and South West Region Mental Health Review Tribunal ex p Moyle (1999) QBD

16.2 Mr Moyle was an asymptomatic patient who was taking medication in hospital. Those treating him were unsure whether he would take medication if discharged into the community. This is one of the most common arguments put by a detaining authority to justify the continuation of a section in a case of an asymptomatic patient suffering from a mental illness.

16.3 In 1990 Mr Moyle had savagely attacked his wife who sustained serious injuries. He was arrested, charged, and remanded in custody to Lewes Prison. There he deteriorated to the extent that he was transferred to Broadmoor Hospital. He was made subject to a hospital order with restrictions under sections 37/41. He was diagnosed as suffering from schizophrenia.

16.4 He made an application to the tribunal and the medical evidence before the tribunal was that were he to be assessed in the community under the Mental Health Act 1983 at the time the tribunal was held he would not be detained under the Act. However, if he stopped taking medication he would quickly relapse and if he did he would pose a danger to himself and to others.

16.5 Latham J said at page 19 of the judgment:

> The correct analysis, in my judgment, is that the nature of the illness of a patient such as the applicant is that it is an illness which will relapse in the absence of medication. The question that then has to be asked is whether the nature of that illness is such as to make it appropriate for him to be liable to be detained in hospital for medical treatment. Whether it is appropriate or not will depend upon an assessment of the probability that he will relapse in the near future if he were free in the community.

16.6 This case was also approved by Lord Phillips MR in *R(H) v Mental Health Review Tribunal North and East London Region*[1] adding to the decision in the High Court:

> The appropriate response should depend on the result of weighing the interests of the patient against those of the public having regard to the particular facts. Continued detention can only be justified if, but only if, it is a proportionate response having regard to the risks that would be involved in discharge.[2]

2 CM v Derbyshire Healthcare NHS Foundation Trust and Secretary of State for Justice [2011] UKUT 129 (AAC)

16.7 The patient, who suffered from paranoid schizophrenia, had been conditionally discharged in 2000. He had been treated in the community since then with a depot medication with which he had always been compliant and had been symptom-free for all of that time. He had been recalled several times for breaching the terms of his conditional discharge as his lifestyle was chaotic due to his drug taking and the associations with other drug users he made due to taking drugs. Despite this the patient had throughout the 10 years been compliant with his prescribed medication.

16.8 The First-tier Tribunal (FTT) found that the patient's condition was of a nature, though not of a degree, to make it appropriate for him to continue to be detained in hospital for treatment. They accepted that taking street drugs did not affect his mental illness but that if his lifestyle became more chaotic it may mean he would fail to keep appointments and this would eventually lead to non-compliance with his treatment.

16.9 The important point made in this case was that for the patient's illness to be of a nature to make it appropriate for him to remain in hospital it had to be likely to relapse in the near future. The evidence was recorded in the FTT decision as 'we conclude therefore that that there is still a very significant chance that within the year, were [the patient] now to be discharged, all the professionals would be facing the same situation then as now and having to decide whether to recall him for the fourth time'. It referred to 'the risk that [the patient's] chaotic lifestyle, continued consumption of drugs, and failure to

1 [2001] EWCA Civ 415.

2 At para 33.

keep appointments with his supervisors will eventually lead to non-compliance with his medication'. The Upper Tribunal found there was no evidence on which the FTT could have found that relapse was likely in the near future.

3 R v Secretary of State for the Home Department and another ex p IH [2003] UKHL 59

16.10 In 1991 IH was convicted of severely mutilating his son. He was dealt with under section 5 of the Criminal Procedure (Insanity) Act 1964[3] and made subject to a hospital order with restriction under that Act and was therefore treated as being detained under sections 37/41 of the MHA 1983. A tribunal which took place in 1999 considered that IH's mental disorder did not necessitate continuing detention in hospital but did consider that he needed to remain liable to recall and needed an after-care plan. As no after-care plan had been prepared the hearing was adjourned, with directions for information and identification of an after-care plan.

16.11 The factual problem in this case was that no psychiatrist could be found who was willing to supervise the patient. The tribunal met again and conditionally discharged the patient deferring the discharge until the conditions were fulfilled. Again no psychiatrist was found. Before this case the deferred discharge simply remained until the conditions were fulfilled and the tribunal did not monitor discharge planning meaning that someone could remain in hospital having been given a deferred conditional discharge sometimes for years.

16.12 The patient appealed alleging his rights under Article 5 ECHR had been violated as his discharge could not be effected. The grounds of appeal were that the tribunal lacked the coercive power of a court to secure compliance with the conditions; the tribunal failed to discharge the patient within a reasonable time and therefore his detention was unlawful. The tribunal could not re-open the case even though the health authority had failed to secure the conditions and the psychiatrist by not agreeing to supervise the patient had acted contrary to the ECHR.

16.13 The House of Lords dismissed the appeal. It said the decision of the tribunal was a provisional decision. The health authority had to

3 As substituted by section 3 of the Criminal Procedure (Insanity and Fitness to Plead) Act 1991.

use its best endeavours to fulfill the conditions which it had done and, when no psychiatrist was found and the conditions could not be fulfilled, the provisional decision was not able to be implemented and the tribunal should at this stage have reconsidered the case.

16.14 The significance of this case for representatives is two-fold. The first is that it established the tribunal practice of monitoring the fulfilment of conditions set by the tribunal on giving a deferred conditional discharge. The original decision is treated as a provisional decision and it asks for a position statement by a set time and can then reconvene to reconsider the case. The tribunal cannot change its mind on discharge at this stage unless there has been a change in the evidence before it such as the patient deteriorating. But, if the conditions are not able to be fulfilled despite the efforts of the authority responsible for providing the after-care, and the tribunal can modify the conditions or if the conditions are a necessary part of the discharge, the tribunal can decide that the patient remains detained.

16.15 Secondly Lord Bingham in his judgment said:

> Indeed, the conditional discharge regime, properly used, is of great benefit to patients and the public, and conducive to the Convention object of restricting the curtailment of personal liberty to the maximum, because it enables tribunals to ensure that restricted patients compulsorily detained in hospital represent the hard core of those who suffer from mental illness, are a risk to themselves or others and cannot be effectively treated and supervised otherwise than in hospital. If there is any possibility of treating and supervising a patient in the community, the imposition of conditions permits that possibility to be explored and, it may be, tried.[4]

16.16 If you take the tribunal to this starting point in your submissions it ensures that it addresses the question could the patient be managed in the community?

4 R (AN) v Mental Health Review Tribunal (Northern Region) and others [2005] EWCA Civ 1605

16.17 The patient in this case sought to argue that the standard of proof in tribunal proceedings should be something higher than the balance of probabilities somewhere between this standard and the criminal

4 [2003] UKHL 59 para 26.

standard beyond reasonable doubt. The High Court and then the Court of Appeal found that the civil standard applied.

16.18 At para 62 Richards LJ said:

> Although there is a single civil *standard* of proof on the balance of probabilities, it is flexible in its *application*. In particular, the more serious the allegation or the more serious the consequences of the allegation is proved, the stronger must be the evidence before a court will find the allegation proved on the balance of probabilities.

16.19 The Court could see no reason to disagree with the guidance of Munby J in the High Court[5] to the evaluation of hearsay evidence although they note the detail had not been argued before them.[6] This is an extremely useful quote to use in the face of reports of conduct the patient denies and was garnered from old reports without reference to the original material. This will happen frequently in tribunals of patients who have a long history of contact with services. The tribunal needs to be reminded of the dangers of accepting hearsay evidence and Munby recognised this and said at para 129 of his judgment in the High Court:

> If the Tribunal is relying upon hearsay evidence it must take into account the fact that it is hearsay and must have regard to the particular dangers involved in relying upon second, third or fourth hand hearsay. The Tribunal must be appropriately cautious of relying upon assertions as to past events which are not securely recorded in contemporaneous notes, particularly if the only evidence is hearsay. The Tribunal must be alert to the well-known problem that constant repetition in 'official' reports or statements may, in the 'official' mind, turn into established fact something which rigorous forensic investigation shows is in truth nothing more than 'institutional folk-lore' with no secure foundation in either recorded or provable fact. The Tribunal must guard against too quickly jumping to conclusions adverse to the patient in relation to past events where the only direct evidence is that of the patient himself, particularly where there is no clear account in contemporaneous notes of what is alleged to have happened. In relation to past incidents which are centrally important to the decision it has to take the Tribunal must bear in mind the need for proof to the civil standard of proof; it must bear in mind the potential difficulties of relying upon second or third hand hearsay; and, if the incident is really fundamental to its decision, it must bear in mind that fairness may require the patient to be given the opportunity to cross-examine the relevant witness(es) if their evidence is to be relied on at all.[7]

5 [2005] EWHC 587 (Admin).

6 At para 77.

7 At para 129.

5 RM v St Andrew's Healthcare [2010] UKUT 119 (AAC)

16.20 RM was being covertly medicated with both anti-psychotic and anti-epileptic medication. If he was told of this covert medication he was likely to reduce his food and fluid and therefore put his mental and physical health at significant risk including a risk of sudden death due to his epilepsy. When taking medication he was largely free of symptoms. His case to the tribunal was that he was largely free of symptoms without taking medication.

16.21 The Upper Tribunal decided that the information should be disclosed despite there being a risk of serious harm set out in rule 14(7) of the Tribunal Procedure (Upper Tribunal) Rules 2008.[8]

16.22 The fundamentally important issue that was identified was whether he could effectively challenge his detention without knowing about the covert medication. They took into account that the tribunal could manage the hearing so that the information was not disclosed, but decided that in this case the patient's lawyers could not obtain relevant instructions if they could not communicate the undisclosed facts to their client.

16.23 The Upper Tribunal concluded that to withhold this information from the patient meant that he could not have a fair hearing as was required by Article 6 ECHR.

16.24 Jacobs J said at para 27:

> The tribunal may hold a hearing with the patient present. If it does, his legal team will not be able to present the real case. They cannot disclose the covert medication. Nor can the medical witnesses or the tribunal. Everyone in the room will know what the patient does not. They will be reduced to performing a mere mummery. Justice will not be done at the hearing; it will only seem to be done. The real proceedings will have to be conducted out of the patient's sight and knowledge.

16.25 This case is unusual on its facts in that the patient could have died as a result of knowing the information. Article 2 and the right to protect life was not argued but again this is only relevant on the particular facts. What is useful about this case is that if the patient cannot argue his case without knowledge of the facts even serious harm may not be enough to withhold that information.

8 SI No 2698.

6 GA v Betsi Cadwaladrv University Local Health Board [2013] UKUT 280 (AAC)

16.26 This patient in this case did not want to take medication. He was subject to a CTO and a condition of the CTO was that he should take the medication prescribed for him.

16.27 It was argued that this was an interference in his right to a private life under Article 8 ECHR and treatment against his will contrary to the consent to treatment provisions in the MHA 1983. Therefore, the tribunal should discharge him under their discretionary power to discharge.

16.28 The Upper Tribunal referred to *SH v Cornwall Partnership NHS Trust*[9] where he had found that the tribunal has no jurisdiction to deal with issues of consent to treatment. The tribunal has the right to release the patient but no more. Judge Jacobs approved his own judgment in this case.

16.29 The different point here was that if there was no consent to treatment, and the condition of the CTO required the patient to take treatment, then the condition was unlawful, and the CTO in turn was unlawful and therefore the FTT should have discharged under their discretionary powers.

16.30 Judge Jacobs said that while he agreed with his judgment in *SH* consent could not be excluded from consideration in that discretion. However, the decision whether to exercise discretionary powers of discharge only arises when the statutory criteria for detention are made out.

16.31 Therefore the tribunal must be satisfied that without the order treatment and protection would still be given otherwise the findings would be perverse and illogical. Judge Jacobs said that this does not deprive the patient of a remedy. All it means is that it is not usually available from the FTT and the patient must go to court.

7 AM v South London and Maudsley NHS Foundation Trust and the Secretary of State for Health [2013] UKUT 365 (AAC)

16.32 This is an attempt to summarise a judgment on the complex interrelationship of the MHA 1983 and MCA 2005. The difficulties in

9 [2012] UKUT 290 (AAC).

doing so are hinted at in paragraph 2 of the judgment. When referring to the MCA 2005 Mr Justice Charles said:

> ... all decision-makers who have to address the application of the provisions of the Deprivation of Liberty Safeguards (DOLS) ... are faced with complicated legislative provisions and their difficulties are compounded when they have to consider the relationship between the MHA at the MCA. Regular visitors to the provisions need to remember the daunting task set for lawyers and non lawyers who have to apply them.

In the recent case of *P v Cheshire West and Chester Council*[10] in the Supreme Court, Lady Hale said at para 9 of the judgment:

> The safeguards have the appearance of bewildering complexity, much greater than that in the comparable provisions for detaining mental patients in hospital under the Mental Health Act ...

16.33 AM was a 78-year-old woman detained under section 2. She was not discharged by the FTT. It was common cause that she has a mental disorder and needed a cognitive assessment and treatment with medication. Her case was that she would remain in hospital as a voluntary patient, that she was sufficiently compliant to be assessed and treated pursuant to the MCA 2005 if necessary and that this would be a less restrictive alternative.

16.34 Charles J grappled with the correct approach in law to the issue of whether the compliance of a person remaining in hospital for assessment or treatment leads to the conclusion that detention under section 2 or section 3 is not warranted if he or she can be detained under the DOLS. He said that this must be a question for the FTT given that the DOLS came out of the case of *HL v United Kingdom*.[11] HL was kept in hospital without a section against the wishes of his carers. As he was a compliant, incapacitated patient he was not sectioned under the MHA 1983. The case made it all the way to the ECHR which found that there was a violation of Article 5(1) in that he was deprived of his liberty and that there should have been procedural safeguards in place. The court noted the striking difference for HL as compared to the safeguards available to those under the Mental Health Act. In addition there was a violation of Article 5(4) as he should have had access to a court to review the lawfulness of his detention. It was to cover the situation of HL that the DOLS came into being. Charles J noted that the DOLS were intended to, and do, provide an alternative to the MHA 1983 (para 28).

10 [2014] UKSC 19, (2014) 17 CCLR 5.

11 App No 45508/99, [2004] ECHR 471, (2004) 7 CCLR 498.

16.35 If the compliant, incapacitated patient can be deprived of their liberty under the DOLS was this a less restrictive and a more appropriate means of detaining a person for medical treatment than detention under the Mental Health Act 1983? If it would – and if it was certain that DOLS would and could be implemented speedily – then detention under MHA 1983 may not be necessary:

> ... the FTT ... [has] to consider whether the MCA and DOLS alternative are applicable and available and, if so, whether and when they should be used.[12]

16.36 The issues for the FTT include the patient's capacity to consent to the admission and treatment (MHA 1983 s131), their compliance with treatment and consideration of what regime would best achieve the objective of assessment or treatment in the least restrictive way. The FTT would also have to look at the actual availability of DOLS.

8 BB v South London and Maudsley NHS Trust and the Ministry of Justice [2009] UKUT 157 (AAC)

16.37 The appellant, a restricted patient, challenged the decision of the First-tier Tribunal not to order his conditional discharge. The appellant's case was that the tribunal's reasons did not give an adequate explanation for its conclusion that he should continue to be detained. Specifically, it was argued that the tribunal failed to give cogent and comprehensible reasons for rejecting the opinion of an independent psychiatrist who, in his written a report and oral evidence, had recommended conditional discharge.

16.38 The Upper Tribunal referred to the legal test when determining the adequacy of reasons and said it is not in doubt. It referred to the fact that it has been fully discussed in the decision of the Court of Appeal in *R (H) v Ashworth Hospital Authority*[13] which adopted what was said in *English v Emery Reimbold & Strick Ltd*:

> ... the essential requirement is that what the [First-tier] tribunal says] should enable the parties and any appellate Tribunal readily to analyse the reasoning that was essential to the decision'. The Tribunal should provide an explanation as to why it has accepted the evidence of one expert and rejected that of another.[14]

12 At para 34.
13 [2003] 1 WLR 127.
14 Para 6 of the judgment.

16.39 The Upper Tribunal then set out at length key paragraphs from the independent psychiatrist's report, which it described as 'a coherent reasoned opinion expressed by a suitably qualified expert'. If, as was the case, the First-tier Tribunal disagreed with the independent expert, it 'needed to state with clarity how and why it disagreed'. In allowing the appeal, the Upper Tribunal concluded that, rather than providing adequate reasons for rejecting the independent psychiatrist's opinion, the First-tier Tribunal had done little more than set out the differences of opinion between him and the responsible clinician and stated that it preferred the evidence of the latter. In support of its preference the tribunal relied on the responsible clinician's greater knowledge of the patient, whom he had known for 25 years, but it failed to give any account of the substantive content of what the responsible clinician had said in answer to the independent psychiatrist's views, and why the tribunal considered it to be a persuasive answer.

9 TW v Enfield Borough Council [2014] EWCA Civ 362

16.40 This case gave leave to TW as is required by section 139(2) of the MHA 1983. The court was considering whether there was an arguable case that consultation with the nearest relative (NR) by the ASW (Approved Social Worker now an Approved Mental Health Practitioner (AMHP)) was practicable before making the application for treatment as was required by section 11 of the MHA 1983. The case imposes a significant responsibility on an AMHP to weigh up a patient's Article 5 rights not to be deprived of her liberty except by a procedure prescribed by law against the right to privacy under Article 8(1).

16.41 TW was admitted to hospital under section 3 in 2007 (before MHA 1983 was amended by the 2007 Act). TW's NR was not consulted on basis that it was not reasonably practical in to do so given TW did not wish family to be consulted. There were unsubstantiated allegations of abuse, she wanted her father removed as NR and there was evidence that this would cause her great distress and may damage her health. The ASW had consulted with TW's father before the first assessment was planned even though TW had made it clear she did not wish them to have meetings with her family. She had dictated letters saying that mental health workers had breached her confidentiality in giving information to parents.

16.42 The court found that the word practicable in section 11(4) means more than just physically possible and that it is legitimate to take into account the result of the proposed action. The consultation with the NR must be construed compatibly with the Convention rights of the person affected. Article 5 allows deprivation of liberty of a person if it is accordance with the law and in accordance with one of the specific exceptions, the relevant one in this case being the lawful detention of persons of unsound mind.

16.43 This means that the ASW needs to properly conduct the statutory procedure which calls for the consultation with the NR. Article 8 and the right to private life also apply but a patient's assertion that the consultation would lead to as infringement of their right to private life cannot lead automatically to the conclusion that it would not be practicable to consult the NR. The consultation of the NR is a vital safeguard for the patient who has no right to object themselves.

> ... when an ASW is considering whether it is 'reasonably practicable' to consult a 'nearest relative,' before making an application to admit ... the section imposes on the ASW an obligation to strike a balance between the patient's Article 5 rights not to be detained unless that is done by a procedure that is in accordance with the law and the patient's Article 8(1) right to her private life.[15]

10 MH v United Kingdom (App No 11577/06) (2013) ECHR 1008

16.44 MH is the long awaited decision from the ECHR following the decision of the House of Lords that many thought was wrong at the time it was handed down. The facts of the case are that MH is a woman with Down's Syndrome who had been living with her mother. She was detained under section 2. As her nearest relative, her mother sought to exercise her right to order that she be discharged from detention (MHA 1983 s23), but MH's RMO issued a 'barring order' (MHA 1983 s25(1)) which certified that MH, if discharged, would be dangerous to herself or others. This had the effect of invalidating MH's mother's discharge order and prevented her from issuing another one for six months. Meanwhile, the local authority began proceedings in the County Court to displace the mother as the NR, which had the effect of extending the detention (MHA 1983 s29), and investigated making a guardianship order for MH.

15 [2014] EWCA Civ 362 para 50.

16.45 For the first 14 days of her detention, MH would have been entitled to apply for a tribunal (MHA 1983 s66). MH did not do this because she lacked legal capacity to instruct solicitors. Therefore the only way MH was able to have her detention reviewed by the tribunal after that 14-day period would have been for someone to request the Secretary of State (MHA 1983 s67) to make a referral.

16.46 The argument was that section 66 was incompatible with Article 5(4) ECHR (the right of persons deprived of their liberty to 'take proceedings by which the lawfulness of his detention shall be decided speedily by a court and his release ordered if the detention is not lawful') as it placed the onus on detainees to make the application and, as MH lacked capacity, she could not do this.

16.47 In the House of Lords section 67 was read to mean that MHA 1983 could be read compatibly with Article 5(4). In the words of Lady Hale, the scheme was 'capable of being operated compatibly'.[16] On the question of whether the right to take proceedings under Article 5(4) is 'theoretical and illusory' rather than 'practical and effective' if the patient is unable to do so, Lady Hale commented:

> ... it does not lead to the conclusion that section 2 is in itself incompatible with the Convention or that the solution is to require a reference in every case. Rather, it leads to the conclusion that every sensible effort should be made to enable the patient to exercise that right if there is reason to think that she would wish to do so.[17]

16.48 The ECHR took a different view of MH's case to the House of Lords, finding one (of a possible three) periods of MH's detention did constitute a violation of her Article 5(4) rights.

16.49 The Court reiterated that to comply with Article 5(4) the remedy 'must be accessible to the person concerned', because 'the Convention requirement for an act of deprivation of liberty to be amenable to independent judicial scrutiny is of fundamental importance in the context of the underlying purpose of Article 5 of the Convention to provide safeguards against arbitrariness'.[18] The question here was whether there were adequate special procedural safeguards to enable MH to exercise her Article 5(4) rights.

16.50 The Court noted that during the first 14 days of her detention, a remedy which would have been available to a 'competent' patient (an application to a tribunal),[19] but this remedy was not in practice

16 [2005] UKHL 60 at para 28.

17 At para 23.

18 At para 76.

19 At para 79.

available to MH 'because she lacked legal capacity'.[20] Although the Court declined to dictate exactly what form the 'special procedural safeguards' for person's in MH's situation should take, it did state that they must 'make the right guaranteed by Article 5(4) as nearly as possible as practical and effective for this particular category of detainees as it is for other detainees'.[21] An automatic review might be one such means, but it was not the only possible means.

16.51 The Court also observed that whilst there were other possible remedies available to MH after that initial fourteen day period (judicial review; habeas corpus or – as she did – asking the Secretary of State for a referral to the tribunal), these too were limited by her lack of legal capacity.[22] Her mother could have initiated habeas corpus proceedings, but the Court held that it was 'wholly unreasonable' to expect her to do so, or requested a referral to the tribunal[23] as the Convention 'does not oblige applicants, after unsuccessfully attempting the obvious remedy at their disposal, to attempt all other conceivable remedies provided for under national law'.[24] Accordingly, the ECHR found that MH's Article 5(4) rights had been violated during the first 27 days of her detention under MHA 1983 s2, because she had not been able to exercise her the right herself and the expectation that her mother or another person or entity should do so on her behalf was unreasonable.

16.52 MH's detention was, as discussed, extended because of the proceedings to displace her mother as NR. During this period of time, MH's mother had instructed solicitors to seek a referral to a tribunal from the Secretary of State. The Court concluded that in this next period of time, her Article 5(4) rights were not violated. However MH's case ended up before a tribunal because her mother had acted upon her own initiative to find solicitors to seek a referral from the Secretary of State, who in turn had agreed to make the referral. There were, thus, two stages in a contingent chain of events which enabled MH to exercise her Article 5(4) rights of appeal. Had either her mother, or the Secretary of State, declined to help MH get to a tribunal, she would have been unable to exercise her Article 5(4) rights.

16.53 In previous cases concerning Article 5(4), the ECHR has, in its own words, 'not looked favourably upon procedures which depend

20 At para 80.
21 At para 82.
22 At para 84.
23 At para 85.
24 At para 86.

upon the exercise of discretion by a third party' (see also *Stanev v Bulgaria*[25] and *Shtukaturov v Russia*[26]). The critical question was – were either of these parties acting upon the exercise of discretion to help MH exercise her Article 5(4) rights, or were they acting upon a duty which obliged them to assist her? Section 67 of the MHA 1983 seems on the face of it to be a discretionary duty.

16.54 However, in the House of Lords Lady Hale had argued that the Secretary of State was exercising functions of a public nature in the meaning of section 6 Human Rights Act (HRA) 1998, and so he was effectively under a duty to ensure compliance with MH's Article 5(4) rights. The ECHR agreed:

> ... the Secretary of State was required under the Human Rights Act to exercise any power compatibly with the rights enjoyed by individuals under the Convention. This means that once a request is made for a referral, rather than enjoying a discretionary power to refer the case to the Tribunal, he is under a duty to do so if not to do so would involve an infringement of the patient's rights under Article 5(4) of the Convention to obtain speedy judicial review of the detention. In such circumstances, the referral to a judicial body cannot be said to be dependent on the goodwill or initiative of the Secretary of State, but rather is a legal consequence flowing from his statutory obligation to act compatibly with the patient's rights under Article 5(4) of the Convention.[27]

16.55 However, the referral from the Secretary of State was as a result of MH's mother requesting it. It cannot be said that MH's mother was under such a duty; nothing in the MHA 1983 obliges a NR to make such a request, and MH's mother is not a public authority in the meaning of HRA 1998 s6, so would not be under the same duty as the Secretary of State to act in accordance with MH's Article 5(4) rights. The Court said:

> The question might be asked whether such a hearing could have taken place had the applicant not had a relative willing and able, through solicitors, to bring her situation to the attention of the Secretary of State.[28]

16.56 However, the Court could not address this hypothetical situation as in this case MH's mother had made such a request, and so MH had been able to exercise her Article 5(4) rights. Whatever the shortcom-

25 [2012] ECHR 46.
26 [2008] ECHR 223.
27 Para 94.
28 Para 95.

ings in the system for others, who were not so fortunate to have a relative who would help them request a referral to a tribunal, MH herself was not deprived of her right to a review of her detention and so she could not claim victim status under the Convention.[29] Accordingly, no violation was found for this period of time in this particular case, but the Court seemed to be implying that in other cases it might be willing to do so.

16.57 The Court also ruled that the for the period following MH's tribunal hearing, where the tribunal had declined to discharge her from her detention, there was no violation of her Article 5(4) rights as it did not guarantee 'a right to take proceedings against an order of detention issued by a judicial body applying an appropriate judicial procedure'.[30]

16.58 In terms of remedying the violation, the government's view is that since MH was detained the MHA 1983 has been amended by introducing provisions on independent mental health advocates under section 130A. In its 'Action Report to the Committee of Ministers at the Council of Europe'[31] the government states:

> An IMHA is there to offer advice as to how the 1983 Act applies to them and give them an idea about what rights they have. They can represent patients including by accompanying them to any meetings and consultations, speak on their behalf and contact a lawyer for them. (MHA 1983 s130B(1), (2))

There is a duty on local authorities to enable an IMHA to be available to help any patient liable to be detained under the 1983 Act.

16.59 The Code of Practice has also been amended to ensure that if a patient lacks capacity to decide whether to seek help from an IMHA, then the hospital manager should ask an IMHA to attend the patient so to explain the help that can be offered.[32] In Wales the Code of Practice provides that the hospital managers should always consider a referral to the tribunal for someone lacking capacity.

16.60 Whether or not these provisions are found to fully implement the judgment remains to be seen.

29 Para 95.

30 Para 98.

31 Action Report concerning *MH v United Kingdom*, 26 February 2015: https://wcd.coe.int/ViewDoc.jsp?id=2293953&Site=CM.

32 Code of Practice chapter 6, specifically para 6.16.

APPENDICES

APPENDIX A

Tribunal Procedure Rules

TRIBUNAL PROCEDURE (FIRST-TIER TRIBUNAL) (HEALTH, EDUCATION AND SOCIAL CARE CHAMBER) RULES 2008 SI No 2699

Part 1: Introduction

1 Citation, commencement, application and interpretation

(1) These Rules may be cited as the Tribunal Procedure (First-tier Tribunal) (Health, Education and Social Care Chamber) Rules 2008 and come into force on 3rd November 2008.

(2) These Rules apply to proceedings before the Health, Education and Social Care Chamber of the First-tier Tribunal.

(3) In these Rules–

'the 2007 Act' means the Tribunals, Courts and Enforcement Act 2007;

'applicant' means a person who–

(a) starts Tribunal proceedings, whether by making an application, an appeal, a claim or a reference;

(b) makes an application to the Tribunal for leave to start such proceedings; or

(c) is substituted as an applicant under rule 9(1) (substitution and addition of parties);

'childcare provider' means a person who is a childminder or provides day care as defined in section 19 of the Children and Families (Wales) Measure 2010, or a person who provides childcare as defined in section 18 of the Childcare Act 2006;

'disability discrimination in schools case' means proceedings concerning disability discrimination in the education of a child or related matters;

'dispose of proceedings' includes, unless indicated otherwise, disposing of a part of the proceedings;

'document' means anything in which information is recorded in any form, and an obligation under these Rules or any practice direction or direction to provide or allow access to a document or a copy of a document for any purpose means, unless the Tribunal directs otherwise, an obligation to provide or allow access to such document or copy in a legible form or in a form which can be readily made into a legible form;

'health service case' means a case under the National Health Service Act 2006, the National Health Service (Wales) Act 2006, regulations made under either of those Acts, or regulations having effect as if made under either of those Acts by reason of section 4 of and Schedule 2 to the National Health Service (Consequential Provisions) Act 2006;

...

'hearing' means an oral hearing and includes a hearing conducted in whole or in part by video link, telephone or other means of instantaneous two-way electronic communication;

'legal representative' means a person who, for the purposes of the Legal Services Act 2007, is an authorised person in relation to an activity which constitutes the exercise of a right of audience or the conduct of litigation within the meaning of that Act;

'mental health case' means proceedings brought under the Mental Health

Act 1983 or paragraph 5(2) of the Schedule to the Repatriation of Prisoners Act 1984;

'nearest relative' has the meaning set out in section 26 of the Mental Health Act 1983;

'party' means–

(a) in a mental health case, the patient, the responsible authority, the Secretary of State (if the patient is a restricted patient or in a reference under rule 32(8) (seeking approval under section 86 of the Mental Health Act 1983)), and any other person who starts a mental health case by making an application;

(b) in any other case, a person who is an applicant or respondent in proceedings before the Tribunal or, if the proceedings have been concluded, a person who was an applicant or respondent when the Tribunal finally disposed of all issues in the proceedings;

'patient' means the person who is the subject of a mental health case;

'practice direction' means a direction given under section 23 of the 2007 Act;

'respondent' means–

(a) in an appeal against an order made by a justice of the peace under section 34 of the Children and Families (Wales) Measure 2010, section 20 of the Care Standards Act 2000 or section 72 of the Childcare Act 2006, the person who applied to the justice of the peace for the order;

(b) in an appeal against any other decision, the person who made the decision;

(c) in proceedings on a claim under section 28I of the Disability Discrimination Act 1995, the body responsible for the school as determined in accordance with paragraph 1 of Schedule 4A to that Act or, if the claim concerns the residual duties of a local education authority under section 28F of that Act, that local education authority;

(d) in proceedings on an application under section 4(2) of the Protection of Children Act 1999 or section 86(2) of the Care Standards Act 2000, the Secretary of State;

(da) in an application for, or for a review of, a stop order under the National Health Service (Optical Charges and Payments) Regulations 1997–

(i) the supplier, where the Secretary of State is the applicant;

(ii) the Secretary of State, where the supplier is the applicant;

(db) in any other health service case–

(i) the practitioner, performer or person against whom the application is made, where the National Health Service Commissioning Board or a Local Health Board is, or is deemed to be, the applicant;

(ii) the National Health Service Commissioning Board or Local Health Board that served the notice, obtained the order or confirmation of the order, where any other person is the applicant; or

(e) a person substituted or added as a respondent under rule 9 (substitution and addition of parties);

'responsible authority' means–

(a) in relation to a patient detained under the Mental Health Act 1983 in a hospital within the meaning of Part 2 of that Act, the managers (as defined in section 145 of that Act);

(b) in relation to a patient subject to guardianship, the responsible local social services authority (as defined in section 34(3) of the Mental Health Act 1983);

(c) in relation to a community patient, the managers of the responsible hospital (as defined in section 145 of the Mental Health Act 1983);

(d) ....

'restricted patient' has the meaning set out in section 79(1) of the Mental Health Act 1983;

'special educational needs case' means proceedings concerning the education of a child who has or may have special educational needs;

'Suspension Regulations' means regulations which provide for a right of appeal against a decision to suspend, or not to lift the suspension of, a person's registration as a childcare provider;

'Tribunal' means the First-tier Tribunal;

'working day' means any day except a Saturday or Sunday, Christmas Day, Good Friday or a bank holiday under section 1 of the Banking and Financial Dealings Act 1971.

2 Overriding objective and parties' obligation to co-operate with the Tribunal

(1) The overriding objective of these Rules is to enable the Tribunal to deal with cases fairly and justly.

(2) Dealing with a case fairly and justly includes–

(a) dealing with the case in ways which are proportionate to the importance of the case, the complexity of the issues, the anticipated costs and the resources of the parties;

(b) avoiding unnecessary formality and seeking flexibility in the proceedings;

(c) ensuring, so far as practicable, that the parties are able to participate fully in the proceedings;

(d) using any special expertise of the Tribunal effectively; and

(e) avoiding delay, so far as compatible with proper consideration of the issues.

(3) The Tribunal must seek to give effect to the overriding objective when it–

(a) exercises any power under these Rules; or

(b) interprets any rule or practice direction.

(4) Parties must–

(a) help the Tribunal to further the overriding objective; and

(b) co-operate with the Tribunal generally.

3 Alternative dispute resolution and arbitration

(1) The Tribunal should seek, where appropriate–

(a) to bring to the attention of the parties the availability of any appropriate alternative procedure for the resolution of the dispute; and

(b) if the parties wish and provided that it is compatible with the overriding objective, to facilitate the use of the procedure.

(2) Part 1 of the Arbitration Act 1996 does not apply to proceedings before the Tribunal.

Part 2: General Powers and Provisions

4 Delegation to staff

(1) Staff appointed under section 40(1) of the 2007 Act (tribunal staff and services) may, with the approval of the Senior President of Tribunals, carry out functions of a judicial nature permitted or required to be done by the Tribunal.

(2) The approval referred to at paragraph (1) may apply generally to the carrying out of specified functions by members of staff of a specified description in specified circumstances.

(3) Within 14 days after the date on which the Tribunal sends notice of a decision made by a member of staff under paragraph (1) to a party, that party may apply in writing to the Tribunal for that decision to be considered afresh by a judge.

5 Case management powers

(1) Subject to the provisions of the 2007 Act and any other enactment, the Tribunal may regulate its own procedure.

(2) The Tribunal may give a direction in relation to the conduct or disposal of proceedings at any time, including a direction amending, suspending or setting aside an earlier direction.

(3) In particular, and without restricting the general powers in paragraphs (1) and (2), the Tribunal may–

- (a) extend or shorten the time for complying with any rule, practice direction or direction, unless such extension or shortening would conflict with a provision of another enactment containing a time limit;
- (b) consolidate or hear together two or more sets of proceedings or parts of proceedings raising common issues, or treat a case as a lead case;
- (c) permit or require a party to amend a document;
- (d) permit or require a party or another person to provide documents, information or submissions to the Tribunal or a party;
- (e) deal with an issue in the proceedings as a preliminary issue;
- (f) hold a hearing to consider any matter, including a case management issue;
- (g) decide the form of any hearing;
- (h) adjourn or postpone a hearing;
  - (i) require a party to produce a bundle for a hearing;
- (j) stay proceedings;
- (k) transfer proceedings to another court or tribunal if that other court or tribunal has jurisdiction in relation to the proceedings and–
  - (i) because of a change of circumstances since the proceedings were started, the Tribunal no longer has jurisdiction in relation to the proceedings; or
  - (ii) the Tribunal considers that the other court or tribunal is a more appropriate forum for the determination of the case; or
- (l) suspend the effect of its own decision pending the determination by the Tribunal or the Upper Tribunal of an application for permission to appeal against, and any appeal or review of, that decision.

6 Procedure for applying for and giving directions

(1) The Tribunal may give a direction on the application of one or more of the parties or on its own initiative.

(2) An application for a direction may be made–

(a) by sending or delivering a written application to the Tribunal; or

(b) orally during the course of a hearing.

(3) An application for a direction must include the reason for making that application.

(4) Unless the Tribunal considers that there is good reason not to do so, the Tribunal must send written notice of any direction to every party and to any other person affected by the direction.

(5) If a party, or any other person given notice of the direction under paragraph (4), wishes to challenge a direction which the Tribunal has given, they may do so by applying for another direction which amends, suspends or sets aside the first direction.

7 Failure to comply with rules etc

(1) An irregularity resulting from a failure to comply with any requirement in these Rules, a practice direction or a direction, does not of itself render void the proceedings or any step taken in the proceedings.

(2) If a party has failed to comply with a requirement in these Rules, a practice direction or a direction, the Tribunal may take such action as it considers just, which may include–

(a) waiving the requirement;

(b) requiring the failure to be remedied;

(c) exercising its power under rule 8 (striking out a party's case);

(d) exercising its power under paragraph (3); or

(e) except in mental health cases, restricting a party's participation in the proceedings.

(3) The Tribunal may refer to the Upper Tribunal, and ask the Upper Tribunal to exercise its power under section 25 of the 2007 Act in relation to, any failure by a person to comply with a requirement imposed by the Tribunal–

(a) to attend at any place for the purpose of giving evidence;

(b) otherwise to make themselves available to give evidence;

(c) to swear an oath in connection with the giving of evidence;

(d) to give evidence as a witness;

(e) to produce a document; or

(f) to facilitate the inspection of a document or any other thing (including any premises).

8 Striking out a party's case

(1) With the exception of paragraph (3), this rule does not apply to mental health cases.

(2) The proceedings, or the appropriate part of them, will automatically be struck out if the applicant has failed to comply with a direction that stated that failure by the applicant to comply with the direction would lead to the striking out of the proceedings or that part of them.

(3) The Tribunal must strike out the whole or a part of the proceedings if the Tribunal–

(a) does not have jurisdiction in relation to the proceedings or that part of them; and
(b) does not exercise its power under rule 5(3)(k)(i) (transfer to another court or tribunal) in relation to the proceedings or that part of them.

(4) The Tribunal may strike out the whole or a part of the proceedings if–
(a) the applicant has failed to comply with a direction which stated that failure by the applicant to comply with the direction could lead to the striking out of the proceedings or part of them;
(b) the applicant has failed to co-operate with the Tribunal to such an extent that the Tribunal cannot deal with the proceedings fairly and justly; or
(c) the Tribunal considers there is no reasonable prospect of the applicant's case, or part of it, succeeding.

(5) The Tribunal may not strike out the whole or a part of the proceedings under paragraph (3) or (4)(b) or (c) without first giving the applicant an opportunity to make representations in relation to the proposed striking out.

(6) If the proceedings, or part of them, have been struck out under paragraph (2) or (4)(a), the applicant may apply for the proceedings, or part of them, to be reinstated.

(7) An application under paragraph (6) must be made in writing and received by the Tribunal within 28 days after the date on which the Tribunal sent notification of the striking out to that party.

(8) This rule applies to a respondent as it applies to an applicant except that–
(a) a reference to the striking out of the proceedings is to be read as a reference to the barring of the respondent from taking further part in the proceedings; and
(b) a reference to an application for the reinstatement of proceedings which have been struck out is to be read as a reference to an application for the lifting of the bar on the respondent from taking further part in the proceedings.

(9) If a respondent has been barred from taking further part in proceedings under this rule and that bar has not been lifted, the Tribunal need not consider any response or other submission made by that respondent and may summarily determine any or all issues against that respondent.

9 Substitution and addition of parties

(1) The Tribunal may give a direction substituting a party if–
(a) the wrong person has been named as a party; or
(b) the substitution has become necessary because of a change in circumstances since the start of proceedings.

(2) The Tribunal may give a direction adding a person to the proceedings as a respondent.

(3) If the Tribunal gives a direction under paragraph (1) or (2) it may give such consequential directions as it considers appropriate.

10 Orders for costs

(1) Subject to paragraph (2), the Tribunal may make an order in respect of costs only–
(a) under section 29(4) of the 2007 Act (wasted costs) and costs incurred in applying for such costs; or

(b) if the Tribunal considers that a party or its representative has acted unreasonably in bringing, defending or conducting the proceedings.

(2) The Tribunal may not make an order under paragraph (1)(b) in mental health cases.

(3) The Tribunal may make an order in respect of costs on an application or on its own initiative.

(4) A person making an application for an order under this rule must–

(a) send or deliver a written application to the Tribunal and to the person against whom it is proposed that the order be made; and

(b) send or deliver a schedule of the costs claimed with the application.

(5) An application for an order under paragraph (1) may be made at any time during the proceedings but may not be made later than 14 days after the date on which the Tribunal sends–

(a) a decision notice recording the decision which finally disposes of all issues in the proceedings; or

(b) notice under rule 17(6) that a withdrawal which ends the proceedings has taken effect.

(6) The Tribunal may not make an order under paragraph (1) against a person (the 'paying person') without first–

(a) giving that person an opportunity to make representations; and

(b) if the paying person is an individual, considering that person's financial means.

(7) The amount of costs to be paid under an order under paragraph (1) may be ascertained by–

(a) summary assessment by the Tribunal;

(b) agreement of a specified sum by the paying person and the person entitled to receive the costs ('the receiving person'); or

(c) assessment of the whole or a specified part of the costs, including the costs of the assessment, incurred by the receiving person, if not agreed.

(8) Following an order for assessment under paragraph (7)(c), the paying person or the receiving person may apply to a county court for a detailed assessment of costs in accordance with the Civil Procedure Rules 1998 on the standard basis or, if specified in the order, on the indemnity basis.

(9) Upon making an order for the assessment of costs, the Tribunal may order an amount to be paid on account before the costs or expenses are assessed.

11 Representatives

(1) A party may appoint a representative (whether a legal representative or not) to represent that party in the proceedings.

(2) If a party appoints a representative, that party (or the representative if the representative is a legal representative) must send or deliver to the Tribunal and to each other party written notice of the representative's name and address.

(3) Anything permitted or required to be done by a party under these Rules, a practice direction or a direction may be done by the representative of that party, except–

(a) signing a witness statement; or

(b) signing an application notice under rule 20 (the application notice) if the representative is not a legal representative.

(4) A person who receives due notice of the appointment of a representative–

(a) must provide to the representative any document which is required to be provided to the represented party, and need not provide that document to the represented party; and
(b) may assume that the representative is and remains authorised as such until they receive written notification that this is not so from the representative or the represented party.

(5) At a hearing a party may be accompanied by another person whose name and address has not been notified under paragraph (2) but who, subject to paragraph (8) and with the permission of the Tribunal, may act as a representative or otherwise assist in presenting the party's case at the hearing.

(6) Paragraphs (2) to (4) do not apply to a person who accompanies a party under paragraph (5).

(7) In a mental health case, if the patient has not appointed a representative, the Tribunal may appoint a legal representative for the patient where–
(a) the patient has stated that they do not wish to conduct their own case or that they wish to be represented; or
(b) the patient lacks the capacity to appoint a representative but the Tribunal believes that it is in the patient's best interests for the patient to be represented.

(8) In a mental health case a party may not appoint as a representative, or be represented or assisted at a hearing by–
(a) a person liable to be detained or subject to guardianship ..., or who is a community patient, under the Mental Health Act 1983; or
(b) a person receiving treatment for mental disorder at the same hospital as the patient.

12 Calculating time

(1) An act required by these Rules, a practice direction or a direction to be done on or by a particular day must be done by 5pm on that day.

(2) If the time specified by these Rules, a practice direction or a direction for doing any act ends on a day other than a working day, the act is done in time if it is done on the next working day.

(3) In a special educational needs case or a disability discrimination in schools case–
(a) if the time for starting proceedings by providing the application notice to the Tribunal under rule 20 (the application notice) ends on a day from 25th December to 1st January inclusive, or on any day in August, the application notice is provided in time if it is provided to the Tribunal on the first working day after 1st January or 31st August, as appropriate; and
(b) the days from 25th December to 1st January inclusive and any day in August must not be counted when calculating the time by which any other act must be done.

(4) Paragraph (3)(b) does not apply where the Tribunal directs that an act must be done by or on a specified date.

13 Sending and delivery of documents

(1) Any document to be provided to the Tribunal under these Rules, a practice direction or a direction must be–

(a) sent by pre-paid post or delivered by hand to the address specified for the proceedings;
(b) sent by fax to the number specified for the proceedings; or
(c) sent or delivered by such other method as the Tribunal may permit or direct.

(1A) If the Tribunal permits or directs documents to be provided to it by email, the requirement for a signature on applications or references under rules 20(2), 22(4)(a) or 32(1)(b) may be satisfied by a typed instead of a handwritten signature.

(2) Subject to paragraph (3), if a party provides a fax number, email address or other details for the electronic transmission of documents to them, that party must accept delivery of documents by that method.

(3) If a party informs the Tribunal and all other parties that a particular form of communication, other than pre-paid post or delivery by hand, should not be used to provide documents to that party, that form of communication must not be so used.

(4) If the Tribunal or a party sends a document to a party or the Tribunal by email or any other electronic means of communication, the recipient may request that the sender provide a hard copy of the document to the recipient. The recipient must make such a request as soon as reasonably practicable after receiving the document electronically.

(5) The Tribunal and each party may assume that the address provided by a party or its representative is and remains the address to which documents should be sent or delivered until receiving written notification to the contrary.

14 Use of documents and information

(1) The Tribunal may make an order prohibiting the disclosure or publication of–
(a) specified documents or information relating to the proceedings; or
(b) any matter likely to lead members of the public to identify any person whom the Tribunal considers should not be identified.

(2) The Tribunal may give a direction prohibiting the disclosure of a document or information to a person if–
(a) the Tribunal is satisfied that such disclosure would be likely to cause that person or some other person serious harm; and
(b) the Tribunal is satisfied, having regard to the interests of justice, that it is proportionate to give such a direction.

(3) If a party ('the first party') considers that the Tribunal should give a direction under paragraph (2) prohibiting the disclosure of a document or information to another party ('the second party'), the first party must–
(a) exclude the relevant document or information from any documents that will be provided to the second party; and
(b) provide to the Tribunal the excluded document or information, and the reason for its exclusion, so that the Tribunal may decide whether the document or information should be disclosed to the second party or should be the subject of a direction under paragraph (2).

(4) The Tribunal must conduct proceedings as appropriate in order to give effect to a direction given under paragraph (2).

(5) If the Tribunal gives a direction under paragraph (2) which prevents disclosure

to a party who has appointed a representative, the Tribunal may give a direction that the documents or information be disclosed to that representative if the Tribunal is satisfied that–

(a) disclosure to the representative would be in the interests of the party; and

(b) the representative will act in accordance with paragraph (6).

(6) Documents or information disclosed to a representative in accordance with a direction under paragraph (5) must not be disclosed either directly or indirectly to any other person without the Tribunal's consent.

(7) Unless the Tribunal gives a direction to the contrary, information about mental health cases and the names of any persons concerned in such cases must not be made public.

15 Evidence and submissions

(1) Without restriction on the general powers in rule 5(1) and (2) (case management powers), the Tribunal may give directions as to–

(a) issues on which it requires evidence or submissions;

(b) the nature of the evidence or submissions it requires;

(c) whether the parties are permitted or required to provide expert evidence, and if so whether the parties must jointly appoint a single expert to provide such evidence;

(d) any limit on the number of witnesses whose evidence a party may put forward, whether in relation to a particular issue or generally;

(e) the manner in which any evidence or submissions are to be provided, which may include a direction for them to be given–

(i) orally at a hearing; or

(ii) by written submissions or witness statement; and

(f) the time at which any evidence or submissions are to be provided.

(2) The Tribunal may–

(a) admit evidence whether or not–

(i) the evidence would be admissible in a civil trial in England and Wales; or

(ii) the evidence was available to a previous decision maker; or

(b) exclude evidence that would otherwise be admissible where–

(i) the evidence was not provided within the time allowed by a direction or a practice direction;

(ii) the evidence was otherwise provided in a manner that did not comply with a direction or a practice direction; or

(iii) it would otherwise be unfair to admit the evidence.

(3) The Tribunal may consent to a witness giving, or require any witness to give, evidence on oath, and may administer an oath for that purpose.

(4) In a special educational needs case the Tribunal may require–

(a) the parents of the child, or any other person with care of the child or parental responsibility for the child (as defined in section 3 of the Children Act 1989), to make the child available for examination or assessment by a suitably qualified professional person; or

(b) the person responsible for a school or educational setting to allow a suitably qualified professional person to have access to the school or educational setting for the purpose of assessing the child or the provision made, or to be made, for the child.

(5) The Tribunal may consider a failure by a party to comply with a requirement made under paragraph (4), in the absence of any good reason for such failure, as a failure to co-operate with the Tribunal, which could lead to a result which is adverse to that party's case.

16 Summoning of witnesses and orders to answer questions or produce documents

(1) On the application of a party or on its own initiative, the Tribunal may–

(a) by summons require any person to attend as a witness at a hearing at the time and place specified in the summons; or

(b) order any person to answer any questions or produce any documents in that person's possession or control which relate to any issue in the proceedings.

(2) A summons under paragraph (1)(a) must–

(a) give the person required to attend 14 days' notice of the hearing, or such shorter period as the Tribunal may direct; and

(b) where the person is not a party, make provision for the person's necessary expenses of attendance to be paid, and state who is to pay them.

(3) No person may be compelled to give any evidence or produce any document that the person could not be compelled to give or produce on a trial of an action in a court of law.

(4) A summons or order under this rule must–

(a) state that the person on whom the requirement is imposed may apply to the Tribunal to vary or set aside the summons or order, if they have not had an opportunity to object to it; and

(b) state the consequences of failure to comply with the summons or order.

17 Withdrawal

(1) Subject to paragraphs (2) and (3), a party may give notice of the withdrawal of its case, or any part of it–

(a) ... by sending or delivering to the Tribunal a written notice of withdrawal; or

(b) orally at a hearing.

(2) Notice of withdrawal will not take effect unless the Tribunal consents to the withdrawal except–

(a) in proceedings concerning the suitability of a person to work with children or vulnerable adults; or

(b) in proceedings started by a reference under section 67 or 71(1) of the Mental Health Act 1983.

(3) A party which started a mental health case by making a reference to the Tribunal under section 68, 71(2) or 75(1) of the Mental Health Act 1983 may not withdraw its case.

(4) A party which has withdrawn its case may apply to the Tribunal for the case to be reinstated.

(5) An application under paragraph (4) must be made in writing and be received by the Tribunal within 28 days after–

(a) the date on which the Tribunal received the notice under paragraph (1)(a); or

(b) the date of the hearing at which the case was withdrawn orally under paragraph (1)(b).

(6) The Tribunal must notify each party in writing that a withdrawal has taken effect under this rule.

Part 3: Proceedings Before the Tribunal other than in Mental Health Cases

[Part 3 not reproduced here as it does not apply to mental health cases]

Part 4: Proceedings Before the Tribunal in Mental Health Cases

Chapter 1: Before the Hearing

31 Application of Part 4

This Part applies only to mental health cases.

32 Procedure in mental health cases

(1) An application or reference must be–
- (a) made in writing;
- (b) signed (in the case of an application, by the applicant or any person authorised by the applicant to do so); and
- (c) sent or delivered to the Tribunal so that it is received within the time specified in the Mental Health Act 1983 or the Repatriation of Prisoners Act 1984.

(2) An application must, if possible, include–
- (a) the name, address and date of birth of the patient;
- (b) if the application is made by the patient's nearest relative, the name, address and relationship to the patient of the patient's nearest relative;
- (c) the provision under which the patient is detained, liable to be detained, subject to guardianship, or a community patient ...;
- (d) whether the person making the application has appointed a representative or intends to do so, and the name and address of any representative appointed;
- (e) the name and address of the responsible authority in relation to the patient.

(2A) A reference must, if possible, include–
- (a) the name and address of the person or body making the reference;
- (b) the name, address and date of birth of the patient;
- (c) the name and address of any representative of the patient;
- (d) the provision under which the patient is detained, liable to be detained, subject to guardianship or a community patient (as the case may be);
- (e) whether the person or body making the reference has appointed a representative or intends to do so, and the name and address of any representative appointed;
- (f) if the reference is made by the Secretary of State, the name and address of the responsible authority in relation to the patient, or, in the case of a conditionally discharged patient, the name and address of the responsible clinician and any social supervisor in relation to the patient.

(3) Subject to rule 14(2) (withholding evidence likely to cause harm), when the Tribunal receives a document from any party it must send a copy of that document to each other party.

(4) If the patient is a conditionally discharged patient–

(a) upon being notified by the Tribunal of an application, the Secretary of State must immediately provide to the Tribunal the names and addresses of the responsible clinician and any social supervisor in relation to the patient; and
(b) upon being notified by the Tribunal of an application or reference, the responsible clinician and any social supervisor named by the Secretary of State under this rule must send or deliver the documents specified in the relevant practice direction to the Tribunal so that they are received by the Tribunal as soon as practicable and in any event within 3 weeks after the notification.

(5) In proceedings under section 66(1)(a) of the Mental Health Act 1983 (application in respect of an admission for assessment), on the earlier of receipt of the copy of the application or a request from the Tribunal, the responsible authority must immediately send or deliver to the Tribunal a copy of–
(a) the application for admission; and
(b) the written medical recommendations on which that application was founded;

and must as soon as practicable send or deliver to the Tribunal the documents specified in the relevant practice direction.

(6) If neither paragraph (4) nor (5) applies, the responsible authority must send or deliver the documents specified in the relevant practice direction to the Tribunal so that they are received by the Tribunal as soon as practicable and in any event within 3 weeks after the responsible authority made the reference or received a copy of the application or reference.

(7) If the patient is a restricted patient, a person or body providing a document to the Tribunal in accordance with paragraph (4)(b) or (6) must also send or deliver a copy of the document to the Secretary of State.

(7A) The Secretary of State must send the information specified in paragraph (7B) and any observations the Secretary of State wishes to make to the Tribunal as soon as practicable and in any event–
(a) in proceedings under section 75(1) of the Mental Health Act 1983 (reference concerning a conditionally discharged restricted patient who has been recalled to hospital), within 2 weeks after the Secretary of State received the documents sent or delivered in accordance with paragraph (7);
(b) otherwise, within 3 weeks after the Secretary of State received the documents sent or delivered in accordance with paragraph (7).

(7B) The information specified in this paragraph is–
(a) a summary of the offence or alleged offence that resulted in the patient being detained in hospital subject to a restriction order or, in the case of a patient subject to a restriction or limitation direction, that resulted in the patient being remanded in custody, kept in custody or sentenced to imprisonment;
(b) a record of any other criminal convictions or findings recorded against the patient;
(c) full details of the history of the patient's liability to detention under the Mental Health Act 1983 since the restrictions were imposed;
(d) any further information in the Secretary of State's possession that the Secretary of State considers relevant to the proceedings.

(8) If the Secretary of State wishes to seek the approval of the Tribunal under section 86(3) of the Mental Health Act 1983 (removal of alien patients), the Secretary of State must refer the patient's case to the Tribunal and the provisions of these Rules applicable to references under that Act apply to the proceedings.

(9) The responsible authority must make records relating to the detention or treatment of the patient and any after-care services available to the Tribunal on request and the Tribunal or an appropriate member of the Tribunal may, before or at the hearing, examine and take notes and copies of such records for use in connection with the proceedings.

33 Notice of proceedings to interested persons

When the Tribunal receives the information required by rule 32(4), (5) or (6) (procedure in mental health cases) the Tribunal must give notice of the proceedings–

(a) where the patient is subject to the guardianship of a private guardian, to the guardian;
(b) where there is an extant order of the Court of Protection, to that court;
(c) subject to a patient with capacity to do so requesting otherwise, where any person other than the applicant is named by the authority as exercising the functions of the nearest relative, to that person;
(d) ... and
(e) to any other person who, in the opinion of the Tribunal, should have an opportunity of being heard.

34 Medical examination of the patient

(1) Where paragraph (2) applies, an appropriate member of the Tribunal must, so far as practicable, examine the patient in order to form an opinion of the patient's mental condition, and may do so in private.

(2) This paragraph applies–
(a) in proceedings under section 66(1)(a) of the Mental Health Act 1983 (application in respect of an admission for assessment), unless the Tribunal is satisfied that the patient does not want such an examination;
(b) in any other case, if the patient or the patient's representative has informed the Tribunal in writing, not less than 14 days before the hearing, that–
(i) the patient; or
(ii) if the patient lacks the capacity to make such a decision, the patient's representative,

wishes there to be such an examination; or
(c) if the Tribunal has directed that there be such an examination.

Chapter 2: Hearings

35 Restrictions on disposal of proceedings without a hearing

(1) Subject to the following paragraphs, the Tribunal must hold a hearing before making a decision which disposes of proceedings.

(2) This rule does not apply to a decision under Part 5.

(3) The Tribunal may make a decision on a reference under section 68 of the Mental Health Act 1983 (duty of managers of hospitals to refer cases to tribunal) without a hearing if the patient is a community patient aged 18 or over and either–

(a) the patient has stated in writing that the patient does not wish to attend or be represented at a hearing of the reference and the Tribunal is satisfied that the patient has the capacity to decide whether or not to make that decision; or

(b) the patient's representative has stated in writing that the patient does not wish to attend or be represented at a hearing of the reference.

(4) The Tribunal may dispose of proceedings without a hearing under rule 8(3) (striking out a party's case).

36 Entitlement to attend a hearing

(1) Subject to rule 38(4) (exclusion of a person from a hearing), each party to proceedings is entitled to attend a hearing.

(2) Any person notified of the proceedings under rule 33 (notice of proceedings to interested persons) may–

(a) attend and take part in a hearing to such extent as the Tribunal considers proper; or

(b) provide written submissions to the Tribunal.

37 Time and place of hearings

(1) In proceedings under section 66(1)(a) of the Mental Health Act 1983 the hearing of the case must start within 7 days after the date on which the Tribunal received the application notice.

(2) In proceedings under section 75(1) of that Act, the hearing of the case must start at least 5 weeks but no more than 8 weeks after the date on which the Tribunal received the reference.

(3) The Tribunal must give reasonable notice of the time and place of the hearing (including any adjourned or postponed hearing), and any changes to the time and place of the hearing, to–

(a) each party entitled to attend a hearing; and

(b) any person who has been notified of the proceedings under rule 33 (notice of proceedings to interested persons).

(4) The period of notice under paragraph (3) must be at least 21 days, except that–

(a) in proceedings under section 66(1)(a) of the Mental Health Act 1983 the period must be at least 3 working days; and

(b) the Tribunal may give shorter notice–

(i) with the parties' consent; or

(ii) in urgent or exceptional circumstances.

38 Public and private hearings

(1) All hearings must be held in private unless the Tribunal considers that it is in the interests of justice for the hearing to be held in public.

(2) If a hearing is held in public, the Tribunal may give a direction that part of the hearing is to be held in private.

(3) Where a hearing, or part of it, is to be held in private, the Tribunal may determine who is permitted to attend the hearing or part of it.

(4) The Tribunal may give a direction excluding from any hearing, or part of it–

(a) any person whose conduct the Tribunal considers is disrupting or is likely to disrupt the hearing;

(b) any person whose presence the Tribunal considers is likely to prevent another person from giving evidence or making submissions freely;

(c) any person who the Tribunal considers should be excluded in order to give effect to a direction under rule 14(2) (withholding information likely to cause harm); or
(d) any person where the purpose of the hearing would be defeated by the attendance of that person.

(5) The Tribunal may give a direction excluding a witness from a hearing until that witness gives evidence.

39 Hearings in a party's absence

(1) Subject to paragraph (2), if a party fails to attend a hearing the Tribunal may proceed with the hearing if the Tribunal–
(a) is satisfied that the party has been notified of the hearing or that reasonable steps have been taken to notify the party of the hearing; and
(b) considers that it is in the interests of justice to proceed with the hearing.

(2) The Tribunal may not proceed with a hearing that the patient has failed to attend unless the Tribunal is satisfied that–
(a) the patient–
(i) has decided not to attend the hearing; or
(ii) is unable to attend the hearing for reasons of ill health; and
(b) an examination under rule 34 (medical examination of the patient)–
(i) has been carried out; or
(ii) is impractical or unnecessary.

40 Power to pay allowances

The Tribunal may pay allowances in respect of travelling expenses, subsistence and loss of earnings to–
(a) any person who attends a hearing as an applicant or a witness;
(b) a patient who attends a hearing otherwise than as the applicant or a witness; and
(c) any person (other than a legal representative) who attends as the representative of an applicant.

Chapter 3: Decisions

41 Decisions

(1) The Tribunal may give a decision orally at a hearing.

(2) Subject to rule 14(2) (withholding information likely to cause harm), the Tribunal must provide to each party as soon as reasonably practicable after making a decision (except a decision under Part 5) which finally disposes of all issues in the proceedings or of a preliminary issue dealt with following a direction under rule 5(3)(e)–
(a) a decision notice stating the Tribunal's decision;
(b) written reasons for the decision; and
(c) notification of any right of appeal against the decision and the time within which, and the manner in which, such right of appeal may be exercised.

(3) The documents and information referred to in paragraph (2) must–
(a) in proceedings under section 66(1)(a) of the Mental Health Act 1983, be provided at the hearing or sent within 3 working days after the hearing; and
(b) in other cases, be provided at the hearing or sent within 7 days after the hearing.

(4) The Tribunal may provide written reasons for any decision to which paragraph (2) does not apply.

42 Provisional decisions

For the purposes of this Part and Parts 1, 2 and 5, a decision with recommendations under section 72(3)(a) or (3A)(a) of the Mental Health Act 1983 or a deferred direction for conditional discharge under section 73(7) of that Act is a decision which disposes of the proceedings.

Part 5: Correcting, Setting Aside, Reviewing and Appealing Tribunal Decisions

43 Interpretation

In this Part–

'appeal' means the exercise of a right of appeal on a point of law under section 11 of the 2007 Act; and

'review' means the review of a decision by the Tribunal under section 9 of the 2007 Act.

44 Clerical mistakes and accidental slips or omissions

The Tribunal may at any time correct any clerical mistake or other accidental slip or omission in a decision, direction or any document produced by it, by–

(a) sending notification of the amended decision or direction, or a copy of the amended document, to all parties; and

(b) making any necessary amendment to any information published in relation to the decision, direction or document.

45 Setting aside a decision which disposes of proceedings

(1) The Tribunal may set aside a decision which disposes of proceedings, or part of such a decision, and re-make the decision or the relevant part of it, if–

(a) the Tribunal considers that it is in the interests of justice to do so; and

(b) one or more of the conditions in paragraph (2) are satisfied.

(2) The conditions are–

(a) a document relating to the proceedings was not sent to, or was not received at an appropriate time by, a party or a party's representative;

(b) a document relating to the proceedings was not sent to the Tribunal at an appropriate time;

(c) a party, or a party's representative, was not present at a hearing related to the proceedings; or

(d) there has been some other procedural irregularity in the proceedings.

(3) A party applying for a decision, or part of a decision, to be set aside under paragraph (1) must make a written application to the Tribunal so that it is received no later than 28 days after the date on which the Tribunal sent notice of the decision to the party.

46 Application for permission to appeal

(1) A person seeking permission to appeal must make a written application to the Tribunal for permission to appeal.

(2) An application under paragraph (1) must be sent or delivered to the Tribunal so that it is received no later than 28 days after the latest of the dates that the Tribunal sends to the person making the application–

(za) the relevant decision notice;

(a) written reasons for the decision, if the decision disposes of–
   (i) all issues in the proceedings; or
   (ii) subject to paragraph (2A), a preliminary issue dealt with following a direction under rule 5(3)(e);
(b) notification of amended reasons for, or correction of, the decision following a review; or
(c) notification that an application for the decision to be set aside has been unsuccessful.

(2A) The Tribunal may direct that the 28 days within which a party may send or deliver to the Tribunal an application for permission to appeal against a decision that disposes of a preliminary issue shall run from the date of the decision that disposes of all issues in the proceedings.

(3) The date in paragraph (2)(c) applies only if the application for the decision to be set aside was made within the time stipulated in rule 45 (setting aside a decision which disposes of proceedings) or any extension of that time granted by the Tribunal.

(4) If the person seeking permission to appeal sends or delivers the application to the Tribunal later than the time required by paragraph (2) or by any extension of time under rule 5(3)(a) (power to extend time)–
   (a) the application must include a request for an extension of time and the reason why the application was not provided in time; and
   (b) unless the Tribunal extends time for the application under rule 5(3)(a) (power to extend time) the Tribunal must not admit the application.

(5) An application under paragraph (1) must–
   (a) identify the decision of the Tribunal to which it relates;
   (b) identify the alleged error or errors of law in the decision; and
   (c) state the result the party making the application is seeking.

47 Tribunal's consideration of application for permission to appeal

(1) On receiving an application for permission to appeal the Tribunal must first consider, taking into account the overriding objective in rule 2, whether to review the decision in accordance with rule 49 (review of a decision).

(2) If the Tribunal decides not to review the decision, or reviews the decision and decides to take no action in relation to the decision, or part of it, the Tribunal must consider whether to give permission to appeal in relation to the decision or that part of it.

(3) The Tribunal must send a record of its decision to the parties as soon as practicable.

(4) If the Tribunal refuses permission to appeal it must send with the record of its decision–
   (a) a statement of its reasons for such refusal; and
   (b) notification of the right to make an application to the Upper Tribunal for permission to appeal and the time within which, and the method by which, such application must be made.

(5) The Tribunal may give permission to appeal on limited grounds, but must comply with paragraph (4) in relation to any grounds on which it has refused permission.

48 Application for review in special educational needs cases

(1) This rule applies to decisions which dispose of proceedings in special educational needs cases, but not to decisions under this Part.

(2) A party may make a written application to the Tribunal for a review of a decision if circumstances relevant to the decision have changed since the decision was made.

(3) An application under paragraph (2) must be sent or delivered to the Tribunal so that it is received within 28 days after the date on which the Tribunal sent the decision notice recording the Tribunal's decision to the party making the application.

(4) If a party sends or delivers an application to the Tribunal later than the time required by paragraph (3) or by any extension of time under rule 5(3)(a) (power to extend time)–

(a) the application must include a request for an extension of time and the reason why the application was not provided in time; and

(b) unless the Tribunal extends time for the application under rule 5(3)(a) (power to extend time) the Tribunal must not admit the application.

49 Review of a decision

(1) The Tribunal may only undertake a review of a decision–

(a) pursuant to rule 47(1) (review on an application for permission to appeal) if it is satisfied that there was an error of law in the decision; or

(b) pursuant to rule 48 (application for review in special educational needs cases).

(2) The Tribunal must notify the parties in writing of the outcome of any review, and of any right of appeal in relation to the outcome.

(3) If the Tribunal takes any action in relation to a decision following a review without first giving every party an opportunity to make representations, the notice under paragraph (2) must state that any party that did not have an opportunity to make representations may apply for such action to be set aside and for the decision to be reviewed again.

50 Power to treat an application as a different type of application

The Tribunal may treat an application for a decision to be corrected, set aside or reviewed, or for permission to appeal against a decision, as an application for any other one of those things.

SCHEDULE: Cases in which the Time for Providing the Application Notice is Within 3 Months After Written Notice of the Decision Being Challenged was Sent to the Applicant

Rule 20(1)(d)

An appeal under section 65A of the Children Act 1989 (appeal against a refusal to give consent for a person who is disqualified from fostering a child privately to carry on, or be otherwise concerned in the management of, or have any financial interest in, or be employed in, a children's home)

An appeal, an application for permission to appeal or an application for permission to have an issue determined under section 4 of the Protection of Children Act 1999 (appeal against inclusion of a person on the list of individuals who are considered unsuitable to work with children or a refusal to remove a person from the list)

An appeal under section 68 of the Care Standards Act 2000 against a refusal to register a person as a social worker under section 58 of that Act (grant or refusal of registration)

An appeal, an application for permission to appeal or an application for permission to have an issue determined under section 86 of the Care Standards Act 2000 (appeal against inclusion of a person on the list of individuals who are considered unsuitable to work with vulnerable adults or a refusal to remove a person from the list)

An appeal under section 74(1)(a) of the Childcare Act 2006 (appeal against a refusal of registration as a childcare provider)

An appeal under section 37(1)(a) of the Children and Families (Wales) Measure 2010 (appeal against a refusal of an application for registration for child minding or providing day care for children)

An appeal under regulation 12 of the Education (Prohibition from Teaching or Working with Children) Regulations 2003 (appeal against a direction, or a refusal to revoke a direction, prohibiting or restricting a person from working in education or in a job which brings them regularly into contact with children).

MENTAL HEALTH REVIEW TRIBUNAL FOR WALES RULES 2008 SI No 2705

Part 1: Introduction

1 Citation and commencement

These Rules may be cited as the Mental Health Review Tribunal for Wales Rules 2008 and come into force on 3rd November 2008.

2 Interpretation

(1) In these Rules–

'the Act' means the Mental Health Act 1983;

'applicant' means a person who–

(a) starts Tribunal proceedings, whether by making an application or a reference, or

(b) is substituted as a party under rule 12 (substitution and addition of parties);

'document' means anything in which information is recorded in any form, and an obligation under these Rules to provide or allow access to a document or a copy of a document for any purpose means, unless the Tribunal directs otherwise, an obligation to provide or allow access to such document or copy in a legible form or in a form which can be readily made into a legible form;

'final determination' means a decision of the Tribunal which disposes of proceedings, including a decision with recommendations or a deferred decision for conditional discharge, but a refusal of an application for permission to appeal under rule 30 (application for permission to appeal) is not a final determination;

'hearing' means an oral hearing and includes a hearing conducted in whole or in part by video link, telephone or other means of instantaneous two-way electronic communication;

'interested party' means a person added as an interested party under rule 12 (substitution and addition of parties);

'legal representative' means a person who, for the purposes of the Legal Services Act 2007, is an authorised person in relation to an activity which constitutes the exercise of a right of audience or the conduct of litigation (within the meaning of that Act);

'party' means the patient, the responsible authority, the Secretary of State (if the patient is a restricted patient), the Welsh Ministers or Secretary of State in a reference under rule 15(7) (seeking approval under section 86 of the Act) and any other person who starts a case by making an application or referring a matter to the Tribunal under the Act;

'registered person' means the person or persons registered in respect of a registered establishment;

'responsible authority' means–

(a) in relation to a patient detained under the Act in a hospital within the meaning of Part 2 of that Act, the managers (as defined in section 145 of the Act);

(b) in relation to a patient subject to guardianship, the responsible local social services authority as defined in section 34(3) of the Act;

(c) in relation to a community patient, the managers of the responsible hospital (as defined in section 145 of the Act);

(d) ...

'restricted patient' has the meaning set out in section 79(1) of the Act;

'Tribunal' means the Mental Health Review Tribunal for Wales;

'working day' means any day except a Saturday or Sunday, Christmas Day, Good Friday or a bank holiday under section 1 of the Banking and Financial Dealings Act 1971.

(2) In these Rules, any reference to a rule or Schedule alone is a reference to a rule or Schedule in these Rules.

3 Overriding objective

(1) The overriding objective of these Rules is to enable the Tribunal to deal with cases fairly, justly, efficiently and expeditiously.

(2) Dealing with a case in accordance with paragraph (1) includes–

(a) avoiding unnecessary formality and seeking flexibility in the proceedings;

(b) ensuring, so far as practicable, that the parties are able to participate fully in the proceedings;

(c) using any special expertise of the Tribunal effectively; and

(d) avoiding delay, so far as compatible with proper consideration of the issues.

(3) The Tribunal must seek to give effect to the overriding objective when it–

(a) exercises any power under these Rules; or

(b) interprets any rule.

Part 2: General Powers and Provisions

4 Preliminary and incidental matters

As regards matters preliminary or incidental to an application or reference, the chairman may, at any time up to the hearing of an application or reference by the Tribunal, exercise the powers of the Tribunal under rules 5, 6, 10, 12, 13, 14, 15, 16, 17, 21, 22, 26, 28 and 29.

5 Case management powers

(1) The Tribunal may give directions at any time in relation to the conduct or disposal of proceedings.

(2) In particular, and without restriction on the general power to give directions under paragraph (1) and any other provisions within these Rules, the Tribunal may by directions–

(a) extend or shorten the time for complying with any rule or direction (unless such extension or abridgement would conflict with a provision of an enactment containing a time limit if–

(i) the party requiring the extension or abridgement has shown a good reason why it is necessary; and

(ii) the Tribunal considers the extension or abridgement to be in the interests of justice;

(b) permit or require a party to amend a document;

(c) permit or require a party or another person to provide documents, information or submissions to the Tribunal or, subject to rule 17 (withholding documents or information likely to cause harm), a party;

(d) provide that an issue in the proceedings will be dealt with as a preliminary issue;
(e) hold a hearing to consider any matter, including a case management issue;
(f) decide the form of any hearing;
(g) stay execution of its own decision pending an appeal of such decision;
(h) stay proceedings.

(3) Rule 6 (directions) sets out the procedures for applying for and giving directions.

6 Directions

(1) The Tribunal may give a direction at any time, including a direction amending or suspending an earlier direction.
(2) The Tribunal may give a direction–
(a) on the application of one or more of the parties; or
(b) on its own initiative.
(3) An application for directions must include the reason for making that application.
(4) An application for directions may be made either–
(a) by sending or delivering a written application to the Tribunal; or
(b) orally during the course of a hearing.
(5) Unless the Tribunal considers that there is a good reason not to do so, the Tribunal must send written notice of any direction to every party and any other person affected by the direction.

7 Failure to comply with rules or directions

(1) An irregularity resulting from a failure to comply with any provision of these Rules or a direction does not of itself render void the proceedings or any step taken in the proceedings.
(2) If a party has failed to comply with a requirement in these Rules or a direction, the Tribunal may take such action the Tribunal considers just, which may include–
(a) waiving the requirement; or
(b) requiring the failure to be remedied.

8 Calculating time

(1) An act required by these Rules or a direction to be done on or by a particular day must be done before 5pm on that day.
(2) If the time specified by these Rules or a direction for doing any act ends on a day other than a working day, the act is done in time if it is done on the next working day.

9 Sending and delivery of documents

(1) Any document to be sent or delivered to the Tribunal under these Rules must be–
(a) sent by prepaid post or delivered by hand;
(b) sent by facsimile transmission to the number specified by the Tribunal; or
(c) sent or delivered by such other method as the Tribunal may permit or direct.
(2) Subject to paragraph (3), a party may inform the Tribunal and all other parties

that a particular form of communication (other than pre-paid post or delivery by hand) should not be used to send documents to that party.

(3) If a party provides a facsimile transmission number, email address or other details for the electronic transmission of documents to them, that party must accept delivery of documents by that method.

(4) Subject to paragraph (3), where any document is required or authorised by these Rules to be sent to any person it may be sent by prepaid post or delivered to the last known address of the person to whom the document is directed.

10 Prohibitions on disclosure or publication

(1) Unless the Tribunal gives a direction to the contrary, information about proceedings before the Tribunal and the names of any persons concerned in such proceedings must not be made public.

(2) The Tribunal may make an order prohibiting the disclosure or publication of–

(a) specified documents or information relating to the proceedings; or

(b) any matter likely to lead members of the public to identify any person who the Tribunal considers should not be identified.

(3) The Tribunal may use the power in paragraph (2) in order to take action under rule 17 (withholding documents or information likely to cause harm) and in such other circumstances as it considers just.

11 Appointment of the tribunal

(1) A person shall not be qualified to serve as a member of a Tribunal for the purpose of any proceedings where–

(a) that person is a member, director or registered person (as the case may be) of the responsible authority concerned in the proceedings; or

(b) that person is a member or director of a local health board or National Health Service trust which has the right to discharge the patient under section 23(3) of the Act; or

(c) the chairman or, as the case may be, president of the Tribunal considers that that person appears to have a conflict of interest or bias of opinion in respect of the patient, or any other member of that Tribunal or party to the proceedings, or has recently been involved with the medical treatment of the patient in a professional capacity.

(2) The persons qualified to serve as president of the Tribunal for the consideration of an application or reference relating to a restricted patient shall be restricted to those legal members who have been approved for that purpose by the Lord Chief Justice after consulting the Lord Chancellor.

(3) The Lord Chief Justice may nominate a judicial office holder (as defined in section 109(4) of the Constitutional Reform Act 2005) to exercise his functions referred to in paragraph (2).

12 Substitution and addition of parties

(1) The Tribunal may give a direction substituting a party if–

(a) the wrong person has been named as a party; or

(b) the substitution has become necessary because of a change in circumstances since the start of proceedings.

(2) The Tribunal may give a direction adding a person to the proceedings as an interested party.

(3) If the Tribunal gives a direction under paragraph (1) or (2) it may give such consequential directions as it considers appropriate.

13 Representatives

(1) A party may appoint a representative (whether legally qualified or not) to represent that party in the proceedings, not being a person liable to be detained or subject to guardianship or after-care under supervision or a community patient under the Act, or a person receiving treatment for mental disorder at the same hospital or registered establishment as the patient.

(2) If a party appoints a representative, that party or representative must send or deliver to the Tribunal written notice of the representative's name and address.

(3) Anything permitted or required to be done by or provided to a party under these Rules or a direction, other than signing a witness statement, may be done by or provided to the representative of that party.

(4) In the event of a representative being duly appointed–
- (a) the Tribunal and other parties may assume that the representative is and remains authorised until receiving written notification to the contrary from the representative or the represented party; and
- (b) the Tribunal must provide to the representative any document which is required to be sent to the represented party, and need not provide that document to the represented party.

(5) The Tribunal may appoint a legal representative for the patient if–
- (a) the patient has not appointed a representative; and
- (b) (i) the patient has stated that they do not wish to conduct their own case or that they wish to be represented; or
  - (ii) the patient lacks the capacity to appoint a representative but the Tribunal believes that it is in the patient's best interests for the patient to be represented.

(6) Unless the Tribunal otherwise directs, a patient or any other party may be accompanied by such other person as the patient or party wishes, in addition to any representative that may have been appointed under this Rule, provided that such person does not act as the representative of the patient or other party.

Part 3: Proceedings before the Tribunal

Chapter 1: Before the Final Determination

14 Procedure for applications and references

(1) An application or reference must be made in writing, be signed (in the case of an application, by the applicant or any person authorised by the applicant to do so) and be provided to the Tribunal so that it is received within the time specified in the Act or the Repatriation of Prisoners Act 1984.

(2) An application or reference must, if possible, include–
- (a) the name and address of the patient;
- (b) in the event of an application being made by the patient's nearest relative, that person's name, address and relationship to the patient;
- (c) the provision under which the patient is detained or liable to be detained, subject to guardianship or after-care under supervision or a community patient;
- (d) whether the person making the application has appointed a representa-

tive or intends to do so, and the name and address of any representative appointed;

(e) the name and address of the responsible authority in relation to the patient.

(3) On receipt of an application or reference, the Tribunal must send notice of the same to–

(a) the responsible authority;

(b) the patient (where the patient is not the applicant); and

(c) if the patient is a restricted patient, the Secretary of State.

15 Statements, reports and documents

(1) Subject to rule 17 (withholding documents or information likely to cause harm), when the Tribunal receives a document from any party it must send a copy of that document to each other party.

(2) When the Tribunal receives an application or reference it must send to the responsible authority or the Secretary of State, as the case may be, a request for the documents and information required to be provided under paragraph (3), (4) or (5).

(3) In proceedings under section 66(1)(a) of the Act (application for admission for assessment), on the earlier of receipt of the copy of the application or receipt of a request from the Tribunal, the responsible authority must send or deliver to the Tribunal by the commencement of the hearing–

(a) the application for admission;

(b) the written medical recommendation or recommendations, as the case may be, of the registered medical practitioners on which the application is founded;

(c) such of the information specified in Part A of the Schedule as is within the knowledge of the responsible authority and can reasonably be provided in the time available; and

(d) such of the reports specified in Part B of the Schedule as can reasonably be provided in the time available.

(4) If the patient is a conditionally discharged patient the Secretary of State shall send to the Tribunal as soon as practicable, and in any event within 6 weeks of receipt by the Secretary of State of a copy of the application or request from the Tribunal, a statement which shall contain–

(a) the information specified in Part C of the Schedule, in so far as it is within the knowledge of the Secretary of State; and

(b) the reports specified in Part D of the Schedule, in so far as it is reasonably practicable to provide them.

(5) If neither paragraph (3) nor (4) applies, the responsible authority must send a statement to the Tribunal as soon as practicable, and in any event within 3 weeks of receipt by the responsible authority of a copy of the application or receipt of a request from the Tribunal, a statement which shall contain–

(a) the information specified in Part A of the Schedule, in so far as it is within the knowledge of the responsible authority;

(b) the report specified in paragraph 1 of Part B of that Schedule; and

(c) the other reports specified in Part B of the Schedule, in so far as it is reasonably practicable to provide them.

(6) If the patient is a restricted patient the responsible authority must also send

the statement under paragraph (5) to the Secretary of State, and the Secretary of State must send a statement of any further relevant information to the Tribunal as soon as practicable and in any event–

(a) in proceedings under section 75(1) of the Act, within 2 weeks of receipt by the Secretary of State of the relevant authority's statement; or
(b) otherwise, within 3 weeks of receipt by the Secretary of State of the relevant authority's statement.

(7) If the Welsh Ministers or Secretary of State wish to seek the approval of the Tribunal under section 86(3) of the Act, the Welsh Ministers or Secretary of State, as the case may be, must refer the patient's case to the Tribunal and the provisions of these Rules applicable to references under the Act apply to the proceedings.

16 Notice of proceedings

When the Tribunal receives the information required by rule 15(3), (4) or (5), the Tribunal must give notice of the proceedings–

(a) where the patient is subject to the guardianship of a private guardian, to the guardian;
(b) where there is an extant order of the superior court of record established by section 45(1) of the Mental Capacity Act 2005, to that court;
(c) unless the patient requests otherwise, where any person other than the applicant is named in the responsible authority's statement as exercising the functions of the nearest relative, to that person;
(d) ... and
(e) to any other person the Tribunal may consider should have an opportunity of being heard.

17 Withholding documents or information likely to cause harm

(1) The Tribunal must give a direction prohibiting the disclosure of a document or information to a person if it is satisfied that–
(a) such disclosure would be likely to cause that person or some other person serious harm; and
(b) having regard to the interests of justice that it is proportionate to give such a direction.

(2) If a party ('the first party') considers that the Tribunal should give a direction under paragraph (1) prohibiting the disclosure of part or all of a document or of information to another party ('the second party'), the first party must–
(a) exclude that part of the relevant document or that information from any document that will be provided to the second party; and
(b) provide to the Tribunal the excluded part of document or information and the reason for its exclusion, in order that the Tribunal may decide whether the document or information should be disclosed to the second party or should be the subject of a direction under paragraph (1).

(3) The Tribunal must conduct proceedings as appropriate in order to avoid undermining a direction given under paragraph (1).

(4) If the Tribunal gives a direction under paragraph (1) which prevents disclosure to a party who has a representative, the Tribunal may give a direction that the document or information be disclosed to that representative if it is satisfied that–

(a) disclosure to the representative would be in the interests of the party; and

(b) the representative would not be likely to act contrary to paragraph (5).

(5) Documents or information disclosed to a representative in accordance with a direction under paragraph (4) must not–

(a) be disclosed either directly or indirectly to any other person without the Tribunal's consent; or

(b) be used otherwise than in connection with the proceedings.

18 Further evidence and submissions

(1) Without restriction on the general powers in rule 5(1) and (2) (case management powers), the Tribunal may give directions as to–

(a) issues on which it requires evidence or submissions;

(b) the nature of the evidence or submissions it requires;

(c) whether the parties are permitted or requested to provide expert evidence;

(d) any limit on the number of witnesses whose evidence a party may put forward, whether in relation to a particular issue or generally;

(e) the manner in which any evidence or submissions are to be provided, which may include a direction for them to be given–

(i) orally at a hearing; or

(ii) by written submissions or witness statement; and

(f) the time in which any evidence or submissions are to be provided.

(2) The Tribunal may–

(a) admit evidence whether or not–

(i) the evidence would be admissible in a civil trial in the United Kingdom; or

(ii) the evidence was available to a previous decision maker;

(b) exclude evidence that would otherwise be admissible where–

(i) the evidence was not provided within the time allowed by a direction;

(ii) the evidence was otherwise provided in a manner that did not comply with a direction; or

(iii) it would otherwise be unfair to admit the evidence.

(3) The Tribunal may require any witness to give evidence on oath or affirmation, and may administer an oath or affirmation for that purpose.

19 Summoning of witnesses and orders to answer questions or produce documents

(1) On the application of a party or on its own initiative, the Tribunal may–

(a) by summons require any person to attend as a witness at a hearing at the time and place specified in the summons, provided that–

(i) the person has been given reasonable notice of the hearing; and

(ii) unless the person is a party to the proceedings, the summons makes provision for the person's necessary expenses of attendance to be paid, and states by whom; and

(b) by order require any person to answer any questions or produce any documents in that person's possession or control which relate to any issue in the proceedings.

(2) A summons under this rule must, if the person to whom it is addressed has

not had an opportunity to object to it, state that the person may apply to the Tribunal to vary or set aside the summons.

(3) When a summons is issued, the Tribunal must send a copy of the summons to each party to the proceedings.

(4) No person may be compelled to give any evidence or produce any document that the person could not be compelled to give or produce on a trial of an action in a court of law in England or Wales.

20 Medical examination

(1) Before the hearing to consider the final determination, a medical member of the Tribunal must, so far as practicable–
  (a) examine the patient; and
  (b) take such other steps as that member considers necessary to form an opinion of the patient's mental condition.

(2) For the purposes of paragraph (1) that member may–
  (a) examine the patient in private;
  (b) examine records relating to the detention or treatment of the patient and any after-care services;
  (c) take notes and copies of records for use in connection with the proceedings.

(3) At any time before the Tribunal makes the final determination, the Tribunal or any one or more of its members may interview the patient, which interview may take place in the absence of any other person.

21 Postponement and adjournment

(1) The Tribunal may at any time postpone or adjourn a hearing for the purpose of obtaining further information or for such other purposes as it may think appropriate.

(2) Before postponing or adjourning any hearing, the Tribunal may give such direction as it thinks fit for ensuring the prompt consideration of the application at a postponed or adjourned hearing.

(3) Where a party requests that a hearing postponed or adjourned in accordance with this rule be reconvened, the hearing must be reconvened if the Tribunal is satisfied that reconvening would be in the interests of the patient.

(4) Save in respect of an application under section 66(1)(a) of the Act, before the Tribunal reconvenes any hearing which has been adjourned without a further hearing date being fixed, it must give to all parties not less than 14 days' notice (or such shorter notice as all parties may consent to) of the date, time and place of the reconvened hearing.

22 Withdrawal

(1) Subject to paragraphs (2) to (3), an applicant may withdraw an application by sending to the Tribunal a written notice of withdrawal stating reasons.

(2) Before making a withdrawal under paragraph (1), the consent of the Tribunal must be obtained.

(3) Where an application is withdrawn, the Tribunal shall so inform the parties and such other persons as the Tribunal considers necessary.

(4) A reference made by the Welsh Ministers or the Secretary of State in circumstances in which they are not by the terms of the Act obliged to make a reference may be withdrawn by the Welsh Ministers or the Secretary of State, as the case may be, at any time before it is considered by the Tribunal and,

where a reference is so withdrawn, the Tribunal shall inform the patient and the other parties that the reference has been withdrawn.

23 Transfer of Proceedings

(1) Where any proceedings in relation to a patient have not been disposed of by the members of the Tribunal appointed for the purpose, and the chairman is of the opinion that it is not practicable or not possible without undue delay for the consideration of those proceedings to be completed by those members, he shall make arrangements for them to be heard by other members of the Tribunal.

(2) Where a patient in respect of whom proceedings are pending moves to the jurisdiction of the First-tier Tribunal, the proceedings shall, if the chairman of the Tribunal so directs, be transferred to the First-tier Tribunal and notice of the transfer of proceedings shall be given to the parties and such other persons as the Tribunal considers necessary.

Chapter 2: Hearings

24 Time and place of hearings

(1) In proceedings under section 66(1)(a) of the Act the hearing of the case must start within 7 days after the date on which the Tribunal received the application.

(2) In proceedings under section 75(1) of the Act, the hearing of the case must start at least 5 weeks but no more than 8 weeks after the date that the Tribunal received the reference.

(3) Subject to paragraph (4), the Tribunal must give the parties reasonable notice, and in any event no less than 14 days' notice, of the date, time and place of any hearing (including any adjourned or postponed hearing) and any changes to the time and place of any hearing, except that in proceedings under section 66(1)(a) of the Act the Tribunal must give at least 3 days' notice.

(4) The Tribunal may give less notice than that required under paragraph (3)–
  (a) with the parties' consent; or
  (b) in urgent or exceptional circumstances.

25 Privacy of hearings

(1) Except where a patient requests a hearing in public and the Tribunal is satisfied that that would be in the interests of the patient, all hearings must be held in private.

(2) Where the Tribunal refuses a request for a public hearing or directs that a hearing which has begun in public shall continue in private, the Tribunal must record in writing its reasons for holding the hearing in private and shall inform the patient of those reasons.

(3) Where a hearing is held in private, the Tribunal may–
  (a) exclude particular individuals from the hearing or part of it; or
  (b) permit particular individuals to attend the hearing or part of it on such terms as it considers appropriate.

(4) The Tribunal may give a direction excluding from the hearing, or part of it–
  (a) any person whose conduct, in the opinion of the Tribunal, is disrupting or is likely to disrupt the hearing;
  (b) any person whose presence the Tribunal considers is likely to prevent another person from giving evidence or making submissions freely; or

(c) any person who the Tribunal considers should be excluded in order to give effect to a direction under rule 17 (withholding information likely to cause harm).

(5) The Tribunal may give a direction excluding a witness from a hearing until that witness gives evidence.

26 Request to appear at and take part in a hearing

The Tribunal may give a direction permitting or requesting any person to–

(a) attend and take part in a hearing to such extent as the Tribunal considers appropriate; or

(b) make written submissions in relation to a particular issue.

27 Hearings in a party's absence

If a party fails to attend a hearing, the Tribunal may proceed with the hearing if–

(a) the Tribunal–

(i) is satisfied that the party has been notified of the hearing or that reasonable steps have been taken to notify the party of the hearing; and

(ii) the Tribunal is not aware of any good reason for the failure to attend; or

(b) the Tribunal otherwise considers that it is in the interests of the patient to proceed with the hearing.

Chapter 3: Decisions

28 Decisions

(1) The Tribunal may give a decision orally at a hearing or may reserve its decision.

(2) The Tribunal must send to each party as soon as reasonably practicable following a final determination–

(a) a notice stating the Tribunal's decision; and

(b) written reasons for the decision.

(3) The documents referred to in paragraph (2) must be sent–

(a) in proceedings under section 66(1)(a) of the Act, within 3 working days of the hearing; and

(b) in other proceedings, within 7 days of the hearing.

(4) Where the Tribunal considers that the full disclosure of the recorded reasons for its decision to the patient would cause the patient or any other person serious harm, the Tribunal may instead communicate its decision to him in such manner as it thinks appropriate and may communicate its decision to the other parties subject to any conditions it may think appropriate as to the disclosure thereof to the patient.

(5) Where the Tribunal makes a decision with recommendations, the decision may specify any period at the expiration of which the Tribunal will consider the case further in the event of those recommendations not being complied with.

(6) Subject to rule 10 (prohibitions on disclosure or publication) the Tribunal may, where appropriate, send notice of a decision or the reasons for it to any person.

Part 4: Correcting and Appealing Tribunal Decisions

29 Clerical mistakes, accidental slips or omissions and irregularities

(1) The Tribunal may at any time correct any clerical mistake or other accidental slip or omission in a decision, direction or any document produced by it, by sending notification of the amended decision or direction, or a copy of the amended document, to all parties.

(2) Any irregularity resulting from failure to comply with these Rules before the Tribunal has determined an application shall not of itself render the proceedings void, but the Tribunal may, and must if it considers that any person may have been prejudiced, take such steps to cure the irregularity as it thinks fit before determining the application, whether by the amendment of any document, the giving of any notice or otherwise.

30 Application for permission to appeal

(1) This rule applies to an application for permission to appeal against a decision of the Tribunal on a point of law under section 78A of the Act (appeal from the Tribunal to the Upper Tribunal).

(2) A party seeking permission to appeal must send or deliver to the Tribunal a written application for permission to appeal so that it is received no later than 28 days after the date that the Tribunal sent written reasons for the decision to the party making the application.

(3) If the party sends or delivers the application to the Tribunal later than the time required by paragraph (2) or by any extension of time under rule 5(2)(a) (power to extend time)–
   (a) the application must include a request for an extension of time and the reason why the application was not provided in time; and
   (b) unless the Tribunal extends time for the application under rule 5(2)(a), the Tribunal must not admit the application.

(4) An application under paragraph (2) must–
   (a) identify the decision of the Tribunal to which it relates;
   (b) identify the alleged error or errors of law in the decision; and
   (c) state the result the party making the application seeks.

(5) Upon considering the application for permission to appeal, the Tribunal must send to the parties as soon as practicable–
   (a) a record of its decision; and
   (b) if the Tribunal has refused to grant permission–
      (i) reasons for such refusal; and
      (ii) notification of the right to make an application to the Upper Tribunal for permission to appeal and the time within which, and the method by which, such application must be made.

(6) The Tribunal may grant permission to appeal on limited grounds, but must comply with paragraph (5)(b) in relation to any grounds on which it has refused permission.

Part 5: Revocations

31 Revocations

The Mental Health Review Tribunal Rules 1983, the Mental Health Review Tribunal (Amendment) Rules 1996 and the Mental Health Review Tribunal (Amendment) Rules 1998 are revoked.

SCHEDULE: Statements by the Responsible Authority and the Secretary of State

Rule 15

Part A: Information about Patients (other than Conditionally Discharged Patients)

1 The patient's full name (and any alternative names used in patient records).

2 The patient's date of birth and age.

3 The patient's language of choice and, if it is not English or Welsh, whether an interpreter is required.

4 The application, order or direction made under the Act to which the tribunal proceedings relate and the date on which that application, order or direction commenced.

5 Details of the original authority for the detention or guardianship of the patient, including the statutory basis for that authority and details of any subsequent renewal of or change in that authority.

6 In cases where a patient has been transferred to hospital under section 45A, 47 or 48 of the Act, details of the order, direction or authority under which the patient was being held in custody before his transfer to hospital.

7 Except in relation to a patient subject to guardianship or after-care under supervision, or a community patient, the hospital or hospital unit at which the patient is presently liable to be detained under the Act, and the ward or unit on which he is presently detained.

8 If a condition or requirement has been imposed that requires the patient to reside at a particular place, details of the condition or requirement and the address at which the patient is required to reside;

9 In the case of a community patient, details of any conditions attaching to the patient's community treatment order under section 17B(2) of the Act.

10 The name of the patient's responsible clinician and the length of time the patient has been under their care.

11 Where another approved clinician is or has recently been largely concerned in the treatment of the patient, the name of that clinician and the period that the patient has spent in that clinician's care.

12 The name of any care co-ordinator appointed for the patient.

13 Where the patient is subject to the guardianship of a private guardian, the name and address of that guardian.

14 Where there is an extant order of the superior court of record established by section 45(1) of the Mental Capacity Act 2005, the details of that order.

15 Unless the patient requests otherwise, the name and address of the person exercising the functions of the nearest relative of the patient.

16 ....

17 In the case of a patient subject to after-care under supervision, the name and address of the local social services authority and NHS body that are responsible for providing the patient with after-care under section 117 of the Act, or will be when he leaves hospital.

18 The name and address of any person who plays a substantial part in the care of the patient but who is not professionally concerned with it.

19 The name and address of any other person who the responsible authority considers should be notified to the Tribunal.

Part B: Reports Relating to Patients (other than Conditionally Discharged Patients)

1 An up-to-date clinical report, prepared for the Tribunal, including the relevant clinical history and a full report on the patient's mental condition.

2 An up-to-date social circumstances report prepared for the tribunal including reports on the following–
   (a) the patient's home and family circumstances, including the views of the patient's nearest relative or the person so acting;
   (b) the opportunities for employment or occupation and the housing facilities which would be available to the patient if discharged;
   (c) the availability of community support and relevant medical facilities;
   (d) the financial circumstances of the patient.

3 The views of the responsible authority on the suitability of the patient for discharge.

4 Where the provisions of section 117 of the Act may apply to the patient, a proposed after care plan in respect of the patient.

5 Any other information or observations on the application which the responsible authority wishes to make.

Part C: Information about Conditionally Discharged Patients

1 The patient's full name (and any alternative names used in patient records).

2 The patient's date of birth and age.

3 The patient's language of choice and, if it is not English or Welsh, whether an interpreter is required.

4 The history of the patient's present liability to detention including details of the offence or offences, and the dates of the original order or direction and of the conditional discharge.

5 The name and address of any clinician responsible for the care and supervision of the patient in the community, and the period that the patient has spent under the care and supervision of that clinician.

6 The name and address of any social worker or probation officer responsible for the care and supervision of the patient in the community and the period that the patient has spent under the care and supervision of that person.

Part D: Reports Relating to Conditionally Discharged Patients

1 Where there is a clinician responsible for the care and supervision of the patient in the community, an up-to-date report prepared for the Tribunal including the relevant medical history and a full report on the patient's mental condition.

2 Where there is a social worker, probation officer or community psychiatric nurse responsible for the patient's care and supervision in the community, an up-to-date report prepared for the Tribunal on the patient's progress in the community since discharge from hospital.

3 A report on the patient's home circumstances.

4 The views of the Secretary of State on the suitability of the patient for absolute discharge.

5 Any other observations on the application which the Secretary of State wishes to make.

APPENDIX B

Practice Directions

First-tier Tribunal: Health Education and Social Care Chamber: Statements and Reports in Mental Health Cases

28 October 2013

1. This Practice Direction is made by the Senior President of Tribunals with the agreement of the Lord Chancellor in the exercise of powers conferred by Section 23 of the Tribunals, Courts and Enforcement Act 2007. It applies to a 'mental health case' as defined in Rule 1(3) the Tribunal Procedure (First-tier Tribunal) (Health, Education and Social Care Chamber) Rules 2008. Rule 32 requires that certain statements and reports must be sent or delivered to the tribunal (and, in restricted cases, to the Secretary of State) by the Responsible Authority, the Responsible Clinician and any Social Supervisor (as the case may be). This Practice Direction specifies the contents of such documents. It replaces the previous Practice Directions on mental health cases dated 30 October 2008 and 6 April 2012, with effect from 28 October 2013.
2. In this Practice Direction 'the Act' refers to the Mental Health Act 1983 (as amended by the Mental Health Act 2007).
3. This Practice Direction contains five separate parts for the following categories of patient:
   A. IN-PATIENTS (NON-RESTRICTED AND RESTRICTED)
   B. COMMUNITY PATIENTS
   C. GUARDIANSHIP PATIENTS
   D. CONDITIONALLY DISCHARGED PATIENTS
   E. PATIENTS UNDER THE AGE OF 18.
4. Responsible Authorities and authors of reports should refer to the relevant part of this Practice Direction, depending on the status of the patient under the Act.

SIR JEREMY SULLIVAN
SENIOR PRESIDENT OF TRIBUNALS
28 October 2013

A. IN-PATIENTS (NON-RESTRICTED AND RESTRICTED)

5. For the purposes of this Practice Direction, a patient is an in-patient if they are detained in hospital to be assessed or treated for a mental disorder, whether admitted through civil or criminal justice processes, including a restricted patient (ie subject to special restrictions under the Act), and including a patient transferred to hospital from custody. A patient is to be regarded as an in-patient detained in a hospital even if they have been permitted leave of absence, or have gone absent without leave.
6. In the case of a restricted patient detained in hospital, the tribunal may make a provisional decision to order a Conditional Discharge. However, before it finally decides to grant a Conditional Discharge, the tribunal may defer its decision so that satisfactory arrangements can be made. The patient will remain an in-patient unless and until the tribunal finally grants a Conditional Discharge, so this part of the Practice Direction applies.
7. If the patient is an in-patient, the Responsible Authority must send or deliver to the tribunal the following documents containing the specified information in accordance with the relevant paragraphs below:

- *Statement of Information about the Patient.*
- *Responsible Clinician's Report, including any relevant forensic history.*
- *Nursing Report, with the patient's current nursing plan attached.*
- *Social Circumstances Report including details of any Care Pathway Approach (CPA) and/or Section 117 aftercare plan in full or in embryo and, where appropriate, the additional information required for patients under the age of 18, and any input from a Multi Agency Public Protection Arrangements (MAPPA) agency or meeting.*

8. In all in-patient cases, except where a patient is detained under Section 2 of the Act, the Responsible Authority must send to the tribunal the required documents containing the specified information, so that they are received by the tribunal as soon as practicable and in any event within 3 weeks after the Authority made or received the application or reference. If the patient is a restricted patient, the Authority must also, at the same time, send copies of the documents to the Secretary of State (Ministry of Justice).
9. Where a patient is detained under Section 2 of the Act, the Responsible Authority must prepare the required documents as soon as practicable after receipt of a copy of the application or a request from the tribunal. If specified information has to be omitted because it is not available, then this should be mentioned in the statement or report. These documents must be made available to the tribunal panel and the patient's representative at least one hour before the hearing is due to start.
10. The authors of reports should have personally met and be familiar with the patient. If an existing report becomes out-of-date, or if the status or the circumstances of the patient change after the reports have been written but before the tribunal hearing takes place (eg if a patient is discharged, or is recalled), the author of the report should then send to the tribunal an addendum addressing the up-to-date situation and, where necessary, the new applicable statutory criteria.

Statement of Information about the Patient – In-Patients

11. The statement provided to the tribunal must be up-to-date, specifically prepared for the tribunal, signed and dated, and must include:
    a) the patient's full name, date of birth, and usual place of residence;
    b) the full official name of the Responsible Authority;
    c) the patient's first language/dialect and, if it is not English, whether an interpreter is required and, if so, in which language/dialect;
    d) if the patient is deaf, whether the patient will require the services of British Sign Language Interpreters and/or a Relay Interpreter;
    e) a chronological table listing:
        - the dates of any previous admissions to, discharge from, or recall to hospital, stating whether the admissions were compulsory or voluntary;
        - the date when the current period of detention in hospital originally commenced, stating the nature of the application, order or direction that is the authority for the detention of the patient;
        - the dates of any subsequent renewal of, or change in, the authority for

the patient's detention, and any changes in the patient's status under the Act;

- dates and details of any hospital transfers since the patient's original detention;
- the date of admission or transfer to the hospital where the patient now is;
- the dates and outcomes of any tribunal hearings over the last three years;

f) the name of the patient's Responsible Clinician and the date when the patient came under the care of that clinician;
g) the name and contact details of the patient's Care Co-ordinator, Community Psychiatric Nurse, Social Worker/AMHP or Social Supervisor;
h) where the patient is detained in an independent hospital, details of any NHS body that funds, or will fund, the placement;
i) the name and address of the local social services authority which, were the patient to leave hospital, would have a duty to provide Section 117 after-care services;
j) the name and address of the NHS body which, were the patient to leave hospital, would have a duty to provide Section 117 after-care services;
k) the name and address of any legal representative acting for the patient;
l) except in the case of a restricted patient, the name and address of the patient's Nearest Relative or of the person exercising that function, whether the patient has made any request that their Nearest Relative should not be consulted or should not be kept informed about the patient's care or treatment and, if so, the details of any such request, whether the Responsible Authority believes that the patient has capacity to make such a request and the reasons for that belief;
m) the name and address of any other person who plays a significant part in the care of the patient but who is not professionally involved;
n) details of any legal proceedings or other arrangements relating to the patient's mental capacity, or their ability to make decisions or handle their own affairs.

Responsible Clinician's Report – In-Patients

12. The report must be up-to-date, specifically prepared for the tribunal and have numbered paragraphs and pages. It should be signed and dated. The report should be written or counter-signed by the patient's Responsible Clinician. The sources of information for the events and incidents described must be made clear. This report should not be an addendum to (or reproduce extensive details from) previous reports, or recite medical records, but must briefly describe the patient's recent relevant medical history and current mental health presentation, and must include:

a) whether there are any factors that may affect the patient's understanding or ability to cope with a hearing and whether there are any adjustments that the tribunal may consider in order to deal with the case fairly and justly;
b) details of any index offence(s) and other relevant forensic history;
c) a chronology listing the patient's previous involvement with mental

health services including any admissions to, discharge from and recall to hospital;

d) reasons for any previous admission or recall to hospital;
e) the circumstances leading up to the patient's current admission to hospital;
f) whether the patient is now suffering from a mental disorder and, if so, whether a diagnosis has been made, what the diagnosis is, and why;
g) whether the patient has a learning disability and, if so, whether that disability is associated with abnormally aggressive or seriously irresponsible conduct;
h) depending upon the statutory criteria, whether any mental disorder present is of a nature or degree to warrant, or make appropriate, liability to be detained in a hospital for assessment and/or medical treatment;
i) details of any appropriate and available medical treatment prescribed, provided, offered or planned for the patient's mental disorder;
j) the strengths or positive factors relating to the patient;
k) a summary of the patient's current progress, behaviour, capacity and insight;
l) the patient's understanding of, compliance with, and likely future willingness to accept any prescribed medication or comply with any appropriate medical treatment for mental disorder that is or might be made available;
m) in the case of an eligible compliant patient who lacks capacity to agree or object to their detention or treatment, whether or not deprivation of liberty under the Mental Capacity Act 2005 (as amended) would be appropriate and less restrictive;
n) details of any incidents where the patient has harmed themselves or others, or threatened harm, or damaged property, or threatened damage;
o) whether (in Section 2 cases) detention in hospital, or (in all other cases) the provision of medical treatment in hospital, is justified or necessary in the interests of the patient's health or safety, or for the protection of others;
p) whether the patient, if discharged from hospital, would be likely to act in a manner dangerous to themselves or others;
q) whether, and if so how, any risks could be managed effectively in the community, including the use of any lawful conditions or recall powers;
r) any recommendations to the tribunal, with reasons.

Nursing Report – In-Patients

13. The report must be up-to-date, specifically prepared for the tribunal and have numbered paragraphs and pages. It should be signed and dated. The sources of information for the events and incidents described must be made clear. This report should not recite the details of medical records, or be an addendum to (or reproduce extensive details from) previous reports, although the patient's current nursing plan should be attached. In relation to the patient's current in-patient episode, the report must briefly describe the patient's current mental health presentation, and must include:

a) whether there are any factors that might affect the patient's understanding or ability to cope with a hearing, and whether there are any adjustments that the tribunal may consider in order to deal with the case fairly and justly;

b) the nature of nursing care and medication currently being made available;
c) the level of observation to which the patient is currently subject;
d) whether the patient has contact with relatives, friends or other patients, the nature of the interaction, and what community support the patient has;
e) strengths or positive factors relating to the patient;
f) a summary of the patient's current progress, engagement with nursing staff, behaviour, cooperation, activities, self-care and insight;
g) any occasions on which the patient has been absent without leave whilst liable to be detained, or occasions when the patient has failed to return as and when required, after having been granted leave;
h) the patient's understanding of, compliance with, and likely future willingness to accept any prescribed medication or treatment for mental disorder that is or might be made available;
i) details of any incidents in hospital where the patient has harmed themselves or others, or threatened harm, or damaged property, or threatened damage;
j) any occasions on which the patient has been secluded or restrained, including the reasons why such seclusion or restraint was necessary;
k) whether (in Section 2 cases) detention in hospital, or (in all other cases) the provision of medical treatment in hospital, is justified or necessary in the interests of the patient's health or safety, or for the protection of others;
l) whether the patient, if discharged from hospital, would be likely to act in a manner dangerous to themselves or others;
m) whether, and if so how, any risks could be managed effectively in the community, including the use of any lawful conditions or recall powers;
n) any recommendations to the tribunal, with reasons.

Social Circumstances Report – In-Patients

14. The report must be up-to-date, specifically prepared for the tribunal and have numbered paragraphs and pages. It should be signed and dated. The sources of information for the events and incidents described must be made clear. This report should not be an addendum to (or reproduce extensive details from) previous reports, but must briefly describe the patient's recent relevant history and current presentation, and must include:

a) whether there are any factors that might affect the patient's understanding or ability to cope with a hearing, and whether there are any adjustments that the tribunal may consider in order to deal with the case fairly and justly;
b) details of any index offence(s) and other relevant forensic history;
c) a chronology listing the patient's previous involvement with mental health services including any admissions to, discharge from and recall to hospital;
d) the patient's home and family circumstances;
e) the housing or accommodation available to the patient if discharged;

f) the patient's financial position (including benefit entitlements);
g) any available opportunities for employment;
h) the patient's previous response to community support or Section 117 aftercare;
i) so far as is known, details of the care pathway and Section 117 after-care to be made available to the patient, together with details of the proposed care plan;
j) the likely adequacy and effectiveness of the proposed care plan;
k) whether there are any issues as to funding the proposed care plan and, if so, the date by which those issues will be resolved;
l) the strengths or positive factors relating to the patient;
m) a summary of the patient's current progress, behaviour, compliance and insight;
n) details of any incidents where the patient has harmed themselves or others, or threatened harm, or damaged property, or threatened damage;
o) the patient's views, wishes, beliefs, opinions, hopes and concerns;
p) except in restricted cases, the views of the patient's Nearest Relative unless (having consulted the patient) it would inappropriate or impractical to consult the Nearest Relative, in which case give reasons for this view and describe any attempts to rectify matters;
q) the views of any other person who takes a lead role in the care and support of the patient but who is not professionally involved;
r) whether the patient is known to any MAPPA meeting or agency and, if so, in which area, for what reason, and at what level – together with the name of the Chair of any MAPPA meeting concerned with the patient, and the name of the representative of the lead agency;
s) in the event that a MAPPA meeting or agency wishes to put forward evidence of its views in relation to the level and management of risk, a summary of those views (or an Executive Summary may be attached to the report); and where relevant, a copy of the Police National Computer record of previous convictions should be attached;
t) in the case of an eligible compliant patient who lacks capacity to agree or object to their detention or treatment, whether or not deprivation of liberty under the Mental Capacity Act 2005 (as amended) would be appropriate and less restrictive;
u) whether (in Section 2 cases) detention in hospital, or (in all other cases) the provision of medical treatment in hospital, is justified or necessary in the interests of the patient's health or safety, or for the protection of others;
v) whether the patient, if discharged from hospital, would be likely to act in a manner dangerous to themselves or others;
w) whether, and if so how, any risks could be managed effectively in the community, including the use of any lawful conditions or recall powers;
x) any recommendations to the tribunal, with reasons.

B. COMMUNITY PATIENTS

15. The Responsible Authority must send to the tribunal the following documents, containing the specified information, so that the documents are received by the tribunal as soon as practicable and in any event within 3

weeks after the Authority made or received the application or reference:

- *Statement of Information about the Patient*
- *Responsible Clinician's Report, including any relevant forensic history.*
- *Social Circumstances Report including details of any Section 117 aftercare plan and, where appropriate, the additional information required for patients under the age of 18, and any input from a Multi Agency Public Protection Arrangements (MAPPA) agency or meeting.*

16. The authors of reports should have personally met and be familiar with the patient. If an existing report becomes out-of-date, or if the status or the circumstances of the patient change after the reports have been written but before the tribunal hearing takes place (eg if a patient is recalled, or again discharged into the community), the author of the report should then send to the tribunal an addendum addressing the up-to-date situation and, where necessary, the new applicable statutory criteria.

Statement of Information about the Patient – Community Patients

17. The statement provided to the tribunal should be up-to-date, signed and dated, specifically prepared for the tribunal, and must include:
a) the patient's full name, date of birth, and current place of residence;
b) the full official name of the Responsible Authority;
c) the patient's first language/dialect and, if it is not English, whether an interpreter is required and, if so, in which language/dialect;
d) if the patient is deaf, whether the patient will require the services of British Sign Language Interpreters and/or a Relay Interpreter;
e) a chronological table listing:
   - the dates of any previous admissions to, discharge from, or recall to hospital, stating whether the admissions were compulsory or voluntary, and including any previous instances of discharge on to a Community Treatment Order (CTO);
   - the date of the underlying order or direction for detention in hospital prior to the patient's discharge onto the current CTO;
   - the date of the current CTO;
   - the dates of any subsequent renewal of, or change in, the authority for the patient's CTO, and any changes in the patient's status under the Act;
   - the dates and outcomes of any tribunal hearings over the last three years;

f) the name of the patient's Responsible Clinician and the date when the patient came under the care of that clinician;
g) the name and contact details of the patient's Care Co-ordinator, Community Psychiatric Nurse, and/or Social Worker/AMHP;
h) the name and address of the local social services authority which has the duty to provide Section 117 after-care services;
i) the name and address of the NHS body which has the duty to provide Section 117 after-care services;
j) the name and address of any legal representative acting for the patient;
k) the name and address of the patient's Nearest Relative or of the person exercising that function, whether the patient has made any request that their Nearest Relative should not be consulted or should not be kept

informed about the patient's care or treatment and, if so, the details of any such request, whether the Responsible Authority believes that the patient has capacity to make such a request and the reasons for that belief;

l) the name and address of any other person who plays a significant part in the care of the patient but who is not professionally involved;

m) details of any legal proceedings or other arrangements relating to the patient's mental capacity, or their ability to make decisions or handle their own affairs.

Responsible Clinician's Report – Community Patients

18. The report must be up-to-date, specifically prepared for the tribunal and have numbered paragraphs and pages. It should be signed and dated. This report should be written or counter-signed by the patient's Responsible Clinician. The sources of information for the events and incidents described must be made clear. The report should not be an addendum to (or reproduce extensive details from) previous reports, or recite medical records, but must briefly describe the patient's recent relevant medical history and current mental health presentation, and must include:

a) where the patient is aged 18 or over and the case is a reference to the tribunal, whether the patient has capacity to decide whether or not to attend or be represented at a tribunal hearing;

b) whether, if there is a hearing, there are any factors that may affect the patient's understanding or ability to cope with it, and whether there are any adjustments that the tribunal may consider in order to deal with the case fairly and justly;

c) details of any index offence(s) and other relevant forensic history;

d) a chronology listing the patient's previous involvement with mental health services including any admissions to, discharge from and recall to hospital;

e) reasons for any previous admission or recall to hospital;

f) the circumstances leading up to the patient's most recent admission to hospital;

g) the circumstances leading up to the patient's discharge onto a CTO;

h) any conditions to which the patient is subject under Section 17B, and details of the patient's compliance;

i) whether the patient is now suffering from a mental disorder and, if so, what the diagnosis is and why;

j) whether the patient has a learning disability and, if so, whether that disability is associated with abnormally aggressive or seriously irresponsible conduct;

k) whether the patient has a mental disorder of a nature or degree such as to make it appropriate for the patient to receive medical treatment;

l) details of any appropriate and available medical treatment prescribed, provided, offered or planned for the patient's mental disorder;

m) the strengths or positive factors relating to the patient;

n) a summary of the patient's current progress, behaviour, capacity and insight;

o) the patient's understanding of, compliance with, and likely future willingness to accept any prescribed medication or comply with any appropriate medical treatment for mental disorder that is or might be made available;

p) details of any incidents where the patient has harmed themselves or others, or threatened harm, or damaged property, or threatened damage;

s) whether it is necessary for the patient's health or safety, or for the protection of others, that the patient should receive medical treatment and, if so, why;

t) whether the patient, if discharged from the CTO, would be likely to act in a manner dangerous to themselves or others;

u) whether, and if so how, any risks could be managed effectively in the community;

v) whether it continues to be necessary that the Responsible Clinician should be able to exercise the power of recall and, if so, why;

w) any recommendations to the tribunal, with reasons.

Social Circumstances Report – Community Patients

19. The report must be up-to-date, specifically prepared for the tribunal and have numbered paragraphs and pages. It should be signed and dated. The sources of information for the events and incidents described must be made clear. This report should not be an addendum to (or reproduce extensive details from) previous reports, but must briefly describe the patient's recent relevant history and current presentation, and must include:

a) whether there are any factors that might affect the patient's understanding or ability to cope with a hearing, and whether there are any adjustments that the tribunal may consider in order to deal with the case fairly and justly;

b) details of any index offence(s), and other relevant forensic history;

c) a chronology listing the patient's previous involvement with mental health services including any admissions to, discharge from and recall to hospital;

d) the patient's home and family circumstances;

e) the housing or accommodation currently available to the patient;

f) the patient's financial position (including benefit entitlements);

g) any employment or available opportunities for employment;

h) any conditions to which the patient is subject under Section 17B, and details of the patient's compliance;

i) the patient's previous response to community support or Section 117 aftercare;

j) details of the community support or Section 117 after-care that is being, or could be made available to the patient, together with details of the current care plan;

k) whether there are any issues as to funding the current or future care plan and, if so, the date by which those issues will be resolved;

l) the current adequacy and effectiveness of the care plan;

m) the strengths or positive factors relating to the patient;

n) a summary of the patient's current progress, behaviour, compliance and insight;

o) details of any incidents where the patient has harmed themselves or others, or threatened harm, or damaged property, or threatened damage;

p) the patient's views, wishes, beliefs, opinions, hopes and concerns;
q) the views of the patient's Nearest Relative unless (having consulted the patient) it would inappropriate or impractical to consult the Nearest Relative, in which case give reasons for this view and describe any attempts to rectify matters;
r) the views of any other person who takes a lead role in the care and support of the patient but who is not professionally involved;
s) whether the patient is known to any Multi Agency Public Protection Arrangements (MAPPA) meeting or agency and, if so, in which area, for what reason, and at what level – together with the name of the Chair of any MAPPA meeting concerned with the patient, and the name of the representative of the lead agency;
t) in the event that a MAPPA meeting or agency wishes to put forward evidence of its views in relation to the level and management of risk, a summary of those views (or an Executive Summary may be attached to the report); and where relevant, a copy of the Police National Computer record of previous convictions should be attached;
u) whether it is necessary for the patient's health or safety, or for the protection of others, that the patient should receive medical treatment and, if so, why;
v) whether the patient, if discharged from the CTO, would be likely to act in a manner dangerous to themselves or others;
w) whether, and if so how, any risks could be managed effectively in the community;
x) whether it continues to be necessary that the Responsible Clinician should be able to exercise the power of recall and, if so, why;
y) any recommendations to the tribunal, with reasons.

C. GUARDIANSHIP PATIENTS

20. If the patient has been received into guardianship the Responsible Authority must send to the tribunal the following documents, containing the specified information, so that they are received by the tribunal as soon as practicable and in any event within 3 weeks after the Authority made or received a copy of the application or reference:
    - *Statement of Information about the Patient*
    - *Responsible Clinician's Report, including any relevant forensic history.*
    - *Social Circumstances Report including details of any Care Pathway Approach (CPA) and, where appropriate, the additional information required for patients under the age of 18, and any input from a Multi Agency Public Protection Arrangements (MAPPA) agency or meeting.*
21. The authors of reports should have personally met and be familiar with the patient. If an existing report becomes out-of-date, or if the status or the circumstances of the patient change after the reports have been written but before the tribunal hearing takes place, the author of the report should then send to the tribunal an addendum addressing the up-to-date situation and, where necessary, the new applicable statutory criteria.

Statement of Information about the Patient – Guardianship Patients

22. The statement provided to the tribunal should be up-to-date, signed and

dated, specifically prepared for the tribunal, and must include:

a) the patient's full name, date of birth, and current place of residence;
b) the full official name of the Responsible Authority;
c) the patient's first language/dialect and, if it is not English, whether an interpreter is required and, if so, in which language/dialect;
d) if the patient is deaf, whether the patient will require the services of British Sign Language Interpreters and/or a Relay Interpreter;
e) a chronological table listing:
   - the dates of any previous admissions to, discharge from or recall to hospital, stating whether the admissions were compulsory or voluntary;
   - the dates of any previous instances of reception into guardianship;
   - the date of reception into current guardianship, stating the nature of the application, order or direction that constitutes the original authority for the guardianship of the patient;
   - the dates and outcomes of any tribunal hearings over the last three years;
f) the name and address of any private guardian;
g) the name of the patient's Responsible Clinician and the date when the patient came under the care of that clinician;
h) the name and contact details of the patient's Care Co-ordinator, Community Psychiatric Nurse, and/or Social Worker/AMHP;
i) the name and address of any legal representative acting for the patient;
j) the name and address of the patient's Nearest Relative or of the person exercising that function, whether the patient has made any request that their Nearest Relative should not be consulted or should not be kept informed about the patient's care or treatment and, if so, the details of any such request, whether the Responsible Authority believes that the patient has capacity to make such a request and the reasons for that belief;
k) the name and address of any other person who plays a significant part in the care of the patient but who is not professionally involved;
l) details of any legal proceedings or other arrangements relating to the patient's mental capacity, or their ability to make decisions or handle their own affairs.

Responsible Clinician's Report – Guardianship patients

23. The report must be up-to-date, specifically prepared for the tribunal and have numbered paragraphs and pages. It should be signed and dated. The report should be written or counter-signed by the patient's Responsible Clinician. The sources of information for the events and incidents described must be made clear. This report should not be an addendum to (or reproduce extensive details from) previous reports, or recite medical records, but must briefly describe the patient's recent relevant medical history and current mental health presentation, and must include:

a) whether there are any factors that may affect the patient's understanding or ability to cope with a hearing, and whether there are any adjustments that the tribunal may consider in order to deal with the case fairly and justly;
b) details of any index offence(s), and other relevant forensic history;

c) a chronology listing the patient's previous involvement with mental health services including any admissions to, discharge from and recall to hospital, and any previous instances of reception into guardianship;
d) the circumstances leading up to the patient's reception into guardianship;
e) any requirements to which the patient is subject under Section 8(1), and details of the patient's compliance,
f) whether the patient is now suffering from a mental disorder and, if so, what the diagnosis is and why;
g) whether the patient has a learning disability and, if so, whether that disability is associated with abnormally aggressive or seriously irresponsible conduct;
h) details of any appropriate and available medical treatment prescribed, provided offered or planned for the patient's mental disorder;
i) the strengths or positive factors relating to the patient;
j) a summary of the patient's current progress, behaviour, capacity and insight;
k) the patient's understanding of, compliance with, and likely future willingness to accept any prescribed medication or comply with any appropriate medical treatment for mental disorder that is, or might be, made available;
l) details of any incidents where the patient has harmed themselves or others, or threatened harm, or damaged property, or threatened damage;
m) whether, and if so how, any risks could be managed effectively in the community;
n) whether it is necessary for the welfare of the patient, or for the protection of others, that the patient should remain under guardianship and, if so, why;
o) any recommendations to the tribunal, with reasons.

Social Circumstances Report – Guardianship Patients

24. The report must be up-to-date, specifically prepared for the tribunal and have numbered paragraphs and pages. It should be signed and dated. The sources of information for the events and incidents described should be made clear. This report should not be an addendum to (or reproduce extensive details from) previous reports, but must briefly describe the patient's recent relevant history and current presentation, and must include:
a) whether there are any factors that might affect the patient's understanding or ability to cope with a hearing, and whether there are any adjustments that the tribunal may consider in order to deal with the case fairly and justly;
b) details of any index offence(s), and other relevant forensic history;
c) a chronology listing the patient's previous involvement with mental health services including any admissions to, discharge from and recall to hospital, and any previous instances of reception into guardianship;
d) the patient's home and family circumstances;
e) the housing or accommodation currently available to the patient;
f) the patient's financial position (including benefit entitlements);
g) any employment or available opportunities for employment;

h) any requirements to which the patient is subject under Section 8(1), and details of the patient's compliance,
i) the patient's previous response to community support;
j) details of the community support that is being, or could be, made available to the patient, together with details of the current care plan;
k) the current adequacy and effectiveness of the care plan;
l) whether there are any issues as to funding the current or future care plan and, if so, the date by which those issues will be resolved;
m) the strengths or positive factors relating to the patient;
n) a summary of the patient's current progress, behaviour, compliance and insight;
o) details of any incidents where the patient has harmed themselves or others, or threatened harm, or damaged property, or threatened damage;
p) the patient's views, wishes, beliefs, opinions, hopes and concerns;
q) the views of the guardian;
r) the views of the patient's Nearest Relative unless (having consulted the patient) it would inappropriate or impractical to consult the Nearest Relative, in which case give reasons for this view and describe any attempts to rectify matters;
s) the views of any other person who takes a lead role in the care and support of the patient but who is not professionally involved;
t) whether the patient is known to any MAPPA meeting or agency and, if so, in which area, for what reason, and at what level – together with the name of the Chair of any MAPPA meeting concerned with the patient, and the name of the representative of the lead agency;
u) in the event that a MAPPA meeting or agency wishes to put forward evidence of its views in relation to the level and management of risk, a summary of those views (or an Executive Summary may be attached to the report); and where relevant, a copy of the Police National Computer record of previous convictions should be attached;
v) whether, and if so how, any risks could be managed effectively in the community;
w) whether it is necessary for the welfare of the patient, or for the protection of others, that the patient should remain under guardianship and, if so, why;
x) any recommendations to the tribunal, with reasons.

D. CONDITIONALLY DISCHARGED PATIENTS

25. A conditionally discharged patient is a restricted patient who has been discharged from hospital into the community, subject to a condition that the patient will remain liable to be recalled to hospital for further treatment, should it become necessary. Other conditions may, in addition, be imposed by the tribunal, or by the Secretary of State (Ministry of Justice).
26. This part only applies to restricted patients who have actually been granted a Conditional Discharge and who are living in the community. In the case of a restricted patient detained in hospital, the tribunal may make a provisional decision to order a Conditional Discharge. Before it finally grants a Conditional Discharge, the tribunal may defer its decision so that satisfactory arrangements can be put in place. Unless and until the tribunal finally grants

a Conditional Discharge, the patient remains an in-patient, and so the in-patient part of this Practice Direction (and not this part) applies.

27. Upon being notified by the tribunal of an application or reference, the Responsible Clinician must send or deliver the Responsible Clinician's Report, and any Social Supervisor must send or deliver the Social Circumstances Report. If there is no Social Supervisor, the Responsible Clinician's report should also provide the required social circumstances information.
28. The required reports, which must contain the specified information, are:
    - Responsible Clinician's Report, including any relevant forensic history.
    - Social Circumstances Report from the patient's Social Supervisor, including details of any Section 117 aftercare plan and, where appropriate, the additional information required for patients under the age of 18, and any input from a Multi Agency Public Protection Arrangements (MAPPA) agency or meeting.
29. The reports must be sent or delivered to the tribunal so that they are received by the tribunal as soon as practicable and in any event within 3 weeks after the Responsible Clinician or Social Supervisor (as the case may be) received the notification.
30. The Responsible Clinician and any Social Supervisor must also, at the same time, send copies of their reports to the Secretary of State (Ministry of Justice).
31. The authors of reports should have personally met and be familiar with the patient. If an existing report is more than six weeks old, or if the status or the circumstances of the patient change after the reports have been written but before the tribunal hearing takes place (eg if a patient is recalled), the author of the report should then send to the tribunal an addendum addressing the up-to-date situation and, where necessary, the new applicable statutory criteria.

Responsible Clinician's Report – Conditionally Discharged Patients

32. The report must be up-to-date, specifically prepared for the tribunal and have numbered paragraphs and pages. It should be signed and dated. The report should be written or counter-signed by the patient's Responsible Clinician. If there is no Social Supervisor, the Responsible Clinician's report should also provide the required social circumstances information. The sources of information for the events and incidents described must be made clear. This report should not be an addendum to (or reproduce extensive details from) previous reports, or recite medical records, but must briefly describe the patient's recent relevant medical history and current mental health presentation, and must include:
    a) whether there are any factors that might affect the patient's understanding or ability to cope with a hearing, and whether there are any adjustments that the tribunal may consider in order to deal with the case fairly and justly;
    b) details of the patient's index offence(s), and any other relevant forensic history;
    c) details and details of the patient's relevant forensic history;

d) a chronology listing the patient's involvement with mental health services including any admissions to, discharge from and recall to hospital;
e) reasons for any previous recall following a Conditional Discharge and details of any previous failure to comply with conditions;
f) the circumstances leading up to the current Conditional Discharge;
g) any conditions currently imposed (whether by the tribunal or the Secretary of State), and the reasons why the conditions were imposed;
h) details of the patient's compliance with any current conditions;
i) whether the patient is now suffering from a mental disorder and, if so, what the diagnosis is and why;
j) whether the patient has a learning disability and, if so, whether that disability is associated with abnormally aggressive or seriously irresponsible conduct;
k) details of any legal proceedings or other arrangements relating to the patient's mental capacity, or their ability to make decisions or handle their own affairs;
l) details of any appropriate and available medical treatment prescribed, provided, offered or planned for the patient's mental disorder;
m) the strengths or positive factors relating to the patient;
n) a summary of the patient's current progress, behaviour, capacity and insight;
o) the patient's understanding of, compliance with, and likely future willingness to accept any prescribed medication or comply with any appropriate medical treatment for mental disorder;
p) details of any incidents where the patient has harmed themselves or others, or threatened harm, or damaged property, or threatened damage;
q) an assessment of the patient's prognosis, including the risk and likelihood of a recurrence or exacerbation of any mental disorder;
r) the risk and likelihood of the patient re-offending and the degree of harm to which others may be exposed if the patient does re-offend;
s) whether it is necessary for the patient's health or safety, or for the protection of others, that the patient should receive medical treatment and, if so, why;
t) whether the patient, if absolutely discharged, would be likely to act in a manner harmful to themselves or others, whether any such risks could be managed effectively in the community and, if so, how;
u) whether it continues to be appropriate for the patient to remain liable to be recalled for further medical treatment in hospital and, if so, why;
v) whether, and if so the extent to which, it is desirable to continue, vary and/or add to any conditions currently imposed;
w) any recommendations to the tribunal, with reasons.

Social Circumstances Report – Conditionally Discharged Patients

33. The report must be up-to-date, specifically prepared for the tribunal and have numbered paragraphs and pages. It should be signed and dated. The sources of information for the events and incidents described should be made clear. This report should not be an addendum to (or reproduce extensive details from) previous reports, but must briefly describe the patient's recent relevant history and current presentation, and must include:

a) the patient's full name, date of birth, and current address;
b) the full official name of the Responsible Authority;
c) whether there are any factors that might affect the patient's understanding or ability to cope with a hearing, and whether there are any adjustments that the tribunal may consider in order to deal with the case fairly and justly;
d) details of the patient's index offence(s), and any other relevant forensic history;
e) a chronology listing the patient's involvement with mental health services including any admissions to, discharge from and recall to hospital;
f) any conditions currently imposed (whether by the tribunal or the Secretary of State), and the reasons why the conditions were imposed;
g) details of the patient's compliance with any past or current conditions;
h) the patient's home and family circumstances;
i) the housing or accommodation currently available to the patient;
j) the patient's financial position (including benefit entitlements);
k) any employment or available opportunities for employment;
l) details of the community support or Section 117 after-care that is being, or could be made available to the patient, together with details of the current care plan;
m) whether there are any issues as to funding the current or future care plan and, if so, the date by which those issues will be resolved;
n) the current adequacy and effectiveness of the care plan;
o) the strengths or positive factors relating to the patient;
p) a summary of the patient's current progress, compliance, behaviour and insight;
q) details of any incidents where the patient has harmed themselves or others, or threatened harm, or damaged property, or threatened damage;
r) the patient's views, wishes, beliefs, opinions, hopes and concerns;
s) the views of any partner, family member or close friend who takes a lead role in the care and support of the patient but who is not professionally involved;
t) whether the patient is known to any Multi Agency Public Protection Arrangements (MAPPA) meeting or agency and, if so, in which area, for what reason, and at what level – together with the name of the Chair of any MAPPA meeting concerned with the patient, and the name of the representative of the lead agency;
u) in the event that a MAPPA meeting or agency wishes to put forward evidence of its views in relation to the level and management of risk, a summary of those views (or an Executive Summary may be attached to the report); and where relevant, a copy of the Police National Computer record of previous convictions should be attached;
v) in the case of an eligible compliant patient who lacks capacity to agree or object to their placement or treatment, whether or not deprivation of liberty under the Mental Capacity Act 2005 (as amended) would be more appropriate;
w) whether the patient, if absolutely discharged, would be likely to act in a manner harmful to themselves or others, whether any such risks could be managed effectively in the community and, if so, how;

x) whether it continues to be appropriate for the patient to remain liable to be recalled for further medical treatment in hospital and, if so, why;
y) whether, and if so the extent to which, it is desirable to continue, vary and/or add to any conditions currently imposed;
z) any recommendations to the tribunal, with reasons.

E. PATIENTS UNDER THE AGE OF 18

34. All the above requirements in respect of statements and reports apply, as appropriate, depending upon the type of case.
35. In addition, for all patients under the age of 18, the Social Circumstances Report must also state:
    a) the names and addresses of any people with parental responsibility, and how they acquired parental responsibility;
    b) which public bodies either have worked together or need to liaise in relation to after-care services that may be provided under Section 117 of the Act;
    c) the outcome of any liaison that has taken place;
    d) if liaison has not taken place, why not – and when liaison will take place;
    e) the details of any multi-agency care plan in place or proposed;
    f) whether there are any issues as to funding the care plan and, if so, the date by which those issues will be resolved;
    g) the name and contact details of the patient's Care Co-ordinator, Community Psychiatric Nurse, Social Worker/AMHP or Social Supervisor;
    h) whether the patient's needs have been assessed under the Children Act 1989 or the Chronically Sick and Disabled Persons Act 1970 and, if not, the reasons why such an assessment has not been carried out and whether it is proposed to carry out such an assessment;
    i) if there has been such an assessment, what needs or requirements have been identified and how those needs or requirements will be met;
    j) if the patient is subject to or has been the subject of a Care Order or an Interim Care Order:
        - the date and duration of any such order;
        - the identity of the relevant local authority;
        - the identity of any person(s) with whom the local authority shares parental responsibility;
        - whether there are any proceedings which have yet to conclude and, if so, the court in which proceedings are taking place and the date of the next hearing;
        - whether the patient comes under the Children (Leaving Care) Act 2000;
        - whether there has been any liaison between, on the one hand, social workers responsible for mental health services to children and adolescents and, on the other hand, those responsible for such services to adults;
        - the name of the social worker within the relevant local authority who is discharging the function of the Nearest Relative under Section 27 of the Act;
    k) if the patient is subject to guardianship under Section 7 of the Act, whether

any orders have been made under the Children Act 1989 in respect of the patient, and what consultation there has been with the guardian;

l) if the patient is a Ward of Court, when the patient was made a ward of court and what steps have been taken to notify the court that made the order of any significant steps taken, or to be taken, in respect of the patient;

m) whether any other orders under the Children Act 1989 are in existence in respect of the patient and, if so, the details of those orders, together with the date on which such orders were made, and whether they are final or interim orders;

n) if a patient has been or is a looked after child under Section 20 of the Children Act 1989, when the child became looked after, why the child became looked after, what steps have been taken to discharge the obligations of the local authority under Paragraph 17(1) of Schedule 2 of the Children Act 1989, and what steps are being taken (if required) to discharge the obligations of the local authority under Paragraph 10 (b) of Schedule 2 of the Children Act 1989;

o) if a patient has been treated by a local authority as a child in need (which includes a child who has a mental disorder) under Section 17(11) of the Children Act 1989, the period or periods for which the child has been so treated, why they were considered to be a child in need, what services were or are being made available to the child by virtue of that status, and details of any assessment of the child;

p) if a patient has been the subject of a secure accommodation order under Section 25 of the Children Act 1989, the date on which the order was made, the reasons it was made, and the date it expired;

q) if a patient is a child provided with accommodation under Sections 85 and 86 of the Children Act 1989, what steps have been taken by the accommodating authority or the person carrying on the establishment in question to discharge their notification responsibilities, and what steps have been taken by the local authority to discharge their obligations under Sections 85, 86 and 86A of the Children Act 1989.

Amendments to the Tribunal Procedure (First-tier Tribunal) (Health, Education and Social Care Chamber) Rules 2008: medical examinations

11th March 2014

The Tribunal Procedure Committee has announced the outcome of the consultation on proposed changes to the HESC Rules. I have decided to issue this guidance under Section 23(2) and Schedule 4, Paragraph 7 of the Tribunals, Courts and Enforcement Act 2007.

The amendments to the Rules continue the previous approach of the committee in relation to CTO paper reviews by putting 'patient choice' at the heart of the process, whilst also making arrangements where the interests of justice require specific provision to be made.

In summary, the tribunal doctor will continue to conduct a pre-hearing examination of the patient in all Section 2 cases unless the patient does not want such an examination, but the tribunal doctor will not conduct such an examination in any other case unless:

- the tribunal is informed in writing by or on behalf of the patient, not less than 14 days before the hearing, that a pre-hearing examination is wanted, or –
- the tribunal has directed that there must be such an examination. This will either be a direction by a salaried judge or Registrar in advance of the hearing, or a direction made by the panel because the patient has failed to attend the hearing.

The new Rule 34 will read –

'Medical examination of the patient

34 (1) Where paragraph (2) applies, an appropriate member of the Tribunal must, so far as practicable, examine the patient in order to form an opinion of the patient's mental condition, and may do so in private.

(2) This paragraph applies–

(a) in proceedings under section 66(1)(a) of the Mental Health Act 1983 (application in respect of an admission for assessment), unless the Tribunal is satisfied that the patient does not want such an examination;

(b) in any other case, if the patient or the patient's representative has informed the Tribunal in writing, not less than 14 days before the hearing, that–

(i) the patient; or

(ii) if the patient lacks the capacity to make such a decision, the patient's representative, wishes there to be such an examination; or

(c) if the Tribunal has directed that there be such an examination.'

The new arrangements will only apply to cases received by the tribunal on or after 6th April 2014. As a transitional measure, general directions will be issued under Rule 34(2)(c) for a pre-hearing examination to be conducted in all cases where the application or reference was received on or before 5th April 2014.

The jurisdiction has drafted a leaflet, which the office will send at an early stage to all Section 2 and unrepresented patients, that advises patients of their rights to legal representation and/or to see the tribunal doctor in advance – and that provides a clear and easy method to promptly inform the tribunal of any wishes.

I expect legally represented patients to receive appropriate and timely advice from their lawyers, and the office will be vigilant in seeking capacity assessments for unrepresented patients to make sure that legal representatives are promptly appointed for patients who do not have the capacity to decide for themselves whether or not to appoint a representative.

Timely requests for a pre-hearing examination will be processed quickly so that tribunal doctors have time to make arrangements to see patients a day or two before the hearing.

In addition, there are two other situations when a pre-hearing examination may arise:

First, a salaried tribunal judge or Registrar can direct that an examination take place in advance of the hearing, as part of their case-management powers. Late requests from or on behalf of patients will be referred for case-management decision (although granting a late request may involve a postponement to give the tribunal doctor time to arrange a visit). Additionally, there may be other cases where, either upon the request of a party or the panel, or on their own initiative, a salaried tribunal judge or Registrar considers whether a pre-hearing examination is required. The test for all such decisions will be whether such an examination is necessary to enable the tribunal to deal with the case fairly and justly.

Second, if the patient completely fails to attend the hearing, the panel itself should direct the tribunal doctor to interview the patient on the ward before proceeding with the hearing unless such an interview is impractical or unnecessary – which it may be if, for example, the patient is too unwell, does not wish to see the tribunal doctor, has gone absent without leave, or lives in the community and has chosen not to attend a hearing. It may also be that the patient's representative agrees that a pre-hearing interview is unnecessary.

A new Rule 39(2) will read –

'39–

(2) The Tribunal may not proceed with a hearing that the patient has failed to attend unless the Tribunal is satisfied that–
- (a) the patient–
  - (i) has decided not to attend the hearing; or
  - (ii) is unable to attend the hearing for reasons of ill health; and
- (b) an examination under rule 34 (medical examination of the patient)–
  - (i) has been carried out; or
  - (ii) is impractical or unnecessary.'

I do not expect that this interview will take too long and, in any event, it should shorten the hearing because the patient will not be giving evidence to the panel as a whole.

If the patient on the ward fails to attend the hearing then a pre-hearing interview provides an opportunity for the patient to be heard. However, all other evidence must be made available to the panel in the usual way. Thus, if the patient has decided not to attend or is unable to attend the hearing, it should not also be necessary to review the patient's records.

Apart from a patient failing to attend, I do not expect panels at the hearing to direct pre-hearing examinations. I recognise that the desirability of a pre-hearing examination may become clear only when the members of a panel read the reports. But it will then be possible for the panel to ask a salaried judge to consider whether or not to direct a pre-hearing examination. Moreover (except in Section 2 cases) if the patient is going to attend at the hearing, even if they have chosen to be unrepresented, there will rarely be time or necessity on the hearing day for a pre-hearing examination as well.

A new Rule 32(9) will read –

'32–

(9) The responsible authority must make records relating to the detention or treatment of the patient and any after-care services available to the Tribunal on request and the Tribunal or an appropriate member of the Tribunal may, before or at the hearing, examine and take notes and copies of such records for use in connection with the proceedings.'

As in all other types of legal proceedings, it is for the parties to draw the panel's attention to any salient records or notes where there is sufficient time to do so. Therefore, if there are any aspects of the records or notes that any party considers the tribunal should consider, then they should prepare an extract and submit it to the tribunal, in advance.

It follows that, in all those cases where there is no pre-hearing examination or where the pre-hearing examination only arises because a patient fails to attend their hearing, tribunal doctors are not expected to routinely inspect the patient's records.

However, with a Section 2 pre-hearing examination or an examination properly requested or directed well in advance, the tribunal doctor should also inspect the patient's records – as has previously been the case. This Rule provides the authority for the tribunal doctor (or the panel as a whole) to have access to records upon request.

Finally, where a pre-hearing interview is not required, panels may consider giving patients an opportunity of speaking first and, again, at the end of the hearing. Many patients have things they want to say at the outset and, of course, much time will be saved by not having to feedback the tribunal doctor's preliminary opinion in such cases.

His Honour Judge Sycamore
Chamber President
(Health, Education and Social Care Chamber)
First-tier Tribunal

APPENDIX C

Guidance

C1 LAW SOCIETY PRACTICE NOTE: REPRESENTATION BEFORE MENTAL HEALTH TRIBUNALS[1]

1 Introduction

1.1 Who should read this practice note?

All lawyers who represent clients before the First-tier Tribunal (Mental Health) in England and the Mental Health Review Tribunal for Wales.

Unless otherwise specified, references to 'the tribunal' includes both tribunals.

2 The right to legal advice and representation before the tribunal

The right of access to a court is a fundamental right at common law under the European Convention on Human Rights (ECHR) and is guaranteed by Article 6 of the Convention.

Article 5(4) of the convention further guarantees the right to legal representation.

When an individual is detained on the grounds of mental disorder, Article 5(4) requires that effective legal representation is provided by the state, free of charge, unless there are 'special circumstances'.

To comply with the state's obligations under Article 5(4) any legal representation that is provided must be 'effective'. That means the legal representative must be suitably qualified and experienced (although not necessarily a qualified lawyer) and must have adequate time and facilities to prepare the case, including sufficient opportunity to visit the client and take instructions.

'Special circumstances' do not include the fact that the detainee's prospects of release are poor or that the detainee has the means to instruct his own lawyers. Even if representation is available (whether at the detainee's or the state's expense) the state must still ensure the detainee is represented unless satisfied that he or she has capacity and has made an informed choice not to be represented. See for example *Megyeri v Germany* (1992) 15 EHRR 584.

In England and Wales, public authorities have duties under the Human Rights Act to ensure that detained patients are represented. In practical terms this will mean that a tribunal should consider appointing a legal representative for an unrepresented patient under rule 11(7) of the First-tier Tribunal Rules in England or Rule 30 in Wales, even where the detainee has chosen not to be represented, unless satisfied that the individual has capacity to make that choice.

See 8.1 Legal and other requirements for further details.

2.1 The role of the hospital

Under the English and Welsh codes of practice, hospital managers must ensure that patients are told how to contact a suitably experienced

1 Published 22 January 2015.

representative (para 2.18 and para 26.5, respectively). The way in which hospitals assist clients to obtain legal representation varies widely.

Under Section 132 of the MHA 1983, hospital managers must ensure that a patient understands 'what rights of applying to a tribunal are available to him in respect of his detention', which would include advice on the right to be legally represented. This information is contained in a leaflet which should be given to patients upon admission.

A list of mental health legal practitioners can be provided by the ward or the Mental Health Act administrator to patients. The tribunal in both England and Wales also holds a list of accredited practitioners as does the Law Society.

You are advised to contact the Mental Health Act administrator at hospitals to check if you or your firm has been included in the list of representatives available to represent detained patients. Details of firms that employ a qualified practitioner in England and Wales can be found using the Law Society's online Find a Solicitor service.

See also a list of Law Society accredited representatives, which is updated monthly.

2.2 Independent mental health advocates

The role of an independent mental health advocate (IMHA) is to help qualifying patients understand the legal provisions to which they are subject under the Mental Health Act 1983 (MHA 1983), and the rights and safeguards to which they are entitled. IMHAs can accompany patients to tribunal and hospital managers' hearings and may speak on their behalf if they are not legally represented. The IMHA may also assist patients to exercise their rights (for example, helping them complete an application to the tribunal).

IMHAs are not the same as legal representatives and are not expected to take over duties currently undertaken by solicitors or other legal practitioners. The following patients are entitled to have access to an IMHA:

- patients detained under the MHA 1983, even if they are currently on leave of absence from hospital, apart from those patients detained under sections 4, 5(2), 5(4), 135 or 136
- patients subject to guardianship under the Act or
- a community patient.

A patient will also qualify for the assistance of an IMHA if:

(i) they discuss with a registered medical practitioner or approved clinician the possibility of being given a form of treatment to which section 57 applies, or

(ii) not having attained the age of 18 years and not being a qualifying patient they discuss with a registered medical practitioner or approved clinician the possibility of being given a form of treatment to which section 58A applies.

In England the tribunal has issued guidance on the role of IMHAs.

You should note that in Wales all psychiatric in-patients have the right of access to an IMHA following implementation of the Mental Health (Wales) Measure 2010.

2.3 Receiving referrals

You must comply with SRA principles when seeking to obtain new instructions. You should also read and abide by any code of conduct issued by the relevant trust or hospital.

If you are a member of the Mental Health Lawyers Association (MHLA) you should look at clause 3 of the MHLA Code of Conduct, which deals with facilitating referrals.

You may:

- contact the Mental Health Act administrator of the hospitals in your area to express willingness to accept referrals for tribunal representation
- contact IMHA service providers in your area to express willingness to accept referrals for tribunal representation.

You must not approach clients on hospital wards without prior appointments to obtain referrals. You should also be mindful of the potential for a conflict of interest to arise should you provide gifts or incentives to members of hospital staff.

If you are in doubt as to how to resolve any issue relating to referrals or gifts you should contact the SRA Professional Ethics Helpline.

If a patient approaches you on a ward seeking representation then you should check with the Mental Health Act administrator to ascertain whether that patient is already legally represented.

If the patient is not already represented, or the Mental Health Act administrator does not know whether or not the patient is legally represented, you can leave your details and invite the patient to contact you for an appointment.

You can take instructions immediately in emergency situations after first checking that no other legal practitioner has been approached. Examples of emergency situations include Section 2 patients where a date has already been set for a hearing or the time limit for appealing is very close.

2.4 Change of solicitor

Under the Civil Legal Aid (Procedure) Regulations 2013, you must not provide legal help to a client who has received legal help for the same matter from another supplier within the preceding six months.

The exceptions to this are:

- there has been a material change in relevant circumstances since the initial determination
- the individual has reasonable cause to be dissatisfied with the services provided under the initial determination
- the individual's usual residence has changed since the initial determination and, as a result, effective communication between the individual and the provider is not practicable; or the provider named in the initial determination has confirmed in writing that no remuneration will be claimed under arrangements made by the Lord Chancellor under section 2(1) of the Act in respect of any services provided under the initial determination.

Where a patient requests a change of solicitor, you should record brief reasons in a file note as to why the patient is seeking to change their legal representative to you. You should write to the firm currently instructed and ask if they object to the change of solicitor.

2.5 Appointing a representative

The tribunal can exercise its power to appoint a representative:

- in England under Rule 11(7) of the Tribunal Procedure (First-tier Tribunal) (Health, Education and Social Care Chamber) Rules 2008 (the FTT Procedure Rules 2008)
- in Wales under Rule 13(5) of the Mental Health Review Tribunal for Wales Rules 2008 (the Tribunal (Wales) Rules 2008)

See 8.2 Legal and other requirements.

The tribunal may exercise this power when a patient either:

- states they want to be represented or does not want to conduct their own case
- lacks the capacity to appoint a representative but the tribunal believes that being represented is in the patient's best interests.

A refusal of representation from a client with capacity to make that decision cannot be overridden. See 4.1 Clients with capacity.

The Upper Tribunal has the power to appoint a representative for the patient under rule 11(7) of the Tribunal Procedure (Upper Tribunal) Rules 2008 (the UT Rules 2008) in the same circumstances as the Tribunal.

The MHA 1983 does not provide for a litigation friend to be appointed for a person who lacks capacity to give instructions to a representative.

For more information, see 4.2 Clients without capacity.

3 Communication with the client

Tailoring the way in which you communicate with clients who have mental health problems is crucial in providing effective representation. The tribunal process can be a daunting process for patients who will often require increased levels of client care, including attendance time, well ahead of significant milestones in their case.

A report by the Administrative Justice and Tribunals Council provides useful analysis and information for you to consider when preparing for and undertaking hearings before the tribunal.

You should:

- be alert to, and seek to overcome, communication challenges which the client faces, including those arising from:
  - lack of capacity or use of medication
  - hearing difficulties
  - learning difficulties
  - oanguage barriers or other cross-cultural issues
- present information in a clear and straightforward manner, avoiding complicated forms and overly legalistic language
- allow extra time to explain issues in the case to clients and, if necessary

attend clients well ahead of a hearing to minimise confusion on the day of the hearing
- ensure clients have timely access to necessary information on their case for example, expert reports where necessary.

3.1 Initial contact with the client

You should make initial contact with the client in a timely manner, to take instructions and give initial advice. You should advise clients on:
- their rights as a detained patient
- the issue of consent to treatment
- entitlement to legal aid
- the strengths and weaknesses of their case
- hearing procedures
- tribunal powers
- timescales
- their right to independent advocacy assistance

You may not be able to communicate all the information above in one meeting – it depends on the unique circumstances of each client. You should refer a client to another specialist legal adviser if you lack expertise on other significant issues for which they might need legal advice. Importantly, this is a requirement of legal aid contracts (see section 2.40 of the 2014 Standard Civil Contract Specification General Rules). Examples of common significant issues include:
- family
- welfare benefits
- debt
- housing
- crime
- public law
- discrimination
- human rights
- community care
- clinical negligence

Legal aid changes have severely restricted or terminated funding in many of these areas. In some cases it may be appropriate to refer clients to the Citizens Advice Bureau.

You should maintain regular contact with the client, and be willing to adjust the level of contact depending on the client's mental health condition. The client's clarity may change during the case as a result of changing mental health or medication.

You should aim to make contact with clients in person as much as possible, rather than relying on telephone or written communication. If your first referral is from a member of staff at the hospital or an IMHA you should try and speak to the client before your first attendance to reassure them that you will be coming to see them. If your client is not detained but lives in the community then you should offer them an appointment at your office. If they are unable to attend your office you should consider what arrangements can be made to meet your client in private at a venue that is appropriate to your client's needs and is safe for you both.

You should be aware that your correspondence, although addressed to the client, may find its way on to the client 's medical notes, thereby breaching solicitor/client confidentiality. It will sometimes be appropriate to visit the client rather than send correspondence by post. If you do so, you should read out the correspondence, offer the client a copy to keep and make a note on your file accordingly. If you find that your correspondence has been put into your client 's records, you should check with your client whether they object to this and if so raise it with staff on the ward.

You must not disclose to the client any documents sent to you by the Tribunal Service or the Tribunal Secretariat in Wales which is marked 'not for disclosure'. You may only disclose such documents to your client if the tribunal authorises you to do so. For more information on disclosure issues see section 5.3.

3.2 Client care letters

Client care letters are especially important when working with clients who have mental health problems. The general rules (set out below) apply but special care and attention may be required.

Chapter 1 of the SRA Code of Conduct 2011 (Client Care) outlines client care requirements.

Chapter 1 provides that solicitors must provide a proper standard of service, which takes into account the individual needs and circumstances of each client. This includes providing clients with the information they need to make informed decisions about the services they need, how these will be delivered and how much they will cost.

Chapter 1 should be interpreted in reference to the 10 mandatory principles in the SRA Handbook.

Your initial letter to the client explaining terms of business is often called the client care letter. It acts as:

- a clear record for you and the client of the instructions given and what will happen next
- a useful guide for your client on your role and responsibilities
- evidence against complaints of insufficient information or inadequate professional service.

You should tailor client care letters to the individual needs of the client, reflecting their communication needs. You should use clear, simple and jargon-free language.

In some cases it may be inappropriate to send a letter, for example if the likelihood of distress to your client is significant. If for any reason you consider it inappropriate to send the client a client care letter you should retain the letter on file and go through the letter in person with the client when appropriate and as far as their comprehension allows.

You should always record the reason for taking this approach. If an IMHA or independent mental capacity advocate (IMCA) is involved, you may wish to make them aware of the contents of the letter, subject to client confidentiality (see below).

For more information see the practice note on client care letters.

4 Taking instructions

4.1 Clients with capacity

The following guidance applies where

- a patient with capacity has instructed you directly,
- you have been appointed to represent them under r 11(7) (a) FTT Rules 2008 or rule 13(5) (a) of the Tribunal (Wales) Rules or r 11(7) (a) Upper Tribunal Rules 2008; namely where the patient 'states they want to be represented or does not want to conduct their own case'.

You must assume that your client has capacity unless the contrary is established (section 1(2) MCA).

The test of litigation capacity is set out in *Masterman-Lister v Brutton & Co* [2003] 1 WLR 1511, namely 'whether the party to legal proceedings is capable of understanding, with the assistance of proper explanation from legal advisers and experts in other disciplines as the case may require, the issues on which his consent or decision is likely to be necessary in the course of those proceedings'. This is sometimes referred to as the client having capacity to instruct a solicitor. It is important to note, as the Supreme Court made clear in *Dunhill v Burgin* [2014] 1 WLR 993, that the test must be applied to the claim that the party in fact has, not to the claim as formulated by their lawyers.

The information that a patient is required to understand to instruct a solicitor in the context of an application to a tribunal is not complex and people severely affected by a mental disorder may still be able to provide instructions if you explain matters simply and clearly.

The question of whether the person is able to provide instructions is a judgment that in many cases an experienced mental health advocate will be able to make themselves. In the rare cases where you are unable to form an opinion you should obtain the opinion of the responsible clinician (RC) – either directly or via the Mental Health Act Administrator – as to the client's litigation capacity by reference to the test in *Masterman-Lister*. You should also ask the RC for his or her opinion of the client 's capacity to appoint you.

If you conclude that your client has the capacity to instruct you, you must take instructions from them and must act in accordance with those instructions, even where they are inconsistent, unhelpful to the case or vary during the preparation of the case, or during the hearing itself. However, the fact that the client's instructions are contrary to their best interests may be evidence that they lack capacity.

You must refuse to advance an argument which is not 'properly arguable', despite instructions to do so, see *Buxton v Mills-Owen* [2010] EWCA Civ 122, para 45. However, a submission may be 'properly arguable' even if it has few, if any, prospects of success (para 43). It will depend upon the context and your judgment. It is highly unlikely that to seek a client's discharge in accordance with his or her express wishes would not be 'properly arguable', even if it is unlikely to succeed.

If you consider that an argument that your client instructs you to advance is properly arguable, you must advance it without reservation. In other words, you should not advance a submission at the same time as signaling to the judge that you may think that it is weak or hopeless, for example by using coded language such as 'I am instructed that '. Such coded language is well understood as conveying that the advocate expects it to be rejected: *Buxton v Mills-Owen* at para 44.

Where you believe your client's instructions are unrealistic or contrary to their interests you should discuss with the client an alternative and more realistic line of challenge.

You may pursue this alternative line only if the client agrees. Your duty to act in accordance with the client's instructions takes precedence over your duty to act in what you perceive to be their best clinical interests. Therefore if your client wishes you to argue for their discharge you should do this, even if in your view your client needs hospital treatment.

The duty to follow the client's instructions is subject to an exception. This is where you believe the client's instructions are affected by either duress or undue influence: see SRA Handbook IB (25) – acting for a client when there are reasonable grounds for believing that the instructions are affected by duress or undue influence.

In those circumstances you must not act on those instructions until you have satisfied yourself that they represent the client's wishes.

As an advocate, you are responsible for decisions about the manner in which you put your client's case to the tribunal, and you must bear in mind your professional responsibilities to the court – in this case the tribunal – as well as to the client. See *R v Farooqi and others* [2013] EWCA Crim 1649.

4.2 Clients without capacity

You must assume that your client has capacity to give you instructions unless the contrary is established. Nevertheless, there will be occasions on which you will not be able to accept instructions directly, or by way of a referral, because the client lacks capacity to instruct you. You may form this view if, for example, the client is profoundly learning disabled and cannot appreciate that they are detained under the Mental Health Act.

If you think that your client lacks capacity to instruct you then you cannot act for this client unless either:

- you are instructed by a properly authorised third party, such as a court-appointed deputy or the donee of a power of property and affairs power of attorney, or
- the relevant tribunal has appointed you to act under the First-tier Tribunal Rules, Tribunal (Wales) Rules or the Upper Tribunal Rules.

See above: 2.5 Appointing a representative.

As set out at paragraph 2.5, the tribunal can appoint a solicitor for a patient if satisfied that the patient lacks capacity to appoint a representative. This is not the same as 'capacity to litigate'. There will be a few patients who lack capacity to litigate at a tribunal but who have capacity to appoint a representative.

The appointment by the tribunal operates as a retainer for the client.

An appointment by the tribunal does not mean that you are also appointed to act as the client's litigation friend: there is no provision for such an appointment within the rules. You should not automatically assume that guidance that may have been prepared for the use of a litigation friend in other court proceedings applies to you as a representative.

Once appointed by the tribunal you have a heightened responsibility to identify and then to act in the interests of the client. The duty to act in the client's best interests is set out in Principle 1 of the SRA Code 2011 and applies to clients with or without litigation capacity.

In our view the client's interest in a fair hearing to determine the lawfulness of their detention is paramount. When your client lacks litigation capacity, you will not take instructions in the same way that you would in respect of a client with capacity. Instead you must do your best to ascertain their wishes and feelings. You must give weight to the wishes that your client expresses.

The closer the patient is to having capacity, the greater the weight you must give to their wishes in seeking to formulate and advance submissions on their behalf. Nonetheless, you remain under the same duty to the tribunal to advance only submissions which are properly arguable as if your client had capacity (see Buxton v Mills-Owen and section 4.1 Clients with capacity).

There are likely to be few cases where a client who is able to express their wish to be discharged by a tribunal will be assessed as lacking capacity to instruct you. Similarly, where a client without litigation capacity tells you they wish to be discharged from hospital, there will be few cases it will not be appropriate to argue for their discharge. This is because of the over-riding importance of the client's right under Article 5(4) to challenge the lawfulness of their detention – a right that exists without the detained individual needing to show that they have any particular chance of success in obtaining their release – see *Waite v UK* (2003) 36 EHRR 54.

Where the client lacks the ability to express their wishes you should:

- ensure that the tribunal receives all relevant material so that it can determine whether the criteria for continued detention are satisfied
- test the criteria for continued detention
- remember your client's right to treatment in the least restrictive setting and alert the tribunal to possible alternatives to detention under the MHA 1983 such as Community Treatment Orders (CTOs) and guardianship
- In the case of a patient who is unable to consent to be detained for purposes of assessment or treatment in hospital but appears to be compliant, you may wish to consider whether the DoLS regime under Schedule A1 to the MCA 2005 might provide a better and less restrictive way of ensuring that your client receives treatment or assessment in hospital: see *AM v SLAM NHS Foundation Trust* [2013] UKUT 365 (AAC).

You should not automatically argue for discharge if you are unable to ascertain the patient's wishes, but you are obliged to test the criteria for detention.

Separate considerations arise if the client is adamant that they do not wish to be represented by you, notwithstanding your appointment by the tribunal under Rule 11(7)(b), the tribunal having assessed the client as lacking capacity to appoint a representative.

If on meeting the client you think that he or she has capacity to appoint you then you should alert the tribunal and ask for the appointment to be discharged. It is then the client's decision whether to instruct you or not.

If you consider that the client lacks capacity to instruct you but think the client is hostile to being represented by you, then in some cases you should consider informing the tribunal and requesting the appointment to be discharged. This may be appropriate where:

- attempting to represent the client would cause them distress or interfere with their ability to participate in proceedings
- the client's hostility is such that you cannot fulfil your professional obligations to them, or
- continuing to attempt to represent the client puts your safety at risk and the risk cannot be managed using local policies at the unit where the client is detained.

For further guidance on obtaining copies of the medical records of a client lacking capacity see section 6.2 Access to medical records.

5 Your duties towards your client

5.1 Duty to act in the best interests of clients

Solicitors must act in the best interests of the client under Principle 4 of the SRA Principles. This duty arises whether the client has litigation capacity or not. It is important to note that the term 'best interests ' here does not necessarily mean the same as 'best interests' for the purposes of the MCA 2005. As set out below, you will need to draw a distinction between what has been termed the client's 'legal best interests' and their 'clinical interests.'

See Professional conduct in the Legal status box above and 8.1 Legal and other requirements

Aspects of the duty to act in the client's best legal interests will include:

- advising clients of the likelihood of being discharged
- advising clients on possible steps towards discharge
- advising clients in respect of disclosure issues
- following the instructions of a client with capacity to instruct you or advocating the views or wishes of a client without capacity to instruct you
- advising on aftercare
- advising on other related issues, for example compulsory treatment provisions, alternatives to detention such as CTOs and Guardianship
- advising on the possibility and consequences of the patient withdrawing the application to the tribunal.

5.2 Situations where legal and clinical interests may conflict

Conflicts may arise because of the nature of the information that you have access to as a representative (regardless of your client 's capacity to give you instructions). For example, in *RM v St Andrew's Healthcare* [2010] UKUT 119 (AAC) the Upper Tribunal ruled that documents revealing the patient was being covertly medicated should be disclosed to the patient because his fair trial rights (which the Upper Tribunal referred to as his best legal interests) required it, even though it was accepted it was likely to affect his health adversely (which the Upper Tribunal referred to as the patient's best clinical interests).

There may be other situations not covered by this practice note. If you are in doubt you should seek guidance from the Solicitor's Regulation Authority's Professional Ethics helpline.

5.3 Duty of confidentiality

5.3.1 Confidential information

This duty is covered in Chapter 4 of the SRA Code of Conduct. You must achieve Outcome 4.1 which requires solicitors to keep the affairs of clients and former clients confidential except where disclosure is required or permitted by law or the client consents.

Practitioners should be aware that the previous version of the code provided for specific exceptions to the absolute duty of confidentiality. These do not appear in the current version of the code and we recognise that this may give rise to difficult questions for practitioners. For example, you are speaking to a client on the ward and as you are about to leave they tell you they have been saving up their medication. They know the ward will be short-staffed tonight and intend to take an overdose and end their life. You know that they have attempted to take their own life before. You suggest that the two of you speak to one of the nurses to tell them this but they will not agree.

In this situation, as the client has refused consent to disclose their intentions, any subsequent disclosure by you would appear to be a technical breach of Outcome 4.1 yet not to do so could also potentially be said to conflict with your duty to act in the best interests of your client.

For guidance as to how you should approach situations such as this you should contact the SRA Ethics Helpline.

5.3.2 Privileged information

You should not disclose information passed to you in circumstances giving rise to a duty of legal professional privilege, which is absolute: see *R v Derby Magistrates ex p B* [1996] AC 487, *L (a minor)* [1997] AC 17 (see 24B-G) and *B v Auckland Law Society* [2003] 2 AC 736.

If you found yourself in this situation – for example, if disclosure of privileged information has been made mistakenly – you should contact the SRA's Professional Ethics Helpline for advice (0370 606 2577).

5.3.3 Duties of disclosure and circumstances where non-disclosure may be appropriate

Chapter 4 of the SRA Code of Conduct 2011 deals with the issue of disclosure.

The relevant outcomes which you must achieve are:

Outcome 4.2: any individual who is advising a client makes that client aware of all information material to that retainer of which the individual has personal knowledge;

Outcome 4.3: you ensure that where your duty of confidentiality to one client comes into conflict with your duty of disclosure to another client, your duty of confidentiality takes precedence;

The relevant indicative behaviours are:

IB 4.4:

where you are an individual who has responsibility for acting for a client or supervising a client's matter, you disclose to the client all information material to the client's matter of which you are personally aware, except when:

(a) the client gives specific informed consent to non-disclosure or a different standard of disclosure arises;

(b) there is evidence that serious physical or mental injury will be caused to a person(s) if the information is disclosed to the client;

(c) legal restrictions effectively prohibit you from passing the information to the client, such as the provisions in the money-laundering and anti-terrorism legislation.

The tribunal can withhold disclosure of documents from a patient if disclosure is likely to cause serious harm to the patient or another person and it is proportionate to do so. In England, this is possible under Rule 14, Tribunal Procedure (First-tier Tribunal) (Health, Education and Social Care Chamber) Rules 2008. In Wales, this is possible under Rule 17, Mental Health Review Tribunal for Wales Rules 2008.

Under these rules, the information can be disclosed to the solicitor on the basis that they do not disclose it to anyone else, including the client. Rule 14(6) prohibits the representative from disclosing documents or the information they contain either directly or indirectly to anyone else, including the representative's client. The rule does not prohibit the representative from informing the client that the representative has a document or information that cannot be disclosed to the client, provided that the representative does not thereby indirectly disclose to the client the information which is being withheld.

If the tribunal has made such a direction then your duty to disclose the information to the client is over-ridden by this legal restriction: see IB4.4. This can be a difficult situation for you to manage – if documents are disclosed to you on this basis you should either:

- consider requesting an earlier hearing which the client does not attend

- consider dealing with disclosure as a preliminary issue without the client on the day of the hearing
- consider making an application for the issue to be considered by a salaried tribunal judge on the papers before the hearing.

Dorset Healthcare NHS Foundation Trust v MHRT (2009) UKUT 4 (AAC) gives guidance on when a responsible authority can resist disclosure of confidential third-party information or when a solicitor wishes to disclose such information to their client.

If you request full access to your client's medical records, the responsible authority should disclose all documents to you subject to an undertaking, if necessary, not to disclose certain specific third-party documents to the patient.

If in 'exceptional circumstances' the responsible authority refuses even to disclose documents to the solicitor, they must show that it is appropriate to do so by serving a skeleton argument to the tribunal office and the tribunal must make a ruling.

You should seek permission from the tribunal to disclose to your client any documents disclosed to you if you consider that it may improve the prospects of a successful outcome. In other words, if the documents are 'material to the client's matter' for the purpose of IB4.4.

You should set out your reasons for disclosure by way of a skeleton argument. In *RM v St Andrew's Healthcare* [2010] UKUT 119 (AAC), also referred to in paragraph 5.2.1 above. In this case the Upper Tribunal ruled that in deciding whether disclosure should be ordered the overriding consideration must be to ensure that the patient has a fair hearing, and that this must take precedence over any concerns that disclosure will harm the patient's health. It would follow that the requirement of a fair hearing can often override considerations of third party confidentiality.

Where a request or refusal of request is not resolved, either party can apply to the tribunal, for an order under Rule 5(d). This can be heard as a preliminary issue on the day of the hearing or a decision can be taken before the hearing following written or oral submissions.

The Upper Tribunal has stressed the desirability of dealing with disclosure issues between the parties without the need to involve the tribunal.

Please note that the guidance above with regard to disclosure which arises from the Dorset case is limited to those cases where there are ongoing proceedings in the tribunal. In other circumstances, if a trust or other body holding data on your client provides you with material that is relevant to your client's case then you must disclose it to the client unless any of the circumstances in IB 4.4 apply.

6 Good tribunal practice

6.1 Avoiding delay

The tribunal's overriding objective is to deal with cases fairly and justly. This includes avoiding delay, so far as compatible with proper consideration of the issues.

Often delay can be caused by late reports from the responsible authority. In this situation it is the responsibility of the Mental Health Act Administrator to secure reports and submit them to the tribunal within the time limit. The tribunal in turn is responsible for issuing directions where reports are late. You should keep an eye on time limits for the submission of reports and ensure that the tribunal issue appropriate directions when it is necessary.

Once statutory reports are received you should ensure they comply with the President's Practice Direction.

These objectives are stated in Rule 2, the Tribunal Procedure (First-tier Tribunal) (Health, Education and Social Care Chamber) Rules 2008 and Rule 3 of the Mental Health Review Tribunal for Wales Rules 2008. This is also the case in the Upper Tribunal as stated in Rule 2, The Tribunal Procedure (Upper Tribunal) Rules 2008.

See 8.1 Legal and other requirements.

You should take all appropriate steps to ensure that tribunal hearings are not delayed.

6.2 Access to medical records

You should examine the section papers as soon as possible after your appointment as this will enable you to scrutinise the legality of your client's detention. For this you will require your client's signed consent authorising you to have access to your client's medical records. This requires the approval of the RC. In some hospitals this will be arranged via the MHAA but practice varies across hospitals.

You must read your client's medical records. These include documents such as progress notes, prescription charts, minutes of ward or CPA meetings, and records held in the community. Again, the means by which you can obtain access will vary across hospitals.

If your client lacks capacity to consent to your access to their section papers or records then you should ask the RC to agree to disclosure on the basis that it is in their best interests to have their case properly prepared. If you cannot resolve this issue with the RC you should apply to the tribunal using CMR1 for an order for disclosure under Rule 5(d). In Wales you should apply for an order under rule 5(c).

6.3 Independent reports

You should always consider whether it is appropriate to obtain independent evidence. Expert evidence may cover a range of issues such as diagnosis, treatment, placement and activities of daily living. You should also maintain an approved list of experts. Prompt instruction of an expert may reduce the need for adjournments and will ensure that your client has a fair hearing. Further guidance is available in the Mental Health Peer Review guidance.

You should request independent reports as soon as possible and in restricted cases send them to the tribunal office and the Ministry of Justice no later than 21 days before the hearing so that the secretary of state can comment on the report.

6.4 Witnesses

You should confirm in advance the availability of all witnesses, including experts, who are expected to attend the tribunal. You should be aware of IB 5.6 which provides that you should not appear as an advocate if you or anyone in your firm will be called as a witness.

6.5 Interpreters

In England Form T110 (Application to the FTT (Mental Health) and the listing form HQ1, you must indicate whether your client will require an interpreter. If you need an interpreter, you should notify the tribunal as early as possible in proceedings. In Wales you should notify the tribunal by email or letter.

6.6 Documents

You should send all relevant documents to the tribunal office no later than seven days before the hearing.

6.7 Pre hearing medical examination

A pre-hearing examination is indicated in all section 2 cases. In all other cases you should always consider whether it is appropriate to request a pre-hearing medical examination by the medical member of the tribunal. You must make such a request on form CMR1 within the prescribed period ie14 days before the date fixed for the hearing. If your client lacks capacity to make the decision you must consider whether or not it would benefit your client 's case for there to be such an examination.

6.8 Applications for postponements

You should avoid applications for postponements wherever possible. The tribunal frequently refuses applications for postponement, especially those made at the last minute. An application for a postponement should be made to the tribunal using Form CMR1. You must use this form where a request is made for any of the following:

- directions
- postponement
- prohibition of disclosure of information
- wasted costs
- permission to withdraw an application
- other applications

If you consider that a postponement is in the interests of the client, you should advise the client accordingly, but leave the final decision to the client if the client has capacity to litigate.

If a postponement appears unavoidable, you should apply as early as possible, setting out the reasons.

Where delay is caused by late reports from the responsible authority, if the tribunal has not already issued directions, solicitors should request directions immediately after the breach of the time limits on submission of statutory reports.

6.9 Withdrawing an application to the tribunal

An application can be withdrawn at any time by the client if the tribunal accepts the withdrawal. A reference cannot be withdrawn.

If the client wants to withdraw the application, you should notify the tribunal office using Form CMR1, giving the reasons.

Early notification allows for other cases to be rescheduled and maximises the use of the tribunal's time.

Where the withdrawal is received directly from the patient and that patient is represented, the solicitor will be approached by the tribunal and encouraged to make contact with the client to discuss the request to ensure the patient has not been put under pressure to withdraw.

The patient may make a fresh application for a tribunal within the same period of eligibility.

6.10 Other codes of conduct

6.10.1 Mental Health Lawyers Association (MHLA) code of conduct

The MHLA has adopted a Code of Conduct. It covers:

- quality of service
- making appointments
- behaviour on the wards
- disputes over representation
- seeking clients
- gifts
- hospital procedures.

6.10.2 NHS mental health trusts – codes of conduct

Some NHS mental health trusts and private hospitals have developed voluntary codes of conduct for solicitors. These codes ask solicitors to:

- contact the ward in advance to inform them of their intention to visit
- produce identification when visiting
- report to the ward office when visiting
- inform a member of staff if they wish to hold an informal meeting with another client whom they are visiting
- respect the operational needs of the unit/ward
- leave the ward following the completion of their appointment with a client.

Solicitors are asked not to:

- make unsolicited visits or telephone calls
- talk to or approach other patients

- hand out publicity materials
- offer gifts or money to service users other than existing clients
- offer gifts to staff

You should find out whether there is such a code in place at the relevant hospital. If you have any concerns about the code, you should contact the relevant trust.

7 Representing children and young people before the tribunal

The tribunal has established a Child and Adolescent Mental Health Service (CAMHS) panel. Its purpose is to ensure that at least one of the tribunal members has special expertise in dealing with cases where a child is either detained under the Mental Health Act 1983 or subject to another order under the act. For the purposes of the CAMHS panel a child is treated as any person under the age of 18 at the time of the application or reference.

Although the Tribunal Rules do not make any specific provision in relation to child patients, the solicitor representing a child should always consider the following:

- the wishes and feelings of the child
- the need to ensure that the child is able to participate fully in the proceedings by, for example, requesting that the proceedings are dealt with in as informal manner as appropriate
- any legal issues that are specific to the child, for example the impact of the Children Act 1989 on decision making in relation to the child and the need to identify the child's entitlement to aftercare services under children's legislation and mental health legislation.

8 More information

8.1 Legal and other requirements

- The Mental Health Act 1983 as amended by Mental Health Act 2007
- The Tribunal Procedure (First-tier Tribunal) (Health, Education and Social Care Chamber) Rules 2008
- The Practice Direction issued 30/10/08 (for England)
- The Mental Health Review Tribunal for Wales Rules 2008 (for Wales)
- The MHA codes of practice (different for England and Wales)
- Mental Capacity Act 2005
- Tribunal Procedure (Upper Tribunal) Rules 2008
- The Equality Act 2010
- Mental Health (Wales) Measure 2010

8.2 Mental Health Accreditation Scheme

The Law Society operates the Mental Health Accreditation Scheme.

If you are a member of the scheme you are authorised to advise and represent clients who have been detained under the Mental Health Act 1983 (the MHA 1983), before the relevant tribunal.

Since 1 August 2014 membership of the scheme is mandatory for advocates appearing before the tribunal other than self-employed counsel, and that all legal aid providers must comply with this (see 7.6(b) Category Specific Rules, 2014 Standard Civil Contract Mental Health Specification). Requirements for membership of the scheme include a good working knowledge of this practice note. The provisions of the Mental Health Act 1983 (the MHA 1983) have been qualified by the following legislation, statutory instruments and Codes of Practice:

- The Mental Health Act 2007
- The Tribunal Procedure (First-tier Tribunal) (Health, Education and Social Care Chamber) Rules 2008 (for England)
- The Mental Health Review Tribunal for Wales Rules 2008 (for Wales)
- The Mental Health Act codes of practice (different for England and Wales)
- Mental Health (Wales) Measure 2010
- Code of Practice to Parts 2 and 3 of Mental Health (Wales) Measure 2010

You should familiarise yourself with all of the above and know which provisions apply, depending on whether you practise in England or Wales.

You should also have knowledge of:

- 2014 Standard Civil Contract Mental Health Specification
- Peer review guidance, Mental Health – 3rd Edition, 2011

Read copies of the relevant practice directions and updates, which all practitioners should be familiar with.

See 8.1 Legal and other requirements for further details.

Find out more about eligibility and membership

8.3 Other products and services

8.3.1 Practice Advice Service

The Law Society 's Practice Advice Service can be contacted on 020 7320 5675 from 09:00 to 17:00 on weekdays.

8.3.2 Solicitors Regulation Authority's Professional Ethics Helpline

Solicitors may obtain further help on matters relating to professional ethics from the Solicitors Regulation Authority's Professional Ethics Helpline (0370 606 2577) from 09:00 to 17:00 on weekdays.

8.3.3 Law Society publications

- Assessment of Mental Capacity, 3rd ed
- Mental Health Tribunals
- Mental Capacity, 2nd ed
- Advising Mentally Disordered Offenders, 2nd ed

8.4 Terminology in this practice note

Must

- A specific requirement in legislation or of a principle, rule, outcome or other mandatory provision in the SRA Handbook. You must comply, unless there are specific exemptions or defences provided for in relevant legislation or the SRA Handbook.

Should

- Outside of a regulatory context, good practice for most situations in the Law Society's view.
- In the case of the SRA Handbook, an indicative behaviour or other non-mandatory provision (such as may be set out in notes or guidance).

These may not be the only means of complying with legislative or regulatory requirements and there may be situations where the suggested route is not the best possible route to meet the needs of your client. However, if you do not follow the suggested route, you should be able to justify to oversight bodies why the alternative approach you have taken is appropriate, either for your practice, or in the particular retainer.

May

- A non-exhaustive list of options for meeting your obligations or running your practice. Which option you choose is determined by the profile of the individual practice, client or retainer. You may be required to justify why this was an appropriate option to oversight bodies.

SRA Code – SRA Code, 2011
OFR – Outcomes-Focused regulation
SRA – Solicitors Regulation Authority
IB – Indicative Behaviour

8.5 Acknowledgements

This practice note has been prepared and updated by the Law Society's Mental Health and Disability Committee. The committee would like to thank the SRA and the Mental Health Lawyers Association for their input into the practice note.

See more at: www.lawsociety.org.uk/support-services/advice/practice-notes/mental-health-tribunals/#sthash.jJFEVD3W.dpuf

C2 MENTAL HEALTH LAWYERS ASSOCIATION (MHLA) CODE OF CONDUCT

All members of the Association have agreed to adhere to the following Code of Conduct.

MHLA CODE OF CONDUCT FOR REPRESENTATIVES

In representing hospital inpatients, particularly those detained by the state against their will, legal representatives carry out an important function for a civilised society. It is therefore important that the highest ethical and professional standards are adhered to.

Status of this Code

The committee of the Mental Health Lawyers Association have adopted this Code of Conduct. Annual renewal of membership, from January 2008, will require an undertaking that the Code will be followed.

This Code is in addition to the general Codes of Conduct made by the Solicitors Regulation Authority and the Institute of Legal Executives. The MHLA is a representative body rather than a regulatory body but, where appropriate, encourages complaints to be made to the SRA and/or ILEX.

Quality of service

1. Representatives should be members of the Law Society's Mental Health Review Tribunal accreditation scheme, or actively seeking membership. The scheme is designed to demonstrate legal knowledge (through the accreditation process) and suitability (including a Criminal Records Bureau check). Unqualified representatives and/or those not on the panel must be closely supervised by a member of the scheme.

2. Representatives should always conduct themselves professionally and courteously, and strive to provide a high standard of work in both advice and representation.

Making appointments

3. Except in exceptional circumstances, representatives should contact ward staff to arrange prior appointments with clients and should arrive punctually. Ward staff should be asked to ensure that a private room will be booked.

Behaviour on the ward

4. The representative should report to ward staff on arrival, and then go straight to the appointment with his client.

5. Unplanned meetings with other existing clients should be arranged via the ward staff.

6. The representative should not loiter on the ward, hand out business cards except where requested, or otherwise approach patients who are not existing clients.

7. If approached by a patient who is not a client, the representative may give a business card for an appointment to be made, but should inform ward

staff and, unless there is good reason to do so, should not accept instructions from a client who already has legal representation. The representative should consider contacting the existing solicitors to invite them to contact the patient again.

Disputes over representation

8. If there is a dispute over which firm should represent a patient, then this should be resolved via an independent third party rather than by revisiting the patient, as usually it is the more impressionable and vulnerable patients who find themselves in this situation.

Seeking clients

9. No representative is to place posters in the hospital to advertise his firm; only standard hospital/Trust/national posters are allowed. Representatives should instead ensure that they are on the hospital's list of firms and/or representatives.

Gifts

10. No gifts of any description should be given to hospital staff, including MHA administrators and nurses, or to clients or other patients.

Hospital procedures

11. Representatives will comply with any lawful hospital procedures such as those relating to searches, identification, protected meal times, and access to medical records.

Dress Code

12. Appropriate attire and footwear should be worn by legal representatives and should be consistent with presenting a professional image. Those representing mental health clients should be sensitive to their client's environment and bear in mind issues of risk at all times.

General

The word 'representative' in this Code includes solicitors, legal executives, and any solicitors' staff who represent clients.

Contact admin@mhla.co.uk with any queries or feedback.

Version 2, June 2013

C3 PEER REVIEW GUIDANCE 2011

Improving Your Quality: a guide to common issues identified through Peer Review (Mental Health)[2]

Foreword to the First Edition

The focus of the delivery of legal aid is firmly on the provision of consistently good quality services for clients.

The introduction of the peer review process provides a unique opportunity with access to a wealth of information directly related to the quality of legal advice and information given to clients. It allows us to identify areas of good practice and areas in need of improvement.

We are pleased to introduce this new edition 'Improving Your Quality – Mental Health', which is intended to give the profession access to peer review findings and help support those wishing to achieve the highest levels of quality of legal advice and work.

The guide makes available common quality issues identified by the Mental Health Peer Reviewers. Derived from the entire body of peer review reports, analysis has concentrated on those issues frequently contributing towards lower ratings at Peer Review. Each issue is divided into 3 parts:

- A brief description of why the issue has been identified as important.
- The process by which an organisation can identify if the quality concern affects their work and advice.
- Outline suggestions on activities/methods which could assist improvement.

These suggestions for making improvements are not suggesting a standard approach nor are they an exhaustive list; they are only some of the ways that improvements can be made. Your organisation may have other ways of resolving the issues raised in the guide, it is not our intention to invalidate those approaches.

Some of the suggestions may lead to a more general debate concerning standard setting, and the best approaches to dealing with specific quality of advice issues for Mental Health work. We continue to welcome the opening up of the world of legal competence to such scrutiny and debate.

Avrom Sherr

Director of Institute of Advanced Legal Studies

Foreword to the Second Edition

The last edition of this guide was published in January 2007. Since that time the number of mental health peer reviewers has expanded and many more files have been reviewed. In addition there have been significant changes to both law and procedure with the introduction of the Mental Health Act 2007, new Rules for the Mental Health Tribunal, now renamed formally as the First Tier Tribunal (Mental Health), and the growth of practice under the

2 Third edition, April 2011.

Mental Capacity Act 2005. Where appropriate this guide has been amended to address these changes. As in the previous edition, it addresses procedures before the Mental Health Tribunal, although some advice would be applicable to other areas of the representation of those with mental health issues.

A recent meeting of peer reviewers considered what might generally be regarded as 'major concerns' in files examined. The following points were agreed:

1. Relevant section or detention papers not being seen or examined

2. Medical records not being examined, or no evidence to support the assertion that they had been examined

3. No evidence of written advice specifically tailored to the client's situation; that is complete reliance on standardised correspondence

4. No evidenced attempt to check the Tribunal decision for legality

5. Where there is a conflict of interest demonstrated on a file, for example by acting for a party opposing discharge as well as for an applicant patient seeking discharge

6. In cases where the Nearest Relative had the power to discharge the client from section where no attempt had been made:

   a) To identify the Nearest Relative with the client

   b) Discuss with the client the Nearest Relative's powers

   c) To seek the client's consent to contact the Nearest Relative

Peer reviewers accept that particular circumstances might prevent these issues from becoming 'major concerns.' Illustrations would include the client refusing consent to access medical records or making it clear he, or she, wanted no, or limited, correspondence.

Similarly, additional issues might be major concerns, such as inadequate attendance, but in the particular context of the file samples.

Following further consideration of advice on the 'merits of the case', peer reviewers accepted this could be a very difficult area in mental health cases. In particular, 'early advice' in this area was frequently felt to be unrealistic. This part of the guide has been re-drafted to reflect this view. This is not to say, however, that peer reviewers felt that the prospects of success should not generally be discussed when appropriate with the client.

Peer reviewers remain concerned to see what effect the introduction of new funding procedures may have on the quality of work carried out in this area of law. However, to date, there is no clear way for reviewers to conclude how these new fees have impacted on files before them, as no straightforward comparative 'before' and 'after' samples files are available. Peer reviewers are aware of the role of 'exceptional cases' within the new fee scheme, which may become more common as advisers conduct a range of work within a client's Tribunal eligibility period.

Peer reviewers feel this guide represents their view of what good practice will generally require in conducting a case before the new Mental Health Tribunal.

This guide assumes knowledge of Tribunal procedure together with the relevant law and should not be used as a substitute for these. It is to be hoped, however, that this guide can assist practitioners to deliver good standards of work, and indeed, despite the pessimism in much of profession, encourage a positive debate about the delivery of this vital work and assist in the improvement of standards.

As in the previous edition, there is some overlap between some sections of the guide, and subsequently some overlap of content. This has again been seen as necessary so that important issues are not missed.

As indicated in the Foreword to the first edition, the suggestions made in this edition are not prescriptive, unless they repeat regulatory obligation, and it is accepted that practitioners may work in a variety of ways to deliver good quality.

Contents

1 Are files organised and legible?

Why does it matter?

- Properly organised and understandable files are an important basis for all subsequent preparation work.
- Files that are disorganised and contain illegible handwriting are difficult to refer back to.
- Disorganised files will not pass the quick 'pick up' test for another adviser who may have to consider the file at short notice.

How can I check this on my files?

- Are files organised?
- Are the documents, letters and file notes in each file arranged in chronological order?
- Are all handwritten file notes and pro forma legible?
- Have file notes and pro forma that contain illegible handwriting been transcribed?

What will help?

- Include this issue in File Review.
- Ensure that the date is clear on all file notes, attendance notes and correspondence so they can be organised in chronological order.
- Consider typing/dictating any handwritten notes that are difficult to read.

'Understandable files are an important basis for all subsequent preparation work'

2 Were the advisers selected to be involved in the matter appropriate?

Why does this matter?

- Mental Health cases require specialist knowledge of:
  - Mental health law;
  - The procedure of the First Tier (Mental Health) Tribunal ('the Tribunal');
  - Mental disorders and treatment;
  - Substantial experience in dealing with clients with mental disorders.
- The use of inexperienced advisers on Mental Health cases raises concerns as to whether the advice given is appropriate, correct, comprehensive and timely. Some cases, for example those where the client is a child, may be particularly complex.
- Without the use of experienced advisers in the preparation of Mental Health cases it is likely that crucial issues will remain unidentified and the client's case may be prejudiced, perhaps even leading to negligence.

How can I check this on my files?

- Has essential information been obtained from the client and been recorded either in statement(s) or by completing appropriate pro forma forms?
- Is there evidence of Tribunal preparation in the form of a case analysis or skeleton argument?
- Is there evidence of thorough preparation, for example, in the form of notes of questions prepared in advance of the hearing, letters sent to Responsible Clinicians ('RCs'), the Nearest Relative, together with other

appropriate third parties, as outlined elsewhere in this guide, before the hearing and evidence that medical notes have been perused?Has consideration been given to provide the client, at an appropriate point prior to the Tribunal hearing written advice on the specific merits of their case and has this been evidenced either in correspondence or in a file note?

What will help?

- Implement initial instructions pro forma tailored to specific cases.
- Undertake frequent and thorough file reviews of files conducted by inexperienced advisers.
- Review use of training and supervision for such advisers.
- Consider the comments and suggestions in subsequent parts of this guide.

'Undertake frequent and thorough reviews of files conducted by inexperienced advisers.'

3 Was the initial contact with the client timely?

Why does this matter?

- When clients are detained in hospital they may feel isolated and vulnerable (particularly in acute admission cases); it is therefore vital that the adviser does not delay visiting the client to take instructions and to give initial advice.
- Delay might lead to a breach of the need for a 'speedy' Tribunal hearing as set down in Article 5(4) European Convention on Human Rights as incorporated into the Human Rights Act 1998.
- Instructions by way of confidential face-to-face meetings are the starting point to the taking of instructions/giving of advice and therefore should be accomplished as soon as possible.
- Some cases (eg Section 2 appeals) must be dealt with very quickly to avoid the right of appeal being lost or the hearing going ahead with inadequate preparation.

How can I check this on my files?

- Does the file record when and how initial contact with firm was made?
- Was it established at an early stage whether there was any particular urgency?
- In a Section 2 case, and any other obviously urgent matter, was the client seen within 2 days of initial contact?
- In other cases, was the client seen within 7 days? If not, was the delay explained to the client?
- If the referral was through an Independent Mental Health Advocate (IMHA), is the advocate aware that an adviser has visited the client?

What will help?

- Ensure that any support staff that receive calls on behalf of advisers are trained to identify new case enquiries and bring them to the advisers' immediate attention.
- Ensure that advisers allow sufficient time in their weekly schedules to be able swiftly to respond to new enquiries.

- Consider whether the firm has the resources to take on a new case, particularly a Section 2 Tribunal case.
- Maintain details of local IMHAs.

'Delay might lead to the breach of the need for a speedy Tribunal hearing.'

4 Are clients who are detained in hospital visited sufficiently regularly to obtain instructions and inform them of progress?

Why does this matter?

- Communication with clients is particularly challenging in mental health cases. A client with mental health difficulties who is detained in hospital has limited opportunity to contact their legal adviser and may find giving instructions difficult.
- It is a requirement of Rule 2.02 of the Solicitors' Code of Conduct 2007 that clients be informed of the objectives, issues, steps to be taken and progress in their case. To ensure compliance with this Rule in mental health cases extensive communication will often be required.
- It is vital that the adviser maintains a good rapport and regular contact with the client so that over time detailed instructions on all aspects of the client's case can be taken.
- A client's instructions, and their clarity, may change during the case on account of changing mental health and/or the effects of medication.
- The client may need an interpreter and/or signer.
- Clients who are completely unable to give instructions raise important conduct issues. A client's position/condition in a mental health setting can be extremely fluid and important developments (positive or otherwise) can be missed without regular contact. However, there are no hard and fast rules and some clients will need more contact than others.

How can I check this on my files?

- Are the client's instructions, as recorded in attendance notes, clear and comprehensive?
- Does the number and frequency of attendance notes, correspondence and telephone calls to the client show that regular contact with the client is maintained?
- Are clients in hospital kept informed of the progress of their case in a timely manner?
- Every client will be different. Certain clients are likely to require more attendances, for example if they have a limited attention span. Other examples include:
  - Those with significant impairment;
  - Those whose mental health is fluctuating in the course of the case;
  - Those who are suffering side effects from changing medication;
  - Those who require interpreters or signers;
  - Those who facing lengthy reports to consider for a Tribunal;
  - Those who strongly contest many of the details of the Responsible Authority's case.
- If the client needs an interpreter or signer, has the hospital accepted that they should provide this service? If so will it be of sufficient frequency to

allow proper communication and can letters also be translated? In addition, is the client satisfied as to confidentiality arrangements?
- Has the Tribunal been informed of the attendance of an interpreter?
- Where clients are completely unable to give instructions, was the Law Society's guidance 'Representation before mental health Tribunals' considered and followed?

What will help?
- Record all visits to clients in hospital on attendance notes divided into instructions, advice and action to be taken.
- Send follow-up letters to clients in hospital confirming their specific instructions after each visit, together with the advice supplied, action agreed and confirmation of progress in the case; unless there is some special noted reason why the client cannot receive this information in writing.
- Monitor the local hospital policy regarding the use of interpreters, and if necessary consider complaint, contact with the Tribunal for a Direction or other remedy.
- If the client is a long way from your office consider referring the case to another solicitor who is nearer and who is likely to provide a better service more easily and be more flexible with regard to visits; although if a client is transferred to another hospital during the currency of a Tribunal application you will want to weigh this against the benefits of consistent representation.
- Where possible, generally attempt to ensure continuity in the adviser visiting the client.
- On a file that has gone to hearing (other than in Section 2 cases), after an initial visit, it is likely that you will need to visit the client several times prior to the hearing to take further instructions, and consider notes, section papers and Tribunal papers. The meeting to discuss Tribunal reports should (except in Section 2 cases) be a sufficient period before the hearing to allow the adviser to follow up any instructions from the client as to the content of the report (for example as to factual inaccuracy).
- Give specific consideration, once any written Tribunal decision is available, to the need to visit the client to discuss this and, if there is no discharge, the subsequent review and appeal possibilities (see also elsewhere in this guide).
- The Independent Mental Health Act Advocates (IMHA) may become increasing involved in certain clients' cases. They may, if appropriate, assist in communication and to this end may, with the client's agreement, be informed of the key advice that has been provided. The client should be made aware, however, that such advocates may not be bound by the same duty of confidentiality as solicitors are under Rule 4 of the Solicitors Conduct Rules 2007. In addition contact with IMHAs in this way will not be a substitute for 'face to face' meetings with the client.
- In Section 2 cases, attempt to obtain reports and meet with the client to discuss the reports before the day of the Tribunal.
- Confirm that the Tribunal is aware of the role of an interpreter and, if necessary, has allowed more time for the case.

'A client with mental health difficulties who is detained in hospital has limited opportunity to contact their legal advisor and may find giving instructions difficult.'

5 Has the client been advised of the merits of their case?

Why does this matter?

- Consideration should be given to advising the client of the strengths and weaknesses of their case. However, it is accepted that such advice may not always be easy to provide, especially if the client's mental state is fragile or changeable.
- As far as possible, the client's expectations regarding the prospects of success need to be managed.

How can I check this on my files?

- Do files show consideration of advice on merits has been given in an attendance note?
- Is consideration of the advice on merits updated to reflect changes in the case?
- Do files satisfy the quick 'pick up' test on this point 'ie' could another adviser pick up the file, without any prior knowledge, and understand what the client's instructions were and what advice had been given)?
- If the client is unable to read, or will be distressed by correspondence, has this been noted on the file?

What will help?

- If the adviser is unable to provide advice to the client (eg for lack of information), the adviser should consider confirming that fact to the client in writing. If the adviser considers that merits advice is inappropriate, at least for this stage in the case, then a note of this should be made on the file.
- Address this issue generally in Supervision.
- Ensure that advice on merits is assessed in File Review.
- Consider discussing merits at key points in the case, for example after the receipt of reports for the Tribunal.
- Where a client is unable to read easily or understand advice (or indeed provide instructions), additional meetings should be considered to discuss prospects of success generally.

'The client's expectations regarding the prospect of success need to be managed.'

6 Are letters and information sheets used appropriately?

Why does this matter?

- It is a requirement of Rule 2.02 of the Solicitors' Code of Conduct 2007 that clients are informed as to the: objectives agreed; issues; steps to be taken; and progress in their case.
- Standard letters can be useful in ensuring clients receive clear and consistent information. However such letters need to be tailored to the client's specific instructions and circumstances and comply with Rule 2.02. If they are not specific they could cause worry and confusion to clients.

- Similarly if information sheets are used, they need to be clearly applicable to the client's situation. Information sheets are not a substitute for tailored correspondence.

How can I check this on my files?

- Are letters to clients tailored to their individual circumstances?
- Do letters comply with the requirements of Rule 2.02?
- Have clients received letters containing unclear and inconsistent information, perhaps based on unedited standard letters?
- Do the information sheets given to clients contain any irrelevant information?
- If the client is unable to receive such correspondence, is this noted on the file?

What will help?

- Make sure that advice letters include a specific record of the client's instructions with some individual reference to the details of the client's case, the advice given and the action that the adviser is to take.
- Ensure that information or fact sheets relate to one type of case only. For example, an information sheet for Section 37/41 cases should not contain information on when a nearest relative can exercise powers of discharge.
- If the client is unable to receive such correspondence, has consideration been given to further meetings to advise and take instructions?

'Are standard letters to clients tailored to their individual circumstances?'

7 Has the client been advised about the powers and the procedure of the Tribunal?

Why does this matter?

- The client needs to be advised about the timescales of a case together with Tribunal powers and hearing procedures. If not advised the client will not know what to expect and may worry unnecessarily.
- Clients may forget or misunderstand advice given in face-to-face meetings; it is therefore important to confirm this advice in writing so that the client can refer to it at a later stage in the proceedings.

How can I check this on my files?

- Is there advice on Tribunal powers and procedures, including the role of the Medical Member visiting the client before the hearing, confirmed in attendance notes and letters to client?
- Is the written advice clear and specific to the client's case? In particular, check that it does not require the client to identify his/her case from a list of possible sections?
- Has the client been advised about how long the procedure should take, with clear explanations as to delays, for example due to adjournments?

What will help?

- Information sheets explaining the powers of the Tribunal and Tribunal procedure, appropriately tailored to the client's specific section.
- Advice re Tribunal powers/procedure etc. is important and is often best

explained in a face-to-face meeting, details of which should be recorded on file, and followed up by a letter confirming the discussion.
- Put headings in template letters to prompt advisers to record advice on Tribunal powers and procedures.

'Are clients advised on timescales, tribunal powers and hearing procedures (where appropriate)?'

8 Have the fundamental issues of the case been analysed appropriately as the case progresses?

Why does this matter?
- A lack of analysis of the fundamental issues relevant to the client's case may lead to incorrect or inappropriate advice being given to the client.
- There may be a critical lack of appropriate preparation work, including necessary enquiries, if this analysis is not carried out.
- There is a risk that cases may drift without direction, perhaps even leading to negligence.

How can I check this on my files?
- Do the attendance notes and client letters show that tailored advice is being given to the client?
- Have the nursing and medical records been considered at the beginning of the case, so that key issues are highlighted as soon as possible? Has the adviser considered all issues arising in the case, based especially on:
  - The client's instructions;
  - Examination of the medical records;
  - Examination of reports;
  - Enquiries from third parties.
- Do cases progress in a timely manner?

What will help?
- Consider drafting a simple case plan and keep it under review, especially after key events in the case such as a s117 meeting or receipt of Tribunal reports.
- Use standard attendance note pro forma, which require the action to be taken and the case objective to be identified.
- Consider other aspects of this Guidance.

'There may be a critical lack of appropriate preparation..... if this analysis is not carried out.'

9 Has the adviser promptly considered the use of independent experts to assist the client's case?

Why does this matter?
- Some cases are more likely to fail without independent expert evidence to challenge the Responsible Authority's evidence and/or to deal with gaps in that evidence.
- Failure to consider independent expert evidence may mean that central issues, including diagnosis, in the case are missed.
- Lack of expert evidence may mean that the case is ill prepared.

- Expert evidence may cover a range of issues. Medical experts can cover diagnosis, treatment, placement, risk and prognosis. Cognitive issues may need to be addressed by a psychologist. An occupational therapist may help on activities of daily living. A social worker may help on placement and funding issues.
- Prompt instruction of an independent expert may reduce the need for postponements in Tribunal hearings, or at least minimise the length of any such delays.

How can I check this on my files?

- Do advisers identify the central issues and consider what independent expert evidence (if any) might assist. Before instructing independent psychiatrists, do advisers consider:
  - Whether the Responsible Clinician's report contains (or is it known that it will contain or be likely to contain), a diagnosis about which there is any reasonable doubt and/or recommendations (for example, as to detention, treatment, transfer and/or aftercare) which are not acceptable to the patient?
  - If so, is it likely that an independent psychiatric report would assist the patient in achieving an outcome more acceptable to the patient in all the circumstances of the particular case, including as to treatment (possibly in another geographical area) and/or hospital leave?
- Are independent experts properly instructed, so that they adequately understand, the criteria for the client's detention and the relevant issues on which they have to comment? In particular have the following areas for instruction been considered:
  - Have the relevant discharge criteria applicable been met?
  - What is the present clinical diagnosis?
  - What further benefits (if any) would arise from further psychiatric or psychological medical treatment and the timescale on which these benefits can be expected to arise?
  - Could future treatment be given in a less restrictive setting and/or can any suggestions be made for alternative arrangements for care and treatment?
  - Could the client live in the community and manage self-care? (You should consider what support would be required);
  - What is the risk assessment model used by the responsible authority?
  - What is the prospect of future dangerous behaviour either to self or to others?
  - What details (if any) appear to have been omitted from other reports already served in the proceedings?
  - What are the meaning and implications of technical diagnosis, prognosis and treatment (including medication) set out in the attached reports/papers?
  - What is the source of reference materials used and can you cite these, and provide references and copies?
- Have the experts been provided with appropriate material to allow them to produce a robust report?

- Have the independent psychiatrists been advised as to their right of access to medical records and the client under the provisions of s76? If other independent experts require access to medical records, has the hospital's policy for access for such experts under the Data Protection Act 1998 been considered?
- Have the experts been instructed promptly when the view of the Responsible Authority and/or the Ministry of Justice has become clear?
- Are clients advised on the use of experts in attendance notes or advice letters?
- Has consideration been given to requesting attendance at the Tribunal by an independent expert whose report supports the client's application? If so have the client's instructions been taken on the prospect, if necessary, of a postponement in the Tribunal's hearing date?

What will help?

- Maintain an approved panel of experts, incorporating specialist experts for unusual cases.
- Review the reports produced by experts instructed.
- Ensure that instruction letters to experts are reviewed by mental health supervisors before being sent.
- On any checklist or pro forma case plan used, ensure that there is a prompt consideration of the instruction of experts.
- Consideration of medical records, prior to the receipt of reports, together with attendance at s117 or other case conferences, may assist to determine the basis for the Responsible Authority's opposition to discharge and enable early informed instruction of experts.

'Failure to consider independent expert evidence may mean that central issues.... of the case are missed.'

10 Has communication been established with third parties who may be able to assist the client?

Why does this matter?

- Communication with third parties is necessary in order to:
  - Proactively gather evidence to properly prepare and conduct a client's case.
  - Gather the information needed to advise the client on the strengths and weaknesses of their case.
- Key third parties include:
  - The Mental Health Act Administrator;
  - The Tribunal;
  - The Nearest Relative;
  - The Responsible Clinician (the 'RC');
  - The Ministry of Justice (in appropriate cases);
  - The Approved Mental Health Act Professional ('AMHP');
  - Hospital Managers;
  - Independent Mental Health Advocates;
  - Previous advisers.
- Contact with the Mental Health Act Administrator at the commencement

of the case will alert them to the application and the need for reports and, if necessary, to liaise with the Tribunal. It might also assist if the Administrator wishes to send reports straight to the adviser, rather than face a delay of going via the Tribunal.

- The Tribunal needs to be informed that the adviser is acting at an early stage, particularly if the client has made his or her own application, and subsequent monitored for their service of reports (see also elsewhere in this guide.) In addition the Tribunal may require information from the adviser by way of a listing questionnaire.
- In some cases the Nearest Relative can apply for discharge from section and can sometimes have rights to apply to the Tribunal for discharge. If a barring certificate has been issued by an RC the subsequent legal test for discharge following an application by a Nearest Relative in s3 cases is principally based on dangerousness.
- The Ministry of Justice, or the RC as appropriate, have the power to discharge the client from section prior to the Tribunal, or grant community leave. In restricted Tribunal cases it might be useful to know the progress of any community leave application made by the RC to the Ministry of Justice.
- The RC has to consider the convening of a 's117 meeting' in accordance with 27.7 of the Code of Practice in order to take reasonable steps to identify aftercare provisions if a Tribunal discharges the client.
- An AMHP will have important information as to plans for aftercare under s117, including any required accommodation and funding, together with any Needs Assessment completed under s47 NHS and Community Care Act 1990.
- Hospital Managers not only have a power to discharge from section in unrestricted sections but will also take evidence, both in written and oral form, from RC, key nurse and AMHP; usually the same individuals who will give evidence at a forthcoming Tribunal.
- Independent Mental Health Advocates are likely to become increasingly involved in clients' cases. If an IMHA is already involved with the client they may be a useful source of information and might have attended ward rounds, meeting with the RC etc. This may be especially helpful if the client's memory is poor.
- Advisers who have acted for the client previously may have invaluable earlier reports, background information and earlier Tribunal decisions. In addition, in cases where a criminal conviction, or finding of fact, is likely to be of significance to a subsequent Tribunal and/or the client disputes the facts surrounding the criminal proceedings, consideration should be given to obtaining the criminal papers from the appropriate previous adviser.
- Advisers currently acting for the client on other parallel matters, such as criminal or family proceedings, may be able to provide important information that is pertinent for the forthcoming Tribunal.

How can I check this on my files?

- Are discussions and/or correspondence with relevant third parties outlined above recorded?

- Are letters sent to RC and AMHP (and perhaps family and friends) raising issues about aftercare planning and support, or accommodation problems that the client might face etc? In particular is a letter sent to the RC asking if a s117 aftercare planning has been arranged?
- Are letters sent to the Nearest Relative, with the client's consent, asking for views regarding discharge from detention (where appropriate)?
- Has there been any attendance at significant aftercare planning meetings (as allowed by paragraph 27.12 Mental Health Act Code of Practice) or case conferences held in accordance with the provisions of paragraph 27.7 of the Code?
- Is there correspondence with the Tribunal, for example:
  - If an application is being sent on behalf of the client, checking that it has been received?
  - If an application has already been sent in by the client, is there a letter to the Tribunal confirming that the firm acts for the client and requesting reports when available?
  - Chasing any late reports which are in breach of Rule 32 of the Tribunal Rules.
- Is there a letter to the Mental Health Act Administrator confirming that the firm acts for the client in a forthcoming Tribunal and asking for assistance with any late reports?
- Is there an application to the Data Controller assigned under the Data Protection Act 1998 requesting access to medical and nursing records in preparation for Tribunal, or, if appropriate, to the authority supervising the client on a Community Treatment Order?
- Has there been consideration of attending a Hospital Managers' Hearing and/or the evidence obtained from these proceedings together with the details and reasons for the decision?
- Are there letters requesting reports and chasing up delays, for example, to Mental Health Act Administrators for both Managers and Tribunal hearing; or, in the case of the Tribunal, an application for a Direction for late reports under Rule 5?
- Are there letters to appropriate previous advisers asking for papers and/or ongoing advisers in other relevant matters?
- Are there any letters to Complaints Officers in hospitals (where appropriate)?
- Throughout has contact with other parties been with the client's consent?

What will help?

- Adopt a practice of routine enquiry with health professionals and other third parties, subject to the client's consent.
- The use of a checklist to ensure that all the relevant options for third party contact have been considered.
- The practice of using standardised letters to third parties may assist, for example to the RC regarding s117 aftercare planning meetings, but only if the letters are adapted to each case.
- Ensure that the firm has sufficient resources to monitor communication with third parties.

- Ensure these issues are covered in File Review, supervision and training.
- For guidance on issues of confidentiality in contacting third parties the following should be consulted:
  - Guide to the Professional Conduct of Solicitors 2007 (especially at principles 4.01 and 4.02);
  - The Law Society's guidance '– 'Representation before mental health Tribunals' ;
  - If necessary, the Ethics Guidance Helpline at the Law Society
- Consideration of the current Mental Health Act Code of Practice.

'Adopt a practice of routine enquiry with health professionals and other third parties, subject to the client's consent.'

11 Have the necessary nursing, medical and, if appropriate, Social Services or Community Health Team, records been obtained and considered?

Why does this matter?

- A failure to check the Section papers carefully may result in the client being detained unlawfully if there are errors on admission or renewal; this may lead to significant prejudice to the client and even negligence on the part of the adviser.
- In Community Treatment Order 'recall' cases the records will show whether procedure and time limits have been properly followed.
- Medical and nursing notes contain vital information that may assist in the preparation of the client's case and their early examination is likely to form a key element for an initial case plan, even before the Responsible Authority's reports have been received.
- Social services records and/or combined Community Mental Health Team Records may be particularly significant in CTO cases.
- Needs Assessments may be on either the medical or social services file and might be of significance for discharge plans.
- Records may contain factual inaccuracies and the client's instructions must be taken in good time so that the records can be corrected.
- Medical records are potentially before the Tribunal as evidence, particularly as the Medical Member of the Tribunal will have examined them, and the RC, AMHP and nurse will all be aware of them. Not to have examined them on behalf of the client is likely to put her/his case at a disadvantage.

How can I check this on my files?

- Are copies of section papers on the file?
- Alternatively, is there a note on the file confirming that section papers have been considered with relevant details recorded on the file?
- In CTO cases, have recall papers been checked?
- Are there detailed file notes and/or summaries of the medical and nursing records on the file?
- Have the medical and nursing records been applied for and considered at an early stage in the case and subsequently close to the time of the

Tribunal's Medical Member's assessment? If there is doubt as to the identity of the Data Controller, or required procedures for access to records, has this been clarified?

- Have there been any attempts by the hospital to restrict access under s7 Data Protection Act 1998 and the Data Protection (Subjects Access Modification)(Order) 2000? If so, has the guidance set out in Dorset Healthcare NHS Foundation Trust v MHRT (2009) UKUT 4 (AAC) been considered with, if necessary, an application made to the Tribunal to obtain full access under the provisions of Rule 5 of the Tribunal Rules?
- Are there attendance notes on the file recording discussions with the client regarding medical and nursing records?
- Does the file include a letter to the client confirming the client's instructions regarding medical and nursing records?
- If relevant, has an application been made for Social Services or Community Mental Health Team records; for example if there are contested details of incidents involving an AMHP in the community prior to detention or in relation to an ongoing Community Treatment Order?

What will help?

- Ensure that the identity of relevant Data Controllers is known, together with any special forms or procedures they wish to use.
- Ensure that requests to access the client's records are made under the provisions of s7 Data Protection 1998 as soon as possible.
- Ensure you promptly discuss medical and nursing records with the client as part of taking instructions.
- If there are difficulties in access to medical and nursing records, consider applying the procedure within *Dorset Healthcare NHS Foundation Trust v MHRT* (2009) UKUT 4 (AAC); making an application under Rule 5 to the Tribunal; and/or complaining to the Chief Executive of the relevant hospital Trust.

'Medical records are potentially before the Tribunal as evidence......not to have examined them on behalf of the client is likely to put his/her case at a disadvantage.'

12 Have the client's Tribunal reports and statements been considered promptly on receipt?

Why does this matter?

- Clinician, Nursing, (including Supervisor in Community Treatment Order cases), and Social Circumstances reports should be obtained and considered well before the Tribunal hearing to ensure that there is time to take instructions and to take any further action that may be required. In section 2 cases, reports should still be obtained as early as possible, together with the section application and medical recommendations.
- The statement from the Responsible Authority, or Ministry of Justice, will contain critical information about the client.
- Any statement from the victim in a relevant case made under the Domestic Violence, (Crime and Victims) Act 2004, as amended by the Mental Health Act 2007 may not comply with any relevant Tribunal Practice or

specific Directions, or may otherwise be inappropriate. In addition, the client may need to be further advised on the role of such statements and the rights of victims in general.

- Reports or statements may contain factual inaccuracies, which may prejudice the client's case, if they remain uncorrected or not examined against medical records or any previous reports used as a source of information. The issue of inaccurate earlier reports and 'institutional folklore' used in Tribunal reports was referred to as a particular area of concern in the case of R (AN&DJ) v MHRT & Others [2005] EWHC 587 (Admin) paragraph 129.
- Reports and statements from the Responsible Authority or Ministry of Justice, may not be sufficiently comprehensive, and in particular not comply with the provisions of the relevant Tribunal Practice Direction. If necessary a request for a Direction under Rule 5, the Tribunal Rules will need to be quickly considered.
- Clinician reports may not be from a qualified doctor. If the client is receiving medication this may not be adequate for evidential purposes. Again a Direction may need to be sought urgently from the Tribunal.
- Social Circumstances reports may raise issues such as funding, placement and disputed catchment area responsibility. If the AMHP report writer is not an appropriate social worker they might not be in the position to provide the required evidence to the Tribunal. In addition issues of perceived risks in the community, including the views of Multi Agency Public Protections Arrangements (MAPPA), and 'restricted areas' in restricted cases, may require urgent further investigation. Reports and statements may contain material which is not disclosed under the provisions of Rule 14, which may require urgent consideration and action.
- Subsequent to receipt and instructions on these reports, independent reports will have to be promptly considered, (or re-considered, if this was done earlier) subsequent to an earlier review of medical records or attendance at a s117 meeting.

'Reports or statements may contain factual inaccuracies, which may prejudice the client's case, if they remain uncorrected or not examined against medical records.'

How can I check this on my files?

- Are there file notes detailing perusal of the reports and statements promptly after their receipt? Are the reports and statements sufficiently comprehensive, and in particular do they comply with the provisions of the relevant Tribunal Practice Direction? In addition is there material not to be disclosed under Rule 14? In either case has a request for a Direction under Rule 5 of the Tribunal Rules been considered?
- Do files show that the client has promptly given specific instructions on issues raised in the reports/statements?
- Has action been taken to address issues arising from the reports in accordance with the client's instructions? Have reports been cross-referenced with notes from records to check for inaccuracies, inconsistencies or omissions? If necessary, have steps been taken to obtain earlier reports if references to them are disputed by the client?
- In applicable cases under the provision of the Domestic Violence (Crime

and Victims) Act 2004 the victim and/or his or her family, may have made a statement. Does the file show that urgent inquires have been made as to whether they wish attendance at the Tribunal hearing and if so the response of the Tribunal to this, including the guarantee of medical confidentiality and whether a Direction is to be made under Rule 38(5)? In addition, does the file indicate that the client has been fully advised as to the role of the victim(s), the Tribunal's arrangements for such victims and the role of the victim's evidence? Has also the latest Tribunal policy on victim's statements been considered? Finally, does the file show whether necessary consideration has been given for a further application for a Direction, or further Direction, from the Tribunal if this is appropriate regarding such arrangements?

- Has the instruction of relevant independent experts been considered subsequent to consideration of these reports and instructions from the client?

What will help?

- Ensure the Tribunal office is pressed for early service of the reports and statements in accordance with the Tribunal Rules. If necessary seek a Direction from the Regional Chair of the Tribunal under the provisions of Rule 5 of the Tribunal Rules if a breach of service under Rule 32 has occurred.
- Ask hospital administrators to send reports to you direct, when they are sent to Tribunal.
- Ensure advisers have sufficient time to visit clients promptly on receipt of reports.
- Ensure early authority is agreed to access medical records, and that necessary earlier papers and reports have been obtained from previous advisers.

'Are there file notes detailing perusal of the reports at an early stage in the case?'

13 Has there been thorough preparation for Tribunal hearings?

Why does this matter?

- Failing thoroughly to prepare for a Tribunal hearing is likely to lead to an unfocussed approach and a poorly presented case.
- Without thorough preparation, fundamental issues in the case are likely to be missed.
- Poor preparation is likely to lead to ineffective cross-examination of health professionals.
- Recent legal developments might have occurred relevant to the client's case, and perhaps his or her liberty. Failure to apply these might result in negligence.
- The Tribunal may require information about the case by way of a listing questionnaire.

How can I check this on my files?

- Is the case objective and action to be taken kept under continuous review as the case progresses, for example after significant events, such as greater community leave, attendance at a s117 meeting, consideration of

medical records or Tribunal reports, together with further instructions from the client?
- Do advisers read through the file, professional reports and medical notes before any hearing?
- Is a case analysis or skeleton argument prepared prior to any hearing, noting that the Tribunal will formally require a skeleton for any Human Rights Act argument?
- Is there evidence of thorough preparation, for example, in the form of notes of questions prepared in advance of the hearing; contact with relevant third parties before the hearing and evidence that medical notes together with section papers have been perused?
- Are pre-hearing discussions held with the client about the issues and the approach to be taken at the hearing?
- Where appropriate, has consideration been given to the use of independent experts to assist the client's case? If so has their attendance at the Tribunal been considered, along with need for any adjournment? Has this, in turn, been discussed with the client?
- Has there been consideration of attendance at a s117 pre-discharge after-care meeting, given that these meetings should take place before Tribunals and will be of considerable importance in some cases?
- Has relevant case law been applied?

What will help?
- Use an attendance note pro forma, which requires the adviser to identify the case objective and any action to be taken.
- Use a pre-hearing checklist to prepare for Tribunal hearings.
- Prepare skeleton arguments for Tribunal hearings.
- Confirm, if possible in writing, the approach agreed with the client.
- Ensure that advisers read through the file, professional reports and medical and other notes before hearings.
- Ensure that the firm subscribes and/or has access to latest relevant case law developments, together the latest edition of standard reference books such as Jones' Mental Health Act Manual.
- As necessary, contact LSC Specialist Advice Line.

'Without thorough preparation, fundamental issues in the case are likely to be missed.'

14 Have all necessary referrals been made in an appropriate way?

Why does this matter?
- Clients with mental health problems are more likely to have other significant issues for which they may need specialist help from legal practitioners in fields such as Welfare Benefits, Debt, Housing and Crime.
- Clients may need referral to the Independent Mental Health Advocacy service for issues which are not appropriate for legal representation.
- If the adviser has no expertise in other areas of law, a failure to make an effective referral to another adviser or firm is likely to prejudice the client.

How can I check this on my files?

- Is there evidence (in attendance notes or correspondence) that the client has raised issues that require specialist help?
- Do the client's social circumstances, clinical and/or nursing reports raise issues that require specialist help?
- Does the file show discussions with the Nearest Relative and/or other family and friends about the possibility that the client may require assistance on other issues?
- Has the client forthcoming issues where advocacy assistance would be appropriate?

What will help?

- Include questions designed to highlight the potential for any such problems into an initial questionnaire or pro forma.
- Keep an up to date list of local advisers who will be able to take on referral work.
- Be aware of the details of the relevant IMHA service.

> ***'Clients with mental health problems are more likely to have other significant issues for which they need specialist help.'***

15 Have the necessary steps been taken to represent children under 18 years at the Tribunal?

Why does this matter?

- Children are especially vulnerable if detained in hospital under the Mental Health Act.
- The relevant law can be complex inter alia with regards to the interaction with the Children Act 1989 and Mental Capacity Act 2005.
- New legal safeguards have recently been introduced to assist in the protection of children in hospital, the operation of which will need to be confirmed.
- The Local Authority in care cases, or the High Court in wardship cases, can be involved as the Nearest Relative.
- The Tribunal has established a specialist Child and Adolescent Mental Health Services (CAMHS) panel, at least one of whom should sit in such hearings.
- Other advisers may also be representing the client on other matters which may impact on the client's case.

How can I check this on my files?

- Have sufficient visits been made to see the client?
- Is correspondence to the client suitable, bearing in mind especially age?
- Has the Tribunal and/or Mental Health Act Administrator, correctly applied the amended law on annual Tribunal references?
- Has the hospital ensured that the accommodation where the child is detained is 'suitable' in terms of the standards proposed under s131A, with which hospitals are encouraged to comply even before formal implementation?
- Have enquiries have been made as to the identity of the Nearest Relative; to include the possibly of the Local Authority and/or the High Court?

- Has the identity of those with Parental Responsibility been established?
- If the Local Authority is the Nearest Relative and/or the child is in care, has the Authority made steps to visit the client in accordance with s116?
- Has the identity of the relevant social worker(s)been established?
- Is an alternative placement under s25 of the Children Act 1989 relevant?
- Has a case conference been organised before the Tribunal and attendance by the adviser been requested?
- Does the Tribunal contain at least one member of the specialist CAMHS panel established to handle children's cases?
- Has Chapter 36 of the Code of Practice been generally considered?
- Has the Law Society guidance 'Representation before mental health Tribunals' been considered?
- Have capacity issues been addressed, in accordance with the principles set down in the Law Society's guidance together with, as appropriate, the Mental Capacity Act 2005 and 'Gillick' competence issues (*Gillick v West Norfolk and Wisbech Area Health Authority* [1985] 3 All ER 402 (HL).
- Has access to the relevant medical records been obtained, especially with respect to capacity issues, or is the application of the procedure set down in *Dorset Healthcare NHS Foundation Trust v MHRT* (2009) UKUT 4 (AAC) appropriate with, if necessary, an application made to the Regional Tribunal Judge to obtain full access under the provisions of Rule 5 of the Tribunal Rules?
- Has contact been made, with consent as appropriate, with any other advisers involved with the client? If so is it possible to receive details of pertinent reports and/or assessments regarding accommodation and/or family situation together with other legal proceedings which might be relevant for Tribunal?
- Has there been consideration of whether a referral, particularly to a family and/or children's adviser, is required?
- Has an adviser of sufficient experience been allocated to the case?

What will help?

- Ensure that advisers have sufficient training in this area.
- Close supervision of the case, if a supervisor does not have direct conduct of the matter.
- Liaison with an adviser experienced in Children's law, if appropriate by way of a referral, or an existing adviser already acting for the child.

'Children are especially vulnerable if detained in hospital under the Mental Health Act.'

16 Have adequate steps been taken to explain the Tribunal's written reasons; their adequacy; the right of review and appeal together with confirmation of the client's current legal status?

Why does this matter?

- • Subsequent to the implementation of Rule 11(4)(a) of the Tribunal Procedure Rules 2008, Tribunal decisions are not sent to the client.
- Final outcome visits and letters to clients should explain the Tribunal's decision, their legal status, time limits for future applications and advice

on the grounds for a review of the Tribunal's decision under Tribunal Rules 44, 45, including, as appropriate permission to apply to the Upper Tribunal under Rule 46 in additional to any prospect of judicial review.

- If clients are not advised of the above issues they may be unsure of their legal position and their right to take the matter further.
- Clients will not be able to make informed decisions about the next steps in their case, including any right to s117 aftercare if discharged from section.

How can I check this on my files?

- Has a visit taken place, or at least consideration of such a visit, to discuss with the client the implications of the Tribunal decision
- Do final outcome letters to clients:
  - Have the Tribunal's written decision enclosed?
  - Accurately reflect the Tribunal's written decision?
  - Explain the Tribunal's reasons for their decision?
  - Advise upon the legality of the decision and the subsequent appeal rights?
- Are clients assisted and represented, if appropriate, in any application for review of a decision to the First Tier Tribunal and to the Upper Tribunal?
- Are clients given advice on continued detention (where appropriate) and of entitlement to aftercare if they are discharged?
- Are clients advised when further applications can be made to the Tribunal or hospital managers as appropriate?
- Are clients given advice on aftercare, especially if they are discharged from detainability?

What will help?

- Consider whether clients should be given post-hearing advice face to face particularly if they remain in hospital, on or off section. This might be particularly appropriate if the client is unlikely to understand the decision and its implications, including the prospect of a review and/or appeal of the decision.
- Put headings in template letters to prompt advisers to record Tribunal's decision and post hearing advice.
- Ensure that final outcome letters to the client explain Tribunal decision reasons and appeal rights, It is not sufficient simply to quote from the decision; further comment is needed.

'Ensure that final outcome letters to the client explain Tribunal decision reasons and appeal rights.'

17 Differences between Welsh and English Law – Appendix

This appendix was written to complement the Mental Heath guide Edition 3 to outline the differences between Welsh and English law in the practice of Mental Health law.

Prior to 3 November 2008 the Mental Health Review Tribunal (MHRT) for Wales in Cardiff was a regional office of the Mental Health Review Tribunal system for England and Wales. The MHRT in Wales had a degree of autonomy, as it had become, administratively, a part of the Welsh Assembly, and it had established its own ways of working, within the overall Tribunal system. However its functions were governed by the Mental Health Review Tribunal Rules 1983 and the Mental Health Act Code of Practice was for England and Wales.

From 3 November 2008 the MHRT in England was absorbed into the Tribunal Service and became the First-tier Tribunal (Mental Health), part of the Health, Education and Social Care chamber, otherwise known as the Mental Health Tribunal (MHT). The Tribunal, Courts and Enforcement Act 2007 that had introduced these changes, had no impact upon the MHRT for Wales, which remains as a stand alone, independent judicial body governing the Mental Health Act appeal process in Wales.

This has particular significance for those who represent patients in both jurisdictions, because although the law is the same (Mental Health Act 1983 as subsequently amended) its procedural implementation is different in Wales. At its simplest, even the statutory forms have different reference letters and numbers.

Representatives should be familiar with the Mental Health Act Code of Practice, published by the Department of Health, but cross-border representatives need also to be familiar with the Mental Health Act Code of Practice for Wales, published by the Welsh Assembly, available in English and Welsh from the MHRT for Wales website at www.wales.nhs.uk/sites3/page.cfm?orgid=816, or via the MHT website www.mhrt.org.uk.

There are no differences of great substance between the two Codes, but there are differences eg the Chapter 1 Guiding Principles in Wales are expressed differently to those in the English Code, although they have the same purpose. The Welsh Code is also set out very differently to the English Code.

Representatives also need to be able to refer to the MHRT for Wales Rules 2008 (SI 2008 No 2705) whereas the MHT is governed by the Tribunal Procedure (First Tier Tribunal) (Health Education and Social Care Chamber) Rules 2008 and subsequent practice directions. Two differences of which to be particularly mindful, although there are others as well, are that the MHRT for Wales do not require the production of a nursing report on an application concerning an inpatient, and the MHRT for Wales Rules make no provision for the Tribunal to set aside the whole or part of one of its own decisions (in contrast to the MHT rule 45).

There are also differences in the approach to case management at the MHRT for Wales of which Representatives, and Peer Reviewers, need to be aware. Case management powers are set out in Rules 5 and 6, in both jurisdictions, but traditionally the MHRT for Wales has always been more reluctant to issue formal directions eg in relation to late reports, preferring to use more informal methods of report chasing, including as the last resort, a complaint letter to the Director/Chair/Chief Executive of the relevant body.

For those representing detained patients in England or Wales, the quality issues and standards to be achieved, in terms of file management, are the same. Those who represent in both countries may, at points, need also to demonstrate on files their awareness of the differences between the two.

Neil P Confrey
April 2011

Mental Health Peer Review Panel Members (as of April 2011)

Sarah Burke
Ian Campbell
Richard Charlton – guide's editor
Neil Confrey
Maureen Grenville
Richard Nicholas
Karen Walton

C4 MINISTRY OF JUSTICE/TRIBUNAL SERVICE (MENTAL HEALTH) GUIDANCE[1]

This guidance has been agreed between the Ministry of Justice Mental Health Unit, the Tribunal Service, Mental Health, and the Tribunal Judiciary. It sets out the respective roles and responsibilities of those involved in hearings by the Mental Health Tribunal of references by the Secretary of State for Justice (SSJ) and applications from restricted patients in England and Wales, so that all parties are aware of their obligations and the level of service they can expect from the other parties. The guidance is set out in three parts: Pre-hearing; Hearing & Post-hearing.

The status of this document is non-statutory guidance. It will be revised annually. Additional copies of this document are available in both electronic and hard copy format from the Ministry of Justice, Mental Health Unit and the Tribunal Service, Mental Health website.

Section 1: Statutory framework

This is covered by the Mental Health Act 1983 (ss69–75), First Tier Tribunal (HESC) Rules 2008 and the practice directions to those Rules. Any reference to the Act in this guidance should be taken as a reference to the Mental Health Act 1983, unless otherwise specified. Any reference to the Rules should be taken as a reference to the Tribunal Procedure (First Tier Tribunal) (Health, Education and Social Care Chamber) Rules 2008 unless otherwise specified.

Section 2: Pre-hearing

Detained Restricted patients

2.1 **Responsible Authority's obligations** – Rule 32(6) states that the Responsible Authority must send or deliver a statement containing the information and documents required by the relevant practice direction to the Tribunal so that it is received by the Tribunal as soon as practicable and in any event within 3 weeks after the responsible authority received a copy of the application or reference.

2.2 'Responsible Authority' means the Managers of the hospital in which the patient is detained (see Rule 1). The Responsible Authority's statement comprises medical, social circumstances and nursing reports which conform to the requirements of Paragraphs B-F of the Practice Direction.

2.3 If the patient is a restricted patient, the Responsible Authority must also send a copy of the statement to the Secretary of State (Rule 32(7))

2.4 **Tribunal office's obligations** – Rule 32(3) obliges the tribunal to send the Ministry of Justice a copy of the documentation it has received from the Responsible Authority in respect of a restricted patient.

2.5 Rule 37(3) requires the Tribunal to give reasonable notice of the time and

1 At the time of going to press this guidance was due to be amended, with a new version expected in mid-2015.

place of the hearing (including any adjourned or postponed hearing), and any changes to the time date and place of the hearing to each party entitled to attend the hearing, including the Secretary of State. The period of notice must be at least 14 days except for those reasons stated in Rule 37(4)(b). It is important that the tribunal office notify the Ministry of Justice as soon as possible once a hearing date is set. This information will be sent electronically to the MHU Tribunal Correspondence mailbox.

2.6 **Secretary of State's obligations** – Rule 32(7) requires the Secretary of State, on receipt of the Responsible Authority's statement, to send a statement of any further relevant information to the Tribunal as soon as practicable and in any event –

(a) in proceedings under section 75(1) of the Mental Health Act 1983, within 2 weeks after the Secretary of State received the relevant authority's statement; or

(b) Otherwise, within 3 weeks after the Secretary of State received the Responsible Authority's statement.

The Secretary's of State's statement must contain the information set out in Section G of the practice direction. This comprises

(i) written comments he wishes to make upon the statement he has received from the Responsible Authority together with any further information relevant to the application as may be available to him and

(ii) the information required in paragraph 21 of the practice direction.

Such reports will be sent electronically to the Tribunal Service, Mental Health restricted mailbox with an electronic copy of previous convictions where necessary.

2.7 The Ministry of Justice's target is to provide the Secretary of State's response to the Responsible Authority's statement within the statutory deadline in 100% of cases. The MHU gives very high priority to the delivery of that target. The Tribunal office should expect that, save for exceptional circumstances, it will receive the SSJ's statement within the statutory deadline. The Ministry of Justice accepts that, if it has failed to provide the SSJ's response to the Responsible Authority's statement within the 21 day statutory deadline, then the Tribunal is entitled to proceed without it (subject always to the Tribunal being satisfied that the Responsible Authority's statement has been received by the SSJ). The Ministry of Justice accepts that an electronically generated acknowledgment of the Responsible Authority's statement sent to the dedicated Tribunal communication email address, or a fax receipt confirmation, will constitute sufficient evidence of receipt by the SSJ.

Late or non-submission of Responsible Authority statements for detained restricted patients

2.8 This can lead to unnecessary delays and adjournments which prejudice the interests of justice. Attention is drawn to the overriding objective contained in Rule 2 of the Rules and the obligation imposed by Rule 2(4) on all parties to help further the overriding objective and to co-operate with the Tribunal generally.

2.9 Rule 7 states that failure to comply with the Rules does not make tribunal proceedings void. If a party has failed to comply with a requirement in these Rules, a practice direction or a direction, the Tribunal may take such action as it considers just.

2.10 **Role of the Tribunal office** – The Tribunal office will chase the Responsible Authority for missing or late reports. The Tribunal will, on its own initiative, make such directions as may be necessary to ensure the prompt provision of the required documents, and the Ministry of Justice is under no obligation to request such directions.

Submission of late Responsible Authority statements to the Ministry of Justice – requests for postponement or adjournment of hearing

2.11 Tribunals will sometimes request a Ministry of Justice response to a Responsible Authority statement that has been submitted less than 3 weeks prior to the hearing date.

2.12 **Position of the Ministry of Justice** – Under the Rules and Practice Direction the Ministry of Justice, although required to respond as soon as practicable, has a maximum of 3 weeks in which to respond to the Responsible Authority statement (2 weeks in the case of Secretary of State references following a recall). The Ministry of Justice, however, fully appreciates the need to avoid adjournments, if at all possible, as they not only cause additional work for all parties involved but can also be unfair to the patient. The Ministry of Justice will make all reasonable efforts to assist the Tribunal in preventing the need for adjournment by providing its response to the Responsible Authority's statement even in cases where this has been provided late.

2.13 It will not always be possible for the Ministry of Justice to respond to every Responsible Authority statement that is submitted late. In particular, this may not be achievable where:
(i) the Ministry of Justice assessment is that the patient poses a potentially serious risk if discharged; and
(ii) the late report increases the likelihood that the tribunal may discharge; and
(iii) the time available does not allow the Ministry of Justice to submit a properly considered response.

2.14 A key determining factor will be the amount of time the Ministry of Justice has to consider the late report before the date of the hearing. Where the Ministry of Justice has at least 5 working days in which to consider the late Responsible Authority statement it will use all reasonable endeavours to provide a response. The Mental Health Unit have agreed that it would be most effective if the TSMH telephone a Higher Executive Officer at the MHU no later than 3 days before a hearing if the SSJ 's statement has not been received, to ascertain whether it is possible for the statement to be prepared in time for the hearing.

2.15 Where the hearing is in respect of a Section 75(1) reference where the Secretary of State has recently recalled the patient to hospital, the provision of a response, even at short notice, will receive greater priority.

Submission of documents other than the Responsible Authority's statement to the Ministry of Justice

2.16 Some supplementary reports, not forming part of the Responsible Authority's statement, are being submitted to the Tribunal only days before the hearing and even on the day of the hearing itself. These are typically either independent reports commissioned by the patient's representatives, victims' statements or addendum reports from the patient's care team. Rule 32(3) provides that that the Tribunal shall send a copy of all such documents to the Ministry of Justice in the case of restricted patients. A failure by the Tribunal to supply copies of such documents to the Ministry of Justice might well give rise to a right to challenge the decision under Rule 45. Tribunal panels should satisfy themselves that the Ministry of Justice has been sent all the documentation. This information should be contained in the 'handover sheet' supplied to the Tribunal Judge with the papers in each case.

2.17 There is no obligation under the Rules on the Ministry of Justice to comment on each supplementary report. Consequently a Tribunal may proceed in the absence of Ministry of Justice comments on supplementary reports and documents, as long as the Tribunal is satisfied that they have been sent to the Ministry of Justice. The Ministry of Justice accepts that an electronically generated acknowledgment of any report sent to the dedicated Tribunal communication email address or a fax receipt confirmation will constitute sufficient evidence of receipt by the SSJ.

2.18 The Secretary of State may however provide a supplementary statement in respect of any further reports that are received if he has any relevant additional information or opinion to offer. The Ministry of Justice response may be an oral, emailed or faxed statement. The statement will contain the patient's name, the Tribunal office and the Ministry of Justice's reference and also identify the reports to which the email or fax refers.

Requests for adjournments by the Ministry of Justice

2.19 The Ministry of Justice may, in common with other parties, make an application to adjourn a Tribunal hearing at any time it sees fit.

No notice evidence

2.20 The approach to 'no notice' oral evidence which directly contradicts the written evidence previously presented eg the Responsible Clinician now supporting discharge counter to his/her previous written reports is a matter for the exercise of judicial discretion. The Tribunal will consider each case on its facts bearing in mind the overriding objective, relevant case law and the power to set aside decisions contained in Rule 45.

Legal representation

2.21 Under Rule 11 any of the parties may be represented at the tribunal hearing. The Ministry of Justice very rarely seeks representation, but will notify the Tribunal at the earliest opportunity where it wishes the Secretary of State to be represented, especially if it needs to request a postponement to instruct Counsel.

Conditionally discharged restricted patients

2.22 **The Secretary of State's obligations** – Where the patient is a conditionally discharged restricted patient, (as defined in the Mental Health Act 1983) the Secretary of State must send or deliver a statement containing the information and documents required by the relevant practice direction to the Tribunal so that it is received by the Tribunal as soon as practicable and in any event within 6 weeks after the Secretary of State received a copy of the application or a request from the Tribunal (Rule 32(4)). It is the Ministry of Justice's responsibility to chase up late or missing reports in respect of conditionally discharged restricted patients.

2.23 As with detained restricted patients, the Ministry of Justice target is to provide the Secretary of State's statement on time in 100% of cases and MHU gives high priority to the delivery of that target. The Secretary of State's statements will be emailed to the Tribunal Service, Mental Health restricted mailbox.

Section 3: The hearing

Role of the Tribunal Service, Mental Health in respect of detained restricted patients

3.1 The role of the Tribunal Service, Mental Health in the case of restricted patients is limited to determining whether or not the statutory criteria for detention in hospital continue to be met, and if not, whether discharge should be absolute or subject to conditions. Tribunal panel members should be aware of the case law relating to restricted patients, and the limitations on their role: for example in contrast to the powers under s72, Tribunals hearing restricted cases have no power to make statutory recommendations in respect of leave or transfer to another hospital. Guidance on the law is given in *Mental Health Tribunals – Essential Cases* (ed. Kris Gledhill) and Richard Jones' *Mental Health Act Manual*, copies of which are supplied to all Tribunal Judges. It is the responsibility of each Tribunal Judge to be familiar with the recent case law developments and to take advantage of the training opportunities offered by the Tribunal Service, Mental Health. In addition guidance on common problems arising in restricted cases is given on the TSMH website.

Re-convened hearings following a deferred conditional discharge

3.2 The House of Lords judgment in *R (IH) v Secretary of State for Health* [2003] UKHL 59 established that a deferred conditional discharge is a provisional decision which the tribunal may re-visit at any point prior to effecting conditional discharge. This means that the Tribunal can rescind their earlier discharge decision, if they subsequently find the criteria for detention are met. Equally, they can discharge absolutely, vary the conditions or uphold the original, provisional, decision.

3.3 Tribunals can, and should, re-convene to chase progress where a deferred conditional discharge is pending. In doing so, however, the Tribunal must not defer the conditional discharge to a specific date. There is no power to do so.

3.4 Where a tribunal re-convenes following the provisional decision to grant a deferred conditional discharge, the tribunal members should, as far as possible, be the same as those who originally considered the application.

Ministry of Justice response to further reports where a deferred conditional discharge decision is pending

3.5 The Ministry of Justice is under no obligation to respond to any further reports that the Tribunal receives following a provisional decision to grant a deferred conditional discharge. The Ministry of Justice will, of course, consider, in every case whether a response is necessary. The Ministry of Justice will normally only offer comments where the further reports raise issues about the patient's detainability. The Ministry of Justice will not normally comment where the further reports are simply detailing progress in meeting the provisional conditions imposed by the tribunal, but do not raise any issues regarding the patient's suitability for conditional discharge.

Attendance of Ministry of Justice as observers

3.6 From time to time staff from the Mental Health Unit of the Ministry of Justice may wish to attend a hearing as observers. Mental Health Unit will request permission to observe at the time of drafting the Secretary of State's statement. They will write to the tribunal office providing them with the name(s) of the proposed observer(s). Attendance at the tribunal as an observer is, of course, subject to the patient's consent, which can be withdrawn at any time. It should also be made clear to the tribunal that those attending from the Ministry of Justice do so solely as observers and should not be called to give evidence.

Section 4: Post-hearing

Notification of decisions

4.1 Rule 41 requires the tribunal to notify all parties, including the Secretary of State of the decision, with reasons, in writing within 7 days of the hearing. The Ministry of Justice will take up with the tribunal offices those cases where no decision has been received within seven days and if no notification has been given, will send a formal request.

4.2 Where a patient has been granted an absolute, conditional or deferred conditional discharge, the Tribunal office will notify the Ministry of Justice within 24 hours of the hearing. This information will be sent electronically to the MHU Tribunal Correspondence mailbox.

4.3 It is especially important that the Ministry of Justice is notified as soon as possible where the patient is discharged conditionally. The Ministry of Justice has a statutory responsibility for the management of conditionally discharged restricted patients. It is self evident that MHU cannot carry out this function unless it knows that the patient has been discharged, under what conditions and under whose supervision.

4.4 This applies equally to confirmation that the conditions have been met following a deferred conditional discharge.

Deferred conditional discharges

4.5 Where the tribunal defers a conditional discharge, the Ministry of Justice has no role either in meeting the conditions or determining whether the conditions are met. It is for the tribunal to decide whether or not its conditions have been met.

4.6 Where the tribunal defers a conditional discharge and there is fresh evidence that the patient meets the criteria for detention in hospital or where it appears that the discharge conditions cannot be met, the Ministry of Justice may write to the Tribunal and ask them to reconsider their decision at a reconvened hearing before the conditional discharge takes place.

Deferred conditional discharges & automatic referrals

4.7 Under section 71(2) of the Mental Health Act 1983 the Secretary of State for Justice is obliged to refer to the tribunal the case of any detained restricted patient that has not been considered by the tribunal for three years. This applies equally to those patients who have received a deferred conditional discharge but where three years have elapsed without the conditions being met or the tribunal re-convening to consider the case. Section 71(2) refers to the case not being considered "whether on his own application or otherwise, within the last three years".

4.8 Where the tribunal has not revisited a provisional decision on discharge for three years, that delay triggers referral under section 71(2).

Section 74 recommendations in respect of prisoners transferred to hospital under the MHA

4.9 Where a tribunal makes a recommendation under section 74 in respect of a prisoner transferred to hospital, the tribunal office must inform the Ministry of Justice immediately of the recommendation decision. The Secretary of State must consider without delay his response to the recommendation.

Section 5: General

Complaints

5.1 This section does not cover complaints about members of the Tribunal Service, Mental Health. Any such complaints are subject to separate procedures and should be directed through to the Customer Service Manager who will notify the relevant Principal Judge.

5.2 Complaints about either the First-tier Tribunal (Mental Health), or the Tribunal Service, Mental Health office should, in the first instance be directed to the Senior Operations Manager of the tribunal office.

5.3 Where the complainant is the Ministry of Justice, the complaint should be referred through a Grade 7 Casework Manager in the Mental Health Unit.

Correspondence

5.4 All correspondence between the tribunal office and the Ministry of Justice must quote both the tribunal reference (where it is known) and the Ministry of Justice "MNP" reference (where it is known). It would also be helpful if any correspondence also quoted the patient's date of birth.

C5 SECTION 17 LEAVE OF ABSENCE GUIDANCE[1]

Minstry of Justice (Mental Health Casework Section) Guidance Section 17 – leave of absence

LEGAL PROVISIONS

1. Section 41(3)(c)(i) of the Mental Health Act 1983 requires a responsible clinician to obtain consent from the Secretary of State before granting section 17 leave to a restricted patient. No patient may leave the hospital or unit[2] named on the authority for detention without such consent.[3]

POLICY ON SECTION 17 LEAVE FOR RESTRICTED PATIENTS

2. The Secretary of State recognises that well thought out leave, which serves a definable purpose and is carefully and sensitively executed, has an important part to play treating and rehabilitating restricted patients. It also provides valuable information to help responsible clinicians, and the Secretary of State, in managing the patient in hospital, and to all parties, including the Tribunal, when considering discharge into the community.
3. To help responsible clinicians provide all the information required by the Secretary of State to assess escorted or unescorted leave proposals, a leave request form is available on www.justice.gov.uk and at Annex A. Responsible clinicians should also submit any additional information that they consider would assist the Secretary of State to reach a decision.
4. The Secretary of State expects leave programmes to be designed and conducted in such a way as to preserve public safety and, where appropriate, respect the feelings and fears of victims and others who may have been affected by the offences.
5. The Secretary of State will often consent to programmes which give responsible clinicians an element of discretion as to leave arrangements. However, there will be circumstances where consent is given on the understanding that the responsible clinicians will limit leave or add certain conditions, for instance, when a patient needs to visit a proposed discharge placement, or where leave at the responsible clinician's discretion is not appropriate for reasons of risk or sensitivity.
6. Once agreed, the Secretary of State's consent to leave remains in operation unless the circumstances of the patient's health or other factors change the risk assessment. This means that the responsible clinician should make a careful risk assessment of the patient before each instance of leave. If there are any doubts that the leave should take place, it should be stopped. The responsible clinician should inform the relevant caseworker in Mental Health

1 Published 16 March 2015.

2 Where section 47 of the Crime (Sentences) Act 1997 applies.

3 Historically, MHCS had entered into agreements with some hospitals for some restricted patients to take leave beyond the hospital perimeter, for the purposes of accessing wider grounds or local shops. These agreements are no longer in force.

Casework Section immediately should any change occur that affects the basis on which the Secretary of State's consent has been given, particularly any factor that changes a patient's risk.

LEAVE REQUEST FORM

7. To help ensure that the Secretary of State receives all of the information necessary to take a decision, a leave request form is provided for responsible clinicians (see **Annex A**).[4] In addition to the details below, the form also asks for a report on leave already taken to be attached and contact with the Victim Liaison Officer, if there is one. This should be supplemented with any additional information that the responsible clinician considers would assist the Secretary of State. Examples of such information would include additional material which explores the context, purpose and therapeutic benefits of proposed leave. Additional requests for progress reports on leave will only be made by MHCS if and when the caseworker requires further information.

8. In support of any request for leave for a restricted patient, the Secretary of State requires the following information:

   - the aims of the proposal and the anticipated benefits for the patient's treatment and/or rehabilitation;
   - the potential risk of harm to the public, taking into account the nature and adequacy of safeguards. Responsible clinicians must also consider any other risk factors which apply individually to the patient, particularly any risks to victims and their families, consulting with the Victim Liaison Office where appropriate.;
   - any potential public concerns or media attention, and any measures proposed in response to such concerns;
   - any concerns which have been expressed, or are likely to be expressed, by victims of the offences committed by the patient, or by families of the victims. In addition, any measures proposed in response to such concerns; and
   - where leave for rehabilitation purposes is proposed, a plan of the periods of leave which are being requested for the patient, setting out:
     - the destinations of the leave;
     - length of absences from the hospital;
     - the escorting arrangements, where applicable;
     - the part which the individual leaves will play in the overall treatment plan;
     - what, specifically, each instance of leave will seek to achieve;
     - how the leave will be monitored, whether by escorting staff or through the patient's own report or both; and
     - how the success or otherwise of the leave will be assessed and measured.
     - any incidents of abscond or escape.

9. MHCS aims to make a decision on all requests for community leave as soon as possible on receipt of all relevant information. Clinical teams should note

4 A shorter version of the form is available for requests for leave for the purposes of medical treatment (see para 19 below).

that relevant information may extend to details that are additional to that provided on or with the application form. For patients who have had any ground leave or previous community leave, a report on this leave is needed to assess any further application for leave.

SPECIFIC TYPES OF LEAVE

'Ground Leave'

10. The responsible clinician has complete discretion to allow the restricted patient access to the grounds of the hospital or unit in which the detention authority requires his detention. The detention authority means here the hospital order, hospital direction, transfer direction, warrant of recall or letter agreeing to trial leave or transfer. That authority may name a complete hospital, a named unit within a hospital, or a specific level of security within a hospital. It is for the hospital or unit to define its own geographical boundaries. If the responsible clinician wants to allow the patient beyond the boundaries of the hospital or unit named on the detention authority, then he needs the Secretary of State's agreement. So, for example, if the responsible clinician has a patient whose order states a particular Unit as the place in which the patient is detained and the responsible clinician wants to allow access to the grounds of the Hospital, an application for section 17 leave into the community must be submitted to the Secretary of State.
11. If the responsible clinician wishes to allow the patient to access wider hospital grounds, beyond the hospital or unit named on the detention authority, MHCS may consider using section 19 to transfer him to a wider range of units. However there is often little difference in public safety terms between access to a whole hospital and to the community at large, so such requests should always be accompanied by a robust risk assessment and be carefully scrutinized.
12. Where the detention authority names an entire hospital, the responsible clinician's discretion extends to all the facilities the hospital comprises. This may include non secure step-down facilities outside the hospital perimeter.

Escorted Community leave

13. If the Secretary of State has given consent for escorted leave to take place, the patient will remain in the custody of the escort who has powers to convey and restrain the patient. It is for the hospital to assess the number of escorts required and the level of training and experience such staff must have. In certain cases, typically where the Secretary of State is giving consent for compassionate or medical leave to a patient who would not otherwise leave the hospital, consent may be granted with additional requirements. These may include a specified numbers of escorts, or other conditions such as requiring travel directly to and from the venue without intermediate stops, or requiring secure transport.

Unescorted community day leave

14. The Secretary of State will generally agree to unescorted leave at the responsible clinician's discretion when satisfied that the patient is sufficiently

rehabilitated to respect the conditions of leave, behave safely in the community and abide by the time limits set for return to hospital. Hospitals are reminded that unescorted community leave is the point at which the MAPPA that 'owns' the case should be notified that a MAPPA eligible offender is approaching the stage at which discharge is possible. Part 2 of the MAPPA 1 form should be used for this purpose.

Overnight leave

15. As patients approach the stage of their rehabilitation where they are close to discharge, it is common for responsible clinicians to ask for overnight leave. As with any application for leave, the Secretary of State will only consent to overnight leave if satisfied the proposal does not put the patient or others at risk. The Secretary of State will consider each application for overnight leave on its merits, but may require that the number of nights away from the detaining hospital is limited where this is necessary for the safe rehabilitation and testing of the patient.

16. Where the Tribunal has made a deferred conditional discharge and the proposed discharge address is a hostel or other housing placement, which insists on a minimum period of overnight assessment of the patient, the Secretary of State will consider any request for overnight leave in the context of that decision, so as not to frustrate the proposed discharge. Nonetheless, the Secretary of State will not grant permission for leave unless he is satisfied that it does not put the public, or patient, at risk.

Holiday type leave

17. As set out above, the Secretary of State expects programmes of section 17 leave to be designed and conducted in such a way as to preserve public safety and, where appropriate, respect the feelings and possible fears of victims and others who may have been affected by the offences. When considering any request for overnight leave to activity centres or any facility offering "holidays" or whose description gives the impression that it is a holiday centre, particular scrutiny will be given to the expected therapeutic benefits of such leave, the proposed arrangements for any escorts and the availability of support for the patient should they become unwell.

Leave outside England and Wales

Scotland

18. Section 17 leave to Scotland from England and Wales can be permitted subject to appropriate assessments of risk. Escorts from both Scotland and England & Wales have the necessary powers of custody in both jurisdictions. Explicit agreement for the period of leave will be sought from the Scottish Executive.

Northern Ireland

19. Section 17 leave to Northern Ireland may also be permitted subject to appropriate assessments of risk with escorts from England & Wales having powers under the MHA to take into custody any patient who absconds or escapes. For unescorted leave, the patient may similarly be taken into lawful custody

should it become necessary, with the intention of returning them to England & Wales.

Compassionate leave

20. Leave may sometimes be sought for compassionate reasons for patients who would not otherwise qualify, either on risk grounds or because they have been in hospital for too short a time to have been assessed for community leave, for example to visit a terminally ill relative or to attend a funeral. These applications tend by their nature to be urgent will be dealt with as a priority. The Secretary of State will look sympathetically on such requests, but must still be satisfied with the risk management arrangements in place.

Leave for the purposes of medical treatment

21. There are occasions when restricted patients are required to attend medical appointments for assessment or treatment. Secretary of State permission is required for a restricted patient to attend such appointments outside the secure hospital, unless permission for escorted or unescorted community leave at the responsible clinician's discretion has been previously granted, and that permission has not been revoked. In the event that a patient is required to attend a medical appointment outside the secure hospital, the responsible clinician should submit a formal request. If satisfied that attendance is necessary and that the risk management arrangements, including physical security are sufficient, the Secretary of State will issue a general permission for a specific patient, subject to the exceptions outlined below, for medical leave to be taken at the responsible clinician's discretion. Requests for Secretary of State permission to allow restricted patients to attend medical appointments/treatment should contain:

- Initial reasons for the appointment/treatment
- Clear evidence that any risk factors have been addressed.
- A full risk management plan including any physical security arrangements.
- Current mental state and compliance.
- Risk of absconding.
- Details, if applicable, of whether the appointment will take the patient into any exclusion zone or into the proximity of any victim
- Further information if there are unusual circumstances e.g. likely to attract national media interest

A form is available for requests for medical leave (see Annex B) although it is acceptable for an email or other communication to be sent, providing it contains all the relevant information.

22. The Secretary of State permission will be a general consent enabling the responsible clinician to arrange for the patient to attend medical appointments when necessary. Any appointments or treatment received by the patient should be recorded and included in the Annual Statutory Report submitted to the Ministry of Justice. If there are incidents of the leave being misused or evidence of behaviours which pose a risk to the public or patient, the leave must be suspended and the Ministry of Justice (MHCS) informed immediately.

NB. It remains the responsibility of the responsible clinician to immediately suspend the general permission for medical leave if there are concerns that the patient's behaviour causes a risk to others or to the patient themselves.

Exceptions to a general permission for medical leave

23. Applications for patients who are considered by the Secretary of State to pose an increased risk to the public will require permission to be obtained for specific appointments as the arrangements will need to be individually agreed, including the duration of the permission. The Secretary of State will indicate whether applications are in this category when he responds to the responsible clinician's initial request. Leave will be granted for the purposes specified in the request for medical leave and in line with a proposed risk management plan. Any changes to the need for the leave or the plan must be notified to the MHCS Casework Manager in writing. Further advice should be obtained from the MHCS Casework Manager.

Leave for emergency medical treatment

24. Aside from routine medical appointments or treatment, there may be occasions when a patient needs to receive urgent or emergency treatment. This will include acute medical emergencies such as heart attack, stroke, serious burns or penetrative wounds but may also include situations which are not life threatening but still require urgent treatment e.g. fractures. Although Secretary of State consent should be obtained wherever possible, it is recognised that patients may have to attend hospital at very short notice. Responsible clinicians may use their discretion, having due regard to the emergency/urgency being presented and the management of any risks. MHCS must however be notified, as soon as is practicable, that the patient has been taken to hospital, what risk management arrangements are in place and must be kept informed of developments, especially the return of the patient to the secure hospital/unit. Outside office hours, hospitals should notify the out of hours switchboard. If the patient is high profile or there are unusual circumstances, the switchboard will contact the MHCS duty officer.

Short-term leave to Scotland

25. Explicit agreement must be sought for any trip across the border. Any leave request will be risk assessed by the Secretary of State in the usual fashion. If the Secretary of State is minded to give consent for such leave, the Scottish Government will be consulted. It is possible for leave to Scotland to be escorted.[5]

REPORTS ON COMPLETED LEAVE

26. In order to consider any request for leave, the Secretary of State will require an up to date report on all previous leave taken. In giving consent for leave, the Secretary of State will consider whether additional reporting is required, and any such requirement will be set out in the letter granting consent for leave. A form is available for reports on completed (see Annex C). This form may also be used to report changes in the patient's circumstances such as:

5 See the Mental Health (Cross-border Visits) (Scotland) Regulations 2008.

- a change or cessation of medication;
- self harming;
- the involvement of the patient in an incident in, or outside, the hospital;
- abuse of substances; or
- the added stress of bad news from outside or from another stressful occasion.

27. Notwithstanding requests for specific reports on leave, details of progress made on community leave should always form part of the annual statutory report.

WITHDRAWING CONSENT FOR LEAVE

28. There will be occasions when it is necessary for the Secretary of State to withdraw consent for leave under section 17. This may be as a result of a patient not complying with conditions of leave, or because their behaviour or actions indicate a real or potential increase in risk to others or themselves. A responsible clinician may also take action to suspend a patient's leave for similar reasons and must advise the relevant caseworker in MCHS immediately. .

29. In making this decision, the Secretary of State will consider matters such as:
- whether the patient's condition has relapsed or, if the problem was a behavioural one.
- whether the incident that caused leave to be rescinded was "one-off";
- whether or not the patient was the main instigator and, if they were, whether the patient shows appropriate remorse which has been consistent and sustained as has a further period of stable behaviour; and
- What the factors were which contributed to the infraction, and how they have been addressed so as to reduce the risk both of any recurrence and of its severity & impact were it to recur.
- any plans that might have been put in place by the responsible clinician requiring the patient to demonstrate certain behaviours before leave can be reinstated.

MHCS is always willing to discuss the best course of action in an individual case.

LEAVE FOR COURT PROCEEDINGS

30. Where a court directs the attendance of a patient, the Secretary of State will rarely refuse consent to leave under s.17. However consent for leave must still be sought. For those patients detained under Section 48 of the Act, general permission will be provided on the assumption that legal proceedings will inevitably need to be completed. This will take the form of a formal notification, on admission, advising that 'Secretary of State permission for the attendance at court for the purposes of legal proceedings is given'.

31. With regard to patients detained under sections 37/41 and sentenced prisoners transferred under sections 47/49 the following details will be required:
- Date(s) when attendance is required.
- Details of the Court, including location.
- Reasons for attendance.

- Whether consideration has been given to the patient attending the hearing via a video-link.
- Arrangements for transporting the patient to court, including physical security e.g. number of escorts/secure van/necessity for handcuffs.
- Details, if applicable, of whether attendance will take the patient into any exclusion zone or into the proximity of any victim.
- Further information if there are unusual circumstances e.g. likely to attract national media interest.

An email to the Mental Health Caseworker will suffice. The expectation is that providing all the relevant information is received, permission will be granted within 48 hours.

Leave to attend Court for legal proceedings other than criminal

32. Some restricted patients may be required to attend court for purposes other than criminal proceedings, for example to attend the Family Court. Secretary of State permission is also required for this purpose and the details above should similarly be provided by email, giving as much prior notification as possible.

33. Where a patient's attendance is not strictly required but is voluntary or may be seen as useful to the administration of justice, the Secretary of State will consider all applications on merit.

34. Restricted patients should not attend court hearing unescorted without the Secretary of State's express agreement.

Restricted patients who become the subject of Police enquiries while an inpatient

35. Occasionally a patient may be the subject of police interest, for example if an alleged offence has taken place while in hospital, or if earlier allegations come to light and are then to be investigated. Were that to occur while the subject is in Prison, the Police are permitted to arrest an individual and take them to a Police station for questioning, returning them to the prison thereafter. In a parallel manner, if the Police decide to arrest a restricted patient in hospital and take them to a Police station for questioning, the consent of the Secretary of State is not necessary. It will however be the responsibility of the Police to transport the patient between Police station and hospital and prior to this occurring the Police should be informed in writing that the person is a detained patient subject to the provisions of the Mental Health Act and who must be returned to the unit at the conclusion of questioning. Arrangements should also be made for an appropriate adult to accompany and assist the patient at the police station as necessary. The MHCS should be informed of the matter in advance of the circumstances, and of the patient's return to hospital.

PRISONERS SUBJECT TO DIRECTIONS UNDER SECTION 45A OR TRANSFERRED UNDER SECTIONS 47 AND 48 OF THE MENTAL HEALTH ACT 1983

Patients Transferred under section 47/49 or patients subject to section 45A directions

36. As a general rule, a patient who was sentenced and directed to hospital by the Court under section 45A or who has transferred from prison under section 47/49 will not be permitted privileges while detained under the Mental Health Act in hospital (example e.g. community leave) that he or she would not have been able to access whilst in prison. The presumption for many of these patients is that their care pathway will see their return to prison to continue their sentence rather than release into the community. However as this is not always the case, discretion is needed and the Secretary of State will consider requests for community leave on an individual basis.

37. As with all patients, when considering a request for community leave for a transferred prisoner, the Secretary of State, will always have in mind the ongoing protection of the public. Factors relevant to this consideration include any history of absconding or escape. For transferred prisoners, it will be necessary to review their history in prison and in hospital. Careful consideration will be given to the potential increase in the patient's risk and the likelihood of them being in the community without the necessary supervision and support. .

Escorted leave

38. Escorted leave may be an important part of treatment and rehabilitation for directed and transferred prisoners. When applying for such leave, responsible clinicians should always have in mind the general principles set out in paragraphs 2-6 above and must ensure, if granted, that the leave is conducted in such a way as to safeguard public confidence in the restricted patient system. Responsible clinicians also need to bear in mind that the granting of escorted leave to transferred prisoners should not be taken as an indication that unescorted leave will follow. However, unescorted leave may be appropriate where a patient is going to be released into the community e.g. if the prison sentence is about to expire.

Compassionate leave

39. Requests for leave for compassionate reasons will be considered in line with paragraph 19 above.

Unescorted leave

40. In line with Prison Service policy on Release on Temporary Licence (ROTL), prisoners directed or transferred to hospital who are likely to be released into the community from hospital will be eligible to be considered for unescorted leave on one of the following dates (whichever is the later):

- 24 months before the prisoner's Parole Eligibility Date (PED) or, where applicable, 24 months before the conditional release date (CRD), or

- once they have served half the custodial period less half the relevant remand time.

41. In order to save misunderstandings or difficulties in calculating the ROTL eligibility date, the H1003 form that MHCS obtains from the prison when a prisoner is transferred now contains a box for the ROTL date and it is the prison's responsibility to complete this. Responsible clinicians should contact the relevant MHCS Casework Manager if they have doubts concerning the relevant date.

Overnight leave

42. Directed or transferred prisoners who are subject to the parole process can be considered for overnight leave if there are clear therapeutic reasons for the leave and the prisoner is three months away from their Parole Eligibility Date or have completed their tariff.

Indeterminate Sentence Prisoners

43. Transferred or directed indeterminate sentence prisoners fall into 2 categories:

"Technical Lifers"

44. These are prisoners whom the Secretary of State agreed, exceptionally, to manage as if the Court had made a restricted hospital order instead of a life sentence. The process was ended in 2005, so the number of such prisoners in hospital has diminished. Applications for section 17 leave for technical lifers should be treated as if they were detained under sections 37 and 41.

Other Indeterminate Sentence Prisoners

45. Most indeterminate sentence prisoners in hospital will be serving life sentences or indeterminate sentences for public protection. They will be subject to hospital directions or transfer directions. Their release will ultimately be ordered on licence by the Parole Board. If the Secretary of State is asked to consider a request for leave, the responsible clinician must also address the question of why the patient should not be remitted to prison.

ANNEX A

Ministry of Justice

Leave application for restricted patients

Mental Health Casework Section

Please send the completed form to the Mental Health Casework Section **at MHCSTeam1@noms.gsi.gov.uk (case letters A-Gile); MHCSTeam2@noms.gsi.gov.uk (case letters Gilf-Nev); MHCSTeam3@noms.gsi.gov.uk (case letters New-Z) or fax on 0300 047 4387 (case letters A – GEO) or 0300 047 4395 (GEP – NEAL and NEAM – Z)**

Patient's basic details

Full name of patient

Date of birth

MHCS reference

Location of index offence

Responsible clinician's details

Responsible clinician

Address

Telephone number

Fax number

Email address

Leave proposal

Please note that any leave taking place outside the designated security perimeter of the named unit, hospital or ward requires Secretary of State approval **unless** the hospital has a current agreement with the Mental Health Casework Section specifically devolving agreement to the Responsible Clinician.

Type of leave proposed ☐ Compassionate ☐ Escorted community
☐ Overnight ☐ Unescorted community

Other (please specify)

Previous types of leave taken ☐ Compassionate ☐ Escorted community
☐ Overnight ☐ Unescorted community

Other (please specify)

Report on current leave (frequency, duration, destination, purpose and conduct)

Please give details of the leave proposal, including:

- the purpose of the leave
- if escorted, the number of escorts
- future leave plans, if proposal agreed
- full address of the leave destination
- means of transport, if any
- views of care team, if different

Patient's condition

Mental state – please describe the patient's mental state, including:

- how long the patient has been stable
- what insight, if any, the patient has into his or her illness

Behaviour – please describe the patient's behaviour, including any incidents of:

- aggression
- self-harm
- substance abuse

State what effect these have had on the patient and how they will be addressed.

Compliance – to what extent does the patient:

- accept the treatment programme?
- comply with medication?

Risk

Risk to victims and others – what is your assessment of the risk (including further offending, or a possible encounter) that the patient would present to:

- past victims?
- any specific group?
- the public in general?

How do you propose to address these risks?

Victim Consideration & VLO contact – have you contacted the VLO to get the victim's views on unescorted leave (please give full and frank account of victim's views)

Name of VLO: **Tel. No.** **Date of Contact:**

Risk of absconding – what is your assessment of the patient's current risk of absconding? How do you propose to address this risk?

Responsible clinician's signature

Date

ANNEX B

Medical Leave application for restricted patients

Mental Health Casework Section

Please send the completed form to the Mental Health Casework Section **at: MHCSTeam1@noms.gsi.gov.uk (case letters A-Gile); MHCSTeam2@noms.gsi.gov.uk (case letters Gilf-Nev); MHCSTeam3@noms.gsi.gov.uk (case letters New-Z) or fax to 0300 047 4387 (case letters A – GEO) or 0300 047 4395 (GEP – NEAL and NEAM – Z)**

With immediate effect, each occasion of leave for medical appointments or treatment will require the written consent of the Ministry of Justice. **If the Secretary of State has previously granted permission for escorted or unescorted community leave at the Responsible Clinician's discretion, and that permission has not been revoked, no further application for leave is required.**

Patient's basic details

Full name of patient	
Date of birth	
MHCS reference	
Location of index offence	

Responsible clinician's details

Responsible clinician	
Address	
Telephone number	
Fax number	
Email address	

Leave proposal

Please note that any leave taking place outside the designated security perimeter of the named unit, hospital or ward requires Secretary of State approval **unless** the hospital has a current agreement with the Mental Health Casework Section specifically devolving agreement to the Responsible Clinician.

Type of medical leave proposed ☐ Hospital ☐ Dental ☐ Other

Other (please specify)	

Reason(s) for appointment:
(The precise nature of the treatment required)

Address of hospital/clinic/surgery etc:

Date(s) of appointments – if available
(Will follow up appointments be required?)

Escorting and transport arrangements (please specify if handcuffs will be used):
(Number of escorts and details of transport that will be used)

Current mental state and compliance:
(Whether in your clinical opinion the problem necessitates a medical appointment?)

Is the leave likely to bring the patient back to the area of the index offence or near to victim(s) of the offence?

Risk of absconding:

Responsible clinician's signature		Date	

C6 PRACTICE GUIDANCE ON PROCEDURES CONCERNING HANDLING REPRESENTATIONS FROM VICTIMS IN THE FIRST-TIER TRIBUNAL (MENTAL HEALTH)[1]

The Tribunal Procedure (First-tier Tribunal) (Health, Education and Social Care Chamber) Rules 2008

Background

1) This Guidance Note is drafted to assist judges and members of the First-tier Tribunal, Mental Health - (the tribunal) - in handling relevant representations from the victims of patients, where such patients have applications or referrals before the tribunal. This guidance has been issued by the Chamber President of the Health, Education and Social Care Chamber and it is intended to promote consistent and high standards in making judicial decisions, particularly in relation to Rule 5 (Case management powers); Rule 15 (Evidence and submissions), Rule 33 (Notice of proceedings to interested persons); Rule 36 (Entitlement to attend a hearing), and Rule 38 (Public and private hearings).

2) The definition of "victim" is taken to include any person in relation to the patient's index offence or offences who appears to the relevant local probation board to be the victim of the offence or offences. This includes a victim's family in a case where the offence has resulted in the victim's death or incapacity and in other cases where the victim's age or circumstances make it more sensible to approach a family member.

Part A: Cases covered by the Domestic Violence, Crime and Victims Act 2004

3) The Domestic Violence, Crime and Victims Act 2004 (DVCVA) made provision for a number of measures improving services and support to victims of sexual or violent offences (see *Definitions*, below). This includes offences committed by people sent from prison to hospital for psychiatric treatment, as well as offenders subject to hospital orders. Under Schedule 6 of the Mental Health Act 2007, which amends the 2004 Act, these rights are extended to the victims of a sexual or violent offence committed by offenders who are detained in hospital but are not subject to special restrictions (unrestricted patients).

4) This Guidance Note suggests how the judiciary should approach requests from victims to make written representations, or to attend a hearing in person or through a representative. The Guidance Note does not address in detail the duty of the tribunal to notify the relevant local probation board if relevant applications or referrals or made, and the Guidance Note does not address in detail the duty of the tribunal to notify the local probation board of certain aspects of the outcome of the proceedings.

1 Issued by the Chamber President under Schedule 4 of the Tribunals, Courts and Enforcement Act 2007.

The Statutory Regime

A victim is not a party to the proceedings. However, where the court sentenced the patient to certain **disposals** the tribunal has a statutory duty to permit a victim to make certain **representations** to the tribunal, so long as sentencing occurred on or after 1 July 2005 or, for non-restricted patients, after 3 November 2008.[2] This duty is not retrospective, and applies only to victims.

The **disposals** include the following:

- those convicted of a sexual or violent offence who are then made subject of a hospital order;
- those found to be
  a) unfit to plead and to have committed the act or made the omission charged as the offence; or
  b) not guilty by reason of insanity, under the Criminal Procedure (Insanity) Act 1964 as amended by the DVCVA in respect of a sexual or violent offence;

  and are then made subject to a hospital order;
- those convicted of a sexual or violent offence, who are then made subject of a hospital direction and limitation direction (if the associated prison sentence is for 12 months or more); and
- those sentenced to 12 months imprisonment or more, for a sexual or violent offence, and transferred from prison to hospital, under a transfer direction.

The **representations** must only relate to the following questions:

- **whether the patient should, in the event of his or her discharge or release from detention, be subject to any conditions and, if so,**
- **what particular conditions should be imposed.**

5) These arrangements also apply to those patients in the above categories who have subsequently been made the subject of Conditional Discharge (restricted patients) or a Community Treatment Order (unrestricted patients). If an offender was subject to a hospital order with restrictions but had those restrictions removed on or after 3 November 2008, or was made subject to a transfer direction without restrictions being made, the victim will continue to enjoy the rights offered by the DVCVA, as long as the offender was sentenced after 1 July 2005.

Restricted Cases

6) The Ministry of Justice (MoJ) Mental Health Casework Section (MHCS) carries out the Secretary of State's responsibilities under the Mental Health Act 1983, and related legislation. It directs the admission to hospital of patients transferred from prison, and considers recommendations from Responsible Clinicians (RCs) in hospitals for leave, transfer or discharge of restricted patients. MHCS also prepares documentation for the tribunal and monitors patients who are conditionally discharged. Each restricted patient has a caseworker at MHCS.

2 Note: PART B below deals with the position regarding disposals prior to these dates.

7) For each new restricted case, including transferred prisoners, the Victim Liaison Officer (VLO), who is a Probation Officer with special responsibility for liaising with victims of sexual or violent offences, will contact the MHCS caseworker. MHCS will then inform the VLO of the details for the care team or RC, where this is known.

8) A detained patient may apply to have his or her case heard by a tribunal once each year. If the patient does not apply, his or her case will be referred to a tribunal every three years. In addition, after a conditionally discharged patient has been recalled, the Secretary of State must refer the case to a tribunal within one month of recall. The tribunal will then consider whether the individual needs to be detained in hospital for the purposes of appropriate and available mental health medical treatment.

9) When the Secretary of State refers a patient to the tribunal, MHCS will forward the details of the relevant VLO to the tribunal office. When an application is made to the tribunal, the tribunal office will obtain the details of the relevant VLO from MHCS. In both circumstances, the tribunal office will then inform the VLO of the **date (but not the venue)** of the tribunal hearing, once it has been set, and also advise of the date by which any written information, representations or submissions from the victim must be received. Note that a victim is not permitted to see the reports prepared for the tribunal by the witnesses in the case.

10) VLOs should consult victims about the information or submissions that they may wish to submit relating to possible discharge conditions, and forward them to the tribunal office by the specified date. VLOs should not encourage victims to make a general 'impact statement' because the tribunal is unable to take account of any representations from victims except those relating to the matters set out above.

11) If a restricted patient ceases to be subject to a restriction order, limitation direction or restriction direction on or after 3 November 2008, the arrangements below for unrestricted cases, involving hospital managers, will apply from the time when the restrictions are removed.

Unrestricted Cases

12) Unrestricted patients whose victims may make relevant written representations are those patients who are convicted of a sexual or violent offence on or after 1 July 2005 and are made subject to an unrestricted hospital order or transfer direction on or after 3 November 2008. In addition, they also include patients (whose victims fall within the scope of the statutory scheme) who were initially subject to a hospital order with restrictions, but in relation to whom restrictions were removed on or after 3 November 2008, whilst they remained detained in hospital.

13) For unrestricted patients, the role of probation services (Area or Trust) is limited to identifying the victim(s) and, if they consent, to passing on their details to hospital managers. For these cases, hospital managers (or staff to whom the function has been delegated) have the statutory duty to liaise with victims. Therefore, it is the hospital managers' responsibility to ensure that the victim is aware of the proceedings and to ascertain whether the victim

wishes to make representations. The managers are required to pass any such representations to the RC, who should then forward them to the tribunal office.

14) Victims continue to fall under the new arrangements even if the relevant patient is subsequently discharged onto a Community Treatment Order (CTO). Note, however, that the tribunal has no power to attach conditions to a CTO or to amend conditions imposed under S.17(B) of the Mental Health Act 1983 (as amended). The tribunal may, however, summarise any relevant representations from a victim in its decision.

Provision of documents, written information or submissions to the tribunal

15) Where a victim wishes to do so, and having submitted a written request to be advised of the **date** fixed for any hearing concerning that patient in advance of the hearing, a victim shall have the right to provide to the tribunal any **relevant** documents, written information or submissions that he or she wishes the tribunal to consider. Documents, information or submissions should only be regarded as relevant if they are capable of amounting to persuasive and cogent evidence, upon which the tribunal would be entitled to rely, relating to the following questions:
- **whether the patient should, in the event of his or her discharge or release from detention, be subject to any conditions and, if so,**
- **what particular conditions should be imposed.**

16) Conditions relevant to victims could, for example, relate to 'no contact' conditions or limited and carefully defined exclusion zones.

17) In the event of any difficulty, the tribunal will consider exercising its case management powers. In particular, under Rules 5 & 15, the tribunal may give directions as to the manner in which any representations are to be provided, which may include a direction for them to be given by written submissions or statement. Alternatively (and exceptionally), the tribunal may take the view that the victim should have an opportunity of being heard in person, or through a representative.

Application to Attend the Hearing

18) Rule 33(e) of the Tribunal Procedure (First-tier Tribunal) (Health, Education and Social Care Chamber) Rules 2008 ("the Rules") compels the tribunal to give notice of the proceedings (i.e. date, time and place) to any person who in the opinion of the tribunal: 'should have an opportunity of *being heard*'.

19) Representations made by a victim can only cover only a limited range of issues (see above) and the victim is not a party to the proceedings. In most cases, therefore, a written statement will be the most satisfactory way for the victim to express his/her views because direct involvement in the proceedings, or a procedure that brings the victim into direct conflict with the patient, is unlikely to be helpful to the victim, to the patient, or to the tribunal. However there may be some cases in which the victim believes that this is not sufficient and may decide to ask to attend the hearing. Any such requests will be treated on a case by case basis applying the principles in the overriding

objective as set out in Rule 2. The victim will have to demonstrate that the opportunity to make written representations is insufficient and that he or she needs an opportunity to be heard in relation to relevant matters (see paragraphs 4 & 15 above).

20) If a victim wishes to contend that he or she needs an opportunity to give oral evidence in relation to relevant matters, they must make a written application to the tribunal in advance of the hearing. The application must explain why the right to provide relevant documents, or relevant information or submissions in writing is not sufficient to enable the tribunal to deal with the case fairly and justly.

21) The victim should understand that the tribunal will be required to consider a large amount of information from different sources, including confidential medical reports which the victim will not be permitted to see. A victim's representations, whilst potentially relevant and helpful, are only part of a constellation of factors that will inform the tribunal's final decision.

22) If the tribunal determines that a victim should have an opportunity of being heard, then the tribunal will advise the victim of the date, time and place of the hearing. Rule 36(2) then permits such a person to attend and take part in the hearing to such extent as the tribunal considers proper. This gives the tribunal a wide discretion to regulate its own procedure, taking account of all the relevant circumstances.

23) Rule 38(4) and (5) may be particularly helpful when a tribunal is deciding what approach to take when dealing with the oral evidence of a victim who is permitted to attend a hearing. In particular, the tribunal has power under Rule 38(5) to exclude a victim from a hearing until the time comes for the victim to give his or her evidence. However, notwithstanding Rule 38(4), the tribunal will be reluctant to exclude a patient from a hearing relating to that patient's liberty, unless there are strong and evidentially supported reasons for doing so. Rule 5 empowers a tribunal judge to consider these matters at any time up to the hearing. Consequently, the manner and format in which the victim's oral evidence is presented to the tribunal (e.g. whether it is in the presence or absence of the other parties to the hearing) can be determined either by the judge dealing with the management of the case in advance of the hearing, or by the panel at the hearing itself.

Disclosure of the Victim's Evidence to the Patient

24) Rule 15 (2) provides that the tribunal may admit in evidence any document or written material, whether or not that such document or material would be admissible in a civil trial. However, the tribunal will generally wish to copy such information or written material to the patient, unless it is satisfied that there are grounds to prohibit disclosure under Rule 14. If the tribunal decides to prohibit disclosure to the patient, it will usually send a copy of the material to the patient's legal representatives. In such circumstances, the representatives will not be permitted to disclose material, or the information contained within it, to the patient.

25) Victims should be made aware that no guarantees can be given that any representations they make will not be disclosed to the patient. The expectation is

that all documents will be disclosed to the patient, and the circumstances in which documents can be withheld are very limited. Rule 14 allows the tribunal to withhold any document from the patient if they are satisfied that:

a) disclosure would be likely to cause that person or some other person serious harm, and
b) having regard to the interests of justice, it is proportionate not to disclose.

26) Rule 14 requires compliance with some important procedural steps. Further guidance is available in the tribunal's *Reports Guidance Booklet* "Reports for Mental Health Tribunals", available on the tribunal's website.

27) When deciding whether it is in the interests of justice to direct that the material must be withheld from the patient, the tribunal must ask itself whether nondisclosure would prevent the patient from participating effectively in all aspects of the proceedings (see *RM v St Andrew's Healthcare* [2010] UKUT 119 (AAC)

Decision of the Tribunal

In restricted cases, the tribunal office should be able to inform the VLO of the relevant aspects of the tribunal's decision, in writing within seven days. In particular, the victim is entitled to know

- whether the patient is to be discharged and, if so, when the discharge will take effect;
- if a restricted patient is to be discharged, whether the discharge is to be absolute, or subject to conditions;
- if a restricted patient is to be discharged subject to conditions, what the conditions are;
- if a restricted patient has previously been discharged subject to conditions, of any variation of these conditions by the tribunal; and
- if the restriction order is to cease to have effect by virtue of action to be taken by the tribunal, of the date on which the restriction order is to cease to have effect.

28) With regard to prisoners who have been transferred to hospital, the tribunal may make recommendations on how they would have acted had the patient not been a transferred prisoner. Therefore, VLOs may forward the victim's representations about possible conditions in these cases, and the tribunal's conclusions in relation to possible discharge and conditions will be forwarded to the Parole Board where appropriate.

29) In unrestricted cases, the hospital managers are responsible for notifying the victim of the relevant aspects of the outcome of the hearing. The managers will have their own arrangements to ensure that they have the information they need to comply with this duty.

30) A victim is not permitted to make an application for permission to appeal on point of law to the Upper Tribunal under S.11 of the Tribunal Courts and Enforcement Act 2007, because this right is limited to parties to the proceedings, and a victim is not a party.

Part B: Cases not covered by the Domestic Violence, Crime and Victims Act 2004

31) As outlined at Part A above, The Domestic Violence, Crime and Victims Act 2004 ('DVCVA') came into force on 1 July 2005, but it does not apply to victims of incidents involving restricted patients where sentencing occurred prior to that date, as the DVCVA is not retrospective. For non-restricted patients, the relevant date is 3 November 2008.

32) The tribunal has given careful consideration to the position of persons who have been subject to a sexual or violent offences committed by persons who were subsequently detained under the provisions of the Mental Health Act 1983, where such offences occurred prior to the introduction of the DVCVA.

33) The tribunal has determined that where a patient's victim wishes to be advised of the date of any pending tribunal proceedings concerning that patient they shall, upon written request, be informed in advance of the **date (but not the venue)** fixed for any hearing concerning that patient. Such request must be in writing, and addressed to HM Courts & Tribunals Service, Mental Health, PO Box 8793, 5th Floor, Leicester. LE1 8BN.

34) The tribunal will log and acknowledge in writing all such requests. The victim will subsequently be informed of the **date (but not the venue)** fixed for the hearing. Note, however, that this is **not** a notification under Rule 33(e), but merely a practice to be adopted in order to allow a victim to know when a tribunal hearing is taking place in order that the victim may have an opportunity of providing written information or submissions to the tribunal, under Rule 5(3)(d) and Rule 15(1)(e)(ii).

Definitions

A "**Sexual or Violent Offence**" falls within one of the following descriptions:

- Murder, attempted murder or conspiracy to murder and any offence in Schedule 15 Criminal Justice Act 2003 (c.44). This includes: manslaughter; kidnapping; false imprisonment; assaults under sections 18, 20 or 47 Offences Against the Person Act 1861 (as amended); child cruelty; possession of a firearm with intent; burglary; robbery; affray; death by dangerous driving; and a wide range of sexual offences;
- An offence which requires that a patient complies with the notification requirements of Part 2 of the Sexual Offenders Act 2003 (c.42). This refers to a large number of offences set out at schedule 3 which includes: rape; indecent assault; sexual offences involving children; and possession of indecent photographs of children;
- An offence against a child within the meaning of Part 2 of the Criminal Justice & Courts Services Act 2000

Restricted Patients are those patients who were given:

- a restricted hospital order (i.e. a hospital order accompanied by a restriction order) (Section 37 and section 41 orders); or
- hospital and limitation directions (Section 45A); or
- a sentence of imprisonment for a qualifying offence but were subsequently

transferred to hospital by a restricted transfer direction (i.e. a transfer direction accompanied by a restriction order) (Section 47 and 49 orders).

His Honour Judge Sycamore,
Chamber President,
Health, Education and Social Care Chamber,
First-tier Tribunal (Mental Health)

1 July 2011

APPENDIX D

Forms and standard letters

CASE MANAGEMENT REQUEST FORM (CRM1)

CMR1
CASE MANAGEMENT
REQUEST FORM

The First-tier Tribunal (Health, Education and Social Care Chamber) Mental Health

Request

The Tribunal Procedure (First-tier Tribunal) Health Education & Social Care Chamber Rules 2008

The tribunal may give a direction at the request of one or more of the parties. The request should be in writing and must give reasons. Directions are provided for in the Rules.

Please provide the information required below, as appropriate, and delete what you don't need.

Case Number: XXXXXX
Date of Application: 5th January 2015
Hearing Date (if fixed): 16th February 2015

Patient: Dean Alexander (born 25th July 1977)
A patient now liable to be detained under Section 3 Mental Health Act 1983

Responsible Authority: Anytown Partnership Trust
Responsible Hospital Anytown Hospital

This request is made by: Sarah Malcolm of Malcolm and Partners LLP on behalf of: Dean Alexander

Postal Address:
Telephone: ; Secure email address:

Request is made for: (Please tick as appropriate, and provide precise details in **Section A** below. Please also complete the other sections as appropriate)

☐ Directions ☐ Postponement ☐ Prohibition of Disclosure of Information

☐ Wasted Costs ☐ Permission to Withdraw an Application ☐ Other

- *If you want the tribunal to make a specific direction, you must provide an exact draft in* ***Section B*** *below, using the precise words you want the tribunal to use and state to whom the direction should be addressed. If you do not provide a draft, the judge may refuse to consider your request.*
- *Postponements are only granted for compelling reasons and, before approaching the tribunal, parties are expected to liaise and agree possible alternative dates that comply with Rule 37. You must answer the further questions in* ***Section C*** *below, relating to postponement requests.*
- *Prohibition of Disclosure is dealt with in Rule 14, and in the tribunal's Reports Guidance Booklet: "Reports for Mental Health Tribunals", available at www.mhrt.org.uk.*
- *An order for wasted costs can only be made against a party's representative, and only if they have behaved in a way that is improper, unreasonable or negligent.*
- *A reference to the tribunal cannot be withdrawn, but an application may be withdrawn if the tribunal consents. If the tribunal does not consent, the case will proceed.*

- *This form may also be used for <u>other interlocutory matters</u>, such as a request for the appointment of a representative on ground of incapacity under Rule 11(7)(b).*

<u>A. The Details of this Request (with full reasons) are:</u>

1. This firm represents Mr Alexander who has applied to the Tribunal following his detention under s3 on 22nd December 2014. Mr Alexander has a longstanding diagnosis of schizophrenia and emotionally unstable personality disorder, which has been associated with self-harm when he is particularly anxious. The report of his responsible clinician (RC) is enclosed with this application and details his history. We draw your attention to paragraph 6 where the RC describes Mr Alexander's documented difficulty in forming relationships with those seeking to work with him and his anxiety when having to explain his background to new people.
2. Mr Alexander has instructed us on three previous occasions within the last two years when he has been detained under the Mental Health Act. Ms Malcolm has represented him at three former hearings prior to the current period of detention. We therefore consider we have a good understanding of his history and are well-placed to promote his participation in the hearing.
3. The hearing has been fixed for 16th February 2015. Please note that our HQ1 was filed on 2nd February 2015 .A copy is attached. It will be seen that we provided 6 dates within the hearing window. 16th February was not one of the dates offered and Ms Malcolm is not available on that date. She is the only solicitor in this firm who is a member of the Law Society's Mental Health Accreditation Scheme.
4. We were notified of the fixture yesterday. We immediately contacted the Mental Health Act Administrator and ascertained that the Responsible Authority does not object to the date being changed. We have identified three possible dates that are convenient to ourselves and the Responsible Authority (see paragraph 3 below).
5. We submit that a postponement in this case would be entirely consistent with the over-riding objective, with particular reference to TPR 2(2)(c), namely ensuring, so far as practicable, that the parties are able to participate fully in the proceedings. Mr Alexander's ability to participate in this hearing, which concerns his liberty, will be significantly compromised if he has to be represented by another advocate with whom he is unfamiliar. This may lead to significant distress on his part. We submit that a postponement would be a proportionate response to this request, given that we have fully co-operated with the pre-hearing procedure, that we have made this request promptly and that other dates that are mutually convenient are available. Furthermore the delay entailed will be minimal.

Do the other parties in the case agree to your request? Yes, see attached copy email.

<u>B. Directions</u>

The directions should be sent to: the Mental Health Act Administrator, Anytown Hospital, and Malcolm and Partners LLP

<u>The exact wording of the direction(s) requested is:</u>

1. The hearing on 16th February 2015 is postponed.
2. This application will now be heard on [date] at [time] with a time estimate of two hours.

C. Postponements

Q. Have you and all the other parties agreed an alternative date that is convenient to everyone? If so, please specify the date. A. Yes, see attached email. All parties are available on 19th, 20th and 25th February 2015.

Q. Does the proposed new date comply with Rule 37? A.

Q. Is the Responsible Authority aware of any other cases that may be ready and suitable to fill the gap? Do not give details here, just answer YES or NO, and the tribunal will contact you. A. No

D. Evidence in Support

(Please indicate if you are attaching any supporting evidence, and say what it is. For example, if a direction is sought prohibiting the disclosure of a document or information to another party, please attach the document or information in compliance with Rule 14 & the tribunal's Reports Guidance Booklet, available at www.mhrt.org.uk. Or, if an appointment of a representative is sought under Rule 11(7)(b) on ground of incapacity, written evidence of incapacity should be attached.)

RC's report (relevant paragraph highlighted)

E. Have there been any previous requests by you, or have any previous directions been made by the tribunal in this case? If so, please give full details.

(Please provide here a full history to enable the judge to take a decision based on all the facts. If you seek to vary or set aside a previous direction or order please clearly identify that direction or order.)

1. No

Signed: Malcolm and Partners LLP
Date: 10th February 2015

Please send this request to the tribunal either by

- Secure email to TSMHCaseManagementRequest@tribunals.gsi.gov.uk

  or, if using a CJSM account, to TSMHCaseManagementRequest@tribunals.gsi.gov.uk.cjsm.net

  or

- First Class Recorded Delivery post to MHT, PO BOX 8793, 5th Floor, Leicester LE1 8BN.

LETTER TO CLIENT RE SECTION 2 ADVICE

Mr

PROTECT: PERSONAL DATA

24 January 2015
Our Ref: AB/11169.002/CD
Your Ref:

Dear

Re: Your application to the mental health tribunal/hospital managers

I was pleased to meet you on [date]. I am writing to confirm what we discussed, the advice that I gave you and the action that we decided that I would take.

You told me that you had been detained under section 2 of the Mental Health Act 1983. An order under section 2 of the Mental Health Act 1983 lasts for up to 28 days.

An approved mental health professional (usually a social worker) can apply for a person to be detained under Section 2 of the Mental Health Act 1983. Two doctors also need to certify that the person concerned is suffering from mental disorder of a nature or degree which warrants that person's detention in hospital for assessment, or for assessment followed by treatment, for at least a limited period. The doctors must also certify that that person ought to be detained in the interests of their own health, or their safety, or with a view to the protection of other people.

As I mentioned above, the order can last for up to 28 days. It cannot be renewed. However, it sometimes happens that during the course of the 28 days the person who has been detained is placed under section 3 of the Mental Health Act 1983. An order under section 3 of the Mental Health Act 1983 allows that person to be detained for up to six months. I will advise you in more detail about this should this situation arise.

We discussed the methods whereby you could be discharged from your section. Firstly, your consultant (sometimes referred to as your responsible clinician or RC) can lift the section at any time.

Secondly, your nearest relative, who I understand is [name], has the power to discharge you from detention under the Mental Heath Act 1983. I would stress, however, that these powers are limited. If your nearest relative attempts to discharge you, and your consultant believes that, if discharged you would act in a way that was dangerous to yourself and other people, then he/she can stop the discharge from taking effect. Additionally, legal action can be taken against your nearest relative to displace them which means that they would no longer act as your nearest relative.

You also have the right to appeal to a hospital manager's hearing or to a mental health tribunal.

The hospital managers have the power to discharge you from detention. If you request it, the hospital managers will hold a hearing at which they consider reports from your consultant, from a social worker and probably a nursing report as well. They will also hear from you and they will decide whether to discharge you from the section or not. I can advise you and accompany you to the hospital manager's hearing.

The mental health tribunal is an independent body whose members are appointed by the Ministry of Justice, the government department which has responsibility for the judiciary. Mental health tribunal members, if you request, visit the hospital to hold a Hearing to decide whether or not you should be discharged from your section. Before any tribunal hearing, reports will be prepared by your consultant, a social worker and probably a member of nursing staff. I will receive copies of these reports and will discuss them with you.

The tribunal consists of a tribunal judge, a medical member who is a consultant psychiatrist and a lay member who is usually a social work professional. The medical member will come and speak to you and look at your notes before the hearing takes place. I will represent you at the hearing.

Agreed action

You told me that you would like to appeal to the mental health tribunal and/ or the hospital managers and i have therefore written to the mental health tribunal and the Mental Health Act administrator at this hospital advising them of your wish.

The mental health tribunal must take place within a week of the tribunal receiving the application. It is likely therefore that the hearing will take place in the very near future.

You have authorised me to look at your medical and nursing file and I have written to your consultant asking him/her if he/she has any objections to this. I will let you know when I receive a response.

Yours sincerely

Sarah Malcolm
Malcolm & Partners LLP

LETTER TO CLIENT RE SECTION 3 ADVICE

Mr

PROTECT: PERSONAL DATA

24 January 2015
Our Ref: AB/11169.002/CD
Your Ref:

Dear

Re: Your application to the mental health tribunal/hospital managers

I was pleased to meet you on [date]. I am writing to confirm what we discussed, the advice that I gave you and the action that we decided that I would take.

You told me that you had been detained under section 3 of the Mental Health Act 1983. An order under section 3 of the Mental Health Act 1983 lasts for up to 6 months. It can then be renewed for a further period of 6 months, then periods of 12 months.

An approved mental health professional applies for an order under section 3 of the Mental Health Act 1983. Also, before someone can be placed under Section 3 of the Mental Health Act 1983, two doctors must certify that the person is suffering from mental disorder and that that person's mental disorder is of a nature or degree which makes it appropriate for him or her to receive medical treatment in hospital. The doctors must also certify that appropriate treatment is available and that it is necessary for the health or safety of the person concerned or the protection of other persons that they should receive the treatment in hospital, and that treatment cannot be provided unless that person is detained under section 3 of the Mental Health Act 1983. The approved mental health professional must also attempt to contact your nearest relative in order to seek their agreement for your detention under section 3 of the Mental Health Act 1983.

We discussed the methods whereby you could be discharged from your Section.

Firstly, your consultant (sometimes referred to as your responsible clinician or RC) can lift the section at any time.

Secondly, your nearest relative, who I understand is [name], has the power to discharge you from detention under the Mental Heath Act 1983. I would stress, however, that these powers are limited. If your nearest relative attempts to discharge you, and your consultant believes that, if discharged you would act in a way that was dangerous to yourself and other people, then he/she can stop the discharge from taking effect. Additionally, legal action can be taken against your nearest relative to displace them which means that they would lose any authority as your nearest relative.

You also have the right to appeal to a hospital manager's hearing or to a mental health tribunal.

The hospital managers have the power to discharge you from detention. if you request it, the hospital managers will hold a hearing at which they consider reports from your consultant, from a social worker and probably a nursing report as well. They will also hear from you and they will decide whether to discharge you from the section or not. i can advise you and accompany you to the hospital manager's hearing.

The mental health tribunal is an independent body whose members are appointed by the Ministry of Justice, the government department which has responsibility for the judiciary. mental health tribunal members, if you request, visit the hospital to hold a hearing to decide whether or not you should be discharged from your section. Before any tribunal hearing, reports will be prepared by your consultant, a social worker and probably a member of nursing staff. I will receive copies of these reports and will discuss them with you.

The tribunal consists of a legally qualified tribunal judge, a medical member who is a consultant psychiatrist and a lay member who is usually a social work professional. The medical member will if you wish come and speak to you and look at your notes before the hearing takes place. I will represent you at the hearing.

Agreed action

You told me that you would like to appeal to the mental health tribunal and/or the hospital managers and I have therefore written to the mental health tribunal and the Mental Health Act administrator at this hospital advising them of your wish.

It is likely that it will be between six to eight weeks before your hearing takes place.

You have authorised me to look at your medical and nursing file and I have written to your consultant asking him/her if he/she has any objections to this. I will let you know when I receive a response.

Yours sincerely

Sarah Malcolm
Malcolm & Partners LLP

LETTER TO CLIENT RE SECTION 37 ADVICE

Mr

PROTECT: PERSONAL DATA

24 January 2015
Our Ref: AB/11169.002/CD
Your Ref:

Dear

Re: Your application to the mental health tribunal/hospital managers

I was pleased to meet you on [date]. I am writing to confirm what we discussed, the advice that I gave you and the action that we decided that I would take.

You told me that you had been detained under section 37 of the Mental Health Act 1983. I advised you that section 37 is an order which can be made either by a magistrates' court or Crown Court. In order to make the order, the court has to receive medical recommendations from two doctors. Both the doctors must agree that the person concerned is suffering from a mental disorder of a nature or degree which makes it appropriate for that person to be detained in hospital for medical treatment. The court must also consider that making a hospital order is the most suitable way of disposing with the case.

The effect of the order is that you must be admitted to hospital within 28 days of the order being made. The order lasts up to a maximum of 6 months from the date of the order. The order can, however, be renewed.

Your consultant can discharge you from your section at any time.

You have the right to appeal against the section to the hospital managers.

In the first six months of a hospital order, you do not have the right to appeal to a mental health tribunal. If after the first six months your section has been renewed then you will acquire the right to appeal to the mental health tribunal.

The hospital managers have the power to discharge you from detention. if you request it, the hospital managers will hold a hearing at which they consider reports from your consultant, from a social worker and probably a nursing report as well. They will also hear from you and they will decide whether to discharge you from the section or not. I can advise you and accompany you to the hospital manager's hearing.

The mental health tribunal is an independent body whose members are appointed by the Ministry of Justice, the government department which has responsibility for the judiciary. mental health tribunal member, if you request, visit the hospital to hold a hearing to decide whether or not you should be discharged from your section. Before any tribunal hearing, reports will be prepared by your consultant, a social worker and probably a member of nursing staff. I will receive copies of these reports and will discuss them with you.

The tribunal consists of a legally qualified tribunal judge, a medical member who is a consultant psychiatrist and a lay member who is usually a social work professional. The medical member will if you wish come and speak to you and look at your notes before the hearing takes place. I will represent you at the hearing.

Agreed action

You told met that you would like to appeal to the mental health tribunal and/or the hospital managers and i have therefore written to the mental health tribunal and the Mental Health Act administrator at this hospital advising them of your wish.

It is likely that it will be between 6 and 8 weeks before any hearing takes place.

You have authorised me to look at your medical and nursing file and I have written to your consultant asking him/her if he/she has any objections to this. I will let you know when I receive a response.

Yours sincerely

Sarah Malcolm
Malcolm & Partners LLP

LETTER TO CLIENT RE SECTIONS 37–41 ADVICE

Mr

PROTECT: PERSONAL DATA

24 January 2015
Our Ref: AB/11169.002/CD
Your Ref:

Dear

Re: Your application to the mental health tribunal/hospital managers

I was pleased to meet you on [date]. I am writing to confirm what we discussed, the advice that I gave you and the action that we decided that I would take.

You told me that you had been detained under sections 37 and 41 of the Mental Health Act 1983. This is an order which can only be made at the Crown Court. Before making the order, the court has to receive medical recommendations from two doctors both of whom must agree that you are suffering from a mental disorder of a nature or degree which makes it appropriate for you to be detained in hospital for medical treatment. Also the court must consider that making the hospital order is the most suitable way of disposing with the case.

Additionally, in your case, the court has attached an order under section 41 of the Mental Health Act 1983. The court can attach an order under Section 41 if the court believes that having regard to the nature of the offence of which you were convicted, your antecedents and the risk of your committing further offences, that it is necessary for the protection of the public from serious harm to attach a restriction order. The effect of the restriction order is that you:

- cannot be discharged by your consultant without the agreement of the Ministry of Justice;
- cannot be discharged by the hospital managers;
- cannot be granted leave or moved to a different hospital without the agreement of the Ministry of Justice.

After your first six months detention under section 37/41 you do have the right to appeal to a mental health tribunal.

The mental health tribunal is an independent body whose members are appointed by the Ministry of Justice, the government department which has responsibility for the judiciary. Mental health tribunal members, if you make an application or have not made an application in a three year period visit the hospital to hold a hearing to decide whether or not you should be discharged from your section.

Before any tribunal hearing, reports will be prepared by your consultant, a social worker and probably a member of nursing staff. I will receive copies of these reports and will discuss them with you.

The tribunal consists of a legally qualified tribunal judge, a medical member who is a consultant psychiatrist and a lay member who is usually a social work professional. The medical member will if you wish come and speak to you and look at your notes before the hearing takes place. I will represent you at the hearing.

Agreed action

You told me that you would like to appeal to the Mental Health Tribunal. I have written to the Mental Health Tribunal and asked them to fix a Hearing.

You have asked me to look at your medical and nursing file and I have written to your Consultant asking him/her if he/she has any objections to this. I will let you know when I receive a response.

Yours sincerely

Sarah Malcolm
Malcolm & Partners LLP

LETTER TO CLIENT RE COMMUNITY TREATMENT ORDER

Mr

PROTECT: PERSONAL DATA

24 January 2015
Our Ref: AB/11169.002/CD
Your Ref:

Dear

Re: Contact-002

Further to our meeting on [date], I write in order to confirm your instructions to us in relation to your application to the [mental health tribunal/hospital managers] against your supervised community treatment order, commonly referred to as a CTO.

You instructed that you were made subject to a community treatment order on [date] further to your detention in hospital under section [XX] of the Mental Health Act 1983 (as amended by the Mental Health Act 2007).

As I advised, a CTO is a community mental health order which can be imposed by your responsible clinician if he/she is of the opinion that you no longer need to be detained in hospital however that you need to be subject to treatment in the community and accordingly your responsible clinician can in those circumstances discharge you from hospital, with conditions in the community and make you liable for recall to hospital for treatment should you breach the conditions of the order.

A CTO is made under section 17A of the Mental Health Act 1983 and can only be imposed by a responsible clinician with the written agreement of an approved mental health professional (AMHP), confirming that the relevant criteria have been met; and (i) the AMHP agrees with the opinion of the responsible clinician; and (ii) that it is appropriate to make the order.

Relevant criteria

(a) The patient must be suffering from a mental disorder of a nature or degree which makes it appropriate for him to receive medical treatment;
(b) It is necessary for the patient's health or safety or for the protection of other persons that such treatment should be received;
(c) Subject to the patient being liable to be recalled, such treatment can be provided without continued detention in hospital;
(d) It is necessary that the responsible clinician should be able to exercise the power of recall to hospital; and
(e) Appropriate treatment is available for the patient.

Conditions

The Community Treatment Order will set out conditions for the purpose of ensuring that a patient

(a) receives medical treatment;

(b) does not pose a risk of harm to the patient's health and safety; and
(c) does not pose a risk to other persons;

In addition the order must specify –

(a) a condition that a patient makes himself/herself available for examination upon renewal of the order; and
(b) that a patient makes himself/herself available for the purpose of a second opinion doctors assessment.

Duration

A Community Treatment Order will initially last for a period of six months following which the order may be renewed for a further period of six months and then renewable for further periods of twelve months.

Recall

A patient who has been made subject to a Community Treatment Order may be recalled to hospital if the responsible clinician is of the opinion –

(a) that a patient requires medical treatment in hospital for the mental disorder, and
(b) that there would be a risk of harm to the health or safety of the patient or to other persons if the patient were not recalled to hospital for that purpose.

The responsible clinician may also recall a patient to hospital if the patient fails to comply with a condition to make himself/herself available for examination upon renewal of the order and to make himself/herself available for the purpose of a second opinion doctor's assessment.

Discharge of community treatment order

A responsible clinician may discharge a patient from a community treatment order at any stage.

Additionally a patient who is made subject to a community treatment order has the right to appeal to the mental health tribunal and/or to the hospital managers once during the period of the community treatment order, in addition to once during each subsequent period in which the community treatment order is renewed.

Your nearest relative also has the right to request the discharge of the community treatment order however upon making the above request; the responsible clinician has the power to prevent that discharge if he/she is of the opinion that the patient may pose a risk to their own safety or to the safety of other persons. If the responsible clinician prevents a nearest relative discharge, that decision will be referred to the hospital managers for review.

Instructions

You instructed that you wished to lodge an application to the [mental health tribunal/hospital managers] against the continuation of your community treatment order and I can confirm that I have submitted your application to the [mental health tribunal/hospital managers].

It should take approximately eight weeks before your hearing is listed for hearing and I shall arrange to meet with you further during that period in order to prepare for your hearing.

Yours sincerely

Sarah Malcolm
Malcolm & Partners LLP

LETTER TO WARD MANAGER RE BENEFITS

FAO: The Ward Manager

PROTECT: PERSONAL DATA

24 January 2015
Our Ref: AB/11169.002/CD
Your Ref:

Dear

Re: Our Client: Mr/MS
DOB:
N.I. Number:

We have been instructed by the above named client. We understand that he/she is in receipt of benefits which may make him/her eligible for free legal representation.

We seek to confirm our client is in receipt of benefits and request the following information:

- Confirmation that our client is in receipt of benefits, including the type of benefit received and date when benefits were commenced
- Confirmation of his/her national insurance number

We enclose our client's signed authority for the release of the above information.

If you are unable to confirm the above information we would be grateful if you would kindly forward this letter along with the attached authority to our client's social worker or care coordinator.

We would be grateful for your assistance in this matter.

Yours sincerely

Sarah Malcolm
Malcolm & Partners LLP

Enc.

CASE MANAGEMENT CHECKLIST

CASE PROGRESS		*DATE(S)*
CLR / LH Form **(signed and completed):**		
Conflict Check Completed:		
Signed Authority by client:		
Client Care Letter / Client Advice Letter Sent:		
Confirmation of Benefits – Requested from Ward: Requested from DWP: Received:		
Access to Medical Notes Requested:		
Application Sent to Tribunal Service:		
Preliminary Chronology / Summary:		
Section Papers Viewed:		
Part A Statement Received:		
Medical Report Received:		
Social Circumstances Report Received:		
Nursing Report Received:		
Tribunal Hearing(s):		
CPA Meeting(s) / s117 Meeting(s):		
Managers Hearing(s):		
Optional Documents		
Independent Psychiatric Report – Requested: Received:		
Independent Social Work Report – Requested: Received:		
FUNDING INFORMATION	*Y or N*	*DATE(S)*
Non MHRT		
MHRT LEVEL 1		
PROGRESSED TO MHRT LEVEL 2		
PROGRESSED TO MHRT LEVEL 3		

Adjourned Hearing Fee(s)	
Remote Payment	N/A
Matter Concluded:	
Date File Billed:	
FILE REVIEWS	
File Reviewed: Date Reviewed: Reviewed By:	Y / N
DISBURSEMENTS	£

APPENDIX E

Section papers checklist

Section 2

The application for a section 2 and is made by the approved mental health practitioner (AMHP). The nearest relative can also make an application but rarely does. There must also be two medical recommendations or a joint medical recommendation.

The application by the AMHP

1. The application must be on a form A2.[1]
2. Check that the applicant is described as an AMHP. There should be no conflicts of interest but this will be difficult to know and should just be borne in mind during the case. It would be unusual for there to be any conflicts.[2]
3. Check that the right patient is identified.
4. Check that the right hospital is identified. A person can only be taken to the hospital named in the application within 14 days on the date on which the patient was last examined by a medical practitioner.[3] A fresh application can be made if the hospital is not available for any reason as long as it is still made writing 14 days of the last examination.
5. Check the nearest relative (NR) is correctly identified under section 26. In a section 2 application the identification of the wrong NR would probably not invalidate the section in any event as there is no power of the NR to object nor any duty on the AMPH to make enquiries. However if there is to be an application for a section 3 the right person needs to be consulted.
6. Check that the applicant has personally seen the patient within 14 days of making the application.[4]

1 Reg 4(1) of the Mental Health (Hospital, Guardianship and Treatment) (England) Regulations 2008 SI No 1184 ('Mental Health Regs 2008') reg 4(1); see 2008 SI No 2439 for Wales.

2 Potential conflicts could be a financial benefit for the applicant (see Mental Health (Conflict of Interest) (England) Regulations 2008 and Chapter 39 of the Code of Practice; Mental Health (Conflict of Interest) (Wales) Regulations 2008 and Chapter 3 of the Code of Practice Wales).

3 MHA 1983 s6(1)(a).

4 MHA 1983 s11(5).

The medical recommendations

7. A3[5] for a joint medical recommendation or two A4s for a single recommendation.
8. The patient must have been admitted to the named hospital within 14 days of the latest dated medical examination[6] (and not the date the recommendation was signed if they are different).[7]
9. The two medical recommendations must have taken place within five days of each other so in effect within a seven-day period. The patient must have been personally examined by those making the recommendations.[8]
10. Check that at least one of the approved clinicians is section 12 approved.
11. If one of the doctors who examines the patient will not recommend admission then the AMHP can approach another doctor to examine the patient and recommend admission.[9]
12. The doctors examining should give reasons for their opinions which includes a description of the symptoms from which the patient is suffering not just a diagnosis.[10]
13. If the application or recommendations are incorrect or defective they can be rectified within 14 days of the date on which the patient was admitted to hospital. This is primarily for errors and could not be used to make a fundamentally defective application lawful.[11]

Section 3

The application by the AMHP

14. The application must be on form A6.
15. See 2 above.
16. See 3 above.
17. See 4 above.
18. The correct identification of the nearest relative is important. However as long as the AMHP applied the test in section 26, did not act in bad faith or reached a decision that was clearly wrong the court would not interfere with the conclusion.[12]
19. The NR must be consulted further to section 11(4) unless it is not 'reasonably practicable' to consult. The meaning of 'practicable' has been extensively discussed in case-law. In *R (E) v Bristol City Council* [2005] EWHC 74 (Admin)

5 Mental Health Regs 2008 reg 4(1)(b)(i); Welsh Regs equivalents under the Welsh Regs are Form HO3: joint recommendation or HO4 for applications under s2.
6 MHA 1983 s12(1).
7 MHA 1983 s6(1)(a).
8 MHA 1983 s12(1).
9 *TTM v London Borough of Hackney* [2011] EWCA Civ 4.
10 Code para 14.75 (England); Code para 2.52 (Wales).
11 MHA 1983 s15, Code para 35.13 (England); Code para 10.2 (Wales).
12 *R (WC) v South London and Maudsley NHS Trust* [2001] EWHC 1025 (Admin).

the Court held that as the patient did not want her NR to act as the NR, the chance of positive harm if she was consulted, and the fact that the NR did not wish to act, taken together meant that it was not 'reasonably practicable' to consult the nearest relative. In *TW v Enfield Borough Council* [2014] EWCA Civ 362[13] the court found that the ASW must consider not only the patients wishes and her right to a private life in accordance with Article 8 ECHR but her right under Article 5 ECHR not to be detained unless that is done in accordance with the law. The fact that the patient says they do not want their NR contacted should not lead to the automatic conclusion that it is not reasonably practicable to consult them.

20. The burden of showing consultation with the NR rests on the AMHP.[14] The consultation needs to be meaningful consultation and therefore the AMHP must provide enough information on the form to make a decision.

21. See 6 above.

The medical recommendations

22. Forms A7 or A8[15] must be used.

23. Then follow the steps in the section 2 list above.

Renewals

1. A section 3, or section 37 must be renewed after the first six months after the date of admission the second six months and then yearly.[16] Check the dates if possible from the original documentation on the MHAA file. If the six-month period starts on 2 January then the first six months ends at midnight on 1 July.

2. The responsible clinician (RC) must examine the patient within two months before the date the section expires.[17]

3. In a case where the patient was on a restriction order which has lapsed, eg when a determinate sentence prisoner is transferred and his early date release has passed, the date of admission is taken as the date on which the restriction expired.[18]

3. Check the RC has furnished a report[19] to the managers informing them that the criteria in section 20(4) are satisfied which mirror the admission criteria under section 3. The RC has to do this and it cannot be delegated.

4. The report must be furnished which means the RC cannot have left it on their desk. It must have been mailed or handed to someone who is authorised by the managers to accept it.

13 See also chapter 16, Top Ten Cases.

14 *B v Cygnet Healthcare* [2008] EWHC 1259 (Admin).

15 In Wales, Form HO7 joint recommendation and HO8 for recommendations under s3.

16 MHA 1983 s20(2).

17 MHA 1983 s20(3). For guardianship if the LA is not the guardian the it is the guardian

18 MHA 1983 s41(5).

19 Ford H5 in England and Form HO5 in Wales.

5. Check that the RC has consulted a professional who is professionally concerned with the patient but who is not a member of the same profession as has agreed with the RC in writing in Part 2 of the form.
6. The RC must consult with 'one or more other persons who have been professionally concerned with the patient.' The other person must be from a different profession and state their agreement that the criteria for renewal have been made out.[20] The section is then renewed on the date that it would have expired.
5. Lastly the managers have to consider the report and whether they should exercise their section 23 powers of discharge. There is no time limit for this. If it is uncontested it may happen on the papers but it must be considered by three managers.[21]

Section 7

This is a rare section which has become less utilised since the advent of the CTO. The renewal section follows that of the section 3 or section 37 except that the appropriate practitioner is the person who examines the patient. The appropriate practitioner is defined as the RC or where the patient is not in the guardianship of the LA the nominated medical attendant.[22] The report must be furnished to the guardian and where the guardian is not the LA then to the LA as well.[23]

Section 37, 37/41, 45A, orders made when unfit to plead[24]

These orders cannot be invalid in the same way that civil sections can. If the order is wrong it can be reissued. Even if an application for judicial review is made the order must be complied with until set aside.

The grounds and duration of these orders are set out in chapter 3.

Check the time from which the order is made and the date of admission. If it is longer than 28 days the detention is unlawful.[25]

Section 47

1. Check that one of the medical practitioners is section 12 approved.[26]
2. Check how long it has taken from the medical recommendations being made until the transfer. There is no statutory time limits between the date of the report and the date of the decision but it may be relevant in terms of fulfilling the criteria for deprivation of liberty under Article 5(1)(e) ECHR.

20 MHA 1983 s20.

21 MHA 1983 s23(4).

22 MHA 1983 s34(1).

23 MHA 1983 s20(6).

24 Criminal Procedure (Insanity) Act 1964, as amended by the Criminal Procedure (Insanity and Unfitness to Plead) Act 1991 as further amended by the Domestic Violence, Crime and Victims Act 2004.

25 *R (DB) v Nottinghamshire Healthcare NHS Trust* [2008] EWCA Civ 1354.

26 MHA 1983 s54(1).

3. There is no time limit for the issue of a warrant from the provision of reports. However the Secretary of State has to consider whether they can rely on the reports and one of the considerations will be how recent the report is.[27]
4. Check that the transfer happened within 14 days of the warrant of being issued.[28]

Community treatment orders

1. Check that the CTO1[29] has been used.
2. Check that the RC has made the CTO. They are the only ones that can.[30]
3. Check that the AMHP has agreed in writing.[31] There is no time limit between this agreement and the putting into effect the CTO by the RC. There is also no requirement for the AMHP to see the patient before agreeing.
4. Check the patient is detained on an unrestricted treatment section. A restricted patient cannot be subject to a CTO.[32]
4. Check the reasons for the opinion that supports the grounds of the CTO, which are set out on the CTO1 from (a)–(e).
5. The two mandatory conditions are printed on the form. In terms of other conditions the have to address the purposes set out on the CTO1 under the box where the conditions are to be written.

If the patient has been recalled

1. A form CTO3 is used[33] to recall a patient and a CTO5 for revocation.
2. The RC need not see the patient themselves but can rely on others reports.
3. The notice of recall must be delivered to the patient but if he refuses to accept it or cannot be found then it should be delivered to his last known address.[34]
4. Check the time of admission as the 72 hours start running when the patient is admitted. If it is later that this and the section has not been revoked the patient is free to leave.[35]
5. Check the written reasons against the criteria which is written on the standard form above the box for the reasons.

Renewal

1. A form CTO7 is used.[36]

27 *R v Secretary of State for the Home Office ex p Gilkes* [1999] EWHC 47 (Admin).
28 MHA 1983 s47(2).
29 In Wales CP1.
30 MHA 1983 s17A.
31 MHA 1983 s17A(4).
32 MHA 1983 s47(3) and Schedule 1 Part 1.
33 In Wales CP5.
34 Code (England) paras 29.53–29.56; Code (Wales) paras 30.67–30.68.
35 17F (8)(a).
36 In Wales CP3.

2. A section 17A must be renewed after the first six months after the date the order was made the second 6 months and then yearly.[37] The Code of Practice in England defines this date as the date on which the order is effective.[38] As for a section 3 check the dates if possible from the original documentation on the MHAA file. If the six-month period starts on 2 January then the first six months ends at midnight on 1 July.
3. The RC must examine the patient within two months before the date the section expires.[39]
4. Check the RC has furnished a report[40] to the managers informing them that the criteria in section 20A(6) are satisfied which mirror the application criteria under section 17A.The RC has to do this and it cannot be delegated.
5. The report must be furnished which means the RC cannot have left it on their desk. It must have been mailed or handed to someone who is authorised by the managers to accept it.
6. A AMHP needs to agree with the renewal in writing and there is provision for this on the form.
7. Lastly the managers have to consider the report and whether they should exercise their section 23 powers of discharge. There is no time limit for this. If it is uncontested it may happen on the papers but it must be considered by 3 managers.[41]

37 MHA 1983 s20A(3).
38 Code para 29.26.
39 MHA 1983 s20A(4).
40 H5 in England; HO5 in Wales.
41 MHA 1983 s23(4).

Index